Revolution remembered

Manchester University Press

Politics, culture and society in early modern Britain

General Editors
PROFESSOR ALASTAIR BELLANY
DR ALEXANDRA GAJDA
PROFESSOR PETER LAKE
PROFESSOR ANTHONY MILTON
PROFESSOR JASON PEACEY

This important series publishes monographs that take a fresh and challenging look at the interactions between politics, culture and society in Britain between 1500 and the mid-eighteenth century. It counteracts the fragmentation of current historiography through encouraging a variety of approaches which attempt to redefine the political, social and cultural worlds, and to explore their interconnection in a flexible and creative fashion. All the volumes in the series question and transcend traditional inter-disciplinary boundaries, such as those between political history and literary studies, social history and divinity, urban history and anthropology. They thus contribute to a broader understanding of crucial developments in early modern Britain.

Recently published in the series

Chaplains in early modern England: Patronage, literature and religion
HUGH ADLINGTON, TOM LOCKWOOD AND GILLIAN WRIGHT (eds)

The Cooke sisters: Education, piety and patronage in early modern England GEMMA ALLEN

Black Bartholomew's Day DAVID J. APPLEBY

Battle-scarred: Mortality, medical care and military welfare in the British Civil Wars
DAVID J. APPLEBY AND ANDREW HOPPER (eds)

Insular Christianity ROBERT ARMSTRONG AND TADHG Ó HANNRACHAIN (eds)

Reading and politics in early modern England GEOFF BAKER

'No historie so meete' JAN BROADWAY

Writing the history of parliament in Tudor and early Stuart England
PAUL CAVILL AND ALEXANDRA GAJDA (eds)

Republican learning JUSTIN CHAMPION

News and rumour in Jacobean England: Information, court politics and diplomacy, 1618–25 DAVID COAST

This England PATRICK COLLINSON

Sir Robert Filmer (1588–1653) and the patriotic monarch CESARE CUTTICA

Doubtful and dangerous: The question of succession in late Elizabethan England
SUSAN DORAN AND PAULINA KEWES (eds)

Brave community JOHN GURNEY

'Black Tom' ANDREW HOPPER

Reformation without end: Religion, politics and the past in post-revolutionary England
ROBERT G. INGRAM

Royalists and Royalism during the Interregnum JASON MCELLIGOTT AND DAVID L. SMITH

Laudian and Royalist polemic in Stuart England ANTHONY MILTON

The crisis of British Protestantism: Church power in the Puritan Revolution, 1638–44
HUNTER POWELL

The gentlewoman's remembrance: Patriarchy, piety, and singlehood in early Stuart England ISAAC STEPHENS

Exploring Russia in the Elizabethan Commonwealth: The Muscovy Company and Giles Fletcher, the elder (1546–1611) FELICITY JANE STOUT

Full details of the series are available at www.manchesteruniversitypress.co.uk.

Revolution remembered

Seditious memories after
the British civil wars

EDWARD LEGON

Manchester University Press

Copyright © Edward Legon 2019

The right of Edward Legon to be identified as the author of this work has been asserted by him in accordance with the Copyright, Designs and Patents Act 1988.

Published by Manchester University Press
Oxford Road, Manchester M13 9PL
www.manchesteruniversitypress.co.uk

British Library Cataloguing-in-Publication Data
A catalogue record for this book is available from the British Library

ISBN 978 1 5261 2465 4 hardback
ISBN 978 1 5261 6073 7 paperback

First published 2019

Paperback published 2021

The publisher has no responsibility for the persistence or accuracy of URLs for any external or third-party internet websites referred to in this book, and does not guarantee that any content on such websites is, or will remain, accurate or appropriate.

Typeset in 10/12 Scala by
Servis Filmsetting Ltd, Stockport, Cheshire

For my parents and Katharine.

Contents

ACKNOWLEDGEMENTS—viii
ABBREVIATIONS—ix

1	Introduction: 'Remember the Good Old Cause'	1
2	Locating seditious memories in England and Wales	17
3	The politics of memory after the Restoration	47
4	Seditious memories: Contestation and cultural resistance	67
5	Sharing seditious memories	89
6	Seditious memories in Scotland and Ireland	110
7	Mis-commemoration after the Restoration	142
8	Seditious memories across generations	172
	Conclusion: Burying the good old cause	199

SELECT BIBLIOGRAPHY—207
INDEX—229

Acknowledgements

I am very lucky to have received the support of colleagues, friends, and family throughout the production of this book. I am indebted to Jason Peacey, who has been a major source of inspiration for this project. He has put up with me much longer than he has needed to. Several people, including Jason, have also gone beyond the call of duty by reading chapters and iterations of this book. For this, I thank Richard Bell, Coleman Dennehy, Eilish Gregory, Wendy Hitchmough, Laura Stewart, and Hillary Taylor. For conversations that have inspired the shape of this book, I am thankful to those mentioned and to Dave Appleby, Catherine Arnold, Ian Atherton, Amy Calladine, Will Cavert, Justin Champion, Tom Cogswell, Stephen Conway, Misha Ewen, Michael Fleming, Sam Fullerton, Joel Halcomb, Clare Haynes, Catherine Hinchliff, Andy Hopper, Julian Hoppit, Ann Hughes, Paul Hunneyball, Lindsey Ilsley, Mark Knights, David Magliocco, Dave Manning, Angela McShane, Jonah Miller, Matthew Neufeld, Imogen Peck, Erin Peters, Tim Reinke-Williams, Robbie Rudge, Jack Sargeant, Talya Sarna, Tim Somers, Elaine Tierney, Ted Vallance, Elliot Vernon, and Alex Walsham. The Institute of Historical Research and Historic Royal Palaces have both provided stimulating environments to think about, research, and write this book and I appreciate the generosity of staff at both. I am also grateful to the staff of other libraries and record offices who have supported my research. I thank Emma Brennan and the series editors at Manchester University Press for guidance throughout the production process and the readers for their helpful comments. Last, but certainly not least, I am truly grateful to my friends and family in London, the West Country, and East Anglia who have offered a great deal of love and support and who have managed to keep me relatively normal. I am especially indebted to Mum, Dad, and Katharine, to whom this book is dedicated.

Abbreviations

CSPD Calendar of State Papers Domestic
DCY   Depositions from the Castle of York
MCR   Middlesex County Records
ODNB Oxford Dictionary of National Biography
RPCS Register of the Privy Council of Scotland

Chapter 1

Introduction: 'Remember the Good Old Cause'

The wars and revolutions in Britain between 1637 and 1660 continued to impact the lives of the people of the Restoration era. This was especially the case in the 1680s when the fault lines that had wrought war and revolution four decades earlier were cleft open once more by the issue of whether, as a Roman Catholic, James, Duke of York, ought to succeed to the throne of his brother Charles II. For members of the emerging Tory party, the efforts of their Whig counterparts to secure York's exclusion from the throne were dangerously reminiscent of the actions of those who, forty years earlier, overthrew the Stuarts and the Church of England.[1] One common manifestation of the Tories' fears was accusations that old Parliamentarians, as well as a new generation of troublemakers, brazenly retained sympathies for their so-called 'good old cause'. In her 1678 comedy *Sir Patient Fancy*, the playwright Aphra Behn depicted the title role – based on the London alderman and Puritan Sir Patience Ward – as yearning for those 'better dayes', or, more specifically, 'the good days of the late Lord Protector [i.e. Oliver Cromwell]'.[2] Three years later, and echoing Behn's drama in starker language, the author of one pamphlet charged the Whigs, or 'factious schismatics', with 'commending and slyly insinuating the good days of the late times [and] the plenty, power, riches, and reputation of *their* dear commonwealth'.[3] In a graphic representation of these accusations, the 1682 broadside *The Whig Rampant* incorporated the image of a dissenting 'tub-preacher' from an earlier work, ascribing to him the words 'remember the good old cause'.[4]

The sympathies for the 'old cause' to which Aphra Behn and others alluded have been largely absent from the recent surge of interest in how the civil wars and revolutions were remembered in Britain.[5] Instead, historians have tended to impute rather different attitudes to the men and women who lived in the three decades after 1660.[6] In these accounts, traumatic memories of civil war and revolution 'imprisoned' Britons with fears of a return to 'rebellion' and 'usurpation'.[7] So ingrained were these fears that they are taken to have comprised an ideological 'middle ground' after the Restoration from which those who failed to conform to the narrow political and religious settlements of the 1660s were sniped at as the heirs of civil war 'fanatics'.[8] This account of the Restoration era's mnemonic landscape – a term that is used in this book to refer to the memories and ways of remembering that defined British society in this era – has dovetailed with analyses of the crisis at the end of Charles II's reign. In studies of the so-called 'Exclusion Crisis', the Tories' evocation of Parliamentarianism and republicanism, such as is evident in the writings of Aphra Behn and others, is held to have had greater potency than the Whigs' warnings about the dangers of 'popery' and 'arbitrary government', thus forestalling the efforts of the latter to prevent the Duke of York from succeeding to the throne and securing toleration for Dissenters.[9] If anyone was remembering the old cause, it was the Tories, while 'the[ir] opposition ... by and large, did not see themselves as the descendants of Cromwell or [John] Pym'.[10]

A willingness to explore the nature and depth of enduring sympathies for the old cause is largely confined to literary studies, especially those of the era's celebrated band of authors and poets; John Milton, Andrew Marvell, John Bunyan, and Richard Baxter were all active opponents of the Stuarts and the established church at various stages between 1640 and 1660. The best of these studies have situated such figures, and some others, within what they have termed a culture of 'defeat'.[11] And yet not everyone has been so willing to identify the continuation of the old cause after 1660, drawing attention instead to the transmutation of revolutionary impulses into 'quietism'.[12] Whatever their differences, the foci of these investigations often converge on the coterie of educated, and thus predominantly elite and male, figures whose testimonies have been bequeathed to us by print. Even then, owing to the hazard of adopting certain political and religious positions publicly after the return of Charles II, enduring sympathies for Parliament and the Republic tend to be synonymised by scholars with radical or republican intentions.[13] By extension, the incorporation of these sympathies into the historical mainstream is usually identified much later: after the Glorious Revolution of 1688–89 when the deposal of James II corresponded with an upswing in critical accounts of the Stuart dynasty.[14] Finally, and most crucially, the individual and social significance of the act of remembering is often subordinated to the contentious issue of how, and indeed whether, the political and religious trajectories of civil war and revolution endured after 1660.[15]

Influenced by theoretical developments in the field of 'memory studies', historians and literary scholars are now addressing some of these lacunae by devoting their attention to the mnemonic and psychological impacts of civil war and revolution across Restoration society.[16] Most notably, Matthew

Neufeld has underscored the tension between remembering and forgetting in England during the reigns of the later Stuarts, the latter having been exemplified by the Act of Free and General Pardon, Indemnity, and Oblivion in 1660, a precursor to modern programmes of reconciliation that forbade 'using any words tending to revive the Memory of the late Differences'.[17] For Neufeld, combatants and others who experienced the 1640s and 1650s wished to exorcise its spectral presence. Rather than 're-fighting the old struggle', Neufeld posits 'public remembering' after 1660 as having entailed 'commending and justifying, or contesting and attacking, the Restoration settlements that underlay the Anglican confessional state.'[18] Prominent in Neufeld's account is a hostile version of Parliamentarianism and republicanism that constructed 'a legal *cordon sanitaire* around the puritan impulse' and 'vindicated an exclusively Anglican confessional polity'.[19] Here, historically minded Whigs are viewed as circumspect when seeking to profit from the recent past, warning their readers of the pitfalls of returning to the 'popish' counsel of the 1630s, rather than identifying more positively with those who opposed, resisted, or overthrew the Stuarts and established church in the following decades.[20]

By highlighting the trauma of early modern warfare, and the government's role in sanctioning certain memories of the recent past, these studies are critical to how we understand the Restoration. However, it has not been within the scope of these works to challenge the prevailing idea that Royalist interpretations of the wars and revolutions were not only dominant, but also widely held. We may infer, then, that a hostile attitude towards the events of the 1640s and 1650s was the inevitable, or even natural, position for people to adopt after the Restoration, save, perhaps, for a radical or republican minority of elite authors.

The main objectives of this book are to build on the emerging interest in the mnemonic landscapes of Restoration Britain by illustrating that they were considerably more diverse than is evident in existing studies, that they were far from consensual, and that there was social depth to enduring sympathies for opposition to and resistance against the Stuarts and Church of England. It does so by acknowledging that the printed evidence in which many historians have located memories of the civil wars and revolution is, as historians have shown, an inaccurate barometer of the full range of opinions about politics and religion in the era that followed.[21] In Peter Lake's concise formulation, we must acknowledge that 'hegemony is not monopoly'.[22] Furthermore, I argue that the hostile version of the civil wars and revolution which characterised the output of the presses after the Restoration must be associated with those who were responsible for its regulation from the early 1660s. Prominent among these was the redoubtable Sir Roger L'Estrange, whose 'anti-fanaticism' and associated hostility to Parliament and the Republic are referred to regularly in the pages that follow.[23]

Given the illusory effect of print, a survey of the diversity of memories in Restoration Britain, one that includes the majority of individuals who were excluded from the traditional 'political nation', must incorporate alternative forms of communication.[24] Inspirational in this, and other, respects is the work of Andy Wood, a historian of early modern politics and society who has looked beyond print, and especially to oral culture, as a way of engaging with plebeian custom and, by extension, the 'popular' memories of subaltern communities.[25] Following Wood's lead, this book engages carefully with sympathies for Parliament and the Republic in England and Wales between 1660 and 1688, the articulation of which in speech and writing by a broad social base was rendered seditious and treasonable, and thus, in many cases, made visible, by the Sedition Act of 1661 and pre-existing legislation.[26] This includes cases that came before assize and quarter sessions courts throughout England and Wales, including those that were communicated to secretaries of state at Whitehall. Given the reliance of this study on evidence of seditious and treasonable speech, its scope is confined to the three decades in which British governments were preoccupied by sympathies for Parliament and the Republic. That, as Paul Kléber Monod has shown, Jacobitism replaced these sympathies as the chief menace to William and Mary's government deems the Glorious Revolution of 1688–89 an appropriate limit for this study.[27]

The legal records and government papers in which alternative opinions about the civil wars and revolution reside have proven fecund for historians of the Restoration, especially those who are interested in the relationship between oral culture and 'popular' politics.[28] Yet the relationship between this evidence and contemporaries' *memories* has not received the attention it deserves. Chapter 2 begins by tapping such material to expose a reservoir of Parliamentarian and republican sympathies in the form of what are referred to collectively as 'seditious memories' of the civil wars and revolution in England and Wales. In doing so, it shows that there were opinions about those events that were targeted specifically by the Sedition Act, as well as others that were vulnerable to treatment as threats to the safety and security of the realms. Chapter 2 also presents a typology of seditious remembering that is employed throughout this book. This includes memories that are characterised by justification of, identification with, and nostalgia for forms of opposition and resistance during the 1640s and 1650s, as well as their 'prospection': that is, the prediction that those events would be re-realised at some stage in the future. In each of these cases, the memories of people after the Restoration are compared with those to which scholars of memory have referred in other chronological and geographical contexts. In doing this, I take several opportunities to reflect on how concepts that have been developed by scholars from a range of disciplines, but especially social psychology, may be transposed fruitfully to early modern Britain.

The second role of chapter 2 is to interrogate the issue of how representative seditious memories were of a more widespread understanding of the recent past. Like those of more famous Restoration authors, sympathies for Parliament and the Republic in evidence of sedition and treason are usually synonymised with the enduring legacy of popular political and religious radicalism.[29] The most notable advocate of this approach was Richard L. Greaves, whose work highlighted dissenting voices during the reigns of Charles II and James II.[30] In doing so, Greaves attracted criticism from historians who have argued that radical and republican communities, insofar as they survived the return of monarchy and episcopacy, were small, sparse, and disunited.[31] Such criticisms are often informed by national war fatigue, the scale of popular support for the return of Charles II, and the abject failure of any subsequent efforts to depose him or his brother (such as in 1661, 1663, 1683, and 1685). Chapter 2 takes heed of these revisionist accounts of the Restoration by arguing that the threat of seditious memories must be understood in relation to the anxieties of those who, having remained loyal to Crown and established church before 1660, acquired the authority to police such opinions. This is borne out by the fact that the range of opinions about the 1640s and 1650s that were actionable as seditious and even treasonable after the Restoration do not always correspond with evidence of radical or republican intent.

In the absence of an explanation for seditious and treasonable sentiments in which they are equated with a popular radical tradition, a trend has emerged of treating these opinions as ineffectual and unrepresentative; what one historian has described as the 'alehouse chatter' of 'a disgruntled minority' and even the 'ordinary anti-authoritarian belligerence of drunk or disgruntled commoners.'[32] Elsewhere, the kinds of language to which Greaves and others referred has been described as reflecting 'a tavern culture where imagined realities could be played out in varying degrees of intoxication in deep, but essentially meaningless, plans.'[33] Tim Harris, whose portrayals of popular politics and religion in the late seventeenth century are otherwise exceedingly rich, has echoed this dismissiveness by labelling seditious and treasonable words as the sentiments of 'a 'radical fringe' and, elsewhere, 'little more than the product of the fertile imaginations of unscrupulous informers seeking to feed off government paranoia'.[34] Few, it is held, were interested in perpetuating the bloodshed and turmoil of the British civil wars beyond the Restoration.

I contend that such evidence deserves to be bestowed with far greater significance. The fact that a range of sympathies for Parliament and the Republic were *vulnerable* to being treated as sedition or treason is viewed here as a reason to suspect that the available evidence of such sentiment is representative of a wider, but necessarily concealed, body of opinion. In the words of Melinda Zook, 'sedition' was a label that was 'applied to numerous ... seventeenth-century folk' whose 'grievances' extended far beyond 'repudiat[ing] the existing order and legitimat[ing] a new one'.[35] This portrayal of seditious memories as intersecting a diverse range of political and religious opinions is borne out by the extent to which other individuals, including those who are often associated with a movement away from the good old cause, secreted away their own sympathies for opposition and resistance before the Restoration in diaries and other 'personal' writings. In all these respects, the book follows the important claim of the sociologist Zsuzsa Gille that 'lamenting the losses that came with the collapse of [a regime] does not imply wishing it back', and that 'favorable, because selective, recollections of the old regime can come from the entire length of the traditional political spectrum'.[36]

This analysis leaves us with a question: given that radical and republican intent is unlikely to account for more than a small proportion of cases of seditious remembering, what is it that motivated individuals to articulate these memories and to risk themselves in the process? The remaining chapters of this book seek an answer, one that avoids dismissing seditious and treasonable words as anti-authoritarian or drunken grumbling. It does so by deducing what the intentions of the speakers and authors of seditious memories were. Necessarily, this involves navigating the assumption of the authorities, and some later historians, that the motivation of such language was *ipso facto* seditious or treasonable – that is, intending to undermine the authority of Crown and established church. Instead, I suggest that conclusions can be drawn about authorial intention from information about the immediate context of seditious remembering, as well as how memories were conveyed to the authorities: namely, that audiences were usually expected to react in a certain way to opinions about Parliament and the Republic. Moreover, the full significance of these expectations becomes apparent only when we acknowledge their inextricability from structures of political, religious, and socio-economic authority that were constituted by the attempts of those with authority – by and large civil war Royalists – to eradicate the 'fanatic' ideology that had motivated their erstwhile enemies.

In this respect, my approach draws inspiration from the work of Phil Withington, who has shown that records of plebeian speech are often expressive of 'a politics ... of social participation involving inclusions, exclusions and the construction of boundaries (both visible and invisible to the historical eye).'[37] It is also underpinned by a conceptualisation of remembering as inextricable from authority and identity (i.e. senses of self), factors that are, in turn, inextricable from each other.[38] Scholars of memory argue that sharing experiences of reality (as a form of what sociologists refer to as 'intersubjectivity')[39] plays a critical role in the formation and reproduction of social identities.[40] Where a society has undergone, or is undergoing, major disunity (along, for instance, political or religious lines), interpretations of experiences of reality (including memories) that are meaningful to a sizable proportion of that society's members are liable to diverge significantly. Moreover, if that society is one in which censorship is regarded as a legitimate tool of authority, it follows that the principal media of communication are vulnerable to appropriation by dominant interests as means of promoting their interpretations of experiences of reality at the expense of others.[41] In doing so, these interests effectively control the means through which the identities of the dominated are publicly and socially reproduced. The upshot is that we arrive at what the historian Berthold Molden has recently described as 'mnemonic hegemony', a situation in which 'one particular narrative' is accepted 'as a quasi-natural universality and delegitimizes alternative forms of reasoning.'[42] But the story does not end here. Hegemony must be regarded as a process, something that is struggled for and, by extension, may act as a source of anxiety for dominant forces within a society.[43] Studies of remembering have shown us that any efforts to promote and demote certain memories are necessarily vulnerable to contestation and subversion.[44] Indeed, any discussion of 'mnemonic hegemony' must include also a discussion of what have been termed variously 'counter-memories', 'popular memories', and 'vernacular memories'.[45]

The remaining chapters of this book unpick the full significance of seditious memories by thinking of them as counter-memories amid attempts by some Royalists to secure mnemonic hegemony. This involves reconfiguring how the transition from forgetting (as embodied by the Act of Free and General Pardon, Indemnity, and Oblivion) to remembering in the early 1660s has been thought about. Whereas historians have seen this transition as a natural response to popular anxieties about political and religious 'fanatics', chapter 3 argues that the Restoration's politics of memory was characterised by the active efforts of 'hard-line' Royalists – those who prescribed a purge of political and religious dissenters to cure Britain of its ills – to achieve mnemonic hegemony. This entailed their seizure of the authority to speak for the past, culminating in the *censorship* of Parliamentarians and republicans (as is evident in the sedition legislation through which seditious remembering becomes visible) and the retrospective *censure* of their actions during the 1640s and 1650s.[46] Censorship and censure are regarded as having been driven by a specifically Royalist impulse to eradicate a 'fanatic' ideology, and with it certain political and religious identities, through the public and social delegitimisation of Parliamentarianism and republicanism. The remainder of chapter 3 shows that censorship and censure comprised a major component of what Christopher Hill and others have referred to as the 'experience of defeat' for those who fought for, and otherwise supported, the old cause.[47] This is reflected in the extent to which some of these figures utilised oblivion as a legitimate, although largely ineffective, foil to Royalist recrimination by re-placing the authority to speak for the past in the hands of Charles II.

Chapter 3 allows us to depict seditious memories as having been, by definition, illegitimate counter-thrusts to these Royalists' pursuit of mnemonic hegemony. Put differently, they are treated not only as alternative memories, but also as *counter*-memories that are inextricable from, and thus potentially counteractive within, a politics of memory in which they were censored and their authors were censured. In this respect, the book draws on Daniel Woolf's acknowledgment that men and women outside the political nation 'were able to hang on to a significant portion of their beliefs about the past'. Whereas Woolf's reference point is 'mounting antiquarian scepticism and the rising tide of printed historical material',[48] the focus of this book is the concerted efforts of some Royalists to secure mnemonic hegemony across various media.

Subsequent chapters analyse in detail the myriad ways in which countermemories could be deployed by people within this politics of memory. They do so by investigating the immediate context in which such memories were expressed and the forms they took. Chapter 4 focuses on evidence of seditious remembering in which the speaker or author was conscious of the hostility of audiences to Parliamentarian and republican sympathies. This is taken to represent how seditious memories served to counteract the censure of Royalists by legitimising the decisions to oppose and resist Crown and established church *publicly*. In doing so, the chapter shows that, outside an early historiography of the civil wars that, as historians have recently shown, was largely Royalist, there was a vibrant debate about the meanings of opposition and resistance during the 1640s and 1650s.[49] Chapter 5 focuses on cases of seditious remembering in which consensus was the expectation of the speaker or author. Accordingly, the sharing of seditious memories is construed as a means by which attempts by Royalists to prevent the *social* circulation of favourable interpretations of opposition and resistance between former Parliamentarians and republicans was reversed and, consequently, identities that were anchored in the events of the civil wars and revolution were reproduced. In this way, the chapter shows that seditious memories mediated the creation of 'communities of memory' that, in turn, acted as sources of solidarity amid experiences of Royalist recrimination.[50]

As well seditious memories that were retrospective in orientation, chapters 4 and 5 consider those that were present oriented and 'prospective' (or 'restorative'): that is, those that made possible the imagination of alternative future realities.[51] In the first of these chapters, claims of enduring allegiance to Parliament and the Republic are shown to have been accompanied regularly by physical and verbal abuse against former Royalists and those in positions of authority. This reveals how the Royalists' pursuit of mnemonic hegemony served to perpetuate the divisions between 'Cavaliers' and 'roundheads', and, more intriguingly, that it imbued statements of identification with Parliament and the Republic with a potency akin to what scholars of hegemony refer to as 'cultural resistance'.[52] Here, the book draws on the work of historians who have highlighted how 'popular' uses of history could be wielded as critiques of *contemporary* politics.[53] Indeed, the chapter concludes by examining how seditious memories, especially insofar as they referred to the future of the Stuart realms, were deployed as means of intimidating former Royalists and those in positions of authority by exploiting the very anxieties that drove the Royalists' pursuit of mnemonic hegemony in the first place. Finally, in chapter 5, these prospective memories are used as evidence that, when circulated socially, sympathies for Parliament and the Republic could indeed inspire acts of rebellion after the Restoration, and that this continued into the reign of James II during the Monmouth Rebellion. Nonetheless, the chapter concludes by eschewing a straightforward synonymisation of shared prospective memories and radical or republican intent by drawing on studies that have highlighted the psychological potency of senses of collective hope.[54]

The first section of this book is confined to England and Wales, and the expression of seditious memories in oral, print, and scribal culture. Moreover, that memories and identities were bound up with each other is related to the fact that those who did the remembering had actually experienced the 1640s and 1650s, including as active Parliamentarians and republicans. In the second half of this book, I push against these self-imposed boundaries by considering alternative ways of articulating sympathies for opposition to, and resistance against, Crown and established church and the extent to which these sympathies, and seditious remembering more generally, existed in other geographical and generational contexts. Chapter 6 uses the methods of earlier chapters to explore the existence of equivalent forms of remembering in two of the Stuarts' other realms: namely, Scotland and Ireland. In Scotland, sympathies for the rebellion against the Crown and established church in the 1630s and 1640s are shown to have endured after the Restoration. These are identified in evidence of language which, like that in England and Wales, was deemed to be 'unlawful' by the government, but which incorporates additional evidence, such as scaffold speeches, and print and scribal cultures. Correspondingly, they are understood as means by which people legitimised opposition and resistance during the Scottish revolution, as well as means of negotiating, resisting, and subverting authority. The same is held for Ireland, where sympathies for the Oliverian conquest can be witnessed in legal records and state papers well into the 1680s. It also expands the definition of seditious memories to include sentiment that was favourable to the rebellion of Roman Catholics in 1641. By examining seditious memories in these two nations, the book hopes to draw an understanding of the extent to which the mnemonic landscapes of the four kingdoms diverged according to different experiences of the 1640s and 1650s, but also converged as result of related political and religious cultures.[55]

The boundaries that the book seeks to expand are not merely geographical. Drawing on studies of how memories can be embodied in physical movement, chapter 7 demonstrates that seditious memories were not only spoken and written, but also performed within a ritual culture.[56] Whereas historians have tended to see commemorative culture after the Restoration as defined by 'loyal' responses to the anniversaries of the regicide on 30 January and the Restoration itself on 29 May, this chapter demonstrates, and seeks to explain, the existence of 'mis-commemorative' activities. Rather than arguing that these activities comprised straightforward performances of alternative opinions about the regicide and the Restoration, however, I associate this behaviour with a range of dissenting opinions about the Restoration settlements, including opposition to the use of the recent past as a stick with which to beat 'fanatics'. Finally, and drawing on studies of cultural, intergenerational, and post-memory, chapter 8 demonstrates that seditious memories were expressed by individuals whose formative political experiences were events that occurred after the Restoration in 1660.[57] In doing so, it suggests that one consequence, and indeed motivation, of the expression of seditious memories by those who had supported Parliament and the Republic was to convey these meanings to a new generation of British men and women.

Gleaning the significance of seditious memories from their oppositional position within the Restoration's politics of memory increases the danger of presenting those views as a homogenous body of opinion. Since the views examined in this book are defined by the 'threat' that they were held to pose to the restored kingdoms by accusers and governors, I refer throughout to 'the wars and revolutions', as well as 'sympathies' for 'Covenants' or 'Parliament' and the 'Republic' or for 'opposition' and 'resistance' to the Stuarts and established church. Nonetheless, I deploy these terms cautiously. That they conceal differences of opinion about a range of political, religious, and socio-economic objectives, as well as how these were to be achieved, is self-evident. So too are the varying degrees with which the 'Covenanter', 'Parliamentarian', and 'republican' causes were owned by people, and, by extension, the propensity of allegiances to shift rapidly and drastically during the wars and revolutions.[58] In what follows, I interrogate these nuances and explore differences of opinion about the significance of Parliamentarianism and republicanism among its confessionally and politically diverse proponents. However, I also explore the ways in which former proponents of these notably fissiparous movements were able to find common ground after the Restoration and how this relates to experiences of censorship and censure.

With these and other claims, a relationship between memory and identity is posited in this book that some historians have suggested could not exist before the modern era. David Lowenthal has argued that, prior to modernity, 'lives were conceived not as diachronic continuities but as instances of constant, universal principles. Individual identity was fixed, consistent and vested wholly in the present.'[59] Another has gone as far as suggesting that 'terms such as "national" or "social", "cultural" or "collective memory" remain anachronistic when used to describe the early modern'.[60] In contrast to these accounts, I draw inspiration from the important recent work of Judith Pollman in acknowledging that early modern identities were bound up inextricably with the events of the past, both within and beyond the horizon of lived experience.[61] In doing so, I offer in this book a response to the calls of early modern historians to bridge a gap with the field of social psychology,[62] and hope to answer Ann Hughes's appeal for seventeenth-century British historians 'to explore the more profound effects of war, revolution and regicide on personal and political identities.'[63] Finally, and perhaps most importantly, by representing memory, authority, and identity as inextricably linked, I hope that this book will also explicate one of the ways in which people were able to actively resist, rather than merely 'negotiate', the terms of their marginalisation after the Restoration in a way that did not necessarily involve repeating the strategies of the 1640s and 1650s.

NOTES

1 M. Knights, 'The Tory Interpretation of History in the Rage of the Parties', *Huntington Library Quarterly*, 58:1–2 (Mar., 2005), 353–373.
2 Aphra Behn, *Sir Patient Fancy: A COMEDY* (London, 1678), pp. 17–18.
3 Cited in P. Jenkins, '"The Old Leaven": The Welsh Roundheads after 1660', *Historical Journal*, 24:4 (1981), 822.
4 Thomas D'Urfey, *The Whig Rampant: OR, EXALTATION. Being a Pleasant New Song of 82* (London, 1682).
5 For notable exceptions, see I. Atherton, 'Remembering (and Forgetting) Fairfax's Battlefields', in A. Hopper and P. Major (eds), *England's Fortress: New Perspectives on Thomas, 3rd Lord Fairfax* (Farnham: Ashgate, 2014), pp. 95–119; M. Harris, 'The "Captain in Oliver's Army" and the Wixford Catholics: Clerical/Lay Conflict in South Warwickshire, 1640–1674', *Warwickshire History* 16:4 (Winter, 2015/16), 170–186; and M. Goldie, *Roger Morrice and the Puritan Whigs* (Woodbridge: Boydell, 2016), p. 161.
6 Tim Harris, for instance, has argued that 'it was not simply that the civil war made political partisans out of people; we have to recognize ... a profound fear of the same thing happening again': 'Understanding Popular Politics in Restoration Britain', in A. Houston and S. Pincus (eds), *A Nation Transformed: England after the Restoration* (Cambridge: Cambridge University Press, 2001), p. 129. For a similar use of this argument, see M. Knights, *Representation and Misrepresentation in Later Stuart Britain: Partisanship and Political Culture* (Oxford: Oxford University Press, 2005), pp. 4, 20.
7 See J. Scott, *Algernon Sidney and the Restoration Crisis, 1677–1683* (Cambridge: Cambridge University Press, 1991), pp. 27–49; and J. Scott, *England's Troubles: Seventeenth-Century English Political Instability in European Context* (Cambridge: Cambridge University Press, 2000), pp. 162–166.
8 J. P. Montaño, *Courting the Moderates: Ideology, Propaganda, and the Emergence of the Party, 1660–1678* (Newark, DE: University of Delaware Press, 2002), *passim*.
9 T. Harris, 'The Legacy of the English Civil War: Rethinking the Revolution', *European Legacy*, 5:4 (2000), 505; and M. Knights, *Politics and Opinion in Crisis, 1678–81* (Cambridge: Cambridge University Press, 1994), p. 11. See also G. Tapsell, *The Personal Rule of Charles II, 1681–85* (Woodbridge: Boydell, 2007), p. 11.
10 M. Zook, *Radical Whigs and Conspiratorial Politics in Late Stuart England* (University Park, PA: Pennsylvania State University Press, 1999), pp. xix–xx.
11 C. Hill, *The Experience of Defeat: Milton and Some Contemporaries* (London: Penguin, 1985); and S. Achinstein, *Literature and Dissent in Milton's England* (Cambridge: Cambridge University Press, 2003).

12 N. H. Keeble, *The Literary Culture of Nonconformity in Later Seventeenth-Century England* (Leicester: Leicester University Press, 1987).
13 S. Bardle, *The Literary Underground in the 1660s: Andrew Marvell, George Wither, Ralph Wallis, and the World of Restoration Satire and Pamphleteering* (Oxford: Oxford University Press, 2012); and D. Norbrook, 'Memoirs and Oblivion: Lucy Hutchinson and the Restoration', *Huntington Library Quarterly*, 75:2 (Summer, 2012), 233–282.
14 B. Worden, *Roundhead Reputations: The English Civil Wars and the Passions of Posterity* (London: Allen Lane, Penguin, 2001).
15 Notable exceptions here are Achinstein, *Literature and Dissent*; A. Hopper, *'Black Tom': Sir Thomas Fairfax and the English Revolution* (Manchester: Manchester University Press, 2007), pp. 225–226; and T. Cooper, *John Owen, Richard Baxter and the Formation of Nonconformity* (Farnham: Ashgate, 2011), p. 296.
16 For the psychological impact of warfare, see M. Stoyle, 'Memories of the Maimed: The Testimony of Charles I's Former Soldiers, 1660–1730', *History*, 88:290 (2003), 204–226; M. Stoyle, 'Remembering the English Civil Wars', in P. Gray and K. Oliver (eds), *The Memory of Catastrophe* (Manchester: Manchester University Press, 2004), pp. 19–30; and E. Peters, *Commemoration and Oblivion in Royalist Print Culture, 1658–1667* (Cham, Switzerland: Palgrave Studies in the History of Media, 2017), especially ch. 4. For the psychological impact of dispossession on Royalist clergymen, see F. McCall, *Baal's Priests: The Loyalist Clergy and the English Revolution* (Farnham: Ashgate, 2013); and F. McCall, 'Children of Baal: Clergy Families and Their Memories of Sequestration during the English Civil War', *Huntington Library Quarterly*, 76:4 (Winter, 2013), 617–638.
17 'An Act of Free and Generall Pardon Indempnity and Oblivion', 12 Car. II, c. 11, *The Statutes of the Realm* (10 vols, n.p.: Great Britain Record Office, 1810–28), v, pp. 226–234 (hereafter 'Act of Indemnity and Oblivion').
18 M. Neufeld, *The Civil Wars after 1660: Public Remembering in Late Stuart England* (Woodbridge: Boydell, 2013), p. 2.
19 *Ibid.*, p. 5.
20 *Ibid.*, pp. 98–120.
21 A. Milton, 'Licensing, Censorship, and Religious Orthodoxy in Early Stuart England', *Historical Journal*, 41:3 (Sept., 1998), 651.
22 P. Lake, 'Calvinism and the English Church, 1570–1635', *Past and Present*, 114 (Feb., 1987), 34.
23 G. Kemp, 'L'Estrange and the Publishing Sphere', in J. McElligott (ed.), *Fear, Exclusion and Revolution: Roger Morrice and Britain in the 1680s* (Aldershot: Ashgate, 2006), p. 69
24 This work thus responds to calls to engage with oral culture as measure of political opinion. See T. Harris, 'Introduction', in T. Harris (ed.), *The Politics of the Excluded, c.1500–1850* (Basingstoke: Palgrave, 2001), pp. 1–29; T. Harris, 'Understanding Popular Politics', p. 128; and L. Bowen, 'Seditious Speech and Popular Royalism, 1649–60', in J. McElligott and D. L. Smith (eds), *Royalists and Royalism during Interregnum* (Manchester: Manchester University Press, 2010), p. 45.
25 Andy Wood, 'Custom, Identity and Resistance: English Free Miners and their Law, c.1550–1800', in P. Griffiths, A. Fox, and S. Hindle (eds), *The Experience of*

Authority in Early Modern England (Basingstoke: Macmillan, 1996), pp. 249–285; Andy Wood, *The 1549 Rebellions and the Making of Early Modern England* (Cambridge: Cambridge University Press, 2007), pp. 209–264; Andy Wood, *The Memory of the People: Custom and Popular Senses of the Past in Early Modern England* (Cambridge: Cambridge University Press, 2013); and Andy Wood, 'Coda: History, Time and Social Memory', in K. Wrightson (ed.), *A Social History of England 1500–1750* (Cambridge: Cambridge University Press, 2017), pp. 373–391. For another historian's work on popular alternative memories, see D. Woolf, *The Social Circulation of the Past: English Historical Culture: 1500–1730* (Oxford: Oxford University Press, 2003), pp. 339–342.

26 For the term 'articulation', see J. Fentress and C. Wickham, *Social Memory* (Oxford: Blackwell, 1988), pp. 26, 47–48.

27 P. K. Monod, *Jacobitism and the English People, 1688–1788* (Cambridge: Cambridge University Press, 1993), p. 233.

28 See, for instance, T. Harris, *London Crowds in the Reign of Charles II: Propaganda and Politics from the Restoration until the Exclusion Crisis* (Cambridge: Cambridge University Press, 1987).

29 C. Hill, *Some Intellectual Consequences of the English Revolution* (London: Weidenfeld and Nicolson, 1980), p. 15; C. Hill, 'Republicanism after the Restoration', in *England's Turning Point: Essays on 17th Century English History* (London: Bookmarks, 1998), p. 67; B. Sharp, 'Popular Political Opinion in England, 1660–1865', *History of European Ideas*, 10:1 (1989), 13–29; Scott, *England's Troubles*, p. 344; A. Hopper, 'The Farnley Wood Plot and the Memory of the Civil Wars in Yorkshire', *Historical Journal*, 45:2 (2002), 281–303; Andy Wood, *Riot, Rebellion and Popular Politics in Early Modern England* (Basingstoke: Palgrave: 2002), p. 176; and D. Cressy, *Dangerous Talk: Scandalous, Seditious, and Treasonable Speech in Pre-modern England* (Oxford: Oxford University Press, 2010), pp. 203–222.

30 R. L. Greaves, *Deliver Us from Evil: The Radical Underground in Britain, 1660–1663* (Oxford: Oxford University Press, 1986); R. L. Greaves, *Enemies under His Feet: Radicals and Nonconformists in Britain, 1664–1677* (Stanford, CA: Stanford University Press, 1990); and R. L. Greaves, *Secrets of the Kingdom: British Radicals from the Popish Plot to the Revolution of 1688–1689* (Stanford, CA: Stanford University Press, 1992).

31 J. C. D. Clark, *Revolution and Rebellion: State and Society in England in the Seventeenth and Eighteenth Centuries* (Cambridge: Cambridge University Press, 1986), p. 98; T. Harris, *London Crowds*, p. 51; and A. Marshall, *Intelligence and Espionage in the Reign of Charles II, 1660–1685* (Cambridge: Cambridge University Press, 1994), pp. 12–17.

32 Cressy, *Dangerous Talk*, p. 203.

33 Marshall, *Intelligence and Espionage*, p. 15.

34 T. Harris, 'The Leveller Legacy: From the Restoration to the Exclusion Crisis', in M. Mendle (ed.), *The Putney Debates of 1647: The Army, the Levellers and the English State* (Cambridge: Cambridge University Press, 2001), p. 228; and T. Harris, *Restoration: Charles II and His Kingdoms* (London: Allen Lane, 2005), p. 97.

35 Zook, *Radical Whigs*, p. xx.

36 Z. Gille, 'Postscript', in M. Todorova and Z. Gille (eds), *Post-Communist Nostalgia* (New York: Basic Books, 2010), p. 286.

37 P. Withington, 'Company and Sociability in Early Modern England', *Social History*, 32:3 (Aug., 2007), 301.
38 Helpful in the conceptual framing of this book have been the following: J. K. Olick and J. Robbins, 'Social Memory Studies: From "Collective Memory" to the Historical Sociology of Mnemonic Practices', *Annual Review of Sociology*, 24 (1998), 105–140; W. Kansteiner, 'Finding Meaning in Memory: A Methodological Critique of Collective Memory Studies', *History and Theory*, 41:2 (May, 2002), 179–197; B. A. Misztal, *Theories of Social Remembering* (Maidenhead: Open University Press, 2003); G. Beiner, *Remembering the Year of the French: Irish Folk History and Social Memory* (Madison, WI: University of Wisconsin Press, 2007), especially ch. 1; and G. Cubitt, *History and Memory* (Manchester: Manchester University Press, 2007).
39 See J. Rydgren, 'Shared Beliefs about the Past: A Cognitive Sociology of Intersubjective Memory', *Frontiers of Sociology*, 11 (2009), 307–330.
40 Fentress and Wickham, *Social Memory*, *passim*; and J. Prager, *Presenting the Past: Psychoanalysis and the Sociology of Misremembering* (Cambridge, MA: Harvard University Press, 1998), ch. 3. On the nature of identity, the following work was particularly helpful: S. Stryker and P. J. Burke, 'The Past, Present, and Future of an Identity Theory', *Social Psychology Quarterly*, 63:4 (Dec., 2000), 284–297.
41 For state control over collective remembering, see J. Wertsch, *Voices of Collective Remembering* (Cambridge, Cambridge University Press, 2002), ch. 4. On the 'promotion' of memories at particular times, see K. Hodgkin and S. Radstone, 'Introduction: Contested Pasts', in K. Hodgkin and S. Radstone (eds), *Memory, History, Nation: Contested Pasts* (New Brunswick, NJ: Transaction, 2003), p. 5. Some of the earliest studies of remembering emphasised the extent to which control over how events were remembered lent itself to the reproduction of capitalist relations of production. See J. Le Goff, *History and Memory*, trans. S. Rendall and E. Claman (New York: Columbia University Press, 1977), p. 54; and E. Hobsbawm, 'Introduction: Inventing Traditions', in E. Hobsbawm and T. Ranger (eds), *The Invention of Tradition* (Cambridge: Cambridge University Press, 1983), pp. 1–14.
42 B. Molden, 'Resistant Pasts versus Mnemonic Hegemony: On the Power Relations of Collective Memory', *Memory Studies*, 9:2 (2016), 125–142.
43 S. Hall, *Cultural Studies 1983: A Theoretical Study* (Durham, NC: Duke University Press, 2016), p. 172.
44 Richard Terdiman describes memory as 'inherently contestatory': *Present Past: Modernity and the Memory Crisis* (Ithaca, NY: Cornell University Press, 1993), p. 20. Barbara Misztal has incorporated these accounts into a broader backlash against the 'invention of tradition' analyses of Eric Hobsbawm and others; see Misztal, *Theories of Social Remembering*, pp. 60–61. For an application of this mode of thinking to early modern Britain, see J. Greenberg and L. Martin, 'Politics and Memory: Sharnborn's Case and the Role of the Norman Conquest in Stuart Political Thought', in H. Nenner (ed.), *Politics and the Political Imagination in Later Stuart Britain: Essays Presented to Lois Green Schwoerer* (Rochester, NY: University of Rochester Press, 1997), p. 121.
45 M. Foucault, 'An Interview with Michel Foucault', trans. M. Jordin, *Radical Philosophy*, 11 (Summer, 1975), 24–29; Popular Memory Group, 'Popular

Memory: Theory, Politics, Method', in R. Johnson, G. McLennan, B. Schwarz, and D. Sutton (eds), *Making Histories: Studies in History-Writing and Politics* (London: Hutchinson in association with the Centre for Contemporary Cultural Studies, University of Birmingham, 1982), pp. 205–252; and J. Bodnar, *Remaking America: Public Memory, Commemoration, and Patriotism in the Twentieth Century* (Princeton, NJ: Princeton University Press, 1992).

46 My use of the phrase 'politics of memory' echoes that of Raingard Esser: 'the appropriation of a version of the past which could accommodate and support present politics and attitudes': *The Politics of Memory: The Writing of Partition in the Seventeenth-Century Low Countries* (Leiden: Brill, 2012), p. 10.

47 C. Hill, *Experience of Defeat*; and B. Adams, 'The Experience of Defeat Revisited: Suffering, Identity and the Politics of Obedience among Hertford Quakers, 1655–65', in C. Durston and J. Maltby (eds), *Religion in Revolutionary England* (Manchester: Manchester University Press, 2006), pp. 249–268. On 'political memory' and experiences of defeat, see A. Assmann, 'Four Formats of Memory: From Individual to Collective Constructions of the Past', in C. Emden and D. Midgley (eds), *Cultural Memory and Historical Consciousness in the German-Speaking World since 1500: Papers from the Conference "The Fragile Tradition", Cambridge 2002*, vol. 1 (Oxford: Peter Lang, 2004), p. 27.

48 Woolf, *Social Circulation*, p. 297.

49 R. Macgillivray, *Restoration Historians and the English Civil War* (The Hague: Martinus Nijhoff, 1974); R. C. Richardson, *The Debate on the English Revolution* (London: Methuen, 1977), ch. 2; and Neufeld, *Civil Wars after 1660*, chs 1 and 3.

50 For uses of the term 'communities of memory', see R. N. Bellah, R. Madsen, W. M. Sullivan, A. Swidler, and S. M. Tipton, *Habits of the Heart: Individualism and Commitment in American Life* (Berkeley, CA: University of California Press, 1985); pp. 153–155; I. Irwin-Zarecka, *Frames of Remembrance: The Dynamics of Collective Memory* (New Brunswick, NJ: Transaction, 1994), ch. 3; and W. J. Booth, *Communities of Memory: On Witness, Identity, and Justice* (Ithaca, NY: Cornell University Press, 2006).

51 See Fentress and Wickham, *Social Memory*, p. 51; and S. Boym, 'Nostalgia and Its Discontents', *Hedgehog Review*, 9:2 (2007), 13.

52 Hall, *Cultural Studies 1983*, especially 'Lecture 8: Culture, Resistance, and Struggle', pp. 180–206.

53 See D. Woolf, 'Two Elizabeths? James I and the Late Queen's Famous Memory', *Canadian Journal of History*, 20:2 (Summer, 1985), 167–191.

54 See C. R. Snyder and D. B. Feldman, 'Hope for the Many: An Empowering Social Agenda', in C. R. Snyder (ed.), *Handbook of Hope: Theory, Measures, and Applications* (San Diego, CA: Academic Press, 2000), pp. 389–412.

55 T. Harris, 'The British Dimension, Religion, and the Shaping of Political Identities during the Reign of Charles II', in T. Claydon and I. McBride (eds), *Protestantism and National Identity: Britain and Ireland, c. 1650–c. 1850* (Cambridge: Cambridge University Press, 1998), pp. 131–156.

56 P. Connerton, *How Societies Remember* (Cambridge: Cambridge University Press, 1989), ch. 2.

57 E. Tonkin, *Narrating Our Pasts: The Social Construction of Oral History* (Cambridge: Cambridge University Press, 1992), ch. 6; J. Assmann, 'Collective Memory and

Cultural Identity', trans. J. Czaplika, *New German Critique*, 65 (Spring–Summer, 1995), 125–133; and M. Hirsch, *The Generation of Postmemory: Writing and Visual Culture after the Holocaust* (New York: Columbia University Press, 2012).

58 A. Hughes, 'A "Lunatick Revolter from Loyalty": The Death of Rowland Wilson and the English Revolution', *History Workshop Journal*, 61 (Spring, 2006), 192–204; and A. Hopper, *Turncoats and Renegadoes: Changing Sides during the English Civil Wars* (Oxford: Oxford University Press, 2012).

59 D. Lowenthal, *The Past Is a Foreign Country* (Cambridge: Cambridge University Press, 1985), p. 198.

60 H. Weber, *Memory, Print, and Gender in England, 1653–1759* (New York: Palgrave, 2008), p. 11.

61 J. Pollman, *Memory in Early Modern Europe: 1500–1800* (Oxford: Oxford University Press, 2017), especially ch. 1.

62 V. Glăveanu and K. Yamamoto, 'Bridging History and Social Psychology: What, How and Why', *Integrative Psychological and Behavioral Science*, 46:4 (2012), 431–439; and D. Woolf, 'Afterword: Shadows of the Past in Early Modern England', *Huntington Library Quarterly*, 76:4 (Winter, 2013), 650.

63 Hughes, 'Lunatick Revolter', 201.

Chapter 2

Locating seditious memories in England and Wales

Studies of how the civil wars and revolution were remembered after the Restoration in England and Wales have tended to focus on retrospective hostility, and how this was marshalled as a means of discrediting forms of political and religious dissent. This chapter differs from these portrayals of the mnemonic landscape after the Restoration by highlighting alternative opinions about the 1640s and 1650s. It does so by largely eschewing print culture as an accurate measure of the full range of opinions about politics and religion in this era. Whereas, as we shall see, seditious material was circulated in print after the Restoration, and some of this even harked back favourably to the decades of conflict and revolution, the output of the English presses more often reflected the opinions of those who controlled them: namely, hard-line Royalists whose antipathy towards Parliamentarianism and republicanism and sympathies for those who had resisted them with their lives, liberties, and estates were undisguised.

Encountering alternative interpretations of the civil wars and revolution requires a careful engagement with evidence of seditious and treasonable speech and writing in legal records and government papers. This includes cases which came before quarter and assize sessions courts and which were conveyed to secretaries of state at Whitehall. The chapter begins by identifying views about the civil wars and revolution that the Sedition Act of 1661 and other legislation of the Cavalier Parliament sought specifically to counteract. Thereafter, we encounter other 'forms' of remembering which, owing to the breadth of what was held by the authorities to be threatening to the safety and security of the Stuart realms, were also suppressed by the authorities. These 'seditious memories', as I refer to them, are distilled into four forms: identification, nostalgia, prospection, and justification. Each of these forms is shown to have resembled, if not actually foreshadowed, modes of past-, present-, and future-oriented remembering to which social scientists and historians of other chronological and geographical contexts have referred.

Throughout, and especially at the end, of this chapter, I grapple with the issue of how representative of a wider body of opinion these seditious memories were. When historians have cited alternative memories of the civil wars and revolution, they are often attributed only to a minority of recalcitrant and violent fantasists.[1] I argue that certain features of seditious memories, and the apparent self-censorship of comparable opinions in scribal form, suggest that these views should be taken seriously as representative of a wider phenomenon. This entails examining the kind of material that is available in legal records and government papers alongside diaries and other writings. We now know that some diarists may have intended for their writings to be read by wider audiences and that, consequently, such records must be read in the light of the author's attempts to fashion an image of her or himself.[2] Care has been taken here to select material for which declared intentions and posthumous publication suggest personal use or that of an immediate family. Through this analysis, the chapter leads us towards an issue with which subsequent chapters tussle: why was it that individuals articulated these opinions when the risks of doing so were considerable?

ENDURING ALLEGIANCES

In the year following Charles II's restoration, England and Wales's new governors displayed little sympathy for those who continued to denigrate monarchy. In February 1661, the radical Robert Danvers found himself in the Tower of London for sympathising with the Fifth Monarchists' rising a month earlier and adding that 'he would be true to his former principles against his ma[j]estie'.[3] His words echoed those of Phillip Leigh, who, at around the same time, was hauled before the Somerset quarter sessions for saying at a Castle Cary inn that 'he had never obeyed the Kings lawes nor ever would'.[4] Yet the kind of language that aroused government suspicions extended well beyond unambiguously republican sentiments. When Thomas Philpott, a corrector of the press, was examined in December 1660, he admitted having taken Parliament's Protestation (1641–42) and the Solemn League and Covenant (1643) and confessed that it was 'honorable for him to keepe [them]'.[5]

Suggesting an eagerness to crack down on the expression of alternative allegiances to the Crown, the newly assembled Cavalier Parliament passed legislation in 1661 that revivified existing legislation against seditious and treasonable speech and writing. The Sedition Act, which came into effect on 24 June 1661, drew on existing treason laws by prohibiting the 'compass[ing] imagin[ing] devis[ing] or intend[ing] death or destruccon or any bodily harm' to the monarch. It was also treasonable to 'deprive or depose' the king 'from the Stile Honour or Kingly Name of the Imperiall Crowne of this Realme ... or to levy war against His Majestie'. Seditious language extended to expressions in 'writing printing preaching or other speaking' of 'any Words Sentences or other thing or things to incite or stir up the people to hatred or dislike of the Person of His Majestie or established Government.'[6]

The Sedition Act also singled out two specific opinions as being seditious and punishable by pains of praemunire: that is, imprisonment and forfeiture of all goods and property to the Crown. The first was the idea, inspired by legislation of 1641, that the Long Parliament of 1640–48 and 1660 had not been, and indeed could not be, dissolved without the consent of its members. The second was the view that 'there lies any obligation upon [a subject] from any Oath Covenant or Engagement whatsoever to endeavor a change of Government either in Church or State'. This passage referred specifically to the Solemn League and Covenant, but it also encompassed the Protestation oath and the 1650 Engagement Oath to the Commonwealth. The act justified these stipulations with respect to several 'assertions' that had been 'seditiously maintained in some Pamphlets lately printed and are daily promoted by the active enemies of our Peace & Happines'.[7] This was a reference to *The Long Parliament Revived* and Zachary Crofton's pro-Covenant pamphlet *Berith Anti-Baal*, both of which had been published in 1660–61.[8]

Through its specific provisions, the Sedition Act of 1661 sought to sever the ties with which men and women had bound themselves to the causes of Parliament and the Republic in the two decades beforehand. Thereby, legislators endeavoured to eliminate allegiances which, as the civil wars and revolution had shown, were incompatible with loyalty to the Crown and established church. Despite these intentions, the execution of the Sedition Act over the remainder of the seventeenth century and its traces within legal records and government papers reveal the survival of seditious allegiances. In 1662, for instance, the Congregationalist minister Edward Bagshaw was arrested and committed to the Tower of London for echoing *The Long Parliament Revived* with his seditious contention that the Long Parliament was 'not yet dissolved, because they had passed an Act that they could not be dissolved save by themselves, so that government was absolutely in that Parliament'. Bagshaw added that 'the people would rather be governed by them than by these new upstarts', a salutary reminder that, for those like Bagshaw who were in their thirties in the early 1660s, the supporters of the Restoration were the true 'upstarts'.[9] References to the Protestation and Solemn League and Covenant also endured. In 1666, a true bill was found against Christopher Marshall at the York assizes for preaching at Horbury in West Yorkshire that 'those who had taken the *Protestation* ... and afterwards attended their parish churches were perjured persons.'[10]

Significantly, most references in legal and state papers to seditious allegiances extend beyond the *specific* provisions of the Sedition Act. In April 1664, for instance, it was reported from Wimborne in Dorset that one Gill, a tucker, had described Oliver Cromwell as having been 'taken away for ye sinnes of ye people'.[11] This information was conveyed to Whitehall by William Constantine, a former Royalist, who wrote that the tucker had been 'brought befor me & my neighbour Savage for speeking words derogating from ye government',[12] suggesting that Gill had been indicted under the Sedition Act for his words. To be sure, since anything that might 'stir up the people to hatred or dislike of ... His Majestie or the established Government' was vulnerable to being charged with sedition, or even treason, under the act of 1661, quarter and assize session records offer numerous references to other forms of enduring allegiance. Commonly, these echoed Gill's sense of allegiance to Oliver Cromwell, the commander-in-chief of the Parliamentarian forces during the civil wars and lord protector from 1653 until his death in 1658. Such cases often entail language which implies that an individual had served Oliver as a soldier or were deploying his name as a placeholder for more general service under Parliament in the 1640s. In August 1662, for instance, a true bill was found against the Londoner Henry Zouch for proclaiming that 'if Oliver were alive, I would fight for him before any man in England for money.'[13] Others made unfavourable comparisons between Oliver Cromwell and Charles II. At the July 1662 quarter sessions in Richmond, North Yorkshire, a yeoman from Westhorpe was indicted for saying that 'Cromwell and [General Henry] Ireton was as good as the King.'[14]

This reference to Henry Ireton, Parliamentarian general and son-in-law of Oliver Cromwell, is suggestive of a broader cast of historical actors to whom people might declare enduring allegiance after 1660. When, in October 1681, the Canterbury resident John Jones was informed against for speaking seditious words, it was for stating his adherence to Oliver's son, Henry, who he believed possessed 'a better title to the Crowne of England, then [sic] the Duke of Yorke'.[15] Similar cases suggest that the government was equally concerned with the citation of allegiances to Major-General John Lambert, a Parliamentarian figurehead whose name was often mentioned in connection with conspiracies after the Restoration. In late summer 1662, it was alleged that, on hearing a report of Lambert's forthcoming trial, the Somerset man John Steevens threatened that 'if [he] were put to death ... there would and should bee bloody noses.'[16] Two years earlier, recognizances were taken at the Middlesex quarter sessions for the appearance of one John Harper to prefer an indictment against William Cox for saying that 'my Lord Lambert deserved the Crowne and to bee King better then King Charles the Second.'[17] Here, we find that Cox's sympathies for Lambert extended to the use of his lordly title, a subversive reference, perhaps, to his having purchased the manor of Wimbledon, a former residence of Henrietta Maria.[18] They also denote how allegiance to Parliamentarian figureheads could be reconciled with monarchical structures. This was evidently not a concern of Dartford man William Burman, who allegedly said in 1678 that 'I am for noe King in England nor for any head of ye church but Jesus Christ' and that 'I was formally acquainted with John Lilbourne, and was privy to all his affaires and undertakeings'.[19]

Perhaps the most famous form of enduring Parliamentarian and republican allegiance was that which cleft to the 'old cause' or 'good old cause'. Allegations that individuals had cited the cause are prominent in government papers throughout the reign of Charles II, especially at moments when its anxieties about republican plotting were most acute.[20] In the wake of the revelation of the Rye House Plot in July 1683, for instance, the regime was sent a list of reasons for apprehending one Samuel Gibson. Notwithstanding his recent admission to the King's Guards, it was explained that Gibson had 'often vindicated ye old Cause and boasted of his Successe against the Then Cavaliers.'[21] This phrase is usually associated by historians with republican opposition to the Protectorate in the mid-1650s and the campaign to restore the Rump Parliament after Oliver Cromwell's death in 1658.[22] Yet the term was also cited during the 1640s and 1650s as a means of evoking the 'good' and 'old' causes with which Puritans had identified their reforming endeavours from the late sixteenth century onwards.[23] While the government, and some recent historians, have equated references to the good old cause after 1660 with the perpetuation of republicanism, it continued to connote the 'reformation' that Parliamentarians had sought in the 1640s. It was with recourse to this framing that the Dissenter Oliver Heywood wrote privately in 1677 of his 'preaching and suffering so much' in his lifetime 'for the good old cause of puritanism and Nonconformity'.[24]

Together with the endurance of the good old cause, the case of Samuel Gibson 'boast[ing] of his Successe against the Then Cavaliers' suggests adherence to Parliament, its oaths, and its leaders were not the only concerns of the authorities after the Restoration. Like him, others were accused of refusing to relinquish ill feeling for the old enemy: those who Gibson termed 'Cavaliers'. William Ivye of Wincanton was informed against in November 1661 by Elizabeth Walter the Younger for asserting that '[i]t had byne noe matter if all the Cavaleires had byne hanged for 7 years agoe, and that [tha]t would have byne the better for him'.[25] Despite the dating discrepancy, Ivye was probably referring to the Royalist rising of 1655 and, more specifically, the failure of the Commonwealth to secure the prosecution of many of the local people who were suspected of participating.[26] Ivye's conception of a lasting enemy was supplemented by anti-episcopacy when the Wiltshire man Jonathan Godby was reported as having spoken seditiously of a future rising against both 'bishops and cavaliers' in 1662.[27]

Equally common in cases like these was the vilification of 'turn coats' or those who were identified as having reneged on the cause of Parliament or the Republic. The insult became common during the civil wars, providing what Andrew Hopper has described as 'an act of self-definition that testified to one's ownership of "the cause" and legitimized one's position.'[28] Following the Restoration, the identification of 'turn coats' reflects the endurance of this process, but it also foreshadows what historians have described as 'myths of betrayal' in the context of the American Reconstruction and Germany between the world wars.[29] By constructing these myths, the downfall of Parliament's cause was attributed to the sabotage of uniquely perfidious individuals rather than to its inherent weaknesses. By far the most frequent target of the 'turn coat' slur was George Monck, Duke of Albemarle, whose perfidy forms a recurring trope in cases of sedition.[30] Monck was the key player in the restoration of Charles II, using his command of the Commonwealth's forces in Scotland to enforce the dissolution of the Rump Parliament in February 1660. For his pains, Charles bestowed Monck with a dukedom, and when he died in 1670 he was given a state funeral of such 'extraordinary Order, Pomp, and Magnificency' that it set back the Treasury over £5,000.[31] Typifying the hostility of some former Parliamentarians and republicans towards Monck, Major Thomas Willoughby, a prisoner in the Fleet, was informed against in early 1662 for having remarked bitterly that 'Monck was a bloody man' and that 'hee broke his Oath to the Parliamt', a reference to the Engagement Oath. Willoughby added that Monck's true intentions had been 'to make himselfe as greate as the Protector, but things hapning otherwise, hee was forc't to bring in the King'.[32] In January 1663, a Welshman named John Morris was accused of saying similarly that Monck was 'a Traytor' for having 'brought in [tha]t Bastard Charles Steward'.[33]

Significantly, Charles II was also accused of treachery. When, in June 1663, the London merchant tailor Samuel Lewys bewailed the Restoration, he cited the fact that 'wee were made to believe when the King came in That we should never pay any more taxes.'[34] Besides fiscal grievances, Charles was also accused of betraying the Dissenters to whom he had promised toleration from exile in 1660.[35] As well as predicting a future plot against the government, John Elliot, prisoner at Ilchester in Somerset, said in December 1662 that 'the kinge made promises while hee was beyond ye seas & was ashamed of what hee had donne.'[36] Such criticisms extended to Charles's subscription to, but later distancing from, the Solemn League and Covenant. In December 1660, for instance, the rector of Westmeston in East Sussex, Nathaniel Jones, was accused, although later cleared, of saying that 'the King had broken the Covenant and made the people to break it.'[37] When Charles was crowned four months later, 'a base, scurrilous, seditious and factious Libel' was posted at Worcester 'in several places of the City', which prayed, 'Lord; in mercy grant' that Charles might 'solemnly ... sware the Covenant.'[38] Such cases suggest that immediately before and after the Restoration (vain) expectations persisted that Charles II would stay true to covenanted reformation.

The cases examined so far illustrate a range of allegiances that, in harking back to the civil wars and Republic, were held to be seditious and treasonable. Taken at face value, this evidence speaks of the enduring force that individual decisions to take up arms – not to mention the various objectives, institutions, oaths, and leaders of Parliament and the Republic that influenced these decisions – exerted over their erstwhile supporters after the Restoration. It suggests that what one *had been* – a supporter of Parliament and the Republic – continued to hold sway over what one was, and what one might be, even when the referents to which those identities clung had legally (as in the case of the Covenant) or vitally (as in the case of Oliver Cromwell) expired. Since, as sociologists have long argued, 'the characteristics of one's group as a whole ... achieve most of their significance in relation to the perceived differences from other groups', these identities were only partly defined by what its members were. What they were not was also important.[39] It is for this reason that we find that cases of seditious allegiance are split equally between identification *with* Parliament and the Republic, and *against* an 'other' that took the form of Royalists (or 'Cavaliers') and so-called 'turn coats'. This suggests that the social psychological impact of the civil wars and revolution was sufficient that political and religious identities continued to be informed by those events long after the Restoration.

PRAISING THE OLD DAYS

Retrospective allegiances and enduring antagonisms are aspects of the Restoration mnemonic landscape that can be identified in records of seditious or treasonable sentiment. Language that compared the government of Charles II unfavourably with that of the Commonwealth and Protectorate was also vulnerable to being treated as dangerous by the former and its supporters. This is illustrated evocatively by the tirade of Charles Browne on Christmas Eve 1663. Browne, a resident of Wickham Market in Suffolk, argued that 'there was a better governement in England by Olivers Dayes then is now And that there were none but a Company of Whores & Rogues now belonging to Whitehall & that formerly he could have eaten & drunke at Whitehall but now ... there would start up a pimping Rogue & say ["]sirra pull of your hatt & say God save the King["].'[40] Browne's comparison of 'Olivers Dayes' with those of Charles II was a common trope of seditious speech after 1660. Five years after the Restoration, they were echoed by one Edward Paige, a barber-surgeon living in the parish of St Katherine's, London. Paige was accused of saying that 'Cromwells government was farr better than this present is', since '[there] was like to be good govment when ye King keepe other mens wyfes and make them in concubynes.'[41] In both cases, references to the half-decade of Oliver's reign brought the sexual licentiousness of Charles II's court, real or imagined, into sharp contrast.

Pro-Cromwellian sentiment appears to have increased during the crisis years of the mid-1660s, and particularly during the Second Anglo-Dutch War of 1665–67, which culminated in the embarrassment of the Dutch raid on the River Medway, Kent, in June 1667. It was during this time that a true bill was found against Henry Northit, a yeoman living in Tottenham, Middlesex, for complaining that soldiers were 'better paid in the days of Oliver'.[42] Opinions such as these were widespread, a fact to which the words of several contemporary commentators testify. One concerned onlooker informed the government in 1666 that 'the comon people ... Curs the King and wish for Crumwell'.[43] Similar reports emerged from Hull a year later when the townspeople were heard to murmur that 'thinges were better ordered in Crumwills time, for then seamen had all their pay, and were not: permitted to swere but were claped in ye bilboes [leg shackles], & if ye: Offisers did the[y] were turned out, & then God gave a blessing: to them.'[44] That the spike in evidence of comparisons between the new government and its predecessor reflected an upsurge in such opinion, rather than merely a government crackdown, is illustrated by the claim of Samuel Pepys that 'everybody doth nowadays reflect upon Oliver and commend him, so brave things he did and made all the neighbour princes fear him'. Pepys compared Oliver with 'a prince,' who had 'come in with all the love and prayers and good liking of his people,' but had 'lost all so soon'.[45]

Pepys's commentary evokes something of a rapprochement between the English people and the Republic during the middle years of the 1660s. Such sentiment often imbued Oliver Cromwell with nigh folkloric status in which his name, his 'days', and his 'time' became euphemistic for the entire era following Parliament's victories in the civil wars and what was held to be the exceptional order, sobriety, abstinence (sexual or otherwise), military prowess, and international standing of Britain at that time. For many, however, religious liberty was the main attribute of Oliver's days. In 1662, a true bill was found against George Taylor of Kendal in Cumbria for saying that 'there hath beene noe peace like as was in Oliver the Protector's time', as well as other republican sentiment.[46] Given Taylor's activities as a Quaker missionary in the 1650s, and his experiences of imprisonment following the Restoration, we might interpret his reference to 'peace' as signifying experiences of relative toleration.[47] We can also attribute similar sentiment to an 'ould rebellious soldier' who was 'secured' in May 1663 for saying 'fare well oulde Olliver', and lamenting that 'in his Days wee had good Lawes better then now'.[48]

Reflecting popular typologies of remembering from across the early modern era, this evidence suggests that Oliver Cromwell embodied a bygone age against which the present could be compared and critiqued. However, references to the comparable godliness of the 1640s and 1650s could be more explicit. In a seditious sermon for which he was later imprisoned, Andrew Parsons, the minister at Wem in Shropshire, told his congregation in 1660 that 'there was more Sin committed now in England in a Month, than was heretofore in seven Years: And that there had been more and better Preaching in England for twenty Years past, than was ever since the Apostles Days.'[49] Elias Pledger, the rector of St Antholin's in London, was reported as having preached similar sentiment in June 1662, holding forth that 'the wise ones now were ruled not by Jesus Christ, but by Macchiavelli'.[50] These kinds of opinion even made it into print. The author of the seditious pamphlet *A Treatise of the Execution of Justice*, for which the printer John Twyn was executed in 1663,[51] informed its readership of the 'dreadful and tremendous Judgment! that ever such a Nation as this, which hath for twenty years together drank of the pure and Crystal streams of living Waters, I mean the pure Worship of God; should at last be compelled to drink of the Whores Poyson!'[52]

Comparison extended to the establishment of Presbyterian ecclesiology during the 1640s and 1650s. One Nicholas Cullen was found guilty at the Maidstone assizes in July 1681 for saying that 'the Presbyterian Government was the best government that ever was used in England', words that were reported to the government as 'The Presbyterian government was ye best Government in ye world.'[53] Cullen's words reflect how long sympathies for the 'reformation' of the 1640s and 1650s endured in England and Wales. They also suggest that Presbyterians were keen to ensure that the baby of ecclesiological reformation was not thrown away with the bathwater of sectarianism and regicide.

Together, these cases tell us that the comparable successes of the 1640s and 1650s continued to influence political discourse after 1660. The atmosphere that this created and the sentiment to which it gave rise bear a strong resemblance to those that followed comparable periods of political and religious turbulence in the early modern era. In the sixteenth century, for instance, seditious and treasonable words often reflected unfavourably on the transformation from Roman Catholicism to Protestantism by evoking the pre-reformation church.[54] Likewise, Parliament's victories in the civil wars led to sympathetic references to the 1630s and earlier decades among Royalists.[55] Similar language can be identified after the Glorious Revolution, when the reigns of the Stuarts were compared unfavourably to the new Dutch king.[56] This kind of sentiment may represent a wider topos of early modern thought in which historical decline was highlighted and lamented.[57] To what extent we can refer to such sentiment as 'nostalgia', the condition of yearning for a former age, is a more challenging question.[58] Cultural theorists and social psychologists usually consider nostalgia to be a product of the accelerated rhythms of life with which the transition from pre-modernity to modernity is associated.[59] Even if what we are witnessing is not a forerunner to the specifically modern psychological condition to which the term nostalgia has been attached, there is clearly a common mode of thinking in which the conflicts and divisions of early modern Britain, and indeed Europe, led to yearning for, and the recovery of, a lost past. 'Nostalgia' is, if nothing else, a useful label for distinguishing this form of remembering.[60]

FROM PAST TO FUTURE

Underpinning the government's anxieties about sedition and treason was the possibility that opposition and resistance would be repeated. It is unsurprising, then, that a sizable proportion of cases that resulted from the Sedition Act, including some of those to which this chapter has referred, entailed the expression of more explicit hopes and expectations about the future. These reflect what scholars of memory have described as 'prospective' or 'restorative' memories.[61] Much of this language is built on the foundations of enduring Parliamentarian and republican allegiances. Hopes for, and expectations of, reprisals against so-called 'Cavaliers' were thus common: Thomas Mayson of Gainsborough in Lincolnshire said in July 1663 that 'there would be warres shortly againe in England, and that there would be fouer for one against the cavaliers.'[62] His words were echoed by Samuel Bagley, the parson of Haslebech in Northamptonshire, who was accused by several witnesses of supposing that 'if [John] Lambert did not ryse & take downe ye Cavaleeres there would bee noe dealing wth them'.[63] Both cases are characterised by self-confidence about the outcome of any future conflict between Parliamentarians and Royalists, suggesting that neither individual was resigned to the notion that the Restoration settlements were permanent.

Like Samuel Bagley, others foresaw the involvement of Parliamentarian and republican leaders in risings against the Crown and established church. Having described Charles II as 'a bastard, and the sonne of a whore', Richard Smith of Halifax was alleged to have proclaimed in 1660 that 'I hope to see Lord Lambert King', words which, as well showing the propensity of former Parliamentarians to cite Lambert's title, reinforce the notion that allegiance to the general did not entail outright republicanism.[64] Two years later, Thomas Herbert, a weaver from the north-east of England, was accused of expressing in a more unambiguously republican manner his disbelief that 'Lambert's armye' had 'been destroyed within three yeares', and his conviction that before 'three yeares goe about he would see an alteration in this government.'[65]

Less exalted figures could be the source of similar convictions about the near future, such as in 1662, when an unnamed individual was bound over by Sir Geoffrey Shakerley, the Royalist governor of Chester, for saying that 'within few years all would would [sic] bee on ... Coll: Croxtons syde or hee would bee hanged for it.'[66] The officer to whom the examinant referred was Colonel Thomas Croxton, a Parliamentarian predecessor of Shakerley as commander of Chester Castle.[67] Even the spirit of Oliver Cromwell could afford posthumous hopes for the future. In November 1663, a true bill was found against a yeoman from Rothwell in West Yorkshire for declaring that 'I served Oliver seaven yeares as a souldier, and if any one will put up the finger on the accompt that Oliver did ingage, I will doe as much as I have done. As for the Kinge I am not beholdinge to him. I care not a fart for him.'[68]

Language that suggests typologies of plebeian remembering was also used in reimaginings of the old cause. This could entail the belief that the 'wheel of time' would 'turn' and restore the conditions of the 1640s and 1650s. Perhaps the most public form that this view took after the Restoration was in the 1661 tract *The Wheel of Time turning Round to the Good Old Way*, a pamphlet which had the subtitle *The Good Old Cause Vindicated*.[69] The trope was deployed again in 1667 by Nicholas Haines, a hosier from Gloucestershire, who argued that one half of MPs '[were] feathermen and the other half of them were whoremasters and drunkards ... and that the times would turn and honest men would rule again.'[70] By 'honest men', Haines may have been referring to members of the Long Parliament, a depiction that was made more explicit in 1666 when John Davis was accused of expressing his hopes that the Long Parliament, which he considered 'the best Parliament that ever was', would 'sitt againe.'[71]

Uses of the recent past to imagine the near future could be considerably more menacing when the bloodshed of the 1640s was reimagined. Statements like these reflect the fact that combatants had been brutalised by their experiences of conflict.[72] When, in October 1661, Captain Lawrence Moyer of Leyton in Essex was heard to say that 'the longest sword would Carry it', his words were described by a witness, William Batten, as 'Aggravating'.[73] Others spoke evocatively of using 'rusty swords' against Cavaliers.[74] One of the most brutal evocations of the civil wars came in 1662, when Francis Cruse of Shoreditch, Middlesex, a former soldier in the regicide Colonel John Okey's regiment, said that 'the Booke of Common Prayer is nothing but Blasphemie & Poperie ... and iff ever their [sic] make a sored drawen againe he wuld Give No q[ua]rter too man wuman or Chyld that wold adhear to itt.'[75] Common to these cases was the belief that, given another opportunity, a more decisive victory would be secured against royalism. This 'uchronia', as it has been labelled, is evident in the words of the radical minister John James, who was executed for treason in November 1661 for saying among other seditious statements that '*when they had Power again they should do the work most thorowly.*'[76]

Sometimes, visions of the future were grounded in a grisly nostalgia, reinforcing the idea that Parliamentarians had undergone brutalisation. When Henry Ashton was accused of promising in 1664 that 'he would doe anything for a livelyhood', he was also indicted for a morbid recollection of his having 'killed twenty-five cavaliers in a day' which 'he thought ... as pleasant ... as killing of bukes or does.'[77] Ashton's deeply personal experience of the civil wars was echoed in 1664 when Henry Alsibrooke the Elder of Church Broughton in Derbyshire said that he 'wish[ed] [tha]t ye bon[d] meadow were full of souldiers and he amongst [the]m', and '[tha]t he should never be light at heart till [the]n [tha]t they may pull downe ye higher powers ... and [tha]t if there were any riseinge if he had noe horse of his owne he would take ye best horse he could light on and hoped to be at ye dealinge.'[78] By evoking memories of 'ye bon[d] meadow', Alsibrooke was likely referring to a nearby plot of land on the banks of the River Dove in which dozens of Royalists had been mown down during the First English Civil War.[79] Cases like these, in which the wars of 1642–51 are themselves the object of memories, are comparatively rare, reflecting, no doubt, the extent of war fatigue in England and Wales after the Restoration.

While opinions about the revolution could prove 'aggravating' to witnesses, few were as troubling to the authorities as those which disclosed an explicit expectation or desire to see Charles II executed as his father had been in 1649. It was for this reason that a true bill was found against Thomas Lunn, a labourer from Bootham in West Yorkshire, for saying shortly after the Restoration that 'the King shall never bee crowned, and, if hee is crowned, hee shall never live long. His father's head was taken [off] with an axe, but a bill [a billhook] shall serve to take of his.'[80] Lunn's words exhibit the confidence with which the lowliest of labourers were instilled by the events of the 1640s, referring, as he did, to the use of a farming implement to sever Charles II's neck. Elsewhere, the use of the plural personal pronoun 'we' implies that individuals felt far from alone in possessing such opinions. Samuel Bagley, whose anti-Cavalierism we encountered earlier, was accused of saying on another occasion that 'wee will serve [the king] as wee did his Father' and 'wee will Cutt off his head'.[81]

Not all images of the future to which sympathies for the 1640s and 1650s lent themselves were hopeful. By alluding to frustrated efforts to achieve political and religious reforms, some individuals were pessimistic about what was politically possible after the Restoration. This was evident in 1661 when Thomas Chapman, who was described as 'a Leveller' who had 'a great Correspondence with such, and indeed of all other factions', poured scorn on the recent 'remonstrance' that had been submitted by London's regiments of horse, trained bands and auxiliaries. '[I]n a scornfull maner', Chapman was alleged to have 'pufft at' the Remonstrance and said that 'he had seen as great a Remonstrance as that come to nothinge.'[82] Given Chapman's Leveller politics, it is likely that he was referring here to the Army Remonstrance that had been adopted in November 1648 with the intention of breaking off negotiations with Charles I. Whereas the ultimate objective of the Remonstrance was successful, the fact that it was rejected by Parliament may have been what Chapman meant by its having 'come to nothinge.' Given the choice of the adjective 'great', it is equally plausible that Chapman was referring to the Grand Remonstrance of December 1641, the document that outlined the Long Parliament's grievances with Charles I, but which was later rejected by the king.

The object of Chapman's memories is significant. If he was referring to the Remonstrance of 1648, the view of his informant that he was 'a very subtle and dangerous fellow' is more understandable than if he had been referring to that of 1641.[83] And yet additional evidence suggests that those foreseeing a repeat of the events of the early 1640s, and even earlier, were vulnerable to allegations of sedition or treason. When, in May 1664, Henry

Phillips of Paddington, then in Middlesex, reacted with hostility to news of a recent Hearth Tax amendment, he was summoned to appear before the assizes for saying that 'the King that now is did take the same waies that his father did to be ill beloved, and that the Chimnie-monie would prove a worse burden than formerly the Ship-monie was.'[84] Others were indicted for language which, while sympathetic to Parliamentarianism, couched these sympathies in avowedly monarchical terms. This is evident in the case of Daniel Winston of Portsmouth, who said in the presence of two of Charles II's servants in 1661 that 'he served the King, but if the King did call a Parliament he would serve the King and Parliament again'.[85] By claiming that he would serve the king *and* Parliament, Winston was evoking the language with which Parliamentarians had legitimised their opposition and resistance in the 1640s. That the words were construed as dangerous to the government almost certainly reflected the fact that, at the time that Winston spoke them, Charles II was escorting his mother and adolescent sister to the town.

That seditious language extended beyond that which was unequivocally radical or republican is further illustrated by the varied grammatical mood of seditious memories. While some former Parliamentarians evidently believed that, since certain events had happened, comparable events would happen again, others framed such language with conditionality. To return to Paddington man Henry Phillips, his views about the future of England and Wales were predicated on Charles II taking 'the same waies that his father did to be ill beloved'. In October 1666, William Duncke of Hawkhurst in Kent was accused, although later found not guilty, of declaring similarly that '[the king that] now is will not leave oppressing of Quakers [until] hee [the king] is served as his father was served.'[86] Much more equivocal was Richard Marsingill, a mariner from North Yorkshire, who was indicted in 1668 for complaining that 'if our Kinge had been right hee would not have imployed such rogues to have beene souldiers', and proclaiming that 'The land is badly ruled, and the King *may* come to make the same end his father made' (my italics).[87]

The conditionality and equivocation of these prospective seditious memories problematises inferences that the accused were actively pursuing the radical or republican ends to which they referred. Indeed, it is plausible that, in talking about what 'may' have happened in certain circumstances, these people were merely 'warning' the government, or its representatives and supporters, about the possible ramifications of certain actions. It is difficult to construe from this evidence whether, by reminding Charles II of what had happened to his father, this particular 'warning' was intended to assist the king rather than to threaten him and his governors. That the charges against William Duncke came to nothing may imply that, even if these words were threatening, uncertainty about intentions could make it difficult to prosecute such language.

RETHINKING REBELLION

The difficulty of construing radical or republican intent from seditious memories is exacerbated when these were oriented to the *past* rather than the present and the future. Nonetheless, there are numerous examples of allegations that individuals had seditiously justified opposition and resistance to Crown and established church during the 1640s and 1650s. Of especial concern to the government was the belief that the trial and execution of Charles I had been a just and legal act. In a well-publicised case from December 1660, Nehemiah Beaton, the rector of Little Horsted in East Sussex, was found guilty for a sermon in which he defended the lawfulness of the regicide.[88] Whereas cases of seditious words overwhelmingly reflect the opinions of men, the example of Margaret Osmond suggests how women might also express seditious memories.[89] In June 1660, Osmond, a native of Ealing, was indicted at the Old Bailey, London, for having said that '[the] Kinges Majestie [who] is dead was lawfully put to death'.[90] Such language might cite specific events as justification for the regicide, such as in March 1679 when Richard Parker was bailed 'for Speaking these Seditious words (vizt) That King Charles the first was a papist which brought him to the Block, and his hand and Seale was at the Rebellion in Ireland And that his death was Just.'[91]

Opinions that differed from common abhorrence of the regicide endured into the 1680s. In 1682, Thomas Hall, a miller from Godalming in Surrey, was fined and condemned to stand in the pillory for having said in February 1681 that 'his late [Majesty] of blessed memory had whatever deserved for running from his parliamt.'[92] While Hall denied that he spoke these words, and produced a witness to swear that the evidence had been malicious, he did not deny the allegation that he had spoken similar words six months later in his native Godalming.[93] The Parliamentarian veteran Ralph Bamford was condemned at the Oxford assizes in April of the same year for expressing the strikingly similar opinion that '[the] late King had a Legall tryall for his life And if hee had not deserved death hee had not had itt and that itt was nothing but what hee deserved.'[94] As late as 1683, a true bill was found against the Kentish man William Fagg for saying likewise that 'Old King Charles dyed according to law'.[95] Rather than explicit justification of the regicide, other individuals reiterated the charges, and indeed abuse, that had been levelled at Charles I in the 1640s and after his death. This was the case in 1660 when Christopher Highton of Southampton was accused of saying that 'King Charles the first ... was a Traytor.'[96] These views were echoed more forcefully some twenty-four years later when, according to the report of a government agent, an old Parliamentarian had said that Charles I was 'the worst of Kings and the worst of Tyrantts.'[97]

The currency of these seditious views about Charles I could reflect the surprisingly wide circulation of such opinions in print shortly after the Restoration. The Licensing Act of 1662 tightened control over the output of the printing presses (see chapter 3). And yet this legislation partly responded to the fact that justifications of the revolution had appeared in print in the form of the transcripts of the trials, final letters, and scaffold speeches of the fourteen men who were executed for their part in the demise of Charles I. Among these was John Carew, who, when asked on the scaffold in October 1660 whether 'he had anything of conviction upon him as to what he was to suffer for?', responded bluntly that he did not, since 'the Lord hath and doth justifie' and 'the Lord hath justified it in the Field once already, in this Nation.'[98] In the two days of bloodshed that followed, similar sentiments were uttered by a number of his fellow regicides.[99] When, for instance, further punishment was meted out upon the three men who were arrested in 1662, the government interrupted any attempts to justify 'that horrid Act.'[100] Despite these efforts, Colonel Okey was as outspoken as his fellow regicides in his belief that the revolution had been 'for the glory of God, and good of his people; and had I had as many lives as hairs on my head, I would have adventured them in that Cause ... I am satisfied as to the Cause.'[101]

As discovered earlier in this chapter, seditious justification of Parliament's cause also took place indirectly through what were termed myths of betrayal. One of the most intriguing of these was the claim that, far from having caused the rebellion, Presbyterians had been consistently Royalist throughout the 1640s and 1650s, and that 'papists' had been responsible for fomenting war, usurping parliament, and executing Charles I in the 1640s. One proponent of this view was Thomas Ludlam, a yeoman living in St Giles-in-the-Fields, Westminster, who confessed to having proclaimed in 1662 that 'the Church of England and Papists were the persons that cutt of [sic] the late King's head, and that the Presbyterians had noe hand in itt, and that the Presbyterians were the King's only Friends, and that he was crowned a Presbyterian.'[102] This theory had been put forward most memorably by the Presbyterian William Prynne in his 1659 tract *The Re-Publicans and Others Spurious Good Old Cause*, which laid the blame for the straits in which the Stuart kingdoms had found themselves on 'discontented Jesuited Papists,' who were 'abetted by the Pope'.[103] Prynne's theory cropped up again during the Popish Plot revelations of 1678, when Titus Oates recalled (spuriously) that the conspirators at the Jesuit college at St Omer had 'expressed that it was now apparent, that the Catholick Religion was to be brought in the same way, that they had used for the destruction of the Father of this King'.[104] That Ludlam's apparent efforts to distance himself from the regicide were regarded as seditious at all could signify the context of the government's sensitivity to disloyalty when they were spoken.

THE 1680s

Whereas the first decade of Charles II's reign has supplied the bulk of the material for this chapter, the case of Thomas Ludlam illustrates the remarkable stamina of Parliamentarian and republican sympathies. The late 1670s and early 1680s, when the Roman Catholicism of Charles II's brother and heir, James, Duke of York, became the dominant issue of political discourse, saw a resurgence of the kinds of opinions listed above. Expectations that the political and ecclesiological revolution of the 1640s and 1650s would recur were restated in May 1679 when Anthony Croft was indicted at the York assizes for saying that 'the Parliament will downe with the Lords and Bisshopps, and will doe with this King as they did with the last; and then wee shall be men.'[105] Two years later, the Yorkshireman William Beever was accused of impugning monarchical government further when he said that 'There was good times when Oliver raigned and I wish there was as good now.'[106] George Cawdron (or Cauldron), steward to the Earl of Clare, was found guilty in 1684 of evoking the Book of Micah in a similar claim that 'in Olivers [time] there was noe such stirr but every man Could sleep quietly under his owne vine & that he hoped ere long to see such times againe.'[107] References to seditious memories peaked in 1683–84 following the revelation of the Rye House Plot to execute Charles II and the Duke of York. It was during this period that Thomas Tutty, a Sussex brewer and former Oliverian lieutenant, had declared that 'hee will never renounce the Coven[an]t.'[108] Meanwhile, the labourer Mathew Webb of St Giles-without-Cripplegate in London was convicted for saying that Charles II would 'looseth his head, And hee will dye as his Father did', but only in the event that he removed the City's charter.[109] By arguing in 1684 that 'the Goverment of Oliver Cromwell was better then the Kings', Thomas Burt of Kingston-upon-Thames in Surrey shows how long such comparisons endured.[110]

The West Country appears to have been particularly fertile ground for Parliamentarian and republican sympathies in the 1680s. Over Christmas 1681, Thomas Parsons of Membury in Devon was held to have said in the nearby villages of Upottery and Offwell that 'as wee did fight agst Charles the 1st & his B[isho]ps for; & in a more Cruell man[ne]r agst this & these B[isho]ps & whoever takes ye Oath of Allegiance & Supremacy is A Roge Knave & Fool'. It was also alleged that one John Trowde, himself resident at Upottery, had said around the same time that 'he did hope to draw & fight as willingly for the parliamt that voted for ye bill of [Exclusion] as ever he did for the old parliamt'.[111] That both men participated in the Monmouth Rebellion in 1685 could suggest that they derived encouragement from their memories of what Trowde described as the 'old parliamt'.[112] To be sure, the recorder of the congregational church at nearby Axminster wrote that they and other rebels had been motivated by 'hope[s] that the day was come in which the good old cause of God and religion that had lain as dead and buried for a long time would revive again.'[113]

Notwithstanding this evidence, the reign of James II witnessed comparably few references to the civil wars and revolution in cases of sedition, reinforcing the idea that the Monmouth Rebellion was the swansong of the good old cause.¹¹⁴ From the summer of 1685, the Duke of Monmouth and his attempt to depose his uncle from the throne became the dominant subjects of seditious and treasonable sentiment.¹¹⁵ Echoing the posthumous reputation of Oliver Cromwell, there are numerous examples of identification with Monmouth after his execution in July 1685.¹¹⁶ One case from 13 July 1685, two days before the duke was beheaded, is suggestive of the waning of Oliver and the waxing of Monmouth in the popular imagination. William Robinson deposed that he had confronted one John Howden about his being 'an Oliver souldier', to which Howden had allegedly responded that 'I served Oliver no longer then he lived', before speaking language that was inferred to reflect his identification with Monmouth instead.¹¹⁷ This case and the comparative absence of references to the civil wars and revolution during the reign of James II suggest that seditious remembering was largely confined to the reign of his predecessor.

HOW REPRESENTATIVE ARE SEDITIOUS MEMORIES?

Long after the Restoration, people continued to justify, identify with, express nostalgia for, and prospect actions and actors that had contributed in various ways to political and religious change in the 1640s and 1650s. Evident in legal records and government papers, these 'seditious memories' correspond with the enduring beliefs that opposition to, resistance against, and the overthrow of the Stuarts and established church had been legitimate and beneficial, and that those actions remained relevant and recoverable. That such views existed at all suggests that the mnemonic landscape after the Restoration was considerably more diverse than a predominantly, although not entirely, Royalist print culture is likely to disclose.

The question that arises at this stage is to what extent this evidence is illustrative of broader opinion after the Restoration. The task of answering this question is complicated considerably by the nature of the evidence from which we glean seditious memories. That accusations of sedition and treason were often denied and solicited through subornation of witnesses or, as the Surrey man Thomas Hall claimed in 1682, were even fabricated out of malice, requires that we approach such material with considerable caution.¹¹⁸ Furthermore, records of cases are often incomplete, making it difficult to identify whether the evidence was deemed credible enough to result in a conviction.¹¹⁹ Much of the material examined so far, and in the remainder of this book, reflects informations, examinations, and indictments, and only irregularly is it clear that the existence of sufficient credible evidence resulted in a true bill or a conviction.

Despite these qualifications, there are reasons to credit allegations of seditious memories. Such sentiment shares the characteristics of popular typologies of remembering that can be identified throughout the early modern era, and, as we have seen, seditious memories have left a more indelible trace in print.[120] Moreover, that we more often encounter allegations than convictions may reflect the fact that the 1661 act did not always lend itself readily to the latter. When Charles Browne was accused of expressing seditious nostalgia for Oliver Cromwell, one local official complained that the Sedition Act 'prescribed' him from 'noe other methode, to deale with such persons, but to secure them, & to acquaint the King or Counsell there withall'.[121] Other magistrates may have been unwilling to prosecute seditious memories out of sympathies with the opinions in question.[122] In 1681, for instance, James Wraight, Mayor of Canterbury,[123] was accused of protecting his 'party' in the city by withholding information regarding seditious memories.[124] David Cressy has added that 'the readiness of juries to find political offenders "not guilty", despite strong evidence of their seditious words, may have inclined some officials not to pursue prosecutions.'[125] That allegations *could* lead to conviction surely reflects the fact that, in the historian Dagmar Freist's words, they were 'plausible, convincing and chargeable'.[126] To be sure, the authorities clearly took accusations of seditious memories very seriously, and considered the credibility of allegations with care.[127] When William Constantine reported the words of the Dorset tucker Gill to the government, he weighed his knowledge that the informer was 'of no good fame' against the fact that the accused associated with 'people [tha]t usually cant in that phrase'.[128]

Most historians have been willing to cut through this evidential thicket and to employ accusations of sedition as evidence of genuine opinions about politics and religion. And yet, given the war-weariness of Charles II's subjects, the popularity of his restoration, and the failure of conspiracies against him and his Church, historians are now less willing than they once were to equate such sentiment with radical or republican intent. While views about the civil wars and revolution were often bound up with opinions about the present and future, the allegiances that they convey evoke the range of political and religious opinions within the Parliamentarian and republican movements of the 1640s and 1650s. Even predictions of the downfall of Charles II and James II tended to be expressed with a conditionality and equivocation that belies actual seditious or treasonable intent. It is rare, in fact, to find sympathies for Parliament and the Republic that were accompanied by hard evidence of radical or republican objectives or actions. Finally, and most importantly, seditious memories were often exactly that, memories, and they tell us more about what people thought about the recent past – respect for parliament's 'reformation', convictions about the legality of the regicide, and nostalgia for the glory of Oliver Cromwell's 'days' to name but a few – than the near or distant futures.

Rather than radical or republican intent, then, seditious memories are most representative of the breadth of what *informants and magistrates* deemed to have threatened the safety and security of the realms, a measure that differed considerably according to who these people were and the domestic context in which they operated. Moreover, the opinions of informants and justices about what constituted sedition or treason varied. When John Reynolds was accused by the apothecary Richard Bracegirdle (or Brasgirdle) of praising Oliver Cromwell in 1669 (see chapter 4), Richard Baxter recalled that Reynolds was later released by justices of the peace who acknowledged that 'mere imprudence' had been 'heightened to a Crime'.[129] We may speculate that those who questioned Reynolds were probably not the kinds of Royalists who, like Richard Bracegirdle, tended to see sedition and treason in any favourable references to Parliament or the Republic.

That the space for subjectivity regarding sedition and treason existed at all derived from the (almost certainly deliberate) vagueness of Sedition Act itself, especially its provisions regarding 'any Words Sentences or other thing or things to incite or stir up the people to hatred or dislike of the Person of His Majestie or established Government.' This ambiguity became a point of contention during the August 1681 trial of Stephen Colledge, a man who, as we shall see in chapter 8, espoused numerous seditious and treasonable opinions about the 1640s and 1650s. Colledge contested the claim of one of his judges, Lord Chief Justice Francis North, that 'the Long Parliaments levying War is declared Rebellion by Act of Parliament.' With a brazenness that did little to endear him to the court, Colledge responded that 'if there hath been an Act since [1660] that says they were guilty of Rebellion, I declare it[,] 'tis more than ever I knew before. This is the first time that ever I heard of it.' Whereas the prosecution, Sir George Jeffreys, condescended to Colledge's claim by saying that 'You are a mighty learned Gentleman to talk of those points indeed', the court did not clarify to which act North had been referring.[130] Indeed, Colledge was almost certainly right to question whether his justification of the Long Parliament, which had provoked North's censure and was being used to corroborate a charge of treason, was actionable under the provisions of the Sedition Act.

Others were warier than Colledge about the pitfalls of expressing anything other than firm denunciation of their actions during the 1640s and 1650s. This became evident in a fascinating case from September 1665 when John Rede of Porton in Wiltshire was examined by Henry Bennet, Earl of Arlington, regarding rumours of plotting. Having identified that Rede 'was governour of Poole' during 'the Late Rebellion', Arlington probed 'whither hee is sorry that hee was soe'. To this, Rede responded that 'hee would bee sorry to comitt an evill action but will not answer to the question.'[131] Rede may well have become aware that his words were in danger of imperilling him, as he later implored Arlington that 'every word sillable Circumstance and clause' of his evidence 'may be expunged.'[132]

The risks attendant on declaring certain opinions about the civil wars and revolution extended beyond government recrimination. Reflecting the fact that seditious memories were necessarily incriminating, many of the cases considered in this chapter are drawn from allegations of a wider range of seditious or treasonable sentiment or were reported to the government at times of heightened anxiety about domestic or foreign conspiracy. Seditious memories might also provoke physical and verbal rebuke. This is evident in a case of seditious words from August 1662 when Charles North was alleged to have declared before his fellow drinkers in Blaxton, South Yorkshire, that 'King Charles was a traitor', a reference, perhaps, to the conspicuous shrinkage of the king from promises made at his coronation at Scone in 1651 and in his Declaration of Breda nine years later. For his troubles, North received 'a boxe of the eare' from John Staunton, a gentleman who hailed from the other side of the Nottinghamshire border. One witness to the assault described how North had dusted himself off, only to declare that 'he was for those men that had murthered the last King, and he would be for them as long as he had life, and that they were honest men, and that the last King did deserve the death he had.'[133] Those who clung on to Parliamentarian or republican allegiances were also vulnerable to shaming by audiences. Eight months after the scuffle involving Charles North, a Mr Child expressed his belief that 'Cromwell was an honester man and a beter ... then he that reules now.' Child was censured by those in his company, who asked him whether he was 'not a shaimed to speake such grouce words?' Apparently unfazed, Child answered with the question: 'what ne[e]d [I? I] know no differance betweene a be[g]gar and he.'[134] As with North, the attempts to silence Child were met with defiance.

The hazards associated with continuing to justify, or identify with, Parliamentarianism and republicanism may have deterred people from articulating opinions that were nonetheless keenly felt. This should lead us to doubt recent accounts of seditious and treasonable language that have dismissed them as the grumbling of a minority.[135] To be sure, anxieties about attracting allegations of sedition or treason, or physical and verbal rebuke, can be used to cast fresh light on the personal writings of better-known former opponents of Crown and established church, many of which include memories that do not differ drastically from those encountered so far in legal records and state papers. When, in 1664, the Presbyterian John Shawe produced an autobiography for his young son (see chapter 8), he did so with recourse to language which, if it had been expressed publicly, may have invoked a charge of sedition, including a reference to the Long Parliament as 'the wonder-working parliament',[136] and a glorification of Parliament's victories in the civil wars as the 'most remarkable victorys in all parts of the land.'[137] That Shawe was conscious of the danger of such language is evident in his confession that 'I write this in much hast, and love not to medle much with state matters that do not concern me; and where, if a man follow truth too near the heeles, he may possibly have his teeth dashed out.'[138]

As a figurehead of dissent in the north of England, Shawe very likely acknowledged that his opinions about his former allegiances were under especially close scrutiny. It is for this reason, no doubt, that the comparable opinions of other notable Dissenters were confined to writings that they intended to publish only posthumously. Richard Baxter's memoirs were written in the 1660s, but not published until 1696, when attitudes towards the 1640s and 1650s had changed considerably owing to the Glorious Revolution of 1688–89. In them, Baxter recalled nostalgically how, in his native Kidderminster during the Commonwealth, 'you might hear an hundred Families singing Psalms and repeating Sermons, as you passed through the Streets.'[139] The memoirs of the Parliamentarian commander Thomas, Lord Fairfax – like those of Richard Baxter, published posthumously – are characterised by what his biographer has termed 'a pride that his modesty struggled to suppress.'[140]

In each of these cases, sympathies for Parliament extended to its reformatory ambitions and certainly not to republicanism or the regicide. Moreover, none of these references to the 1640s and 1650s were explicitly restorative. Thomas Larkham, another Dissenter, differed in this latter respect. Writing in 1661, Larkham recorded his prayers that God might 'once againe restore the glory of England. Amen Amen Amen.'[141] These prayers were echoed a year later when he wrote that 'The Light's puffd out / (deare Lord) that shin'd so bright / And now in England tis a pitteous night / Descend (our Joshua) with all thy Might / And set thy churches and cause now at right.'[142] Elsewhere in his diaries, Larkham asked Christ to 'Raise up thy slaine witnesses from the dead' and 'Restore the nation Lord wee Cry.'[143] That Larkham's diary was not intended for public scrutiny during his lifetime is suggested by the fact that 'from February 1651 until his death in December 1669, he kept the paperbook beside him in Tavistock'.[144]

In addition to nostalgia, personal writings also recorded more direct justification of support for Parliament in the 1640s. Richard Baxter was one erstwhile Parliamentarian who remained willing to defend what he described as 'Parliaments good endeavours for Reformation ... [which] much swayed my Judgment in the Matter of the Wars.'[145] Baxter also shared the opinion of other Parliamentarians that blame for the downfall of their endeavours for 'reformation' lay not with themselves, but with others; namely, the radicals who usurped Parliament and the Crown in the late 1640s. In his *Reliquiae*, Baxter explained with obvious emotion that 'never were such fair opportunities to sanctifie a Nation, lost and trodden under foot, as have been in this Land of late! Woe be to them that were the Causes of it.'[146] Such views should be read positively as firm identification with what Baxter called 'fair opportunities' for 'Reformation', rather than negatively as a complement to his regular efforts to distance himself from the revolution of the late 1640s. Nonetheless, these views differed considerably from those that Baxter *did* make public before the Glorious Revolution. Writing to the former active Royalist Richard Allestree in December 1679, he said regretfully that he had been 'one of those that were glad that Parliament, [in] 1640, attempted a reformation ... which I expressed, perhaps, too openly'.[147]

The private writings of other former Parliamentarians imply that the animus directed at George Monck and other so-called traitors had a broader base. Writing at the time of Monck's death in 1670, the Parliamentarian diarist Sir Bulstrode Whitelocke recorded in his diary, which was intended 'for his private family only',[148] that '[T]he Duke of Albemarle dyed, unlamented by many.'[149] Philip Henry, a Presbyterian who had supported the Restoration, copied into his private diary the following mock epitaph for Monck, suggesting that his views had since changed: 'Here lyes Monk / Who dy'd Drunk / And left his Trunk / To his old Punk [prostitute]'.[150]

Private writings also contain evidence of continued identification against Royalists or those who were perceived as having inherited their opinions. In a letter to Richard Baxter, for example, Josiah Whiston, the Presbyterian minister of Hoggs Norton in Leicestershire, implored him to 'stop the mouthes of [Cavaliers] against that sweet way of Holynesse which you so eminently hold forth.'[151] Such identification might be more positive. This included suggestions that individuals continued to adhere to the Solemn League and Covenant and even the Long Parliament. In November 1661, for instance, Philip Henry spoke of the hesitation of 'many' of the godly at obeying an order to publish the Sedition Act in their churches 'wherein ye Covenant is declar'd an unlawful Oath & ye Cause of ye long Parliamt nullifyd'. In an uncharacteristically resistive remark, Henry wrote in his diary 'lord, break snares.'[152]

The surprisingly widespread adherence to the Covenant of which Philip Henry speaks is borne out further by evidence arising from infringement of the Corporation Act (1661) and the Act of Uniformity (1662). The historian Paul Halliday has suggested that over fifty-three per cent of those who were ejected from English and Welsh corporations under the terms of the Corporation Act (263 office holders) were ejected because of their refusal to take the oath to abjure the Covenant.[153] The strength of the Covenant's ties further down the social scale can be measured by their precipitation of acts of conspicuous nonconformity. The divine Richard Baxter explained in May 1666 that 'a sense of obligation under the covenant' was one reason that his erstwhile parishioners in Kidderminster, Worcestershire, refused to receive the sacrament under their new minister, Francis Wheeler.[154]

Despite the acts of 1661 and 1662, the reign of Charles II saw a steady flow of complaints regarding individuals who had not yet publicly renounced the Covenant. In January 1662, a petition was sent to Whitehall containing information that Joseph Crabb, the vicar of Netherbury in Dorset, was 'disaffected' since he 'still suppose[d] himselfe obliged by the Covenant'.[155] During a disturbance at Newbury Church at Easter 1664, the minister, Joseph Sayer, was accused of having 'never renounct' the Covenant.[156] The Privy Council was informed a year later of three burgesses in Leicester who refused to renounce the Covenant,[157] and a grocer in Chester was fined £100 for the same transgression in 1666.[158] By 1668, it was reported that several members of Yarmouth's corporation had not met the requirements of the Corporation Act concerning the Covenant.[159] Together, this evidence raises the intriguing possibility that sympathies for Parliament and the Republic were even more widespread than evidence of seditious and treasonable speech is likely to suggest.

CONCLUSION

Contrary to the efforts of the government, people throughout England and Wales, and from across the social spectrum, continued to espouse sympathies for their opposition to, and resistance against, the Stuarts and established church in the 1640s and 1650s. By looking beyond print culture, we see how men and women continued to view their Parliamentarianism as having been justifiable. Moreover, we find that individuals continued to identify with opposition and resistance before the Restoration or to express nostalgia for the era to which it had given rise. Most concerning to the government, however, were those opinions in which the civil wars and revolution, and their consequences, were prospected as alternative future realities.

And yet, as we have seen, these were not the opinions of a minority of recalcitrant fantasists. The relationship between seditious memories and radicalism and republicanism is much blurrier than the Restoration government and modern historians have, in turn, deduced. Much of the language to which evidence of seditious and treasonable sentiments refers did not necessarily entail or signify anti-government conspiracy. Moreover, there is considerable evidence to suggest that the kinds of memories that were susceptible to being cast in a seditious light cut across a broad cross-section of political and religious constituencies. It was for this reason that notable Dissenters who had supported Parliament, and perhaps even the Republic, secreted away opinions which, owing in part to their notoriety, were liable to land them in hot water.

What seditious memories connote, then, is that a wide range of sympathies for Parliament and the Republic were vulnerable to being charged with sedition or treason, censured by neighbours, or, most frequently, used to corroborate the possession of radical or republican intentions. We might suppose that these opinions were considerably more widespread after the Restoration than available evidence is likely to disclose. Necessarily, the threats of indictment under the Sedition Act, surveillance by the government, or the censure of neighbours would have discouraged many individuals from publicising their truthful opinions about the events of the 1640s and 1650s. That, despite these hazards, Charles II's subjects continued to express seditious memories is a phenomenon for which the next three chapters of this book seek an explanation.

NOTES

1 Marshall, *Intelligence and Espionage*, p. 15; and Cressy, *Dangerous Talk*, p. 203.
2 For a useful summary of discussions around this issue, see L. Sangha, 'Personal

Documents', in L. Sangha and J. Willis (ed.), *Understanding Early Modern Primary Sources* (London: Routledge, 2016), pp. 118–121.
3   The National Archives, London (hereafter TNA), SP29/28/80.
4   Somerset Heritage Centre, Taunton (hereafter SHC), Q/SR99, fol. 23r. See also ibid., fol. 23v.
5   TNA, SP29/24/105.
6   'Sedition Act', *Statutes of the Realm*, v, pp. 304–305. For a helpful discussion of the intricacies of sedition and treason laws in the early modern period, see Cressy, *Dangerous Talk*, 208–210; and M. Pittock, *Material Culture and Sedition, 1688–1760: Treasured Objects, Secret Places* (Basingstoke: Palgrave Macmillan: 2013), pp. 5–11.
7   'Sedition Act', *Statutes of the Realm*, v, p. 305.
8   Thomas Phillips, *The Long Parliament REVIVED: OR, An Act for Continuation, and the Not Dissolving the Long Parliament (call'd by King CHARLES the First, in the Year 1640.) but by an Act of Parliament* (London, 1660); and [Zachary Crofton], *Berith Anti-Baal, OR Zach. Croftons Appearance Before the Prelate-Justice of Peace, Vainly pretending to binde the Covenant and Convenanters to their good Behaviour* (London, 1661). For a discussion of the Covenants after the Restoration, see E. Vallance, *Revolutionary England and the National Covenant: State Oaths, Protestantism and the Political Nation, 1553–1682* (Woodbridge: Boydell, 2005), ch. 8.
9   *CSPD, 1661–62*, pp. 531–532. See also W. D. MacRay and F. J. Routledge (eds), *Calendar of the Clarendon State Papers Preserved in the Bodleian Library* (5 vols, Oxford, 1872–1970), v, p. 279; and N. H. Keeble, 'Bagshaw, Edward (1629/30–1671)', in *ODNB*, iii, p. 247.
10 A. G. Matthews, *Calamy Revised: Being a Revision of Edmund Calamy's Account of the Ministers and Others Ejected and Silenced, 1660–2* (Oxford: Clarendon, 1934), p. 340.
11 TNA, SP29/96/37.
12 *Ibid.*
13 *MCR*, iii, p. 326.
14 J. C. Atkinson (ed.), *Quarter Sessions Records [North Riding of Yorkshire]* (9 vols, London: North Riding Record Society, 1888), vi, p. 58.
15 TNA, SP29/417/30.
16 SHC, Q/SR102, fol. 68r. Steevens denied that he had spoken these words.
17 *MCR*, iii, p. 304.
18 D. N. Farr, 'Lambert [Lambart], John (*bap.* 1619, *d.* 1684)', in *ODNB*, xxxii, p. 323.
19 TNA, SP29/406, fol. 122.
20 See, for instance, TNA, SP29/75/54, I; TNA, SP29/85/31; TNA, SP29/91/69; TNA, SP29/103/124, I; TNA, SP29/114/22; and TNA, SP29/167/68.
21 TNA, SP29/429/162.
22 A. H. Woolrych, 'The Good Old Cause and the Fall of the Protectorate', *Cambridge Historical Journal*, 2:13 (1957), 133–161; and A. Patterson, *Reading between the Lines* (London: Routledge, 1993), pp. 207–272.
23 See E. Legon, 'Remembering the "Good Old Cause"', in E. Vallance (ed.), *Remembering Early Modern Revolutions* (London: Routledge, forthcoming).

24 Oliver Heywood, *The Rev. Oliver Heywood, B.A., 1630–1702; His Autobiography, Diaries, Anecdote and Event Books*, ed. J. Horsfall Turner (4 vols, Bingley: T. Harrison, 1883), ii, p. 297.
25 SHC, Q/SR101, fol. 33r.
26 I am grateful to Catherine Lazo for her expert guidance on this matter.
27 Royal Commission on Historical Manuscripts (ed.), *Report on Manuscripts in Various Collections* (8 vols, London: [HM Stationery Office (HMSO)], 1901–1913), i, p. 144.
28 Hopper, *Turncoats*, p. 9.
29 W. Schivelbusch, *The Culture of Defeat: On National Trauma, Mourning, and Recovery*, trans. J. Chase (London: Granta, 2003).
30 Greaves, *Deliver Us from Evil*, p. 23.
31 *London Gazette* (28 April 1670), pp. 1–2; W. A. Shaw (ed.), *Calendar of Treasury Books: Preserved in the Public Record Office* (32 vols, London: HMSO, 1904–57), iii, *1669–1672*, pt 1, p. 407.
32 TNA, SP29/49/18.
33 TNA, SP29/67/105. For suspected assassination plots against Monck, see *CSPD, 1660–61*, p. 413; and P. Hines Jr (ed.), *Newdigate Newsletters: Numbers 1 through 2100 (3 January 1673/4 through June 1692)* (n.p., 1994), 277 (18 January 1675).
34 Cited in Harris, *London Crowds*, p. 61.
35 [Charles II], *King CHARLES II. his DECLARATION To all His Loving SUBJECTS of the KINGDOM OF ENGLAND. Dated from His Court at Breda in Holland, the 4/14 of April 1660* (Edinburgh, 1660).
36 TNA, SP29/65/19.
37 Matthews, *Calamy Revised*, p. 302.
38 Henry Townsend, *Diary of Henry Townsend of Elmley Lovett, 1640–1663*, ed. J. W. Willis Bund (2 vols, London: Mitchell Hughes and Clarke, 1930), ii, p. 71.
39 H. Tajfel, *Differentiation between Social Groups: Studies in the Social Psychology of Intergroup Relations* (London: Academic Press, 1978), p. 66. For an application of 'out-grouping' to an early modern context, see P. Lake, 'Anti-popery: The Structure of a Prejudice', in R. Cust and A. Hughes (eds), *Conflict in Early Stuart England: Studies in Religion and Politics, 1603–1642* (Harlow, 1989), pp. 72–106.
40 TNA, SP29/90/88, I.
41 TNA, SP29/159/7, I.
42 *MCR*, iv, pp. 2–3. Northit was found not guilty.
43 TNA, SP29/160/104.
44 TNA, SP29/205/128. See TNA, SP29/178/92 for a similar report from Hull.
45 Samuel Pepys, *The Diary of Samuel Pepys: A New and Complete Transcription*, ed. R. Latham and W. Matthews (11 vols, London: G. Bell and Sons, 1983), viii, p. 332.
46 *DCY*, p. 94.
47 R. L. Greaves and R. Zaller (eds), *Biographical Dictionary of British Radicals in the Seventeenth Century* (3 vols, Brighton: Harvester, 1984), iii, pp. 227–228.
48 TNA, SP 29/74/48.
49 White Kennet, *A REGISTER AND CHRONICLE Ecclesiastical and Civil: CONTAINING MATTERS of FACT, Delivered in the WORDS of the most*

Authentick BOOKS, PAPERS, and RECORDS; Digested in Exact Order of TIME (London, 1728). p. 543.
50 Matthews, *Calamy Revised*, p. 392.
51 T. B. Howell (ed.), *A Complete Collection of State Trials and Proceedings for High Treason and Other Crimes and Misdemeanours from the earliest period to the year 1783, with notes and other illustrations* (34 vols, London: T. C. Hansard, 1816–28), vi, pp. 513–539.
52 *A Treatise of the Execution of Justice, wherein is clearly proved, that the Execution of Judgment and Justice, is as well the Peoples as the Magistrates Duty; And that if Magistrates pervert Judgement, the People are bound by the Law of God to execute Judgement without them, and upon them* (n.p., [1663]), p. 17.
53 J. S. Cockburn (ed.), *Calendar of Assize Records: Kent Indictments, Charles II, 1676–1688* (London: HMSO, 1997), p. 142; and TNA, SP29/416/173, 173, I.
54 Andy Wood, *Memory of the People*, passim.
55 D. Cressy, *England on Edge: Crisis and Revolution, 1640–1642* (Oxford: Oxford University Press, 2006), p. 14; A. Hughes, *Gender and the English Revolution* (Abingdon: Routledge, 2012), p. 69.
56 Monod, *Jacobitism*, p. 261.
57 R. Starn, 'Meaning-Levels in the Theme of Historical Decline', *History and Theory*, 14:1 (Feb., 1975), 1–31.
58 See C. Routledge, *Nostalgia: A Psychological Resource* (New York: Routledge, 2016).
59 Boym, 'Nostalgia', 8.
60 Judith Pollman has used the term in her recent *Memory in Early Modern Europe*, pp. 54–56, 194–196. Likewise, Erin Peters has examined Royalist-inflected nostalgia as a palliative to trauma after the Restoration in her *Commemoration and Oblivion*, ch. 4.
61 Fentress and Wickham, *Social Memory*, p. 51; and Boym, 'Nostalgia', 13.
62 *DCY*, pp. 98–99. For a similar case from Somerset, see SHC, Q/R103, fol. 8r.
63 TNA, SP29/88/44.
64 Hopper, 'Farnley Wood', 292–293.
65 *DCY*, p. 93.
66 TNA, SP29/90/23.
67 See J. H. Hanshall, *The History of the County Palatine of Chester* (n.p., 1823), p. 569.
68 *DCY*, pp. 115–116.
69 *THE Wheel of Time turning Round TO THE GOOD OLD VVAY; OR, The Good Old Cause Vindicated* (n.p., [1661]).
70 Quoted in Bardle, *Literary Underground*, p. 122.
71 TNA, SP29/187/169.
72 G. L. Mosse, *Fallen Soldiers: Reshaping the Memory of the World Wars* (New York: Oxford University Press, 1990), pp. 159–164.
73 TNA, SP29/31/51, I.
74 TNA, SP29/57/42, I. Elsewhere, William Fenn of St Martin-in-the-Fields 'said "that he hoped to wash his hands in the king's blood" and offered to thrust "an old rusty sword ... up to the hilt in his heart"': Cressy, *Dangerous Talk*, p. 206.
75 TNA, SP29/61/1.

76 *A NARRATIVE OF THE APPREHENDING, COMMITMENT, ARRAIGNMENT, CONDEMNATION, And EXECUTION of JOHN JAMES Who Suffered at TIBURNE, Novemb. the 26th 1661* (London, 1662), p. 16. For 'uchronia', see A. Portelli, 'Uchronic Dreams: Working-Class Memory and Possible Worlds', in R. Samuel and P. Thompson (eds), *The Myths We Live By* (London: Routledge, 1990), pp. 143–160.
77 DCY, p. 130.
78 J. C. Cox (ed.), *Three Centuries of Derbyshire Annals. As Illustrated by the Records of the Quarter Sessions of the County of Derby, From Queen Elizabeth to Queen Victoria* (2 vols, London: Bemrose and Sons, 1890), ii, p. 68.
79 See TNA, IR30/8/87, 'Tithe Map & Apportionment of Egginton, Derbyshire'; and S. Glover and T. Noble (eds), *The History of the County of Derby* (2 vols, Derby: H. Mozley and Son, 1829), i, [appendix], p. 66.
80 DCY, p. 85.
81 TNA, SP29/88/44.
82 *THE CITY'S REMONSTRANCE AND ADDRESSE TO The King's MOST EXCELLENT MAJESTY* (London, 1661).
83 TNA, SP29/40/10.
84 MCR, iii, pp. 338–339.
85 M. J. Hoad and R. P. Grime (eds), *Portsmouth Record Series: Borough Sessions Papers, 1653–1688: A Calendar* (Chichester: Phillimore, 1971), pp. 20–21.
86 J. S. Cockburn (ed.), *Calendar of Assize Records: Kent Indictments, Charles II, 1660–1675* (London: HMSO, 1995), p. 176.
87 DCY, p. 124.
88 Nehemiah Beaton, *NO TREASON TO SAY, Kings are Gods Subjects: OR THE SUPREMACY OF God, opened, asserted, applied, In some Sermons preached at Lurgarshal in Sussex by N.B. then Record there* (London, 1661), sig. A3v.
89 For women and seditious-words allegations, see Andy Wood, '"The Queen Is a Goggyll Eyed Hoore": Gender and Seditious Speech in Early Modern England', in N. Tyacke (ed.), *The English Revolution c. 1590–1720: Politics, Religion and Communities* (Manchester: Manchester University Press, 2007), pp. 81–94. For the politicisation of women during the English Revolution, see K. Lindley, 'London and Popular Freedom in the 1640s', in R. C. Richardson and G. M. Ridden (eds), *Freedom and the English Revolution: Essays in History and Literature* (Manchester: Manchester University Press, 1986), p. 139; and D. Freist, *Governed by Opinion: Politics, Religion and the Dynamics of Communication in Stuart London, 1637–1645* (London: I. B. Tauris, 1997), p. 178.
90 MCR, iii, pp. 304–305.
91 H. Stocks and W. H. Stevenson (eds), *Records of the Borough of Leicester: Being a Series of Extracts from the Archives of the Corporation of Leicester, 1603–1688* (Cambridge: Cambridge University Press, 1923), p. 549.
92 Hines, *Newdigate*, 1257 (8 August 1682).
93 Surrey History Centre, Woking, LM1058, fols 1–3.
94 TNA, ASSI5/5. Following information provided by two women in whose company he had been in Lichfield, Staffordshire, Bamford was found guilty and fined '200 marks' later that year: Shaw, *Calendar of Treasury Books*, vii, pp. 307, 332.

95 Cockburn, *Calendar of Assize Records ... 1676–1688*, p. 153.
96 S. D. Thomson (ed.), *The Book of Examinations and Depositions before the Mayor and Justices of Southampton 1648–1663* (Southampton: Southampton University Press, 1994), p. 186.
97 TNA, SP29/438/79.
98 *The SPEECHES AND PRAYERS OF Some of the late King's Judges, viz. Major Gen. Harrison, Octob. 13. Mr. John Carew, Octob. 15. Mr. Justice Cooke, Mr. Hugh Peters Octob. 16. Mr. Tho. Scot, Mr. Gregory Clement, Col. Adrian Scroop, Col. John Jones, Oct. 17. Col. Dan. Axtell, Col. Fran. Hacker, Octob. 19. 1660* ([London], 1660), p. 12.
99 Ibid., pp. 28–36, 68–73, 74–76, 78–80, 88–96.
100 *THE SPEECHES AND PRAYERS Of JOHN BARKSTEAD, JOHN OKEY, and MILES CORBET* (London, 1662), pp. 2–3.
101 Ibid., p. 4. See also *THE TRYAL OF Sir Henry Vane, Kt. AT the KINGS BENCH, Westminster, June the 2d. and 6TH. 1662* (n.p., 1662), pp. 88–92.
102 MCR, iv, pp. 187–188.
103 William Prynne, *THE RE-PUBLICANS AND OTHERS SPURIOUS Good Old Cause, briefly and truly Anatomized* (n.p., 1659), p. 5. See also J. Collins, 'Restoration Anti-Catholicism: A Prejudice in Motion', in C. W. A. Prior and G. Burgess (eds), *England's Wars of Religion Revisited* (Farnham: Ashgate, 2011), pp. 301–302. For uses of the 'Prynne Theory' during the Popish Plot of 1678, see Harris, *London Crowds*, p. 97; and J. Miller, *Popery and Politics in England: 1660–1688* (Cambridge: Cambridge University Press, 1973), pp. 155–156.
104 *A TRUE NARRATIVE OF THE Horrid PLOT AND CONSPIRACY OF THE POPISH PARTY Against the LIFE of His Sacred Majesty, THE GOVERNMENT, AND THE Protestant Religion* (London, 1679), p. 15. See also M. Goldie, J. Spurr, T. Harris, S. Taylor, M. Knights, and J. McElligott (eds), *The Entring Book of Roger Morrice 1677–1691* (7 vols, Woodbridge: Boydell, 2007), ii, p. 5.
105 DCY, p. 238.
106 Cited in Sharp, 'Popular Political Opinion', 17.
107 Hines, *Newdigate*, 1530 (1 May 1684).
108 TNA, SP29/429/27.
109 MCR, p. 227. For another similar case, see TNA, SP29/430/95.
110 Hines, *Newdigate*, 1620 (29 November 1684).
111 TNA, SP29/420/36. See also TNA, SP29/421/30.
112 W. M. Wigfield, *The Monmouth Rebels* (Gloucester: Sutton, 1985), pp. 127, 173.
113 K. W. H. Howard (ed.), *The Axminster Ecclesiastica 1660–1698* (Sheffield: Gospel Tidings, 1976), pp. 93–94, cited in E. Vallance, *The Glorious Revolution: 1688 – Britain's Fight for Liberty* (London: Abacus, 2006), p. 49.
114 See, for instance, B. Capp, *The Fifth Monarchy Men: A Study in Seventeenth-Century Millenarianism* (London: Faber, 1972), p. 221.
115 See numerous cases between 1685 and 1688 in MCR, iv, pp. 284–327; and DCY, pp. 274–284. See also W. J. Hardy (ed.), *Hertford County Records, Notes and Extracts from the Sessions Rolls, 1581–1698* (4 vols, Hertford: Simon, 1905), i, pp. 355, 359; Cockburn, *Calendar of Assize Records ... 1676–1688*, pp. 220, 237; and *Borough Sessions Papers*, pp. 123–124.

116 See *MCR*, iv., p. 312; *DCY*, pp. 283, 283n; and Cockburn, *Calendar of Assize Records ... 1676–1688*, pp. 236–237.
117 *DCY*, p. 276.
118 For these concerns, see Monod, *Jacobitism*, pp. 234–235; and Andy Wood, '"Poore Men Woll Speke One Day": Plebeian Languages of Deference and Defiance in England, c.1520–1640', in T. Harris, *Politics of the Excluded*, pp. 81–82.
119 Monod, *Jacobitism*, p. 234.
120 Andy Wood, 'Poore Men', pp. 81–82.
121 TNA, SP29/90/88. This was a reference to the fourth article of the act, which stipulated that 'No Person [is] to be prosecuted for any Offences in this Act (other than Treason) unless by special Order from His Majesty.' See 'Sedition Act', *Statutes of the Realm*, v, p. 305.
122 See T. Harris, 'Introduction', p. 14. For the possibility that 'disaffected judges and juries' may have let Jacobites off the hook after the Glorious Revolution, see Monod, *Jacobitism*, p. 236.
123 W. Urry and C. R. Bunce, *The Chief Citizens of Canterbury: A List of Portreeves (Prefects, Prepositi) from A.D. 780 until c.1100 of Prepositi (Bailiffs) from the 12th Century until 1448 and of Mayors from 1448 until 1978* ([Canterbury]: Canterbury City Council, [1978]), p. 56.
124 TNA, SP29/417/30.
125 Cressy, *Dangerous Talk*, pp. 209–210.
126 Freist, *Governed by Opinion*, p. 182.
127 For a similar view regarding accusations of pro-Jacobite sentiment, see Monod, *Jacobitism*, pp. 235. 238–239.
128 TNA, SP29/96/37.
129 Richard Baxter, *Reliquiae Baxterianae: OR, Mr. Richard Baxters NARRATIVE OF The most Memorable Passages OF HIS LIFE AND TIMES*, ed. Matthew Sylvester (London, 1696), [iii], p. 48.
130 *THE ARRAIGNMENT, TRYAL AND CONDEMNATION OF Stephen Colledge FOR HIGH-TREASON, IN Conspiring the Death of the KING, the Levying of WAR, and the Subversion of the GOVERNMENT* (London, 1681), p. 83.
131 TNA, SP29/132/2.
132 TNA, SP29/132/30.
133 *DCY*, p. 95.
134 TNA, SP29/97/91.
135 Cressy, *Dangerous Talk*, p. 203; and Marshall, *Intelligence and Espionage*, p. 15.
136 C. Jackson (ed.), *Yorkshire Diaries and Autobiographies in the Seventeenth and Eighteenth Centuries* (2 vols, Durham: Andrews, 1877), i, p. 133.
137 Ibid., p. 146.
138 Ibid., p. 160.
139 Baxter, *Reliquiae Baxterianae*, [i], p. 84.
140 Ibid., p. 225.
141 Thomas Larkham, *The Diary of Thomas Larkham, 1647–1669*, ed. S. H. Moore (Woodbridge: Boydell, 2011), p. 248.
142 Ibid., p. 259.
143 Ibid., p. 284.
144 S. H. Moore, 'Introduction', in *ibid.*, p. 7.

145 Baxter, *Reliquiae Baxterianae*, [i], p. 39.
146 *Ibid.*, p. 97.
147 N. H. Keeble and G. F. Nuttall (eds), *Calendar of the Correspondence of Richard Baxter* (2 vols, Oxford: Clarendon, 1991), ii, p. 211.
148 R. Spalding, 'The Diary and Whitelocke's Other Writing', in Bulstrode Whitelocke, *The Diary of Bulstrode Whitelocke, 1605–1675*, ed. R. Spalding (Oxford: Oxford University Press, 1990), p. 27.
149 Whitelocke, *Diary*, p. 750.
150 Philip Henry, *Diaries and Letters of Philip Henry of Broad Oak, Flintshire, 1631–1696*, ed. M. H. Lee (London: Kegan Paul, Trench, 1882), p. 220.
151 Keeble and Nuttall, *Calendar*, ii, p. 94. See also Ralph Josselin, *The Diary of Ralph Josselin, 1616–1683*, ed. A. Macfarlane (Oxford: Oxford University Press, 1991), p. 501.
152 Henry, *Diaries*, p. 99.
153 P. D. Halliday, *Dismembering the Body Politic: Partisan Politics in England's Towns, 1650–1730* (Cambridge: Cambridge University Press, 1998), p. 95.
154 Keeble and Nuttall, *Calendar*, ii, p. 52. See also *ibid.*, pp. 49–50.
155 TNA, SP29/49/115.
156 TNA, SP29/96/110, I.
157 Stocks and Stevenson, *Records of the Borough of Leicester*, pp. 498, 506.
158 TNA, SP29/182/6.
159 TNA, SP29/250/70, 96; and TNA, SP29/258/181.

Chapter 3

The politics of memory after the Restoration

In legal records and government papers, we can identify sympathies for Parliament and the Republic which survived the restoration of Charles II and which endured well into the 1680s. The threat posed by these opinions does not regularly tally with the government's anxieties about the legacy of what was, by its estimation, seditious or treasonable intent. Given the risks, then, why did individuals express these views? In subsequent chapters, this question is answered by reading evidence of seditious remembering for signs of how audiences were expected to react to such sentiment and, correspondingly, by construing the intentions of its speakers or authors.

The fullest understanding of these intentions and expectations relies on a portrayal of the Restoration era as one in which the events of the 1640s and 1650s were far from being forgotten, as mandated by the famous Act of Free and General Pardon, Indemnity, and Oblivion in 1660. Instead, we must think of the era 1660–88 as one in which the meaning of the events of the civil wars and revolution remained unresolved among those who had fought for, or otherwise supported, king and Parliament. It also entails thinking of these differences as a function of the very political and religious identities whose incompatibility had fomented rebellion and bloody conflict in the first place.

This chapter characterises this fallout of civil war and revolution as the Restoration's characteristic 'politics of memory'; that is, a struggle over the authority to speak for the civil wars and revolution as a means of achieving certain political and religious objectives.[1] It does so by reconfiguring the traditional understanding of the immediate aftermath of the civil wars and revolution as having been characterised by a popular transition between a national urge to forget civil conflict – as enacted through a programme of 'oblivion' – and a 'partial public remembering' that 'provided historical justification for the proscription of the puritan impulse from an exclusively Anglican polity.'[2] Drawing on studies of the Restoration that highlight a transition from reconciliation to recrimination within government itself, I argue that hard-line Royalists saw oblivion as a dangerous capitulation to 'fanaticism', the political and religious impulse that, by their estimation, had resulted in 'rebellion' and 'usurpation' in the early 1640s.[3] I suggest that the election of the Cavalier Parliament in early 1661 provided these Royalists with an opportunity to alleviate such anxieties by effectively seizing the authority to speak for the past from Charles II and those who had supported a conciliatory settlement a year earlier. This took the form of legislation like the Sedition Act of 1661, which, as we saw in chapter 2, censored sympathies for opposition and resistance during the 1640s and 1650s by specifically targeting them or using them to corroborate the possession of radical or republican intent. In parallel, Royalists who controlled access to press, and – following the Act of Uniformity in 1662 – the pulpit, liberated a censorious interpretation of the civil wars and revolution.

That the Restoration was typified by censorship and the censure of opposition to the Crown and established church is not a new conclusion. On the contrary, recriminations against Parliamentarians and republicans have underpinned recent interest in the mnemonic landscape of the Restoration.[4] Together with a closer examination of how these circumstances derived from a conciliatory programme of oblivion, one contribution that this chapter hopes to make concerns the measurable impact of these attacks on their targets. The speeches and writings of those who, as former opponents of Crown or established church, were targeted by censorship and censure represent concerns about, and efforts to counteract, the reversal of oblivion. Through this analysis, the 'experience of defeat' to which Christopher Hill famously referred is reconfigured as one in which what people had done in the past came to shape how they lived in the present and the future.[5] Throughout, I consider the struggle over the authority to speak for the civil wars and revolution at all levels of society, particular insofar as this extended to concerns about being silenced by erstwhile enemies. In doing so, I draw attention to the deep divisions that conflict wrought on communities throughout England and Wales.

FORGETTING OBLIVION

The first decade of Charles II's reign witnessed the reversal of the revolution in England and Wales, and, with a few notable exceptions, the political ascendency of men who had remained faithful to the Stuarts and the Church of England throughout the 1640s and 1650s. And yet one of the most striking aspects of Restoration politics is the reticence of a number of these Royalists to acknowledge their 'victory'. Instead, a deep vein of resentment characterises elements of Royalist discourse in the immediate wake of Charles II's return. Their dissatisfaction was occasioned by what they regarded as the conciliatory atmosphere with which the Restoration had been ushered in and, with it, the excessive favour that erstwhile 'rebels' and 'usurpers' had been shown by the king at the expense of those who had sacrificed their lives, liberties, and fortunes for him. Referring to the famous Act of Free and General Pardon, Indemnity, and Oblivion, which became law in August 1660, Charles's supporters protested that 'if there were an *Act of Oblivion* past of the King's Friends,' 'His Adversaries' had been offered 'an *Act of Indemnity*'.[6] For those who had lost their estates in the revolution, the provisions of the act for indemnifying Parliamentarians was an especial cause of indignation, since, in Paul Seaward's words, it appeared to '[perpetuate] the results of the war by impoverishing royalists and enriching their enemies'.[7]

The provisions of the 1660 act regarding indemnity were not the only causes of Royalist resentment. Equally contentious was the act's promise to 'putt into utter Oblivion' 'all names and termes of distinction'. Depending on social status, fines of £10 or 40s. were to be levied on 'any person or persons' who, within the first three years of the act, 'shall presume maliciously to call or alledge of, or object against any other person or persons any name or names, or other words of reproach any way tending to revive the memory of the late Differences or the occasions thereof'.[8] Here, the Convention Parliament of 1660 effectively appropriated the authority to speak for the civil wars and revolution from the thousands of people who had been actively involved in the conflict, and vested that authority in Charles II alone. His was an account of the civil wars and revolution that highlighted the trial and execution of his father, and the subsequent 'usurpation' of his authority, and that largely excised the contentious issue of what had led Britain there. Remembering, if it was to take place at all, would take stipulated forms on designated occasions, such as the annual commemoration of the regicide on 30 January (see chapter 7).

By mandating a peculiarly truncated narrative of the civil wars and revolution, and appointing Charles as the sole arbiter of his kingdoms' transition into a post-conflict society, the policy of oblivion attempted to forestall the reproduction of conflictual political and religious identities via 'names and terms of distinction' and to exchange these for common allegiance to a godly king.[9] As the act's preamble explained, Charles viewed his Free and General Pardon as the best method of 'bury[ing] all Seeds of future Discords and remembrance of the former' out of 'a hearty and pious Desire to put an end to all Suites and Controversies that by occasion of the late Distractions have arisen and may arise betweene all His Subjects'.[10] In these ways, the act foreshadowed more recent efforts to seek peace and reconciliation through forgetting, such as those that have been encouraged by the governments of Spain and Northern Ireland in the twentieth and twenty-first centuries.[11] Charles's sponsorship of oblivion discloses an apparently sincere belief in its capacity to bring peace to his kingdoms. This is evident in his fierce and sometimes melodramatic defences of the act, such as his warning to would-be opponents of oblivion that they 'would find such an Acceptation from Me as he wou'd have who shou'd persuade me to burn Magna Charta, cancel the old Laws, and erect a new Government after my own Invention and Appetite.'[12]

And yet, for all its commendable intent, the appeal to a form of 'collective amnesia' stirred only resentment in some of Charles's staunchest allies. Royalists felt that oblivion perpetuated another result of the war; namely, the censorship under which they had strained during the Commonwealth.[13] This argument often entailed metaphorical allusions to how oblivion had 'buried' or rendered 'invisible' their version of events. In the words of the Royalist Andrew Cooper, his experiences, and those of his colleagues in arms, were now consigned to be 'Lighted' only 'out from Oblivion's Cell / To which they were condemn'd, the world to tell'.[14] Cooper's sentiments were echoed in the words of his fellow former Royalist George Wharton, who entreated 'That the lively Copy of a truly Loyal subject may not be buryed in Oblivion, but be brought to light afresh, for the encouragement of others to persevere according to Allegiance, in Loyalty, Duty and Obedience.'[15] The arch-Royalist Sir Roger L'Estrange went further than these writers, asking the author of one conciliatory pamphlet whether others like him were 'obliged by the Act of *Oblivion*, to quit our *Nature*, and our *Reason* with our *Passions*: – to such a Losse of *Memory*, as utterly defaces the very *Images* of things *Past*, and robs us of the benefit of our dear-bought *experience*[?]'[16] The words of L'Estrange underscore the basis of Royalist resentment. By burying 'dear-bought *experience*', oblivion smothered the 'natural' and 'reasonable' impulse to save England and Wales from the recurrence of war and regicide.

For these Royalists, oblivion was dangerous exactly because it prolonged the 'memory' – by which they meant the accessibility – of seditious and treasonable principles. As the Church of England minister Thomas Tomkins put it shortly after the Restoration, 'I could heartily wish the Parliament could passe such an act of Oblivion, that all that is past may be not only pardoned but forgot.'[17] Perspectives like these derived from an interpretation of opposition and resistance to the Stuarts and established church that had developed during the civil wars and the revolution. Here, Parliament's 'rebellion' and usurpation', as Royalists often described the wars and revolution, were certainly not the result of some inherent popular antagonism to the Stuarts or the Church of England. Rather, the mobilisation of Parliamentarian support, and its subsequent victories, were the culmination of an entryist takeover of mainstream English Protestantism. The culprits – Presbyterians and Congregationalists in particular – were followers of an anti-monarchical variant of the reformed faith, to whom the ubiquitous signifier of 'fanatic' was bestowed. Between 1640 and 1642, these men had inveigled the ignorant into rebelling against, and then murdering, their monarch. The danger of oblivion was that it provided inadequate protection against their doing so again.

This conception of 'fanaticism' predates, but shares the characteristics of, that which the critical theorist Alberto Toscano has identified in the modern West. Like his fanatics, those labelled by Royalists after the Restoration were deemed to be 'outside the frame of political rationality, possessed by a violent conviction that brooks no argument and will only rest, if ever, once every rival view or way of life is eradicated.'[18] The author of one 1661 ballad – tellingly entitled *The Cavaleers Letany* – used uncannily similar words in its condemnation of religious Dissenters as the 'Brethren, who must still dissent, / Whose froward Gospell brook no Lent', and who would 'recant, but n'ere repent'.[19] Evidence like this shows how far anti-fanaticism came to rival the much-studied discourse of anti-popery within the first few months of the Restoration.[20] It was this anti-fanaticism that drove the beliefs of some Royalists that oblivion would make the recurrence of civil war and regicide an inevitability.

The opening months of Charles II's reign thus witnessed arguments in favour of more or less conciliatory approaches to how the civil wars and revolution should be remembered. One promised to consign all but the most shocking acts of the recent past – the regicide and the establishment of the Commonwealth – to oblivion. The other threatened to call the actions of the Stuarts' opponents to account. Both arguments describe attempts to bestow an interpretation of the civil wars and revolution with what Berthold Molden has described as 'a quasi-natural universality' that 'delegitimize[d] alternative forms of reasoning'. They were, in fact, efforts to secure 'mnemonic hegemony'.[21] The pursuit of this hegemonic project required control of how the past was spoken about. Through oblivion, and its promises to punish anyone who raked over the coals of the recent past, members of the Convention Parliament vested this authority in Charles II. The Convention was a coalition of men whose interests converged on a desire to rescue peace and stability from the jaws of millenarian and republican – what they termed fanatic – chaos.[22] And yet the first twelve months of Charles's reign witnessed the election of members of parliament who, broadly speaking, favoured a more recriminatory approach to remembering the civil wars and revolution.

Historians often regard the election of the Cavalier Parliament as a direct consequence of the Fifth Monarchists' rising in London in January 1661, an event that appeared to vindicate Royalist claims that fanaticism constituted an enduring threat to the safety and security of the Stuart realms. To this should be added a more deliberate redistribution of authority into the hands of hardline Royalists throughout England and Wales in the immediate aftermath of the Restoration.[23] This 'coup' afforded certain Royalists an opportunity to seize the authority to speak for the civil wars and revolution. In few places is this more evident than the scope, and indeed the tone, of the parliament's legislation in the first five years of its sitting: what Mark Kishlansky described as its 'history lesson in the causes of the Civil War'.[24] The penal code of the 1660s – often described as the Clarendon Code – embodied Royalist anti-fanaticism by debarring religious Dissenters from places of public trust and preventing the dissemination of their 'fanatic' ideology.[25] It included the Corporation Act of 1661, the Act of Uniformity in 1662, the Conventicle Acts of 1664 and 1670, and the Five Mile Act of 1665. An act of 1661 also identified 'Tumultuous and other Disorderly solliciting and procuring of Hands by private persons to Peticons' as 'a great meanes of the late unhappy Wars Confusions and Calamities'.[26]

The Cavalier Parliament also passed legislation that effectively superseded the Act of Free and General Pardon, Indemnity, and Oblivion. The first of these acts was the Sedition Act of 1661. In chapter 2, we discovered that it was under this act that individuals were often chargeable for opinions about the civil wars and revolution that, in the eyes of magistrates, were seditious and treasonable. Since there is not a single example of seditious remembering that held the Royalist cause of the 1640s and 1650s in esteem, it would be entirely reasonable to describe this as a form of anti-Parliamentarian and anti-republican censorship. More specifically, the act provided Royalists with a means of censoring opinions about the civil wars and revolution that, under the provisions of oblivion, were treated no differently from their own 'dear-bought experience'. It was, in fact, a method by which magistrates were able to forestall the social legitimisation of Parliamentarianism and republicanism via speech and writing.

The Sedition Act was complemented by similar efforts to censor the outputs of the press. The extent to which censorship of print after the Restoration is comparable with that of modern totalitarian regimes has been a matter of considerable historiographical debate.[27] Nonetheless, as Lois Schwoerer has shown, a series of more or less formal measures were taken by the government in order 'to repress printed material that was critical of the settlement in state and church.'[28] This included the royal appointment of two notable hard-line Royalists – Sir John Birkenhead and Sir Roger L'Estrange, whose antipathy to oblivion was encountered earlier – as successive licensers (and, in L'Estrange's case, also surveyor) of the press.[29] The powers vested in Birkenhead and L'Estrange dovetailed with the provisions of the Licensing Act of 19 May 1662, which outlawed the production of 'seditious' material and limited the number of official printers.[30] The monarch's prerogative powers and the common law of seditious libel were also used to crack down on the production of specific works.[31] Local initiatives even led to book burnings in Devon and Dorset.[32] The Licensing Act was allowed to lapse in 1679, but the government acted swiftly to prevent the spread of seditious material with recourse to orders of council and royal proclamation.[33] In July 1685, shortly after the accession of James II, the act was renewed.[34]

The Sedition Act of 1661 and the Licensing Act of 1662 comprised the principle means by which Royalists in the Cavalier Parliament seized the authority to speak for the civil wars and revolution. In doing so, these acts effectively superseded the provisions of the Act of Free and General Pardon, Indemnity, and Oblivion. This may be the reason that, as Ronald Hutton has shown, there was only one recorded prosecution under the Act of Free and General Pardon. Whereas Hutton described this as a measure of the act's 'almost complete formal success', it is more likely to reflect its futility.[35] To the Sedition Act and Licensing Act should be added different forms of censorship that were encountered in chapter 2. These included the extent to which seditious memories could prove incriminating at moments of domestic conspiracy, and might even provoke hostile responses from neighbours and efforts to shame former Parliamentarians and republicans. That the avowedly Royalist rejoinders of neighbours to seditious memories, and corresponding efforts to censor those who articulated them, were often recorded by the authorities as natural responses to such language is highly suggestive of whose purposes the Sedition Act was serving.

The Royalists' seizure of the authority to remember did not consist solely of the censorship of Parliamentarian and republican sympathies. These men also sought to counteract what they felt was the censorship of their own interpretations of the civil wars and revolution. Corresponding with the sedition and licensing legislation was the unfettering of the principal media of communication – the press and pulpit – as channels for broadcasting anti-fanaticism. Matthew Neufeld's recent work has measured the extent of the government's efforts to 'sanction' an essentially Royalist version of the wars and revolution in various genres.[36] This included the publication of histories, of which the vast majority were avowedly Royalist in tone until the Glorious Revolution.[37] The Restoration also witnessed the publication of government newspapers, including L'Estrange's own the *Intelligencer* and the *Newes*, the pages of which are filled with more or less explicit references to the disorder of the 1640s and 1650s. That, as licenser, L'Estrange intended to deregulate the publication of his 'dear-bought experience' is evident in his claim in August 1661 that, while he approved of '*an Act of OBLIVION, which forbids the MALICIOUS revival of past Differences,*' he and other Royalists were '*allow'd* ... to defend the justice of our Cause, against the publick enemies of it.'[38] More recently, Erin Peters has shown that these kinds of interpretations of the civil wars and revolution were able to reach wider audiences via the wealth of cheap print that flooded the market in the early 1660s.[39] Together with the press, the ejection of thousands of dissenting ministers from their livings freed up the pulpit as a means of lambasting 'rebellion' and 'usurpation'.[40] Indeed, as John Patrick Montaño has argued, the pulpit was favoured by Royalists for its ability to penetrate society where print could not.[41]

In lockstep with censorship, then, was censure. While the former sought to forestall the social legitimisation of opposition and resistance during the 1640s and 1650s, the latter ensured that these actions were delegitimised publicly. In this way, Royalists pursued mnemonic hegemony where their anti-fanatical version of the civil wars and revolution was bestowed with 'quasi-natural universality', as Molden describes it. That this process was tangible to Royalists is evident in print from 1661 onwards. Ballads published during the Cavalier Parliament's opening session imply that Royalists were now free to speak for the civil wars and revolution. One of these, which was published at the some point in May 1661, took great pleasure in proclaiming that '*Fanaticks*' ought now to 'be quiet' so 'That *Truth* and *Peace* may reign'.[42] This triumphalism is also evident in popular speech. When John Cooch was hauled before the Essex quarter sessions for seditious words, one of his accusers, Edward Sayre of Burnham, recalled his own boast that 'Now ... wee have liberty to speak as well as you'.[43] The historian Andy Hopper has recorded a similar case in September 1666 when John Waddington, a Yorkshireman, told Frances Wythes that 'now Oliver is dead wee dare speake to you And now we have a King god blessed him'.[44]

Another direct consequence of the Royalists' seizure of the authority to speak for the civil wars and revolution was that former allegiances – even if they were unspoken – became incriminating in and of themselves. Government papers from the reigns of Charles II and James II are replete with references to former 'disloyalty'. Following a rising in Berkshire against the repeal of the Triennial Act in 1664, which had mandated that parliament should meet every three years, it was noted by Sir Thomas Doleman that the leader had 'beene A Rebell in ye Armies from his cradle'.[45] At around the same time, Sir Philip Musgrave informed the government that one Robert Atkinson of Mallerstang in Westmorland 'was a Capt: of horse in the tyme of Oliver & ... an active man for secureing the Kings freinds in that County when he had power'.[46] Richard Bower, a Great Yarmouth coffee seller, was one of the most actively anti-Parliamentarian government agents during the 1660s and 1670s, and dozens of examples of his surveillance of local 'fanatics' can be found in government papers.[47] In one of these, Bower conveyed to Whitehall a copy of the town's address to Richard Cromwell in 1658, upon which he had marked a 'P' (for 'Presbyterian') next to the names of those who remained 'at large' in the town.[48] Bower was not alone in maintaining such lists. The painstaking efforts of the authorities in London, Staffordshire, Derbyshire, and Hertfordshire provided the government with lists of local men who had been in arms for Parliament.[49] In Wrexham in Denbighshire, meanwhile, two separate warnings were made in 1661 and 1662 about the town's infidelity during the wars and revolution.[50]

Even the *families* of those who had been disloyal to the Stuarts during the revolution became vulnerable to surveillance. In October 1665, for example, Sir Thomas Gower referred one William Sykes to the Earl of Arlington as 'an Agent for ye Fanatiques, and disaffected party in Forraign partes', but also as 'Brother to Rich: Sykes who maryed ye Traytor Tho[mas] Scots Daughter'.[51] Such familial connections could even be manipulated as means of ensnaring suspected radicals. One of the most intriguing examples of this kind of espionage occurred in 1681 when Elizabeth Lilburne, the daughter of the famous Leveller John Lilburne, wrote to the Earl of Shaftesbury to tell him of a meeting she had had with George Savile, Marquess of Halifax, who, having discovered whose daughter she was, asked her if she 'did not know the Duke of Buckingham and Major Wildman.' Lilburne responded to Halifax in the affirmative, leading him to tell her that 'it was in my power to get a great sum of money if I would undertake a business he would put me upon.' According to Lilburne, Halifax sought her help in infiltrating a republican faction which included sometime Leveller John Wildman, the Duke of Buckingham, and Francis Jenks (son-in-law of the notorious Leveller William Walwyn).[52] She added that Halifax had said 'they would make no scruple of trusting me, being Lilburne's daughter'.[53]

THE EXPERIENCE OF DEFEAT REVISITED

Through censorship and censure, Royalists aimed at rather more than merely providing historical justification for an attack on Dissenters, although this was certainly one motivation. By censoring seditious memories, Royalists also sought to control how 'fanatics', as they described them, could reproduce their political and religious identities by sharing, and thus legitimising socially, their experiences of opposition to, resistance against, and the overthrow of the Stuarts and Church of England. In parallel, Royalists unfettered frequent public delegitimisation of these 'rebels' and 'usurpers' from pulpit and press. The mnemonic landscape of Restoration England and Wales was not, then, a level playing field. On the contrary, sympathies for Parliament and the Republic were vulnerable to recrimination while those that lauded the cause of Crown and established church were not only unregulated, but also positively encouraged.

This politics of memory goes some way towards providing the context from which we can deduce the full significance of the articulation of seditious memories after the Restoration. And yet it is equally important to demonstrate that, far from passing over their heads, Royalist censorship and censure impacted upon their targets in a measurable way. The remainder of this chapter renders visible experiences of public and social delegitimisation and some of the ways that these were counteracted. In doing so, it adds an extra dimension to Christopher Hill's influential notion that supporters of Parliament and its revolution underwent 'experiences of defeat' in the 1660s.[54]

Some of the most powerful evidence of the impact of Royalist censorship and censure takes the form of the writings of those who were targeted in print. The Puritan Matthew Newcomen was one of many whose conditional support for the Restoration resulted in profound disappointment following the gradual return of episcopacy thereafter. This disappointment was compounded, no doubt, by the ridicule that he and the other members of the Puritan 'Smectymnuus' group (an acronym comprised of the initials of their names) had suffered since the Restoration.[55] Writing to Richard Baxter, another of those who had expected much from the Restoration, but had received largely derision, Newcomen expressed his worries that 'wee are not onely Like to suffer but to suffer as Evill doers'.[56] His concerns were echoed by one Mr Hooke, who wrote to John Davenport, founder of the New Haven colony, in March 1662, complaining that 'the Presbiterians are in extreme contempt [and] there [sic] former forwardness to bring in the K[ing] not at all regarded'.[57]

Puritan ministers also wrote of attacks at a local level, suggesting thereby that anti-fanaticism took oral, as well as printed, forms. Just before the Restoration, for instance, Thomas Gilbert, the vicar of Upper Wichendon in Buckinghamshire, complained that although he had 'never carry'd incivilly in the least toward the cavalier party', he felt that he was 'so much threatened by them, that I cannot (as they apprehend) be long safe among them.'[58] These words were echoed by Samuel Smith, rector at Stanford Dingley in neighbouring Berkshire, who lamented that 'after the turn of the Times, he met with great unkindness from several of the Episcopal Party, whom he before had screen'd.'[59] In both cases, the censure of Royalists was described as contrasting markedly with the mercy of their enemies before the 'turn of the Times'.

In these cases, we sense the feeling of wretchedness that resulted from 'Cavalier' censure. That such experiences extended beyond personal attacks in print and speech is illustrated by an emotive diary entry by the Essex minister Ralph Josselin, formerly an ardent supporter of Parliament. On 3 May 1661, Josselin recorded a visit to London, where he rode past one of the triumphal arches that had been built to celebrate Charles II's coronation on 23 April.[60] Josselin wrote of his having been 'troubled' by the arch, specifically its depiction of Charles I and his father, James I, and the inscription: 'to the divine James, to the divine Charles, I give endless power'. Josselin also noted what he described as other 'divers sad particulars on the face of the arch', including the Virgilian inscription 'En quo Discordia cives' (Lo! [Into what miseries] hath discord brought the citizens), and the depiction of 'an effigie of stakes and fagots to burne people of the Heads of the regicides on poles. and warrelike Instruments broken.' Far from sharing in the celebratory mood that had consumed London over the previous fortnight, Josselin spoke of his 'sad reflections on the vain flattery' and he prayed that 'the lord [might] prevent villanous wickednes, but if surely it will not be sine fine [endless].'[61]

The diary of Sir Bulstrode Whitelocke, the former Parliamentarian and lord keeper of the privy seal under the Commonwealth, suggests that he shared Josselin's disquiet about Royalist censorship and censure. In fact, his writings offer a rare glimpse into the effect that government surveillance had on those whose former 'disloyalty' was not forgotten by their erstwhile enemies. While Whitelocke had evaded attempts to except him from the Free and General Pardon in 1660, much of the remaining fifteen years of his life was spent in anxiety about his association with other 'fanatics'.[62] On 10 January 1661, for example, Whitelocke's house was searched in connection with the Fifth Monarchists' uprising of the previous week, for which Whitelocke wrote that he 'was sorry'.[63] In November 1663, amid government recriminations following the Farnley Wood Plot, allegations against Whitelocke gave him 'much perplexity of thoughts.'[64] Notwithstanding his concerns, Whitelocke appears to have been luckier than others; his contacts with individuals at the highest level of government provided him with 'tip-offs' that, we may assume, were not afforded to those lower down the social hierarchy. In May 1662, Edward Hyde, Earl of Clarendon, warned him that his association with the 'Phanatickes in the Citty ... might prove of ill consequence.'[65]

Not all former Parliamentarians chose to secrete away their concerns about the overthrow of oblivion. Some made their experiences known and appealed to the act of 1660 as a legal barricade against Royalist abuse. One of the most famous of these appeals to oblivion took the form of a passage in Andrew Marvell's 1672 satirical work, *The Rehearsal Transpros'd*, in which he responded to Samuel Parker's anti-toleration tract, *A Discourse of Ecclesiastical Polity* (1669).[66] Defending oblivion, Marvell reminded Parker that, by raking over the coals of Dissenters' actions in the 1640s and 1650s in order to counter their claims for toleration, he was referring to events that were 'four and twenty years ago, and after an *Act of Oblivion*', adding that, 'for ought I can see, it had been as seasonable to have shown *Casars* bloody Coat, or *Thomas a Beckets* bloody Rochet.' Marvell also spoke of his (apparently vain) hopes that, since 'The chief of the offenders have long since made satisfaction to Justice', he 'might in all this while have satiated your mischievous appetite.' Significantly, Marvell also made an appeal to the fact that the authority to remember lay not in the hands of Royalists, or indeed Parliamentarians, but in Charles II, whose Free and General Pardon had sanctioned oblivion. Marvell explained that 'his Majesty ... is the best Judge [of] how long the revenge ought to be pursued.'[67]

Others took advantage of Royalists' public concerns about the return of civil war by appropriating the argument upon which oblivion had hinged in the first place: that the downfall of reconciliation, rather than toleration, was most likely to spell disaster for the Stuart realms. In 1662, for instance, Edward Bagshaw spoke out against the abuse to which he and Richard Baxter, on whose behalf he wrote, had been subjected since the Restoration. In response to the Bishop of Worcester's demand that Dissenters ought to make '*honourable amends ... by Confession and Recantation*',[68] Bagshaw reiterated the importance of the Act of Oblivion, which was described as being 'so much forgotten'.[69] In fact, he went as far as warning the bishop that Dissenters would 'resent this Malicious and Ill-grounded Fancy' and that it might 'make men Desperate, and thereby render the Peace of the Nation, and, in that, the prosperity and Welfare of His Majesty Insecure and Hazardous. For what can more enrage Men to take Wild and Forbidden Courses', asked Bagshaw, 'than to see even Preachers of the Gospel [i.e. Puritan ministers] strive to widen their Wounds, and contrary to their own former Professions, to pull of that Plaister, which the Wisdom of our State Physicians had provided to heal our Distempers[?]'[70]

Public appeals to oblivion re-emerged in the 1680s amid Tory claims that the Whigs were the inheritors of civil war Parliamentarianism and republicanism. Loyal addresses to Charles II in 1681 were accused of 'reviving the memory of the late unhappy troubles, which it is the interest both of His Majesty and the whole kingdom to have buried in perpetual oblivion', and served 'to make men remember three hasty Dissolutions of Parliaments, and Twelve years want of one [i.e. Personal Rule]'.[71] This view was echoed by Arthur Annesley, Earl of Anglesey, whose 1681 edition of Sir Bulstrode Whitelocke's *Memorials* included a preface that spoke of his opposition to what he described as the Tories' 'habit of publicly invoking party labels from a past civil war'.[72] Echoing Edward Bagshaw's warning from two decades earlier, John Phillips, the nephew of John Milton, urged Tories to 'let *Six Hundred Forty One* sleep in the Bed of *Oblivion*, lest you wake *Five Hundred Eighty Seven* [a reference, perhaps, to the destruction of Jerusalem in 587 BCE] about your Ears: Who, should he be once *conjur'd* up, will hardly be *laid* a gain'. Phillips went on to compare Tory priests to 'certain People in the World, called *Pharisees*, Persons that always extoll'd their *Own* Holiness and Vertues, and laid Crimes and Miscarriages to the Charge of Other Men; perhaps, not so guilty as Themselves.'[73]

The inclusion of appeals to oblivion within ballads suggest that concerns about censure and censorship possessed social depth.[74] In 1674, an anonymous balladeer published *An Answer to the Geneva Ballad*, which highlighted the involvement of Dissenters in the restoration of Charles II and thus demanded that Royalists 'Cease ... impertinently to Rant'. The author presented Dissenters as more reticent than those who censured them, since they chose 'not [to] *Recriminate* the case, / Nor make *boast* of our Loyalty, / But still with *thankful* hearts embrace, / Our Gracious *princes* clemency'.[75] The ballad was a direct response to *The Geneva Ballad* from earlier that year, which condemned Dissenters as those who did 'cry, they love the King, / And make boast of their Innocence'.[76] Opposition to Royalist censure through appeals to oblivion might also occur in everyday speech. In May 1661, for instance, an alehouse in the village of Derwent in Derbyshire witnessed a spat about the king's Free and General Pardon. Witnesses claimed, in fact, that John Hague had 't[aken it] uppon him[self] to speake of ye act of oblivion', saying that 'ye Kinge was a foole and a knave if he made it not voyde, and hanged not upp all ye Roundeheads'. Significantly, some of those present 'warn[ed]' Hague of the 'dangerous Consequence' of his words, suggesting a widespread awareness of the provisions of the 1660 act.[77]

The Act of Oblivion was not the only defence to which former Parliamentarians and republicans had recourse as a means of forestalling

Royalist censure. Others, such as the authors and readers of the *Mirabilis Annus* tracts of 1661–62 saw God's hand in the grizzly fates of those who contravened the Act of Oblivion. Reflecting the extent to which the theatre provided a venue for anti-fanatical censure, the authors of one of the tracts related how a play had been acted out in Ilminster, Somerset, in derision of what 'they call the Rump Parliament', or that which brought Charles I to trial.[78] So hasty was one woman to go and see the play, or so it was claimed, that she forgot to put out a fire that eventually burned down her house and twenty-six others.[79] The tracts also contained references to the deaths of those who spoke ill of former Parliamentarians and 'fanatics'. When, for instance, a lady living near Charing Cross in Westminster had given 'very bitter Invectives against the Parliament party' to 'A Gentleman of good quality', she was found to have died shortly afterwards.[80] A similar case recalled how an apothecary from the City of London named Russell, perhaps William Russell of St Mary Colechurch, menaced that 'we must have the blood of more of them [i.e. former Parliamentarians] yet', and 'named divers persons who were formerly active for the Parliament', before declaring that 'if they might have the blood of those men he believed then they should be all satisfied, but not till then'.[81] It was reported that Russell fell ill and died shortly afterwards.[82] Gloating was also subjected to providential punishment, suggesting, perhaps, that God's hand could act to censor Royalist censure even if the law would not. The third edition of *Mirabilis Annus* reported how a 'Prelatical Priest' from Derbyshire had died shortly after he had preached 'how the Episcopal Cause *had been dead and buried, yea, a seal had been set upon the Sepulchre, yet this Cause had a glorious Resurrection,* &c.'[83]

We are fortunate enough to possess the explanations of some individuals for their objections to Royalist censorship and censure. Richard Baxter referred in his memoirs to the fact that the Restoration had allowed certain individuals 'to cast the Odium of Civil Broils upon Religion, and of other Mens Faults upon the innocent; so that there Interest will certainly lead them to call all those Rebels that swear not to their Words'.[84] His thoughts were echoed by his friend William Bates, who, in his 'farewell sermon' before his ejection from his living at Tottenham in Middlesex, lamented how 'promises' had been 'made to bury all differences as rubbish under the foundation', but that 'nevertheless the great work of many persons [had been] only to revive those former animosities, to make those exasperations fresh and keen upon their own spirits.' Bates went on to explain that this had been done 'to promote divisions and disturbances amongst us, clothe their enemies with the livery of shame and reproach', in order they might 'precede the storm of persecution.'[85] These cases suggest that Baxter and Bates saw oblivion not merely as a way of protecting Dissenters, but also as a way of distinguishing between Parliament's well-meaning 'reformation' and the abhorred revolution of the late 1640s. As such, they were defending the version of oblivion to which Charles had lent his support in 1660, whereby a minority of hardened ideologues were blamed for bringing down monarchy and true religion.

Interpretations like these crystallised into something akin to an early modern conspiracy theory. In the 1675 tract *Two Seasonable Discourses*, the former Parliamentarian and republican Anthony Ashley Cooper, Earl of Shaftesbury, lamented those 'who to compass their Revenge, and repair their broken Fortunes, would hope to see the *Act of Oblivion* set aside, and this happy *Monarchy* turned into an *absolute, Arbitrary, Military Government*.'[86] This theory of oblivion continued to hold sway into the 1680s. In 1682, for instance, one anonymous pamphlet argued that 'a sort of Men' were seeking 'to turn the *Act of Oblivion* into an *Act of Remembrance*'. In the author's opinion, this was because there was 'no Act that ever the King Pass'd more grievous to them than that; and the reason is not, because the King has Pardoned His Enemies, but because they cannot by his power wreck their malice upon their hated Neighbours.'[87] Samuel Amy attacked Sir Roger L'Estrange directly, condemning his labours 'to revive the Memory of forty, in contemptof [sic] the *Act of Oblivion*'.[88] Appealing to memories of Puritan support for the Restoration, Richard Baxter continued to criticise Tory attacks on 'fanatics', arguing in 1682 that the 'Prelacy and Clergy' continued to 'rub over all the healed wounds, and strive again what ever it cost us to ulcerate the peoples minds, and resolve that the Land and Church shall have no Peace, but by the destruction of such as restored the King.'[89]

Further evidence suggests that oblivion could be used to defend individuals against more personal recrimination. In September 1660, Colonel William Sydenham of Clapham, Surrey, was paid a visit by Ursulah Clerke, the daughter of a Royalist soldier, and Theophilus Woodnoth (or Wodenote), a Church of England minster who had been ejected from the rectorship of Linkinhorne in Cornwall in the mid-1640s.[90] The pair bore an order to seize goods that Sydenham, formerly a colonel in the New Model Army, was accused of having plundered from Clerke's father during the civil wars.[91] Sydenham was defiant, however, refusing to relinquish anything to Clerke and arguing instead that 'if the lawe were ag[ains]t. him yet the Act of Oblivion tooke him off, though he knew not how long it would hold, and for his p[ar]te he car'd not'.[92] In the same month, John Caethnes, formerly a lieutenant in Oliver Cromwell's lifeguard, responded to similar efforts to remind him of 'his former expressions' against the Stuarts by citing that 'there was an Act of Indempnitie'.[93]

By deploying Charles II's pardon to prevent Royalists from using their former actions against them, Sydenham and Caethnes were doing exactly what some hard-line Royalists suspected of those who had supported Parliament and the Republic: shielding themselves from being held to account for their actions during the 1640s and 1650s. Writing as late as 1670, the staunch anti-Calvinist Patrick Simon questioned what he and other former Royalists were to do if their old enemies 'begin to talk of the *Holy cause*, and the *Good old cause*'. 'Must we,' asked Simon, 'deal up our lips, and make as if we never heard of such a thing before? What? may we not so much as write a true History of what is past?' Here, Simon theorised the true ends to which the Stuarts' enemies were to put oblivion: 'This is the thing, no doubt, they [i.e. Parliamentarians] would be at. *We must forget ... all that is past, and now believe you cannot err, nay,* were always innocent.' Simon concluded that 'This will be a fine way to keep posterity in Ignorance, that you may do the like again, and never be suspected, till it be too late to prevent it.'[94] Three years later, Richard Leigh concurred that 'the Instruments of our late Miseries' sought to pardon 'not only for what is past, but to come; and so having cancel'd all their old Scores, they might now begin upon a new.' But he also accused them (somewhat hypocritically) of seeking to 'waken the memory of those Crimes, that might (but for them) have slept eternally in the *Act* of *Oblivion*'.[95]

From the writings of Simon and Leigh two paradoxes of the Restoration's mnemonic landscape become apparent. The first is that, even as late as the early 1670s, oblivion was held to have been obstructive to the 'true', Royalist account of the 1640s and 1650s. This was despite the fact that the provisions of the act concerning oblivion were set to expire in 1663. The second paradox is that, for all the protestations of former Royalists, the very fact that it was possible for them to impugn Parliamentarians and republicans as what Richard Leigh called 'the Instruments of our late Miseries', suggests that he and other Royalists had been rather more successful in undermining oblivion than they were willing to admit.

CONCLUSION

The rapid transition from forgetting to remembering after the Restoration was not the result of popular anxiety about Puritanism. The conciliatory programme of oblivion was deliberately overthrown by Royalists who feared that the lessons of 'rebellion' and 'usurpation' had been insufficiently imbibed by the populations of England and Wales. This struggle between proponents of oblivion and those of anti-fanaticism comprised competing attempts to secure what has been described in this chapter as mnemonic hegemony. On the one hand, Charles II, with the support of the Convention Parliament, aimed at eradicating identities that were inextricable from conflict. On the other, hard-line Royalists, seeing reconciliation as a dangerous concession, sought the total eradication of the 'fanatic' ideologies and, with them, identities that had, by their estimation, wreaked only havoc in the Stuart realms. The consequence of the Royalist coup in 1660–61 was the seizure of the authority to speak for the civil wars and revolution by Royalists through legislation that censored and censured Parliamentarians and republicans. This politics of memory had a measurable impact on its targets, some of whom had (largely ineffectual) recourse to oblivion as a method of counteracting the Royalists' pursuit of mnemonic hegemony.

One person who appears to have been acutely conscious of the futility of appeals to oblivion was William Sydenham, the army officer whose doorstepping by reparation-seeking Royalists was recorded earlier. When he was provoked by his visitors – Ursulah Clerke and Theophilus Woodnoth – to cite the Act of Oblivion, he admitted that 'he knew not how long it would hold'. Sydenham's next statement – that 'for his p[ar]te he car'd not' – becomes significant when we discover that he was also charged by Clerke and Woodnoth of speaking seditious words. It was alleged, in fact, that Sydenham chose to justify 'his former illegal proceedings and not repenting in the least of what he had done', stating that 'he lookt upon wt was then don by him or his souldiers just, and that the p[ar]ties father deserv'd justly to suffer beeing of the Kings p[ar]ty.'[96] If Sydenham had little faith in oblivion, he was convinced nonetheless that his decision to fight for Parliament had been the right one. With these words, he did more than merely speaking into the void – he counteracted the efforts of Clerke and Woodnoth to delegitimise what he had done before the Restoration. With the Restoration's unique politics of memory in mind, this book now turns to uncovering the motivations that lay behind the expression of seditious memories.

NOTES

1. I draw here on the use of this term by Esser in *Politics of Memory*. Others refer to 'public memory' and 'public remembering'. See, for instance, A. Assmann on 'political memory' in 'Four Formats of Memory', pp. 19–38.
2. Neufeld, *Civil Wars after 1660*, p. 2.
3. Particularly influential have been P. Seaward, *The Cavalier Parliament and the Reconstruction of the Old Regime, 1661–1667* (Cambridge: Cambridge University Press, 1988); and R. Hutton, *The Restoration: A Political and Religious History of England and Wales, 1658–1667* (Oxford: Clarendon, 1985).
4. Montaño, *Courting the Moderates*; Neufeld, *Civil Wars after 1660*.
5. C. Hill, *Experience of Defeat*.
6. Griffith Williams, *SEVEN TREATISES, Very necessary to be observed in these very bad Days To prevent the Seven last Vials of God's wrath, that the Seven Angels are to pour down upon the Earth* (London, 1661), sig. D1r.
7. Seaward, *Cavalier Parliament*, pp. 196–197.
8. 'Act of Indemnity and Oblivion', p. 230.
9. For an illuminating discussion of the policy of oblivion, including its relationship to identity, see Peters, *Commemoration and Oblivion*, ch. 2.
10. 'Act of Indemnity and Oblivion', p. 226.
11. M. Davis, 'Is Spain Recovering Its Memory? Breaking the "Pacto del Olvido"', *Human Rights Quarterly*, 27:3 (Aug., 2005), 858–880; N. C. Johnson, 'The Contours of Memory in Post-conflict Societies: Enacting Public Remembrance of the Bomb in Omagh, Northern Ireland', *Cultural Geographies*, 19:2 (Nov., 2011), 237–258; and A. Rigney, 'Reconciliation and Remembering: (How) Does It Work?', *Memory Studies*, 5:3 (Jul., 2012), 251–258.

12 *The History and Proceedings of the House of Commons from the Restoration to the Present Time* (London, 1742), i, p, 29.
13 J. McElligott, *Royalism, Print and Censorship in Revolutionary England* (Woodbridge: Boydell, 2007), ch. 8.
14 A[ndrew] C[ooper], *STATOLOGIA OR THE HISTORY OF THE ENGLISH CIVIL VVARS, In English Verse* (London, 166[0]), sigs. A4r–v.
15 [George Wharton], *Select and Choice POEMS Collected out of the LABOURS OF CAPTAIN George Wharton* (London, 1661), p. 2.
16 [Roger L'Estrange], *A CAVEAT TO THE Cavaliers* (London, 1661), p. 10. L'Estrange's pamphlet was a response to James Howell's *A CORDIAL FOR THE CAVALIERS* (n.p., [1661]).
17 [Thomas Tomkins], *The Rebels Plea, OR. Mr. Baxters judgement, Concerning the late Wars* (London, 1660), p. 45.
18 A. Toscano, *Fanaticism: The Uses of an Idea* (London: Verso, 2010), p. xi.
19 *The Cavaleers Letany* (London, 1661). See also A. J. McShane, *Political Broadside Ballads of Seventeenth-Century England: A Critical Bibliography* (London: Pickering and Chatto, 2011), no. 388.
20 R. Clifton, 'The Popular Fear of Catholics during the English Revolution', *Past and Present*, 52 (Aug., 1971), 23–55; Lake, 'Anti-popery', pp. 72–106; and C. Walker, '"Remember Justice Godfrey": The Popish Plot and the Construction of Panic in Seventeenth-Century Media', in D. Lemmings and C. Walker (eds), *Moral Panics, the Media and the Law in Early Modern England* (Basingstoke: Palgrave Macmillan, 2009), pp. 117–138.
21 Molden, 'Resistant Pasts', 126.
22 C. Hill, *A Turbulent, Seditious and Factious People: John Bunyan and his Church, 1628–1688* (Oxford: Clarendon, 1988), pp. 10–11; and T. Harris, *Politics under the Later Stuarts: Party Conflict in a Divided Society, 1660–1715* (London: Longman, 1993), p. 32.
23 For this transferral of power on a local level before the Restoration, see Halliday, *Dismembering*, p. 73. For the composition of the Cavalier Parliament, see Seaward, *Cavalier Parliament*, pp. 36–37.
24 M. Kishlansky, *A Monarchy Transformed: Britain 1603–1714* (London: Allen Lane, 1996), p. 229.
25 Seaward, *Cavalier Parliament*, ch. 7.
26 'An Act against Tumults and Disorders upon p[re]tence of p[re]paring or p[re]senting publick Peticons or other Addresses to His Majesty or the Parliament', 13 Car. II, c. 5, *Statutes of the Realm*, v, p. 308.
27 I. Atherton, 'The Press and Popular Political Opinion', in B. Coward (ed.), *Companion to Stuart Britain* (Malden, MA: Blackwell, 2003), p. 93.
28 L. Schwoerer, 'Liberty of the Press and Public Opinion: 1660–1695', in J. R. Jones (ed.), *Liberty Secured?: Britain before and after 1688* (Stanford, CA: Stanford University Press, 1992), p. 200.
29 *Ibid.*, pp. 200, 206.
30 *Ibid.*, pp. 202–203.
31 *Ibid.*, p. 207.
32 Hutton, *Restoration*, p. 156.
33 Schwoerer, 'Liberty of the Press', pp. 215–218.

34 Ibid., p. 221.
35 Hutton, *Restoration*, p. 135.
36 Neufeld, *Civil Wars after 1660*, especially chs 1 and 3.
37 Richardson, *Debate*, p. 18.
38 Roger L'Estrange, *A Modest Plea Both for the CAVEAT, AND The AUTHOR of It* (London, 1661), pp. 16–17.
39 Peters, *Commemoration and Oblivion*, passim.
40 J. Spurr, *The Restoration of the Church of England, 1646–1689* (New Haven, CT: Yale University Press, 1991), pp. 39–42.
41 Montaño, *Courting the Moderates*, p. 15.
42 *A COUNTREY SONG, INTITULED THE RESTORATION* ([London], 1661). For the dating, see McShane, *Political Broadside Ballads*, no. 391. See also [Thomas Jordan], *Here is some comfort for Poor Cavaleeres* (London, [1661]); for the dating, see McShane, *Political Broadside Ballads*, no. 381.
43 Essex Record Office, Chelmsford (hereafter ERO), Q/SR388/26.
44 Hopper, 'Farnley Wood', 292.
45 TNA, SP29/96/129.
46 TNA, SP29/95/111.
47 See TNA, SP29/212/74; TNA, SP29/221/17; TNA, SP29/235/86; TNA, SP29/293/19, 101; TNA, SP29/363/93; TNA, SP29/379/46; TNA, SP29/382/42, 42, I, 87; TNA, SP29/383/74, 74, I; and TNA, SP29/400/19.
48 TNA, SP29/383/74, 74, I.
49 TNA, SP29/44/134; R. M. Kidson (ed.), 'Active Parliamentarians during the Civil Wars', in Staffordshire Record Society (eds), *Collections for a History of Staffordshire*, fourth series, vol. II (Shrewsbury: Wilding and Son, 1958), pp. 43–70. See also TNA, SP29/58/73; TNA, SP29/66/35; TNA, SP29/101/29, II; and TNA, SP29/143/138.
50 TNA, SP29/41/2; and TNA, SP29/59/23.
51 TNA, SP29/135/25.
52 G. S. De Krey, 'Jenks, Francis (bap. 1640, d. 1686)', in *ODNB*, xxix, p. 92.
53 Victoria and Albert Museum, London F.48.G.3/9. With thanks to Professor Jason Peacey for this reference.
54 C. Hill, *Experience of Defeat*.
55 Sir Roger L'Estrange referred to Smectymnuus in 1661 as 'the Sworn Patrons of the Cause' whose inclusion in the king's pardon might not serve them so well 'before the Great Tribunal' in Heaven, [L'Estrange], *CAVEAT*, p. 27.
56 Keeble and Nuttall, *Calendar*, pp. 15–16.
57 *Collections of the Massachusetts Historical Society*, vol. VIII, fourth series (Boston, MA: Wiggin and Lunt, 1868), p. 195.
58 Cited in Matthews, *Calamy Revised*, p. 221.
59 Ibid., p. 448.
60 See John Ogilby, *THE ENTERTAINMENT OF His Most Excellent MAJESTIE CHARLES II, IN His PASSAGE through the CITY of LONDON TO HIS CORONATION* (London, 1662), p. 21.
61 Josselin, *Diary*, p. 479.
62 Whitelocke, *Diary*, pp. 600, 610.
63 Ibid., pp. 622–623.

64 Ibid., p. 676.
65 Ibid., p. 647.
66 Greaves, *Enemies under His Feet*, p. 151.
67 [Andrew Marvell], *THE REHEARSAL TRANSPROS'D; Or, Animadversions Upon a late Book, Intituled, A PREFACE SHEWING What Grounds there are of Fears and Jealousies of Popery* (London, 1672), p. 139.
68 [Edward Bagshaw], *A LETTER unto a PERSON of Honour & Quality, Containing some ANIMADVERSIONS upon the Bishop of Worcester's LETTER* (London, [1662]), p. 7.
69 Ibid., p. 7.
70 Ibid., p. 8.
71 *AN Impartial Account OF THE NATURE and TENDENCY Of the Late ADDRESSES, IN A LETTER TO A Gentleman in the COUNTRY* (London, 1681), pp. 25–26. See, for example, *CSPD, 1680–81*, 'Address of the city of Exeter to the King', pp. 659–660.
72 Neufeld, *Civil Wars after 1660*, p. 118.
73 [John Phillips], *Speculum Crape-Gownorum, THE SECOND PART* (London, 1682), p. 23. See also [John Phillips], *New News from TORY-LAND AND Tantivy-Shire* (London, 1682), p. 3.
74 See A. J. McShane, '"Ne Sutor Ultra Crepidam": Political Cobblers and Broadside Ballads in Late Seventeenth Century England', in P. Fumerton, A. Guerrini, and K. McAbee (eds), *Ballads and Broadsides in Britain, 1500–1800* (Farnham: Ashgate, 2010), p. 209; and A. J. McShane 'Broadsides and Ballads from the Beginnings of Print to 1660', in J. Raymond (ed.), *The Oxford History of Popular Print Culture*, vol. 1, *Britain and Ireland to 1660* (Oxford: Oxford University Press, 2011), p. 342.
75 *AN ANSWER TO THE GENEVA BALLAD* ([London], 1674).
76 [Samuel Butler], *THE GENEVA BALLAD. To the Tune of 48* (London, 1674).
77 Cox, *Derbyshire Annals*, ii, p. 68.
78 See D. Bywaters, 'Representations of the Interregnum and Restoration in English Drama of the Early 1660s', *Review of English Studies*, 60:244 (2009), 255–270.
79 [George Cockayne, Henry Danvers, and Henry Jessey], *ENIAUTOS TERASTIOS MIRABILIS ANNUS, OR The year of Prodigies and Wonders, being a faithful and impartial Collection of several Signs that have been seen in the Heavens, in the Earth, and in the Waters; together with many remarkable Accidents and Judgments befalling divers Persons, according as they have been testified by very credible hands; all which have happened within the space of one year last past, and are now made publick for a seasonable Warning to the People of these three Kingdoms speedily to repent and turn to the Lord, whose hand is lifted up amongst us* ([London], 1661), p. [75].
80 [George Cockayne, Henry Danvers, and Henry Jessey], *MIRABILIS ANNUS SECUNDUS: Or, The SECOND YEAR OF PRODIGIES* ([London], 1661), p. [76].
81 TNA, PROB11/303/521, will of William Russell, apothecary of St Mary Colechurch, City of London.
82 [George Cockayne, Henry Danvers, and Henry Jessey], *MIRABILIS ANNUS SECUNDUS: OR, THE SECOND PART Of the SECOND YEARS PRODIGIES* ([London], 1662), p. [77].
83 Ibid., p. [41].
84 Baxter, *Reliquiae Baxterianae*, p. 217.

85 *Farewell Sermons of Some of the Most Eminent of the Nonconformist Ministers Delivered at the Period of their Ejectment by the Act of Uniformity in the Year 1662* (London: Gale and Fenner, 1816), p. 164.
86 [Anthony Ashley Cooper], *TWO SEAONSABLE DISCOURSES Concerning this present Parliament* (Oxford, 1675), p. 10. For a similar argument see [Anthony Ashley Cooper], *A LETTER From a Person of QUALITY, To His FRIEND In the COUNTRY* (n.p., 1675), p. 1. Whether Shaftesbury was responsible for this tract has also been debated, see R. Milton, 'The Unscholastic Statesman: Locke and the Earl of Shaftesbury', in J. Spurr (ed.), *Anthony Ashley Cooper, First Earl of Shaftesbury, 1621–1683* (Farnham: Ashgate, 2011), pp. 165–166.
87 J. W., *Some REMARKS UPON A SPEECH MADE TO THE GRAND JURY For the County of MIDDLESEX CONCERNING THE Execution of PENALTIES UPON THE Churches of Christ, Which worship God in MEETING-HOUSES, For their so doing* (London, 1682), p. 4.
88 S[amuel] Amy, *A Præfatory DISCOURSE TO A Late PAMPHLET Entituled, A MEMENTO FOR English PROTESTANTS, &c.* (London, 1682), pp. 17–18.
89 Richard Baxter, *THE TRUE HISTORY OF COUNCILS Enlarged and Defended* (London, 1682), p. 44.
90 J. McElligott, 'Wodenote, Theophilus (*bap.* 1588, *d.* 1662)', in *ODNB*, lix, p. 933.
91 TNA, SP29/9/87.
92 TNA, SP29/19/34.
93 TNA, SP29/14/74.
94 [Patrick Simon], *A Further CONTINUATION AND DEFENCE, OR, A Third Part OF THE Friendly Debate* (London, 1670), p. 118.
95 [Richard Leigh], *THE TRANSPROSER REHEARS'D: OR THE Fifth ACT OF Mr. BAYES's PLAY* (Oxford, 1673), pp. 76–77.
96 TNA, SP 29/19/34.

Chapter 4

Seditious memories: Contestation and cultural resistance

The first months of the Restoration saw the rapid seizure of the authority to speak for the past. The beneficiaries were a group of hard-line Royalists who had objected vocally to the conciliatory atmosphere that defined Charles II's return to England. Through the passage of legislation that effectively supplanted the programme of oblivion and its clarion call for a process of forgetting, the aptly named Cavalier Parliament unleashed the systematic censure of their erstwhile enemies through press, pulpit, and other principal means of communication. Correspondingly, opinions about the civil wars and revolution that differed from their own excoriation of the 'rebellion' and 'usurpation' were censored. In so doing, Royalists hoped to eradicate the 'fanatic' ideology which, by their estimation, had been employed as a means of inveigling subjects into the sin of regicide, and which, corresponding with the innate tenacity of this cancer, continued to pose a threat to the health of the body politic. Rather than passing over their targets, these attacks were registered, provoking appeals to oblivion as the cornerstone of the Restoration settlements that can be identified across society.

These equal and opposite endeavours to exhume and to reinter the events of the 1640s and 1650s describe a politics of memory in which, perhaps to an unprecedented extent in England and Wales, political and religious authority was mediated by the authority to interpret the past publicly. The seditious memories that were identified and typified in chapter 2 can be understood as an additional component of this politics. Whereas appeals to the programme of oblivion, and its formalisation in Charles II's Free and General Pardon, were legitimate, the expression of alternative opinions about the civil wars and revolution were most certainly not. Consequently, as we have seen, sympathies for opposition to, resistance against, and the overthrow of the Stuarts and Church of England in the 1640s and 1650s always had the potential to be, and often were, regarded as 'seditious', 'treasonable', incriminating, and shameful by the government and its well-wishers. Put differently, seditious memories were anathema to hard-line Royalists in their pursuit of mnemonic hegemony.

By exploring how seditious memories contravened and counteracted mnemonic hegemony – how they acted as what have been referred to by scholars of memory as 'counter-memories' – the next two chapters explain why men and women endangered themselves by articulating them.[1] In doing so, they exchange a simplistic, and problematic, equation of these opinions with radical or republican intent and popular complaint for a consideration of the social and cultural significance of such language. First, though, we must acknowledge that, rather than being cast into the void, seditious memories were usually expressed before an audience and that the speaker or author anticipated (rightly or wrongly) how the audience would react. Whether the reaction was expected to be sympathetic or otherwise is a detail of cases of sedition and treason for which we have more information than those considered so far. Correspondingly, subsequent chapters involve a more detailed consideration of a smaller selection of cases that allows us to probe why it was that people articulated alternative opinions about the events of the 1640s and 1650s. In this way, these chapters draw inspiration from Phil Withington's studies of popular speech as a means of identifying forms of early modern sociability.[2]

In this chapter, evidence is considered that implies that people who spoke or wrote seditious memories acknowledged that one or more members of their audience were unsympathetic, or indeed hostile, to these opinions. The significance of these necessarily conflictive seditious memories is shown to have depended on exactly what provoked the expression of those views in the first place and whether they were oriented towards past, present, or future. To begin with, seditious memories are explored for which the circumstance of their expression was the denigration of Parliament and the Republic, or the acclamation of royalism, by someone then present. Thereafter, seditious memories are examined that accompanied physical or verbal abuse and intimidation. The chapter concludes with an examination of seditious memories that, by imagining the recurrence of civil war and revolution, were evidently intended to be intimidating in and of themselves. The culminating portrayal of seditious memories highlights their roles in contesting Royalist censure and thus public delegitimisation of Parliamentarianism and republicanism. However, equally important is a characterisation of seditious memories as having constituted two forms of early modern 'cultural resistance' to mnemonic hegemony via the appropriation and exploitation of the very anxieties which drove the pursuit of Royalist mnemonic hegemony in the first place.

Once more, this approach to sympathies for Parliament and the Republic eschews their problematic equation with seditious or treasonable intent by construing their significance from social and cultural contexts. It does so by drawing on understandings of 'public memory' or 'public remembering' in which divided societies fight over the authority to speak for the past.[3] In this instance, oral communication is highlighted as a medium through which former Parliamentarians and republicans contributed to the shape of the mnemonic landscape. Through this analysis, the chapter penetrates beneath the debate about the civil wars and revolution after the Restoration insofar as it has been made visible to historians by print culture. Consequently, the chapter exposes a lively and long-lasting, but necessarily largely oral, debate about the civil wars that has been neglected by historians and historiographers of the late seventeenth century. Furthermore, by drawing on sociological understandings of 'cultural resistance', the chapter proposes that the divisions of the 1640s and 1650s were a more fundamental aspect of English and Welsh society after 1660 than some historians have suggested.[4]

CONTESTING MEMORIES

Historiographers of the 1640s and 1650s often look to the turbulent 1680s as the decade in which the controversy regarding the origins of civil war began. Following a long period of Royalist martyrology in the 1660s and 1670s, the opening salvos of the debate are traced to Whig historians who sought historical legitimisation for their opposition to 'popery and arbitrary government' via comparisons between their own times and those of Charles I's Personal Rule, an era that was blamed for having drawn the Stuart realms into bloody conflict.[5] References to what happened *between* 1642 and 1660 are generally absent in these early Whig histories.[6] Yet we should not be led to construe the absence of a wider contestation of the meaning of the civil wars and revolution during, and indeed before, the 1680s. Contextual details from cases of seditious remembering illustrate that Parliamentarian or republican sympathies were often expressed with the explicit intention of *contesting* the main claims of Royalist censure. These included the ideas that the civil wars and revolution were a 'rebellion' and 'usurpation', and that the trial and execution of Charles I had been a particularly abhorrent and execrable sin. This evidence allows us to access a vibrant debate about the myriad reasons why men and women opposed, resisted, and overthrew the Stuarts and established church, one which, having been mediated by oral culture, was less easy to pre-empt, and thus muzzle, than printed versions of the same sentiment.

The experiences of Rosamund Bower in March 1664 offer an intriguing means of accessing this debate. Bower was confronted in her home at Bradford in Yorkshire by John Lyley, a man who had been arrested by her husband, Jeremy, for alleged involvement in the radical Farnley Wood Plot and who demanded to know upon 'what authority' he had acted. Unperturbed by Lyley's physical and verbal intimidation, Bower answered matter-of-factly that her husband 'had an order to show for what he did therein.' Unconvinced by her explanation, Lyley proposed that 'your husband sought my life, or he would have my head upon the toll-booth of Bradford,' and threatened that 'if his head went, more should goe with it.' When Bower pointed out that 'he would not have suffered unles he went contrary to the law and government,' and added that 'some had suffered unjustly, for the late King had soe suffered', Lyley corrected her, explaining that Charles I had 'suffered justly, and had a fair tryall, and just witnesses; but soe had not they.' Lyley went further, in fact, asking rhetorically, 'Did not the late King and Earle of Strafford bring all this trouble upon the land?'[7]

Lyley's justification of the regicide can be characterised as a direct response to Bower's claim that Charles I had 'suffered unjustly'. Countermartyrological narratives like these are identifiable elsewhere in the archive. Whereas Lyley had recourse to legality when justifying the regicide, others were less clear about why they had supported the events of 1648–49. In March 1668, for instance, several gentlemen who had met at the house of a William Mason at Bigg Market, Newcastle, accused one of those present, John Lee, of contesting their opinions regarding 'his late Ma[jes]ties unjust and unlawful sufferings'. Lee, a yeoman, proposed that, since 'he had often spoke to his Ma[jes]tie,' meaning Charles I, he knew that 'Newcastle could not afford soe ill-favoured a face as he had.' Despite being urged to be quiet or leave, Lee continued his tirade, asking the other guests 'what better is the present King, for there hath been no grace in the land since he came to it[?]' Quite who John Lee was and why he had 'spoke' to Charles I, if indeed he actually had, is unclear. That Lee's accusers were keen to highlight that he had been 'not att all spoke to' suggests that the house of William Mason was an alehouse and that Lee had been seated elsewhere within it.[8]

If John Lee had been in an alehouse when he justified the regicide, then the words may have been lubricated by alcohol. Further evidence suggests that drunkenness, and its susceptibility to speak a sober heart, were utilised by well-wishers to the government as a means of teasing incriminating sentiments from the mouths of known former Parliamentarians and republicans.[9] This seems to have been the case in December 1660 when Richard Prickett, constable of Canterbury in Kent, gave evidence before the city's mayor that a local shoemaker named Simon Oldfield had expressed pro-regicidal sentiment while in his company.[10] The provocation of Oldfield's outburst had been Prickett's reference to 'the death of the late King Charles the First,' which, in the constable's opinion, had been committed by 'Traytors' who had been 'executed for that horrid Treason.' Challenging Prickett's version of events, Oldfield explained that 'King Charles the First had a fayre and legall Tryall: and that those persons wch were lately executed for the same: were executed & suffered wrongfully.'[11] That the discussion occurred in an alehouse is suggested by the presence of another informer, Thomas Briggs, who corroborated Prickett's evidence, and whose profession was listed as 'Beerebrewer'.[12]

The regicide was not the only bone of contention to provoke the articulation of seditious memories. Posthumous attacks on Parliamentarian and republican leaders, such as Oliver Cromwell, were also liable to receive firm rebuttals from those who remembered the late lord protector more fondly. This was the case in July 1660, when Edmond Bullock was accused of challenging 'sum in [his] cumpany' regarding their opinions about 'the rebles and murdrers of our late lord and sufforant [Charles I]'. It was alleged, in fact, that Bullock had 'semed to be very much trubled' when those present had broached the idea that Oliver was 'the bl[oodiest] reble & rogue in the whol world' and a 'fool', replying that the late lord protector 'was a galant brave man.' Bullock was also accused of having said that Oliver 'could wine [win] any thing by power and kepe it [and] twas galant all though to the murdring of Kinges', a remark that, perhaps owing to its potential to undermine the charge of sedition, was later redacted from the evidence that made its way to the secretary of state.[13]

If Bullock had spoken the redacted words, he may have been clarifying that his sympathies for Oliver Cromwell extended only to his 'galantry' and certainly not as far as the regicide. Bullock was not the only individual who, while keen to salvage Oliver's reputation from reproach, distanced himself from the overthrow of the Stuarts. In 1669, the ejected minister John Reynolds was 'tempted' to respond to 'bitter words' that had been spoken by one Richard Bracegirdle (or Brasgirdle), an apothecary and 'formalist' who lived in Reynolds's former parish of Wolverhampton. Although there is no record of the content of Bracegirdle's words, that he had criticised Cromwell directly is implied by Reynolds's response that 'the Nonconformists were not so contemptible for Number and Quality as he [Bracegirdle] made them, that most of the people were of their mind, [and] that *Cromwel*[,] tho an Usurper[,] had kept up *England* against the *Dutch*, &c.'[14]

Besides censure of the regicide and Oliver Cromwell, the valorisation of those who had brought about the Restoration also provoked testy disagreement. This was particularly the case when General George Monck, who as we saw in chapter 2 became the archetypal 'traitor' of Parliament's cause, was the object of Royalist acclaim. One colourful case of this kind occurred at Lammas in 1664 when William Coulson, a mill owner of Jesmond, Northumberland, and William Carnes, his tenant and millwright, discussed Monck while the pair walked over Town Moor, a grazing land which belonged to the Freemen of Newcastle-upon-Tyne. Carnes deposed that Coulson had said Monck was 'a trator for by his bringing in ye king', since 'it had cost [him] Fiftene pounds in pruneing [bribing] a peer to free him from trouble because he sett his hand to ye Late Kings death'. Coulson was a member of Newcastle's council throughout the civil wars and revolution, and his having 'sett his hand to ye Late Kings death' may refer to his subscription to the Engagement Oath in 1650.[15] Carnes explained that Coulson's words, for which he was later gaoled, had been provoked by his belief that Monck was 'a brave man' and had

71

'gallantly ... brought in his Maiestye without the spilling of any blood or soe much as one sword drawen'.[16] We might speculate that reflections on Monck had been inspired as the men approached the town that Monck had himself passed on his march to London in early 1660.[17] Coulson was not alone in his willingness to contest Royalist praise for Monck. In September 1660, John Cathnes (or Caethnes), then living in Eltham in Surrey, was accused of having quipped that Monck 'deserved a Roope', when three Scottish merchants in his company had said that the General 'was honoured much and will [well] deserved it'.[18]

In each of these cases, individuals contested Royalist censure and the associated valorisation of those who had brought about the Restoration. That they did so, and risked their lives and liberties in the process, is very likely to reflect their own erstwhile allegiances. We do not possess information about all those mentioned above, but we do know that John Caethnes had been a lieutenant in Oliver Cromwell's lifeguard.[19] William Coulson, meanwhile, appears to have referred to his having taken the Engagement Oath and is recorded elsewhere as having 'recouped his financial position during the Cromwellian period.'[20] Elsewhere, John Reynolds, the ejected minister who was accused of defending Oliver Cromwell, had been admitted to the living at Wolverhampton under the late lord protector's regime in February 1658.[21] References to the regicide, Oliver Cromwell, and General Monck comprised indirect, and indeed vicarious, allusions to the fact that each of the individuals had supported, or in some way benefitted from, Parliament or its revolution. This is borne out by further detail from the allegation of sedition that was made against John Caethnes. Not only was the old officer provoked into espousing his scepticism about the portrayal of Monck, his interlocutors also informed against his justification of taking up arms against Charles I. The conversation between him and the three Scottish merchants had begun, in fact, with their pointing out 'ye unjustnesse' of Parliament's 'quarrell' with the king, to which Caethnes responded that 'their cause was just', since those who had participated in the revolution 'fought for ye peoples liberty but they were betrayed'. In response to Caethnes's invocation of Monck's betrayal, one of his detractors, Robert Meine, 'answered he was noe Traytor' and that, in fact, 'he was acting against Traytores, for his ma[jes]tie and ye Cuntry'.[22]

Caethnes's justification of his Parliamentarianism was steeped in what he described as 'ye peoples liberty'. Elsewhere, individuals made sense of their participation in Parliament's opposition to the Crown and established church in rather different ways. In October 1663, for instance, Michael Blackburne of Almondbury in West Yorkshire explained to a neighbour, Thomas Gibson, that he and other Parliamentarians had 'fought for God and a Good Cause.' These words formed a response to an attempt by Blackburne's neighbour to censor him by saying that 'you must [now] keep a good tongue in your head, for you caused us to do so formerly'.[23] Other defences of Parliamentarianism deferred to the language of oaths, such as the Protestation (1641) or the

Solemn League and Covenant (1643). This was the case in 1666 when Malachi Dudeine (or Dudeney), a gentleman of Upton Grey in Hampshire who was being tried for inciting the destruction of a maypole, responded angrily to a reference by the judges to his having been in arms under Sir William Waller. Dudeney retorted that 'he took up arms for the preservation of ... the true Protestant religion'. When pushed on whether it had been 'for the Protestant religion then established', Dudeney stated only that 'I have spoken'.[24]

Whereas Michael Blackburne's defence of his Parliamentarianism was limited to a single neighbour, Malachi Dudeney uttered his self-justification before an entire court. Self-justification could take place before even larger audiences. If we return to the regicides who were executed in 1660 and 1662, their references to why they fought for Parliament and took part in the trial and execution of Charles I can be regarded as challenges to the more or less explicit condemnation and criminalisation of those decisions by their accusers. We can also read the words of the condemned plotter Thomas Tonge in this light. Despite the basis of his conviction being his part in the eponymous plot of 1662, on the scaffold Tonge delved deeper into the past, suggesting that he may have seen his execution as retaliation against the revolution. With his final breaths, Tonge declared that 'I was, and had been sometimes in the Army; and I have looked upon this Cause to be good.'[25] When these kinds of opinions were printed, they had the potential to reach even larger audiences. *A Treatise of the Execution of Justice*, published in 1663, justified the regicide with recourse to 'several examples of the Lords Peoples executing Justice upon their own kings, according to the Law of God.'[26] The potential damage that the dissemination of such language could do is implied in the government's response. When the treason trial of the pamphlet's publisher, John Twyn, was itself published in 1664, the epistle to the reader explained that its audience might thus '*see the Hazzard of Dispersing of Books, as well as Printing of them*'.[27]

Most concerning to Twyn's prosecution was the idea that, by dispersing these kinds of opinions, the probability of a second regicide increased exponentially. Lending credence to these anxieties are cases of seditious remembering in which Parliamentarians and republicans argued that, since war and revolution had been legitimate, they were *ipso facto* repeatable. In August 1665, for instance, an apparently affable encounter between William Andrews and George Webb in Bulford, Wiltshire, turned sour when the former described the latter as 'a knave' for 'fighting against the King.' Webb's response was to proclaim that 'if that bee all, I will doe it againe to morrow upon the same account.'[28] Robert Nicholas, another Wiltshire man, who was described as 'one of the Barrons to ye Late Usurper', expressed similar seditious memories when his role in the revolution was questioned in late 1664. Witnesses claimed that Nicholas had boasted that 'he was the Man that drew up the Charge against his Late Ma[jes]tie.' Unmoved by the hostile reception of these words, Nicholas explained that 'hee would doe the same, for his

Ma[jes]tie was of the Norman Race and unfit to Reigne.'[29] Whereas this case, like that of George Webb, evokes the perpetuation of Parliamentarian and republican identities after the Restoration, Nicholas's words can be read as an affirmation of the justice of the regicide; it was so just that it could be repeated. His particular justification of the regicide – that Charles I had been of the 'Norman Race' – was a commonplace of anti-Stuart rhetoric at the time of the regicide.[30]

The evidence which has been examined so far is characterised by unguardedness about expressing sympathies for Parliament and the Republic. Common to the allegations against Michael Blackburne and the Newcastle man John Lee, in fact, was defiance in the face of censorship. While Blackburne was told to 'keep a good tongue in [his] head, for you caused us to do so formerly', Lee was told to 'hold his peace or begon'.[31] What these cases represent, then, are moments in which former Parliamentarians and republicans transgressed expectations of silence in order to contest what was, owing to the pursuit of mnemonic hegemony by hard-line Royalists, an increasingly unimpeded assault on opposition to and resistance against the Stuarts and Church of England. We should be open to the fact that, occasionally, this contestation took more evasive forms. When, for instance, Malachi Dudeney was pressed on whether he had fought for the 'religion then established', he responded with silence. Silence was not always salvific, however. In chapter 2, we saw that former Parliamentarian governor of Poole, John Rede, refused to answer the Earl of Arlington's probing question about whether he was 'sorry' for his role in the revolution, and later requested that 'every word sillable Circumstance and clause' of his evidence, including, one suspects, the telling silence, 'may be expunged.'[32]

Notwithstanding Rede's circumspection, the examples above reveal that former opponents of Crown and established church were willing to risk a charge of sedition in order to express their opinions about the recent conflict. This risk should be measured against the speakers' (or authors') acknowledgment that their audience was, or was likely to have been, unsympathetic to such sentiment. Rather than 'preaching to the converted', then, or contributing to an 'echo chamber', these individuals were attempting to contend that opposition to, resistance against, and even the overthrow of the Stuarts and Church of England were legitimate before audiences who were convinced otherwise. This objective was supplemented by a series of normative statements about the events of the 1640s and 1650s that were, or were expected to be, salient to individuals who shared conceptions of, for instance, honesty, legality, liberty, and providence. Consequently, seditious memories are characterised by claims that the regicide was just, fair, and legal; that Oliver Cromwell was gallant and brave; and that George Monck was a traitor. The wars themselves, meanwhile, had been fought for God, the Protestant religion, and the people's liberties. By attempting to legitimise Parliamentarianism and republicanism, seditious memories comprised an unequal, but opposite, move against one of the principal objectives of Royalist mnemonic hegemony: the public delegitimisation of fanaticism through the censure and ridicule of fanatics. When former Parliamentarians and republicans defended the past, they opened up a space in which a different public conception of the civil wars and revolution became possible from that which pervaded print culture.

The question that emerges at this point is whether former supporters of Parliament and the Republic were successful in converting any of their former enemies to thinking differently about the civil wars and revolution. Potentially revealing in this respect are the events of 30 January 1683, when MP Brome Whorwood spent the day at work on his Oxfordshire estate. Over the course of the day, Whorwood was approached by one James Eustace, who scolded him for his failing to observe the thirty-fourth anniversary of Charles I's martyrdom (see chapter 7). Whorwood's original response appears to have been well mannered, telling Eustace that he might have observed the anniversary had he known what day it was. Later, however, and seemingly exasperated by Eustace's haranguing over the subject, Whorwood testily enquired of him how he 'should be such a fool for [I] was once endeavouring a mocon in the house [of Commons?] agst [tha]t day.' Eustace responded that 'he was sorry to hear him say soe for [tha]t itt was a day for ever to be marked with a black letter.' In response to this martyrological account of the regicide, Whorwood protested that 'the old King deserved what he had'.[33] By casting an eye over Whorwood's service during the civil wars and revolution, we find that he had been a staunch supporter of the Stuarts. Brome's long-suffering wife, Jane Whorwood (née Ryder), corresponded with Charles I during his imprisonment in 1648, and their relationship may have been sexual.[34] It is possible that her husband's knowledge of the affair, combined with his later association with radical Whigs, engendered a change of heart concerning the trial and execution of Charles I.

ABUSIVE MEMORIES

The cases of seditious remembering that have been examined so far speak of attempts to convince audiences of the legitimacy of opposition to and resistance against Crown and established church during the 1640s and 1650s. The impulse to do so has been viewed as a function of the immediate context within which such views were expressed and indeed provoked: that is, the censure and public delegitimisation of Parliamentarianism and republicanism. But not all evidence of conflictual seditious memories suggest that those views had been provoked by Royalist interpretations of the civil wars and revolution. The contextual information that accompanies other examples of seditious remembering, particularly when these took the form of *identification with* Parliament and the Republic, speaks of their accompaniment by apparently unprovoked antagonistic behaviour, such as physical and verbal abuse. When, for instance, John Diches, a labourer from Somerset, was accused of assaulting a fellow drinker, it was noted that he had done so because his victim had been 'in the King's army' and had spoken 'against ye Anabaptists' while Diches identified himself as being 'in ye Parliament Army'.[35] Here, violence was a manifestation of Parliamentarian identity.

Violence that was informed by anti-Cavalierism is a recurrent feature of evidence of seditious words after the Restoration. In August 1669, for instance, Thomas Hodson (or Hudson) was beaten by William Oliver and his two sons, Richard and Thomas, on a road at Bromley Regis (now King's Bromley) in Staffordshire. Hodson explained that the brutal attack had occurred 'wthout any provocation', and that his assailants had called him a 'Cavalleir Rogue', adding that 'before it was longe, they should see his throate cutt and all his fellow Rogues.'[36] Remarkably, these kinds of attacks continued well into the 1680s. In March 1683, for instance, Emanuel Ford, and Philadelphia and John Bickerton, residents of Hoddesdon, Hertfordshire, were accused of assaulting an elderly man called Robert Humberstone (or Hummerstone) from neighbouring Broxbourne with 'brickbats, stones, and bones'.[37] Humberstone had been indicted for a raft of anti-Parliamentarian speeches during the 1640s,[38] and the assailants referred to him as 'an old cavilere, beggarly rougue,' adding that 'none but rouges served the king – meaning King Charles the First.'[39] Given Humberstone's (presumably) advanced years, this case suggests how deeply the animosities of the 1640s and 1650s could run in local communities.

Whereas evidence of seditious and treasonable speech can often leave a great deal to the imagination, the implication of these indictments was that enduring Parliamentarianism, republicanism, and anti-Cavalierism were associated with, and perhaps even constitutive of, the decision to commit acts of violence. Fascinating evidence from 1662 suggests how imaginative this violence could be. In October 1662, Thomas Gunn of Tuttle Street in Westminster was accused by John Tremaine Esq. not only of having 'kept [him] prisoner as a cavelleir', but also of declaring that 'he was a Roundhead and would so continue.'[40] This may have been the Thomas Gunn who was arrested in January 1641 by Sir John Lenthall, and even the man of the same name who signed London's 'humble Petition of divers free-born People of *England*' in April 1650.[41] Gunn's reference to his having kept Tremaine prisoner 'as a cavelleir' is intriguing. It may refer to actions before 1660, although this is belied by the fact that the Act of Free and General Pardon, Indemnity, and Oblivion cleared all 'Imprisonment ... done by reason of the late Troubles'.[42] Unless this provision was ignored by Tremaine, he was probably referring to his having been imprisoned by Gunn after the Restoration as a form of elaborate revenge.

Those who were deemed to have turned their backs on Parliament's cause were also subjected to abuse. In 1663, Simon Douglas of Fremington told local justices that he and his father had been censured by one James Arrundell, a yeomen, as 'rogues and traitors', since, in Arrundell's conception, 'all is traitors that doth fight for the King'.[43] Although Douglas's evidence spoke only of verbal abuse, further evidence suggests that 'turn coats', like Cavaliers, could be subjected to violence. In July 1662, Thomas Hill of Creech alleged that he was 'beaten and abused' by, among others, Lawrence Carter and Henry Hughes, for refusing to toast local Parliamentarian figurehead Colonel Richard Buffett at the Taunton house of one Andrew Sesse. Suggesting that this toast was a manifestation of enduring Cromwellian identities, the assailants had apparently declared '[tha]t olde Dick [Cromwell] should be old Dick still: and that they would bee for the old Olivers Creation'.[44] When, in a remarkably similar case from a little under a year later, Samuell Potter of Taunton was accused by Henry Duddwill of having toasted 'old Cromwell & Lambert & the rest of his friends', it was added that he had intended to 'hinder' Duddwill by 'putt[ing] his hand upon his thigh as if he were going to thraw [draw?] a sword'.[45] The evidence of Hill and Duddwill illustrates how perceived infidelities might be treated. It also evokes how the subversive Royalist drinking culture of the 1650s was carried on by former Parliamentarians following the Restoration.[46]

In these cases, physical and verbal attacks were accompanied by identification with Parliament and the Republic, and against those who were identified as Cavaliers or turn coats. The image of Restoration society evoked by such evidence is one in which the conflict of the 1640s and 1650s continued to inform societal division well into the 1680s.[47] Indeed, in contrast to recent interpretations of the mnemonic landscape after the Restoration, it appears that some individuals really were continuing to fight old battles.[48] We might imagine, in fact, that name-calling and explicit identification with the factions of the 1640s and 1650s informed scuffles between veterans after the Restoration, such as those to which the historian David Appleby has recently referred.[49] Historians have often highlighted the extent to which Royalist identities outlived the Restoration, perpetuated as they were by the 'Cavalier' trope in balladry and other literature.[50] What this evidence suggests is that the Parliamentarian and republican identities which we encountered in chapter 2 existed in lockstep with Restoration Cavalierism. To be sure, the kinds of abuse to which we have referred here constituted violent forms of 'outgrouping' through which these Parliamentarian and republican identities were constituted long after swords had been sheathed.

Continued senses of allegiance to Parliament and the Republic did not always inform identification against former Cavaliers. Further evidence suggests that attacks on individuals in positions of authority might be framed with recourse to similar sentiments. When, in 1681, the Essex landowner Henry Francis appeared on the jury that heard the case of the beaten minister David Jenner, he was accused of a stream of abuse against both bishops and judges. Jenner recalled that, having become exorcised about what he felt to be the minister's preferential treatment, Francis held forth that he deserved no damages because he was 'a Papist' and deserved instead 'to have [his] Gown pulled off.' Francis elaborated that he thought 'all or most of the Bishops and Clergy' to be 'papists or popishly affected,' and 'that they ruined the Nation and strove to bring in popery.' In the event, Jenner was awarded 5s. in damages, a judgement which provoked Francis to 'Rayl Bitterly against the present Government of Church and State,' even telling the judge, a Mr Lenthall, that 'Olivers and the Comon-Wealths days were better than these' and that the regicides of 1649 'were honest, godly men, and that the men of 40 or 41 were men of sound & honest principles.'[51]

Bishops and judges were not the only objects of abuse that was informed by identification with Parliament and the Republic. In August 1667, Sir Jonathan Trelawney reported to Sir Joseph Williamson, Secretary of State, that the townspeople of Dartmouth had labelled his troops 'papest[s], the scum of Goring, and Trepanners of poore peepell for Tangers.'[52] Drawing on local memories of the civil wars, Trelawney's soldiers were identified with those of the Royalist general George Goring, who had become notorious for the pillaging of Devon's communities.[53] Their abusers also cited the English possession of Tangiers in Africa, part of the dowry of Catherine of Braganza's marriage to Charles II, and, owing to its expense, a source of rancour in the mid-1660s. Thomas Guy, who was involved in policing the Yarmouth coast during the Third Anglo-Dutch War, spoke of having been confronted with similar abuse in September 1672 by the Corporation of Yarmouth. Guy explained that Sir George England, a member of the corporation and a well-known 'fanatic', had exasperated him 'soe farr [tha]t: I was forced to bid him kiss [my arse].' Suggesting the kind of language that may have provoked this outburst, Guy reported that 'they are boasting w[ha]t: a brave fellow Cromwell was but despisinge ye Kinges Captns'. From Guy's point of view, this language was characteristic of what was the most 'rebellious ... corporation' in Charles II's dominions.[54]

The evocation of Oliver Cromwell was common in verbal attacks on government troops. Anthony Hunter told the assizes at York that, in July 1664, he had been confronted with similar abuse in his own home at Birkenside, County Durham, when James Wright of nearby Darlington 'begun to give ill languages, saying he valued none of the King's officers, and that Oliver Cromwell was a better man than the King.'[55] This was presumably the same Anthony Hunter who had discovered a meeting of Quakers in nearby Sunderland earlier that month.[56] Verbal abuse could be accompanied by the physical variety. In June 1663, one John Whorrow (*alias* Barber) was accused of an assault upon Gilbert Luther, 'one of his majestys guards'. Luther deposed that Whorrow had struck him with 'the barr of his doore' before shouting that 'ye king keepes none but house=breaking Rogues about him; ... it was better for us when Oliver his people were heere,' and that he 'wished them heere againe for then every one might keepe his owne'.

Whorrow had apparently justified the act on several robberies that the king's troops had 'donne every night'.[57]

Defiant women also cited adherence to Oliver Cromwell. This was the case in March 1672, when the wife of Robert Baxter, ensign to Sir John Robinson, lieutenant of the Tower of London, was accused of having said that she and her husband were 'not soe abused' and 'lived better in Olivers time', and hoping 'that the Lieu[tenant] ... would be carried out of the Tower'. Baxter was referring to the fact that her husband had been recently court-martialled for a series of offences, including his having 'deprive[d] his ma[jes]ty of his [customs] duties' by bringing 'greate quantities of wine' into the Tower of London.[58] The case is an interesting one, not least because the words were spoken by a woman to troops who were then in the process of confiscating her husband's goods. Moreover, it suggests that restorative nostalgia for the Oliverian era might inform economic, as well as religious, grievances. The threat that Robinson 'would be carried out of the Tower' may have been intended to evoke memories of events that had occurred almost exactly three decades earlier when, in response to Charles I's attempts to arrest five MPs in the House of Commons, the London militia blockaded the Tower, thus securing the resignation of the Royalist lieutenant, Sir John Byron.

Given the government's emphasis on exorcising the spectre of 'fanaticism' after the Restoration, we are provoked to ask why the names and slurs of the civil wars and revolution continued to inform male and female hostility towards the authority of Crown and established church. We come closer to an answer to this question if we turn to another accusation of sedition, one made against John Adcock, a Norfolk tailor, in February 1678. The tailor was accused of having upbraided Colonel William Paston (an MP and Royalist who lived at Oxnead Hall) with 'severall reproachfull & undervaluing Words' while discussing a recent local by-election. One of those who disapproved of Adcock's words was Leonard Robinson, a woollen draper, who told him 'none but such as [he] & his party would be against ye election of ye said Colonel Paston'. Robinson described Adcock as being 'one of Cromwells Gang', to which Adcock responded that 'Cromwell was better bred then ye King of England' and 'a very good man' who had 'ruled very well'.[59]

Here, John Adcock subverted Robinson's attempt to discredit him by assuming the very Oliverian identity that was negatively imputed to him. When disobedience was accompanied by identification with Parliament and the Republic, such as in the cases described above, similar forms of appropriation were taking place. In chapter 3, the context of seditious remembering was described as the pursuit of mnemonic hegemony by hard-line Royalists who sought to expound the threat that, from their point of view, 'fanaticism' continued to pose to the Stuart realms. In doing so, they 'hailed', or 'interpellated' the identities of governors and governed as 'Cavalier' and 'fanatic', respectively. Identification with Parliament and the Republic effectively appropriated this negative interpellation – one that was anchored in the events of the 1640s and 1650s – to express opposition to authority, whatever form it took.[60] Seditious remembering thus comprised a form of 'cultural resistance' in which the identities of the civil wars and revolution not only formed enduring antagonisms between former combatants, but also defined the terms of political, religious, and socio-economic struggle in a post-conflict era.

THREATENING MEMORIES

In the evidence above, the contextual information that people gave when they testified against seditious memories illustrates that the expression of those views had accompanied physical and verbal intimidation. Further evidence shows that seditious memories could be intimidating in and of themselves.[61] In these examples, the prospection of the *recurrence* of certain elements of the 1640s and 1650s constituted direct threats against individuals who, as Cavaliers or turn coats, were to suffer misfortune or even death for their disloyalty to Parliament and the Republic. In October 1663, for instance, Nicholas Myas accused a fellow labourer, William Moulthorpe of Pontefract, of having told a seditious tale concerning 'one George Marre'. Moulthorpe had apparently told Myas that Marre 'was sworne never to bee a cavalier againe', to which Myas responded that 'T'was a pitty but such rogues should be hanged that could not let the Kinge alone, and meddle with their owne matters.' Myas's response provoked a remarkable tirade from Moulthorpe, who asked 'What is the Kinge better than another man?' and explained that one Robin Bulman, another labourer from Pontefract, who was 'a seaventh sonne', could 'cure seaven evils,' while the 'the Kinge can but cure nine, soe that the Kinge is but two degrees better than Robin Bulman.' Reaching his peroration, Moulthorpe predicted that 'Thou shalt see that before the moneth end as many will arise in England and Scotland as will cutt the throats of all those that were for the Kinge, and to bee sure thy throate will be cutt for that thou hast beene soe long a cavalier, and now art in armes for the Kinge!'[62]

The circumstances of other prospective references to the 1640s suggest that such threats were not always as direct as Moulthorpe's. Evoking the downfall of the Stuarts could be pregnant with meaning when uttered to Royalists. Shortly before parliament met in Oxford in September 1665, one John Pengelly was accused by Dr Nathaniel Eaton of a seditious reference to Charles I's attempted coup in January 1642. The significance of Pengelly's words becomes clearer when we discover that, a day before the meeting, Eaton had made another allegation of sedition for words that had been spoken in parliament by Pengelly's master, Francis Buller, the MP for Saltash in Cornwall, for whom Eaton had once acted as chaplain.[63] Eaton had responded to his chance encounter with Pengelly on the road between Saltash and nearby St Stephens with his hopes that 'notwithstanding all ye ire & malice agt. him', he and Buller might meet on good terms at the forthcoming parliament. Pengelly's seditious response was 'if Mr. Buller were tryed in Parliamt. he did not feare, but hee should find freinds enough there to take his parte, but if he ... were questioned out of Parliamt. he did not knowe but it might Cost the King as much as the Five members did his father.'[64] Pengelly was undoubtedly aware of Eaton's vehement royalism.[65] It is likely, then, that he deliberately invoked the events of January 1642 in order to dissuade Eaton from proceeding against Buller in a way which breeched parliamentary privilege.[66]

The case of John Pengelly demonstrates once more how deeply memories of allegiances during the civil wars and revolution ran in local communities and how these could inform threats about the future. This is further illustrated by a case from Yorkshire, shortly before Whit Sunday in 1663, when William Jackson, a joiner, testified against the seditious speeches of George Parkin, a local knife maker, before the York assizes. Parkin, who was later acquitted, had allegedly encountered Jackson and one John Dixon while standing at Dixon's shop window. Jackson explained that 'when Dixon saw [Parkin] come, hee went away', leading Parkin to say that 'John Dixon will not stay if hee see me come'. To this, Jackson warned Parkin that he 'must bee civill,' since Dixon was 'an honest poore man and the King's servant.' Parkin's reaction was imprudent, arguing that 'wee were better without a King then with one, for though wee have a Kinge, the old block remains still.' These words were informed by Parkin's resentment of taxation and the harsh suppression of the Farnley Wood Plot. That Parkin's words were aimed at Jackson is implied by two further allegations of seditious remembering in which the knife maker had remarked 'that there would come a change ere long, and then hee would banish both [Jackson] and all his like, kebbs as they were', and that 'before the twelve month's end wee shall see Kinge Charles his head in a poke, as his father's was.'[67] 'Kebb' is an archaic word which means 'a sheep culled out of the flock for any cause', and would have been particularly meaningful to the members of this rural community.[68]

The cases above represent encounters between individuals whose former allegiances were evidently intimately known to one another. Elsewhere, threatening invocations of the civil wars and revolution were informed by a recognition of where an audience stood politically that only became apparent in the course of a conversation. In June 1667, Dorcas Comber of Chatham in Kent, the location of a recent raid by the Dutch navy, told of having been approached by one John Croscomb. Croscomb explained to her that he wished 'to sattisfy his eye as concerning the fortifications now made there' and that he liked them '(slightly) well enough.' Comber was rather more effusive about the works, describing how they had been 'made by order of my Ld: Generall' – that is, George Monck, Duke of Albemarle and the commander in chief of the armed forces. Comber's invocation of Monck provoked Croscomb to thunder 'that [Monck] was a turncoat' and that 'within three months [she] should see an Army brought from all places against London & should take it,

& turne out the present parliamt. & put in the old one, and then they would take the King and try him as they did his Father'.[69] That Croscomb saw fit to refer to the 'old' parliament – that is, the Rump Parliament that Monck had forcibly dissolved in February 1660 – derived, perhaps, from his conclusion that, as someone who was willing to praise Monck, Comber was a well-wisher to the government.

Croscomb's seditious words are redolent of the fact that, when they were spoken, 'the present parliamt.' was still only six years old. That his evocation of the temporal brevity of the reign of Charles II provided a method of sharpening the edges of his threat is borne out by further evidence. John Caethnes, whose opinions about Monck were encountered earlier, responded to the censure of his company by saying 'Cum, Cum, wee stood 10 yeares and ye King hath not stood one yeare neither doe you knowe how long hee would stand'.[70] The capacity of such language to be threatening may help us to explain the words of which a yeoman living in Keld, North Yorkshire, stood accused in 1661. In evidence that was given before North Yorkshire's justices of the peace, it was alleged that the yeoman had said to a neighbour 'thou had best be quiet, for those that thou buildest upon, I hope they will not last long, and that I lived as well when there was no King and I hope to do so again, when there will be no King.'[71] In this instance, the threat of the recurrence of civil war involved a demand of censorship, suggesting perhaps that his words had served as a rejoinder to a request that the yeoman himself, as a Parliamentarian, ought to hold his tongue.

What exactly the yeoman of Keld meant when he referred to 'those that thou buildest upon' is unknown. He may have been referring not simply to his antagonist's having supported the new regime, but his or her having benefitted financially from it, perhaps as a holder of local office. This supposition is borne out by evidence of how the events of the 1640s and 1650s, and their recurrence, were often wielded against those who derived their authority from the government. In April 1683, John Trevanion, a Hearth Tax collector, entered the house of a Somerset innkeeper, Gabriell Cox. When Trevanion told Cox 'that hee was about to take distress in one of the Neighbours houses for not paying the duty of Hearth money', Cox's wife responded that 'ye. Kings Officers would never give over levieing the tax upon the Kings subjects until they had brought this present Kings head to the Block as his Fathers was; for it was the Officers exacting and levieing hard taxes on ye. People which made him lose his head'.[72] That the informant of the words was a Hearth Tax collector implies that, out of neighbourly solidarity, Cox's words were intended to threaten. This kind of weaponisation of the regicide may also explain why William Gervase, an opponent of the drainage of the Lincolnshire Fens, responded to a claim that 'what was done' to the fenland 'was done by his Ma[jes]ties Lawds [laws]', with the threat that 'if these bee the Kings Lawds[,] God Curse light uppon his heart for that it was likely hee would bee a Traytor as his father was, and [I wish] him hang'd.'[73]

Threats could be particularly fierce when wielded at those who, having supported Parliament or the Republic and since served the new government, were deemed to be 'turn coats'. Such a case occurred in September 1661, when one Lieutenant Wadden was accused of responding to news that had reached the George Inn at Bridport in Dorset that the county troops were to be sent to Scotland with the menacing remark that 'the people of god' might thus have an opportunity to 'hang all turne-coates rogues, meaning such as haveing formerly byn in rebellion [but] did now serve his Ma[jes]tie[.]' Another of those present, Richard Muston, took offence at the words, and made a point of highlighting that Wadden had himself refused to serve Oliver Cromwell and was thus also a turn coat. Unmoved by this effort to silence him, Wadden responded 'noe, for hee disowned that power as much as hee did this, & would as soone fight against it.' When Muston told Wadden that he would have to 'informe his Captaine' of his words, one Colefox, another of the inn's patrons, was heard to say that 'hee hoped to see a change of the Governmt., & that in a short tyme ... such honest men as hee would be lookt upon againe, & not such Turne-coate rogues as [Muston].'[74] This case is significant for showing how debates about what constituted the 'true' cause in the 1640s continued to divide Parliamentarians after the Restoration.

Together with knowledge of whose service an individual had been in before and after the Restoration, seditious references to the return of civil war and revolution resulted from what was described earlier in this chapter as the appropriation of Royalist anti-fanaticism. Two additional cases demonstrate, in fact, that the term 'fanatic' became a way of identifying against the new regime. In 1663, Jonathan Shackleton was accused of having responded to abuse by asking 'am [I] a phenattick?' and stating that 'Yow shall know yet before March wind be blowne that we phenatticks will looke all those in the face which now doe oppose us, for the Kinge is a bloudy Papist, or else he would never have give consent to the putting to death of soe many honest men as he hath.'[75] The Leeds labourer William Lawson may have been responding to similar abuse when, two years earlier, a true bill was found against him for expressing his hopes that 'the phanaticks will disperse his Majesties trained bands like the chafe before the wind', and declaring that 'It was justly done that the late King was beheaded.'[76] William Stanley, a Baptist preacher who had been ejected from the parish of Shinfield in Berkshire, appears also to have been assuming the role imputed to him when, by the orders of Humphrey Henchman, bishop of Salisbury, his house was searched for arms on 18 October 1661. One Mr Garrard, who had been sent by Henchman, explained that, having searched his house, he had been followed by Stanley who had then 'bragd of ye time w[he]n hee was ... Judge Advocat in Col Birches Regiment' of the New Model Army, and 'adding wth much relish [tha]t ["]Those were good daies["]'.[77]

This evidence shows that the references to the civil wars and revolution, and the invocation of its recurrence, served to threaten and intimidate Royalists, and those who supported, benefited from, or acted on behalf of the new regime. The case of William Stanley is particularly evocative of how a former Parliamentarian might, in his accuser's words, 'relish' the opportunity of summoning memories of the 1640s and 1650s as a means of threatening individuals who held positions of authority. The key to understanding these uses of seditious memories involves returning once more to the nature of Royalist mnemonic hegemony. Indeed, what the evidence considered above shows is that speakers or authors were often acutely aware that the recurrence to which they alluded was a cause of anxiety for their audience. Put differently, the former Parliamentarians and Royalists in question were exploiting the very instability upon which the pursuit of Royalist mnemonic hegemony, and thus their particular experience of authority, was founded. If we return to the case of Simon Oldfield, who challenged Richard Prickett's version of the regicide, we learn that these were not the only seditious words of which he was accused. It was also alleged by Prickett that he had responded to the 'hope[s]' of those present that they would 'never ... see the tymes againe to turne' with the words: 'they would not last long for they were now almost att an end'.[78] Here, Oldfield's evocation of the (then very recent) past to inform a version of the future was predicated directly on the fears of his audience that 'the tymes' would 'againe to turne'.

Once more, then, seditious memories constituted a form of cultural resistance which, rather than necessarily evoking seditious or treasonable intent, offered a powerful way of turning the tables against those who had acquired authority since the Restoration. Intriguingly, further evidence suggests that this form of resistance was appropriated by individuals whose religion had put them at odds with Parliament's objectives in the 1640s. In November 1666, it was reported by one Thomas Holton, a gentleman from Halifax, that, while he was 'drinkeing a cupp of ale at Egton', he had heard William Kirke of Eskdale say to the landlord of the alehouse, 'being one of [his] soldiers', that 'Their major is growne so high that he saith never a papist shall weare a sword, not soe much as a stick in his hand. I say never a cavalier shall weare a sword. Within a few daies thou shalt not se[e] a King in England.'[79] If, as the evidence implies, this William Kirke was himself a 'papist', then this case represents a rare one in which the speaker's identification against Cavaliers, and his threats of a return to Commonwealth, were informed by Catholicism rather than Protestant dissent.

CONCLUSION

When sympathies for Parliament and Republic were expressed to individuals who were expected not to concur with that sentiment, the significance of those memories is disclosed by the immediate context of their utterance. When seditious memories were used to contest the meanings of the civil wars and revolution, they can be understood as efforts to legitimise publicly

Parliamentarianism and republicanism in the face of hard-line Royalist censure. When these seditious memories were accompanied by physical and verbal abuse, and were characterised by identification with an individual's part in the events of the 1640s and 1650s, they can be taken to reflect the extent to which the divisions of those decades were perpetuated by the pursuit of mnemonic hegemony. Moreover, the summoning of those identities before individuals whose authority derived from the Restoration settlements implies that 'fanaticism' was a category that could be appropriated subversively by former Parliamentarians and republicans. Finally, the prospection of the recurrence of civil wars and revolution fed off the anxieties in which the pursuit of mnemonic hegemony, and the experience of authority, were grounded.

By examining the context and detail of cases of seditious remembering, this chapter has proposed ways of understanding such language which do not assume radical or republican intent on the part of those who spoke or wrote it. Indeed, when we meet with the looming presence of individuals such as Oliver Cromwell and General George Monck, institutions such as Parliament and the Republic, oaths like the Solemn League and Covenant, and events like the outbreak of civil war and regicide after 1660, we are often encountering something rather more interesting than statements of political or religious belief. While, as we shall discover in the next chapter, these figures could certainly inspire rebellion in people, their survival after the Restoration was often only perpetuated by the government's efforts to delegitimise them. Put differently, that seditious memories are often characterised by the laudation of certain figures, institutions, objects, and events is, above all else, a measure of how these underpinned Royalist anxieties about 'fanaticism' in the wake of 'rebellion' and 'usurpation' and how their posthumous public desecration (both literal and metaphorical) typified experiences of Royalist censure.[80]

NOTES

1 Molden, 'Resistant Pasts'.
2 Withington, 'Company and Sociability', 291–307.
3 See, for instance, Hodgkin and Radstone, 'Introduction: Contested pasts', pp. 1–21.
4 Hall, *Cultural Studies 1983*, especially 'Lecture 8'.
5 Neufeld, *Civil Wars after 1660*, pp. 97–103, 108–120. For an earlier study, see Macgillivray, *Restoration Historians*. R. C. Richardson has termed 1660–88 the 'Royalist-dominated period of historiography', in *Debate*, ch. 2.
6 Melinda Zook argues that Thomas Hunt's use of his POSTSCRIPT FOR *Rectifying some* MISTAKES *in some of the Infèriour* CLERGY, *Mischievous to our* GOVERNMENT *and* RELIGION (London, 1682) to blame Royalists for fomenting the civil war 'was unique' among his fellow Whigs. See her *Radical Whigs*, p. 49n. However, Matthew Neufeld's work has cited the blaming of Charles I's

counsellors as a common trope of early Whig writing; see Neufeld, *Civil Wars after 1660*, pp. 98–103, 110.
7 *DCY*, pp. 118–119.
8 Ibid., p. 158. Lee was acquitted at the next assizes.
9 Marshall, *Intelligence and Espionage*, pp. 233–234.
10 Richard Prickett is mentioned at the Maidstone assizes of 12 March 1661 and those of 30 July 1661 as the constable for Westgate parish (a large area west and north-west of Canterbury). See Cockburn, *Calendar of Assize Records ... 1660–1675*, pp. 4, 17.
11 TNA, SP29/24/42. See also Cockburn, *Calendar of Assize Records ... 1676–1688*, pp. 4, 17.
12 TNA, SP29/24/42.
13 TNA, SP29/7/145.
14 Baxter, *Reliquiae Baxterianae*, [iii], p. 48.
15 See R. Howell, *Newcastle upon Tyne and the Puritan Revolution: A Study of the Civil War in North England* (Oxford: Clarendon, 1967), pp. 16–17.
16 TNA, SP29/125/51, I. For Coulson being gaoled for the words, see TNA, SP29/125/51.
17 Monck stayed in Newcastle on his way to London in January 1660, see H. Reece, *The Army in Cromwellian England, 1649–1660* (Oxford: Oxford University Press, 2013), p. 212.
18 TNA, SP29/14/74.
19 *Ibid.*
20 R. Howell, *Newcastle upon Tyne*, p. 17.
21 Matthews, *Calamy Revised*, p. 409.
22 TNA, SP29/14/74.
23 Cited in Hopper, 'Farnley Wood', 292.
24 Royal Commission on Historical Manuscripts, *Manuscripts in Various Collections*, i, p. 149.
25 William Hill, *A BRIEF NARRATIVE Of that Stupendious Tragedie Late intended to be Acted by the Satanical SAINTS of these Reforming Times* (London, 1663), p. 60.
26 *Treatise of the Execution of Justice*, p. 10.
27 *An Exact NARRATIVE OF THE Tryal and Condemnation OF John Twyn, FOR Printing and Dispersing of a Treasonable BOOK* (London, 1664), sig. A4v.
28 Webb denied the charges, *CSPD, 1664–65*, p. 539.
29 TNA, SP29/106/9.
30 See, for instance, *A DECLARATION OR REPRESENTATION Of the Actions, Intentions, and Resolutions of divers of the Inhabitants of the County of Hartford, which always have, and still intend to stand to their first declared Parliamentary Principles, in Order to Common Right and Freedom* (London, 16[50]), p. 7.
31 *DCY*, p. 158.
32 TNA, SP 29/132/2.
33 TNA, SP29/431/89. See also Greaves, *Secrets of the Kingdom*, p. 257.
34 S. Poynting, 'Deciphering the King: Charles I's Letters to Jane Whorwood', *Seventeenth Century*, 21:1 (2006), 128–140.
35 R. Clifton, *The Last Popular Rebellion: The Western Rising of 1685* (Harlow: Maurice Temple Smith, 1984), p. 47.

36 TNA, SP29/264/139, I.
37 Hardy, *Hertford County Records*, i, pp. 326–327.
38 *Ibid.*, p. 87.
39 *Ibid.*, p. 330. Cf. *ibid.*, pp. 326–327.
40 *MCR*, iii, p. 328.
41 For the arrest, see *Journal of the House of Lords* (n.p., n.d.), iv, pp. 133–134; and John Rushworth, *Historical Collections* (8 vols, London, 1721), iv, pp. 143–144. For the petition, see *Journals of the House of Commons. From September the 2d 1648, In the Twenty-fourth Year of the Reign of King Charles the First, to August the 14th 1651* (n.p., 1803), p. 399. I am very grateful to Richard Bell, who drew my attention to this Thomas Gunn.
42 'Act of Indemnity and Oblivion', p. 227.
43 Atkinson, *Quarter Sessions Records*, vi, p. 67.
44 TNA, SP29/57/123.
45 SHC, Q/SR103, fol. 38v.
46 See M. Keblusek, 'Wine for Comfort: Drinking and the Royalist Experience, 1642–1660', in A. Smyth (ed.), *A Pleasing Sinne: Drink and Conviviality in Seventeenth-Century England* (Cambridge: Boydell and Brewer, 2004), p. 63; Bowen, 'Seditious Speech', p. 57.
47 Clifton, *Last Popular Rebellion*, pp. 46–47; Seaward, *Cavalier Parliament*, p. 50; D. J. Appleby, 'The Restoration County Community: A Post-conflict Culture', in J. Eales and A. Hopper (eds), *The County Community in Seventeenth-Century England and Wales* (Hatfield: University of Hertfordshire Press, 2012), pp. 100–124; and D. J. Appleby, 'Veteran Politics in Restoration England, 1660–1670', *Seventeenth Century*, 28:3 (2013), 323–342.
48 See, for instance, Neufeld, *Civil Wars after 1660*, pp. 15–16.
49 Appleby, 'Veteran Politics', 329–330.
50 See, for instance, Bywaters, 'Representations', 255–270.
51 TNA, SP29/416/123.
52 TNA, SP29/211/88.
53 See M. Stoyle, *Loyalty and Locality: Popular Allegiance in Devon during the English Civil War* (Exeter: Exeter University Press, 1994), pp. 120–121; and I. Roy, 'Royalist Reputations: The Cavalier Ideal and the Reality', in McElligott and Smith *Royalists and Royalism*, p. 110.
54 TNA, SP29/315/210.
55 *DCY*, p. 94.
56 For Anthony Hunter, see *ibid.*, pp. 88n., 94n., 194, 196, 199–201.
57 TNA, SP29/75/44.
58 TNA, SP29/303/235, I.
59 TNA, SP 29/401/35, II.
60 Hall, *Cultural Studies 1983*, especially 'Lecture 8'.
61 For other explorations of this idea, see J. Walter, 'Grain Riots and Popular Attitudes to the Law: Maldon and the Crisis of 1629', in J. Brewer and J. Styles (eds), *An Ungovernable People: The English and Their Law in the Seventeenth and Eighteenth Centuries* (London: Hutchinson, 1980), 47–84; and Andy Wood, *Riot*, pp. 19–20.
62 *DCY*, pp. 100–101.

63 D. Gilbert, *Parochial History of Cornwall* (4 vols, London: J. B. Nicholas and Son, 1838), iii, pp. 463–464.
64 TNA, SP29/138/70.
65 See, for example, Nathaniel Eaton, *De Fastis Anglicis, SIVE CALENDARIVM SACRUM* (London, 1661), pp. 3–5, 11–12, 40–43.
66 Thomas Scot argued at the trial of the regicides in October 1660 that 'whatever I say in Parliament, the Privilege extends to no more than this, that I may be lawfully secured till the Parliament hath been acquainted with it, but not finally concluded till the Parliament have heard it'; see [Heneage Finch], *THE INDICTMENT, ARRAIGNMENT, TRYAL and JUDGMENT, at large, Of Twenty-Nine REGICIDES, THE MURTHERERS Of His Most SACRED MAJESTY King CHARLES I* (London, 1729), p. 75.
67 *DCY*, pp. 117–118. Parkin was acquitted at the next assizes.
68 R. Trow-Smith, *A History of British Livestock Husbandry, to 1700* (London: Routledge, 1957; repr. 2006), p. 153.
69 TNA, SP29/209/150, I.
70 TNA, SP29/14/74.
71 Atkinson, *Quarter Sessions Records*, vi, pp. 42–43.
72 SHC, Q/SR155, fol. 4r.
73 House of Lords Record Office, London (hereafter HL)/PO/JO/10/1/293. See also, HL/PO/JO/10/1/298A. Both cited in K. Lindley, *Fenland Riots and the English Revolution* (London: Heinemann, 1982), p. 234.
74 TNA, SP29/42/1. As Muston was the only witness who was willing to testify against him, Wadden appears to have been lucky to escape the charge of treason for these words; see TNA, SP29/43/1. A letter of 1 October 1661 from Secretary Nicholas implored Lord Holles to bring Wadden before the next assizes, by which point more witnesses might be found against him. Nicholas also mentioned that Colefox's absconding 'implyes ... a confession of guilt': TNA, SP29/43/1a.
75 *DCY*, p. 100.
76 *Ibid.*, p. 88.
77 TNA, SP29/43/84.
78 TNA, SP29/24/42.
79 *DCY*, p. 147.
80 On the vilification of figures like Oliver Cromwell after 1660, see Neufeld, *Civil Wars after 1660*, p. 35; and Peters, *Commemoration and Oblivion*, ch. 3.

Chapter 5

Sharing seditious memories

Not all audiences were hostile to seditious memories. To assume so would be to presuppose the isolation of those who sympathised with Parliament and the Republic. In this chapter, I focus on expectations of a more favourable reception of seditious memories, highlighting thereby moments at which consensus was sought, and sometimes reached, about opposition and resistance in the 1640s and 1650s. Such an analysis entails examining the context and content of seditious and treasonable language to show that speakers or authors expected their audience to share, rather than to contest, those opinions. It is clear from depositions that those who expressed seditious memories were liable to misconstrue how such views would be received. Such misconstrual derived both from misassumptions about an interlocutor's political and religious identities and from the deliberate effort of hostile parties to foster such misapprehension. Elsewhere, the language of seditious remembering itself – its evocation of an imagined community of fellow travellers and its characteristic formulaicity – offers evidence of how far such views were shared. Finally, the social circulation of seditious memories in sermons, scaffold speeches, and, above all, print discloses efforts by speakers and authors to commune with sympathetic audiences.

Together, this evidence is taken to reflect the efforts of men and women to legitimise the events of the 1640s and 1650s socially and, by extension, to reproduce the political and religious identities of which the legitimacy of opposition and resistance had, in the course of those events, become constitutive. In this endeavour, these individuals are shown to have resisted the government's efforts to forestall this process through censorship and censure. The remainder of the chapter uncovers how remembering what came before the Restoration could expand what was imagined to be possible in the realms of politics and religion thereafter. Rather than equating these prospective memories with rebellious intent, however, I associate them with the creation of hope, a psychological phenomenon that is treated here as a meaningful historical category.

Once more, the chapter draws inspiration from recent developments that have occurred outside the historical discipline, especially within the fields of political science and social psychology. By drawing on studies of what has been described variously as 'collective', 'social', and 'communicative' memory, the impulse to reach consensus about the meanings of civil wars is associated with the reproduction of collective identity and resultant experiences of solidarity.[1] The upshot is a new methodology in which the content and context of cases of seditious remembering, as well as the manner in which they were conveyed to the authorities, are utilised to uncover their significance at the level of social psychology. Such an approach enables us to think about the power of remembering in a way that eschews the equation of such sentiment with seditious or treasonable intent and imagines instead the social and cultural efficacy of its communication. In doing so, we find that the power of evidence of seditious and treasonable language is located less in the events to which people referred, and more in the narratives that they spun with other men and women.[2] The implications of this argument include the likelihood that numerous 'communities of memory' existed in Restoration England and Wales whose efforts to conceal themselves have rendered them largely invisible from historians.

COMMUNITIES OF MEMORY

That seditious memories were shared with individuals who were expected to agree is often implicit in how they were detected by the authorities. We often know of these opinions only because one or more of the individuals with whom those memories had been shared in confidence decided to inform against the speaker. In May 1663, for instance, Matthew Morgan of Carrington in Bedfordshire informed against George Cockayne for words that were spoken by the radical preacher while he was visiting his family at Cople in Bedfordshire. Cockayne had been one of the most vocal proponents of bringing Charles I to justice in 1648–49, using a parliamentary sermon in November 1648 to implore the Commons to punish those 'who are the Lords and the Peoples known Enemies.'[3] Morgan deposed that Cockayne had expressed similar opinions at Cople over fifteen years later, including 'that the old K[in]ge did deserve to be beheaded, & why should he not be beheaded as well as another'.[4] That Morgan spoke of having been privy to treasonable speeches and sermons by Cockayne 'severall' times 'in sumer last heare' suggests that the preacher had expected – and, perhaps, hitherto secured – consensus from those in whose company he spoke, including his accuser. What lay behind Morgan's betrayal of Cockayne's trust is a matter of speculation. We cannot discount the possibility that his information comprised part of some unknown vendetta against the preacher, although it is equally plausible that he felt a sense of duty to inform against Cockayne's words.

George Cockayne fell victim to the *ex post facto* decision of an acolyte to betray the preacher's trust. Other cases of seditious remembering suggest that these views were brought to the attention of the authorities via the deliberate fabrication of consensus by an informant. The strange case of Thomas Lintwaits (or Linthwaite), a brazier and member of the Corporation of Stamford in Lincolnshire, seems to represent a botched effort at this kind of provocation. It was reported in August 1683 that Lintwaits had unexpectedly blurted out his hopes to 'see ye Presbiterians look up againe' and that 'they who were conserned in the Death of ye. late Old King did it for the good of ye. Nation.' Lintwaits was defended by one of those then 'in his Company' as 'in very good repute' and it was added that he 'hath always showne himselfe Loyall to ye. King.' Given the apparent improbability that Lintwaits possessed the regicidal sympathies that he was heard to utter, it was speculated that his motivation had been 'to pump one he suspected in ye. Company who he thought to be a Presbiterian.'[5] The role which Lintwaits appears to have assumed in this episode, then, was one of *agent provocateur* (or 'trepanner' to use the language of contemporaries). Where he failed in this capacity, others operated to devastating effect.[6] When Edward Riggs, an ex-army chaplain, ingratiated himself with a group of fellow former Parliamentarians in 1662, he accumulated enough evidence to implicate several men in hatching a plot against the government. This evidence included an allegation that Thomas Kelsey had spoken of his hopes that his fellow conspirators might '"see their error ... [that] in setting up Oliver the[y had] brought in the Kinge"'.[7]

That Thomas Lintwaits was a less successful *agent provocateur* than Edward Riggs may derive from his misassumption that the Presbyterians in his company would be receptive to pro-regicidal language, a notion that belies what we know of Presbyterian opinion before and after the Restoration. And yet Lintwaits lacked something else that Riggs had in his favour as an *agent provocateur*: known, and apparently unquestionable, sympathies for Parliament and the Republic.[8] Elsewhere, conspicuous Parliamentarianism and republicanism proved a rather more effective tool in teasing out seditious memories from unsuspecting individuals. During the winter of 1664–65, James Browne, a prisoner of both the Fleet and, more recently, the King's Bench, was accused of sharing several seditious sentiments with his fellow prisoner, Edward Parrott. Parrott alleged that he had been asked by Browne whether 'Hee had bene a soldier, or not.' Parrot explained that, in order 'to insinuate Him selfe with Browne, and to find His intents', he answered that 'Hee had bene a soldier in the Parliament Armye; although (in truth) Hee never was.' Two weeks later, this insinuation bore fruit when a conversation about 'the present Times' led Browne to complain that 'men were growne more wicked and more suffice to appeare soe, then they were before the Kinge came in'. That, by luring Browne into articulating his opinions about the recent past, Parrott's intentions had been to secure his liberty from the King's Bench may be inferred from the fact that he supplied this information to the prison's chief justice, Sir Robert Hyde.[9] To that end, Parrott acknowledged that declaring his former employment in 'the Parliament Armye' would fill Browne with the confidence that his fellow inmate was someone with whom sympathies for the time 'before the Kinge came in' might be shared.

Other cases of seditious remembering can reflect rather more careless misconstrual of an audience's sympathies for Parliament or the Republic. In December 1663, three members of the Vigures family of Liskeard informed against James Harris, a journeyman fuller from nearby Pelynt. The informants described how Harris had entered the Vigures's household with one Margaret Allen, his master's daughter, where he had entered into a monologue about having been 'a souldier in Cromwells Army' and having seen 'the last Kinge Charles beheaded att London,' which, in Harris's view, he had deserved 'for goeinge from his Parliament and for poisoning of his Father.' Implying, perhaps, that these words had not been very well received by his audience, Harris's accusers described how 'suddenly after this discourse about seaven of the Clocke att night', Harris absconded 'to the howse of one John Hoblyn in Liskerd ... where one Grace Allen brought [him] some meate & drinke'.[10] The historians Thomas Cogswell and Alastair Bellany have recently interpreted Harris's words in the context of the enduring rumour that Charles I had been responsible for the murder of his father James I.[11] However, these words are also significant for suggesting the potential for misjudgement about what an audience wanted to hear and, given the 'meate & drinke' that was enjoyed at the house of John Hoblyn, the intriguing possibility that the same sentiment was more welcome elsewhere. On this occasion, foreknowledge that Samuel Vigures possessed Parliamentarian sympathies – he signed the Protestation in Cornwall – may account for Harris's misjudgement.[12]

These cases of seditious remembering represent the failure of individuals to achieve consensus because of the premeditated or *ex post facto* betrayal of confidence or the misconstrual of shared sympathies for Parliament and the Republic. Other aspects of evidence of seditious memories are suggestive of more successful endeavours to reach agreement about the recent past. We have encountered several cases so far in which seditious memories were expressed by ministers before congregations in parish churches. It is highly unlikely that, in these circumstances, a minister articulated seditious memories from the pulpit without expecting the approval of at least a proportion of his audience. This was surely the case in October 1660 when the minister John Sympson was accused by a sole witness, William Rowland, of preaching at Bishopsgate that 'though the unjust Judges had now condemned the Saints [i.e. the regicides] to death, yet they were justifyed before God: and that what they had don their Consciences did beare them witnesse that it was just and right.'[13]

The idea that seditious memories were shared is much less ambiguous when it formed the basis of charging more than one individual with seditious or treasonable intent. This was the case in April 1661, when Mathew Hall and Thomas Wood, respectively commander and 'master mate' of the flagship *Royal Charles*, were accused of sharing similar regicidal sympathies to those of Sympson. The charge against the sailors was made by Jacob Reynolds, the commander of another ship, the *Saint Luis*, who had been 'Invited abord' the *Royal Charles* while it was moored off the coast of Portugal. Deposing before Thomas Maynard, the English consul at Lisbon, Reynolds explained that the men had described as martyrs the regicides who, in recent months, had been 'inhumanly put to death without having liberty to speake for themselves, wch if they could have had, they would have made all theyre accussers asham=ed, Cleareringe themselves befor God and ye Congregation.' Crucial to Reynolds's allegation was that these views had been exchanged in a 'discourse' and that they were 'spoken by ye one and confirmed by ye other'.[14]

Further detail from this case illustrates that the issue of whether seditious memories were *actually* shared by two or more individuals could be a matter of controversy. Since, under the Sedition Act, a conviction of treason relied on the testimony of 'two lawfull and credible Witnesses',[15] the successful conviction of Mathew Hall and Thomas Wood depended on the testimony of Robert Hatherly, the surgeon aboard the *Royal Charles*. While Hatherly was willing to testify that he had heard Wood say, among other treasonable speeches, that '[Thomas] Harreson and ye rest ... had cleared themselves and theyre Conscience befor god', his deposition fell short of implicating Mathew Hall in those sentiments. Indeed, a month later, Hatherly, along with two of his shipmates, provided additional testimonies that he had *not* heard 'Mathew Hall say any thinge Irreverently or treasonably or preiudiciall to his Ma[jes]tie'. His colleagues – Joseph Cracknell, the boatswain's mate, and Christopher Watson, the carpenter's mate – went further, deposing that they had 'never heard the said Mathew Hall, nor Thomas Wood speake any thing Treasonable or Preiudiciall to his Ma[jes]tie'.[16]

What actually happened aboard the *Royal Charles* on 7 April is unknown. In the event, only Wood was sent home to England as prisoner, reflecting the fact that, as we have seen, Maynard possessed no corroborating evidence against Hall.[17] As such, Wood's conviction was based on the scenario that he had spoken the alleged words without reaching the consensus with his shipmates upon which Maynard's evidence hinged. This, combined with inconsistencies between the evidence of Reynolds and that of Hatherly, Cracknell, and Watson, may imply a conspiracy of silence among the latter three by which they sought to save the neck of their commander, and social superior, Mathew Hall.[18]

Besides the detail of accusations of seditious remembering and the manner of their conveyance to the authorities, there are other reasons to suspect that those who expressed these views did so with the intention of sharing them.

By inspecting how seditious memories were expressed, we are given additional grounds to suspect that, as is probable in the case of Thomas Wood, more of those named in the evidence had agreed with the memories that had been articulated. One common linguistic feature of seditious memories is the apparent willingness of a speaker to exchange the first person singular pronoun 'I' with the equivalent plural pronoun 'we' when referring to some aspect of the civil wars or revolution. Such language is significant because it implies that, in the words of the historian of memory Guy Beiner, 'personal accounts' were grounded 'in a collective, community-based experience'.[19] On 24 August 1660, for example, several men and women deposed that one John Cleverley, a box maker and erstwhile Parliamentarian informer, had shared the news that seven men were to be excepted from Charles's Free and General Pardon. It was reported by those present that Cleverley had followed this revelation with the remark that 'wee cutt off their side againe and they cutt off our heads of this side, and ere long they'l cutt off their side againe and soe we shall have cutting off of heads againe as long as I live.'[20] Whereas all those named as being present eventually informed against Cleverley, his use of the plural pronoun may disclose his belief that those present would share his identification with 'this side' (Parliamentarians) against 'their side' (Royalists). That he spoke these words in August 1660, and thus only three months after the Restoration, suggests that Cleverley was caught unawares by the unwillingness of his company to continue to identify with the conflicting parties of the recent past.

Other linguistic features of seditious remembering suggest that such views were shared. In chapter 2, the articulation of Parliamentarian and republican sympathies was shown to have been highly formulaic. While this formulaicity may be attributed, in part, to the way that such evidence was recorded, the standardisation derived also from the nature of their *communication*. Scholars of memory have argued that oral communication plays a critical role in the reproduction of the traditions that underpin societies.[21] This is particularly true in societies such as seventeenth-century England and Wales, which were, in Dagmar Freist's framing, 'still dominated by oral habits of thought and expression'.[22] Evidence from the Tower Hamlets area of Middlesex in late 1661 is highly suggestive of how this kind of communication may have contributed to the formulation of seditious memories. Within a week of each other, two cases of sedition were heard by the Middlesex quarter sessions in which the speaker reflected positively upon Oliver Cromwell. In the first instance, William Hammond was accused by four men of saying 'that Oliver was as good a man as King Charles was, and that he had lent Oliver a thousand pounds, and that King Charles was as very a knave as Oliver was.'[23] In the second, George Appleby was accused by another man of saying that 'the Lord Protector was as good a man as the King.'[24] While little information about the accused was recorded, two wills from 1688 and 1695, belonging respectively to the mariners William Hammond of Ratcliff and George

Appleby of St Paul, Shadwell, suggest that these accused were employed in the same industry, at the same time, and within the same locale.[25] If this is true, then it would not be far-fetched to infer that the similarity of how these memories were expressed derived from communication between the pair or, at the very least, membership of a broader professional, and perhaps confessional, network.

The production of printed material also played an important role in the standardisation of political discourse.[26] Whereas the main foci of this study are alternative opinions about the civil wars and revolution insofar as they were expressed orally, we must appreciate that printed material that reflected sympathetically on the events of the 1640s and 1650s could slip through the net of Restoration censorship and shape how the civil wars and revolution were remembered.[27] Among the most famous of these was *A Treatise of the Execution of Justice*, a tract that was published anonymously in late 1663.[28] The tract revisited the charges that had been laid against Charles I in the 1640s and which, in the mind of the author, were 'yet fresh in our memories'. These included how the late king had 'made poor England Groan by Illegal Taxes, and unjust Exactions, Episcopal Tyranny, and Prelatick Encroachments, which occasioned a bloody war, wherein many Myriads of men were Sacrificed to his Lust, and the Land miserably Impoverished'.[29] The circulation of seditious memories in pamphlets like *A Treatise of the Execution of Justice* is some of the most tangible evidence that the intention of the author was to share these views and to secure consensus. What makes the circulation of seditious memories in print so different from that which occurred via orality is that it was impossible for – and, presumably, not an intention of – the author to ensure the confidentiality of expression. Consequently, these tracts made their way into the hands of people who might not agree with, and could be openly hostile to, such sentiment (see chapter 4). That print had the potential to reach such large audiences is likely to have offset the concerns of unfavourable reception.

Before *A Treatise of the Execution of Justice*, the publication of the regicides' *Speeches and Prayers* conveyed the seditious memories that were characteristic of the speeches to even larger audiences.[30] The speeches included justifications of the regicide, but also the decision to support Parliament when war had broken out. In the dying words of Daniel Axtell, the officer of the guard at Charles I's trial, the 'Cause' had been fought 'for common Right and Freedom, and against the Surplis and Common-prayer-book.'[31] There is evidence to suggest, in fact, that the *Speeches and Prayers* contributed to a topos of behaviour on the executioner's scaffold that proved influential after 1662. In chapter 2 we encountered the demise of Thomas Tonge, whose defence of his Parliamentarianism from the scaffold strongly echoed that of the regicides. Much later, Algernon Sidney's dying defence of his 'old cause' in 1683 led one reader to describe the old republican as having 'made his Exit like a perfect second [Thomas] Harrison.'[32] Reflecting how far the

Speeches and Prayers travelled, the regicide Edmund Ludlow – then exiled in Switzerland – transcribed the entirety of Major-General Thomas Harrison's printed scaffold speech into his famous memoirs.[33] The original medium of the *Speeches and Prayers* was, of course, oral, and it is likely that some of those who witnessed the hanging, drawing, and quartering of the regicides were also sympathetic to at least some of the content of their dying testimonies. John Sympson's defence of the regicides (see above) was preached on the Sunday following the execution of Thomas Harrison, and may well have been informed by his presence at the spectacle.

Further evidence raises the tantalising possibility that the dying speeches of the regicides were received favourably by individuals who did not share Sympson's or Ludlow's radical proclivities. Ralph Josselin not only failed to condemn the speeches of the three regicides who were executed in April 1662, he actually took heed of Colonel John Okey's mnemonically charged warning 'that prophanes was at such a height that ... England could not stand 3 yeares', writing that 'indeed man knows not to morrow[,] its not for us to prophesy.'[34] Samuel Pepys was equally struck by the last dying speech of Sir Henry Vane, who was executed in June 1662, which he described as 'a very excellent thing, worth reading and [Vane] to have been a very wise man.'[35] Efforts to prevent the circulation of Vane's speech beyond London in June 1662 suggest that the authorities were cognisant of, and indeed anxious about, the surprisingly broad base of sympathies for the regicides' speeches and prayers.[36] That those who were usually outspoken in their abhorrence of the regicide, like Ralph Josselin, found common cause with the former Parliamentarians may reflect the fact that their dying testimonies were often characterised by the justification of actions that were carried out long before the regicide, such as the taking up of arms in 1642. To this should be added the altered political atmosphere of 1662, especially the impending enforcement of religious uniformity throughout England and Wales. It may have been for this reason that Thomas Watson, the vicar of St Stephen's Walbrook, London, and a Presbyterian, preached a sermon that identified with the 'cause' of the regicides Miles Corbet and John Barkstead on 19 April 1662.[37]

Others took greater care in concealing views that had the potential to be seditious by sharing them in private letters. Richard Baxter's epistolary communication was under constant surveillance after the Restoration.[38] Nonetheless, in January 1669, Baxter was provoked to share his memories of having guided his parishioners along the path of godliness during the 1640s and 1650s in a letter to his missionary friend John Eliot. Declaring his success in this endeavour, Baxter explained that 'since I came from them, even in these times, [there were] few ... that professe not the way of strictnesse, and few indeed that oppose it'.[39]

How Parliamentarian and republican sympathies were shared in oral, print, and scribal cultures implies that an immediate objective of expressing such views was to secure consensus about the meanings of the civil wars and revolution. The identification of consensus as an objective of seditious remembering takes on significance if we regard it as a manoeuvre within what was described in chapter 3 as the efforts by hard-line Royalists to secure mnemonic hegemony by censuring, and thus seeking to delegitimise, the decisions to oppose, resist, and overthrow the Stuarts and established church during the 1640s and 1650s. Within this context, seditious memories acted as a foil to Royalist censure by enabling former supporters of Parliament and the Republic to 'reach out' to others and, thus, to legitimise Parliamentarianism and republicanism *socially*. Certain aspects of the pursuit of consensus suggest that, rather than confronting censure head on, the social circulation of Parliamentarian and republican sympathies took place within the shadows of Restoration discourse. For instance, much of the evidence above reflects a dependence on confidentiality as a means of avoiding the interception of seditious memories by agents of, or well-wishers to, the government. Expectations of confidence derived both from the perceived integrity of those with whom seditious memories were shared (i.e. those who were construed to be fellow travellers) and from the 'sequestered' (i.e. hidden) nature of the sites in which sharing took place (e.g. alehouses, churches, conventicles, prisons).[40]

By legitimising elements of the civil wars and revolution socially, people were reproducing political and religious identities that were anchored in the notions that opposing, resisting, and overthrowing the Stuarts and established church before the Restoration had been legitimate acts. Such self-justification was, as the historians Christopher Hill and Austin Woolrych have illustrated in their work, a nigh-obsessive feature of Parliamentarian and republican speech and writing during the 1640s and 1650s.[41] This was a function of the unprecedented nature of opposition and resistance during the civil wars and revolution – whether against the Crown in the 1640s or against the Protectorate in the 1650s – and the corresponding necessity to bestow legitimacy upon those decisions by grounding them in contemporary notions of, for instance, godliness and legality. The social circulation of seditious memories perpetuated this process and, by extension, militated against the efforts of hard-line Royalists to forestall the reproduction of Parliamentarian and republican identities via censorship and censure. In this way, seditious memories became the building materials of what scholars of memory have called 'communities of memory', or those that allow 'the comfort of feeling at home with people we are with.'[42] These were, in fact, sources of solidarity in the face of the intentionally isolating experiences to which Royalist censorship and censure lent themselves.

By conceiving of the social legitimisation of Parliamentarianism and republicanism as a function of consensus, and by identifying the reproduction of identities that were anchored in the 1640s and 1650s as a direct consequence, a series of claims can be made about the kinds of evidence to which this chapter has referred. The first is that what was described in chapter 2 as enduring identification with Parliamentarianism and republicanism is a direct manifestation of seditious remembering and its role in reproducing certain political and religious identities. Secondly, since the available evidence speaks only of communities of memory insofar as their integrity was compromised, it is surely the case that evidence of seditious memories forms the visible tip of a much larger, but concealed, variety of memory. Fortunately for those involved, there were many occasions when men and women shared seditious opinions about Parliamentarianism out of the earshot of government agents and well-wishers. The Lancastrian Dissenter and diarist Roger Lowe seems to have recorded exactly such an occasion on 16 August 1664, when he wrote in his diary of having been in the company of James Woods, a Presbyterian who became curate of Ashton-in-Makerfield in 1645,[43] and William Hasleden, who had chatted long into the night about 'wars and troubles that [they] had beene in togather'.[44]

Collective identification, and thus solidarity, manifested itself in ways that were less vulnerable to allegations of sedition or treason. Some of these may have derived from the occupation of what were described above as sequestered sites. For instance, the historian Andy Hopper has shown that Parliamentarian veterans continued to meet in an inn named after their former general Robert Greville, Baron Brooke.[45] The ways in which people addressed one another could also serve as subversive markers of group identity. There are several references after the Restoration to uses of 'old boys' as a colloquial name for those who fought in the New Model Army (see below). Elsewhere, former Parliamentarian soldiers continued to cite their military rank. One of the reasons for the Commons' rejection of the Lords' amendments to the Bill of Supply in 1680 was the omission of MP John Birch's New Model Army rank of colonel from its text.[46] Elsewhere, as we saw in chapter 2, Major-General John Lambert was often referred to by the title 'Lord'. Places and words were not the only means by which the past bound people together. I have suggested elsewhere that the adoption of coloured ribbons and other identifying clothing may well have signalled former allegiances during the Exclusion Crisis.[47] What this all suggests is that, while the New Model Army may have been officially disbanded after the Restoration, its camaraderie and hierarchy continued to structure senses of self well into the 1680s.[48]

COMMUNITIES OF HOPE

Seditious memories provided people with means of legitimising Parliamentarianism and republicanism, something that perpetuated those identities into the Restoration era. And yet not all seditious memories dwelled on the past. When, as we saw in chapter 1, sympathies for Parliament and the Republic informed predictions about the future of the Stuart realms, the credibility gap between memories and the seditious or treasonable intent of which they were supposed to be emblematic was rather easier to bridge. To return to a case that we encountered earlier in this chapter, the treason that Thomas Reynolds claimed to have heard aboard the *Royal Charles* in April 1661 was not confined to reflections on the regicide; it extended to a shared conception of the accused that 'ye kinge of England would not Reyne one yeare to an end, be=cause ye former government keepte the subiects more in subiection then he doth, and that ye kinge is a greate favorer of Papists'.[49] Likewise, the case against James Browne did not rest solely on his belief in national decline, but also in his apparent 'Hope' that 'The wheele would turne about' and that 'things woulde grow better.'[50]

These cases suggest that there was more to seditious remembering than mere solidarity. Its significance to those who expressed it derived also from their conception of what might be realised in the future. That, as the authorities feared, this future was to be achieved by recreating their 'rebellion' and 'usurpation' is borne out by a series of cases in which individuals reported having been solicited to take part in plots against Crown and established church. In November 1661, for instance, the Yorkshireman Peregrine Corney informed the government that he had been approached by one John Atkins with a 'Declaration in Caracters' that was infused with seditious memories. The 'Declaration' outlined a range of grievances including the claim that 'they had a good Cause which was never lost by the Sword, But that Treacherus Dealers had Delt Treacherusly as George Munke by Sweareing and forsweareing brought in Charles the second'.[51] Here, the myth of betrayal that former Parliamentarians and republicans directed at George Monck was employed as a basis of faith in what had been a 'good Cause'.

The audience size, and thus radical potential, of prospective memories was directly proportional to the reach of the media through which they were expressed. For this reason, the government was particularly wary of the expression of seditious memories to large audiences. In 1684, for instance, Thomas Rosewell, minister at Rotherhithe in Surrey, was accused of treason for evoking the revolution in a way that he flatly denied. Rosewell was alleged to have preached that 'We have had two wicked Kings now together, who have suffered popery to come under their Noses' and that 'if they', which was construed to mean Rosewell's congregation, 'would stand to their Principles, then he did not doubt but they should overcome their Enemies as in former times'.[52] Samuel Starkey, formerly the clerk of the radical lawyer Aaron Smith, heard similar sentiments at a conventicle in the 1680s when the minister prayed that 'once again they might be possessed of their Late Libertyes, & then [tha]t the Gospell of Christ might shine forth in its anciente Splendour.'[53] The Fifth Monarchist Jeremiah Marsden (*alias* Ralphson) was alleged at the same time to have led his congregation in singing a Psalm to the words: 'By Babel, Once Confusion came; / Lord send it Once again: / And in Confusion rayse thy name, / Let Nimrod end his Reign.'[54] These cases suggest a slippage between biblical and more recent frames of reference, one that was, perhaps, employed deliberately in order to disguise seditious references to the 1640s and 1650s.

Print spread prospective memories to even larger audiences than sermons. In his 1660 tract *The Temple of Lively Stones*, the Baptist and radical Thomas Tillam rallied the saints '(like Daniel) TO DO AS AFORETIME'.[55] Three years later, the former Parliamentarian soldier Roger Jones used his *Mene Tekel* to urge his readers to 'be wiser for time to come, make choice of a better Pilot and Mariners for thy next Voyage.'[56] While we can only speculate about whether these particular sermons and pamphlets provoked actual rebellion against the government, additional evidence illustrates their potential to do so. When the Fifth Monarchists rose in the streets of London in January 1661, their declaration, entitled *A Door of Hope*, contained several references to the 1640s and 1650s, including a reminder that their opponents were 'but an old conquered Enemy' who 'has been beaten in the Field times often'.[57] Likewise, the participants in the Farnley Wood Plot in October 1663, including the aforementioned Peregrine Corney, declared their 'ready mind ... to hazard our lives and all that is or may be dear or near unto us, for the Reviving of the *Good Old Cause*.'[58] If the Monmouth Rebellion of 1685 was, as historians have claimed, 'the last bid ... for the "Good Old Cause"' and 'the last blow struck on behalf of the Good Old Cause', then the declaration of the rebels was rather less willing to espouse it than those of 1661 and 1663.[59] Nonetheless, the mobilisation of old veterans and others who sympathised with Parliament and the Republic was encoded in the declaration's call for the rebels to remember 'our noble & generous *Ancestours*, who conveyed our *Priviledges* to us at the expence of their blood & treasure'.[60] The 'expense' or 'purchase' of 'blood and treasure' was a motif that can be found in Parliamentarian and republican literature throughout the late 1640s.[61]

Like 'blood and treasure', the 'good old cause' was itself deployed to evoke memories of the 1640s and 1650s. While it may have been perfectly clear to old soldiers like Peregrine Corney which particular 'cause' was being recalled, the ambiguity of the phrase was probably deliberate. One of the many examples of references to the good old cause that can be found in the state papers occurred in August 1664, when the apprentice Thomas Caulton attested under examination that his master, Captain Lockyer, had spoken of his plans to join a rising in Yorkshire on account of 'ye olde cause.'[62] Four years later, it was alleged that Captain Nicholas Cordey had attempted to conscribe one Cullum to a plot for 'ye good old cause & something that would doe them good', an allegation that Cordey later denied.[63] In these cases, the ambiguous meaning of the old cause was utilised as a means of overcoming the notorious political and religious fissiparousness of Parliamentarianism and republicanism. This kind of language had the potential to unify, and indeed to mobilise, opposition to the Restoration settlements.

Indeed, one of the most intriguing aspects of evidence of plotting after the Restoration is how former involvement in the civil war on Parliament's side was taken not only as evidence that an individual was likely to agree with seditious memories, but also that they would be receptive to involvement in conspiracy. This is apparent in an episode from October 1660, when one William Sharpe solicited a Cambridgeshire ropemaker named Edward Kater to join him in a plot against the government because he 'had beene abroad in these troubles' (i.e. he had fought for Parliament).[64] It was further alleged by Thomas Kater, also a ropemaker, that Sharpe had threatened that 'if the Kinge would lett them doe as they had done before tyme, it would be a means for him to live the longer'.[65] In February 1665, Edward James recalled an experience similar to the Katers' when he had entered the house of Cornet Graves, a former Parliamentarian who was also a resident of Cambridgeshire. For reasons that remained undivulged, Graves assumed that the informant had also fought for Parliament. The consequence was that Graves bade James 'good cheere for once againe we shall eat roast meat, for I have comanded 60 men that are now in the towne of old Olivers boyes and ... we shall have a day for it for all this.'[66]

The indiscretion of Cornet Graves represents how an unawareness that a fellow veteran was unwilling to take up arms 'once again' could result in an accusation of sedition. It also illustrates that the failure to gauge the receptiveness of an audience to anti-government plotting may well have derived from the conception that a large community of fellow travellers – those to whom he referred as 'old Olivers boyes' – lay in waiting. This 'imagined community' was clearly inspiring and, perhaps, comforting to those who longed to see the downfall of the Restoration settlements.[67] It was for this reason, no doubt, that the informant Edward Massey was reassured by a Mr Blake of Taunton in Somerset in May 1682 that 'we have sum of Ollifers [Oliver's] ould offissers to command us still.'[68] Two months later, George Kettle, a victualler and Fifth Monarchist from Southwark, was more explicit when he confided misguidedly in the ironically named Constant Oates that 'he had one good horse', that 'he feared no man, & if calld to it againe (as he was before) he knew how to rewle his sword' since 'the Non=Conformists were provided with Arms, and that he himselfe was suffitiently provided herewith besides many more old Oliverian boyes whoe knew how to Ride'.[69]

The conception of a dormant community of old soldiers was equally powerful to women who sympathised with Parliament and the Republic. In March 1663, Katharine Gregory, the wife of Cromwellian captain John Gregory, was accused of having reassured an unnamed gentlewoman with the expectation that '500 sword men' were ready 'to kill the King and[,] as for that false villaine Moncke[,] he should be put in an Iron Cage and sett upon Paules Church [i.e. St Paul's Cathedral] and [tha]t they will not give quarter to any of the Kings party not so much as to their wives and children.'[70] Here, the common vilification of George Monck took the particularly brutal form of foreseeing a punishment akin to that of the leaders of the 1535 Münster Rebellion. Gregory's case also depicts how collective identification with the old cause perpetuated the divisions between supporters of Crown and Parliament that we encountered in chapter 4. This is even clearer in a case from December 1662, when two prisoners at Ivelchester (Ilchester) in Somerset provided information that one John Elliot had approached them with details of a plan to 'break up the prison', adding that he would 'release all ye prisoners' bar two, 'because they are Cavalieres'.[71]

Together, this evidence portrays a clear link between the expression of prospective seditious memories and the encouragement of rebellion against Crown and established church after the Restoration, confirming thereby Royalist anxieties about seditious and treasonable language. And yet radical politics and religion were not the only means of securing the alternative future realities to which sympathies for Parliament and the Republic might lend themselves. When, for instance, Caleb Trenchfield lectured his congregation at Lee in Kent in September 1660, he held forth 'that you are not so willing to ingage and to sufor for the Cause of god as you were at first' and that '[you] must be willing to sufor for the Cause of god'. Here, how we understand the intention of Trenchfield's words depends on our interpretation of his choice of the verb 'to suffer'.[72] Given the language of other Dissenters in the immediate wake of the Restoration – that the time had come to 'suffer under the cross' – Trenchfield may have been advocating more 'quietist' behaviour.[73] Even if the future involved cleaving to 'the Cause of god', this did not necessarily entail repeating the violence of 'rebels' and 'usurpers'.

Samuel Pepys's famous diaries display numerous references to the recent past which, in sharing Caleb Trenchfield's emphasis on the future, had the potential to be seditious, and yet were clearly not intended to provoke radical political action. Pepys's position at the Navy Board after the Restoration owed itself to the patronage of a former Parliamentarian, his cousin Sir Edward Montagu. Consequently, the diarist was in contact with colleagues and friends whose opinions about Parliament and the Republic tended towards some of those considered so far in this book.[74] One particular occasion illustrates how, as Daniel Woolf has demonstrated, references to former monarchs were intended to impress the need for policy change on the current occupant of the throne; they were certainly not intended to be seditious or treasonable.[75] On 27 February 1665, Pepys recorded in his diary how he had heard several members of the Privy Council, including the former Royalist soldier Baron Berkeley of Stratton, 'cry up the discipline of the late times here ... and wishing that the same law and severity were used against drunkenness as there was then – saying that our evil-living will call the hand of God upon us again.'[76] Clearly these were not individuals who desired the imminent overthrow of episcopacy or monarchy. Here, a comparison of past and present was intended as advice rather than admonition.

There are other reasons to complicate the association of Parliamentarian identification with seditious or treasonable objectives. In some of the cases encountered in this chapter, the words of men and women speak not of intentions, but of hopes. In December 1680, for instance, John Zeale, who was working as a government agent,[77] provided information that he had been approached in the Marshalsea prison by a Mr Haitor (possibly Thomas Hayter) who suborned him to give testimony against the king for a plot to seize 'the Citty Treashury'.[78] Zeale also explained how Haitor had expressed his opinion that 'had it not been for the Bishops the bill [i.e. the Exclusion Bill] had pased the hous of Lords against the Duke [of York]' and that 'hee hoped to see the times againe: that there should bee noe such persons as Bishops; and that hee him selfe did not doubt butt to have as Good an Imploy as ever hee had: by the Earl of Shaftesbureys means'.[79] The hopes of others were couched in terms of local memories of the civil war, such as in November 1684 when an agent with ties to London's dissenting communities reported having heard hopes expressed that, as during the civil war, 'the Citty Gattes' would be once again 'puld down and the Lead melted to make bullets'.[80] Others shared an *expectation* that the Restoration settlements would fail, although they did so without implicating themselves in this failure. In May 1660, for instance, Edward and Alice Jones of St Martins-in-the-Fields were indicted for sharing the belief that 'it was the King's time now to raigne, but it was upon sufferance for a little time, and it would be theres ag[a]ine before itt be long.'[81]

Not all predications about the future involved these levels of certainty. As we saw in chapter 2, other people couched prospective memories with a distinct sense of conditionality. In 1661, for instance, Captain Owen Cox testified that he had been told by Captain William Pestell that, should the king make further exceptions from the Free and General Pardon, then he 'must expect to goe the same way his Father ... went.'[82] In the same year, Enoch Hinton and his relative John were accused of holding beliefs similar to those of Captain Cox 'That many m[e]n were putt to death & that ye same axe that cutt off the old Kings head doth hang over this Kings head.'[83] These kinds of warnings were shared throughout England and Wales after the Restoration. The Somerset husbandman William Springe deposed to the county's justices that, having entered the house of William Goddard, he had found himself 'accidentallie in the companie of one Jeremy Cole of Curland', who was heard to warn 'this younge Rogue', that is, Charles II, to 'take heed that his head be not cutt of [sic] as his fathers was.'[84] The words of the wiredrawer Simon Urlin illustrate how idiosyncratic these evocations of the past could be. It was alleged of Urlin that, while addressing a meeting of his fellow craftsmen in February 1664, he had said 'in passion' that the granting of monopolies 'was ye Cause (for ought hee knew) that the last king lost his head.' The context of Urlin's words was the controversial bestowal of a patent on John Garill relating to the wiredrawing process.[85]

Rather than statements of intent to overthrow the Restoration settlements, these cases imply that prospective seditious memories were often little more than shared hopes, expectations, and threats. Whereas these forms of prospection were encompassed within the government's roomy definition of what was seditious or treasonable, they share the spatial and temporal dissociation of the speaker from the political or religious transformation that was foreseen. Put differently, it was always someone else who would overthrow the monarchy or episcopacy, or at some other time. By emphasising this deferral of praxis, we might speculate that the intention of sharing these kinds of seditious memories was not always to encourage or to mobilise radical action. This is not to say that these views were mere 'bluster' or posturing.[86] Clearly this kind of language represents the extent to which alternative future realities could be imagined and, as we have seen, this might eventually lead people to take part in anti-government plotting or open rebellion. Nonetheless, if we emphasise once more that the *sharing* of prospective seditious memories may have been of significance in and of itself, then the radical potential of such opinions takes a different form. Rather than being preparatory to anti-government plotting, the sharing of these kinds of opinions offered hope that an alternative future was possible if only some element of the recent past was repeated.

If we consider the kind of future to which the politics of memory (as it was described in chapter 2) lent itself, then the significance of these senses of hope becomes apparent. By emphasising the unnaturalness of rebellion and usurpation, and the providential inevitability of the return of the Stuarts in 1660, Royalists were making claims about the certainty of the Restoration settlements. To adapt language that has been used to describe the twenty-first-century political imaginary, Royalist mnemonic hegemony resulted in a 'Royalist realism' in which the politically possible was limited to divine-right monarchy, episcopal ecclesiology, and a neo-Laudian liturgy.[87] Yet by anchoring the Restoration settlements in the delegitimisation of Parliamentarianism and republicanism, Royalists inadvertently lent credence to the notion that, by imitating opposition to and resistance against Crown and established church in the 1640s and 1650s, a different world from that of the persecution, penury, or disempowerment of the Restoration became achievable. In this way, the social circulation of prospective seditious memories foreshadowed what the psychologists David Feldman and Charles R. Snyder have described as 'revolutionary hope', or that which, 'under dire circumstances', serves as a 'pacifying mentality that enables people to endure.'[88] By creating communities of memory, then, Royalists also created 'communities of hope'.[89]

CONCLUSION

When individuals expressed seditious memories, they usually had an audience. Much of the available evidence of seditious memories suggests that the intention of the speaker or author of seditious memories was to share them and to achieve consensus. The kinds of opinions that were circulated ranged from reflections on the events of the 1640s and 1650s to predictions that history was likely to repeat itself. How we understand what such language meant to its authors depends on how much credence we lend to the claims of the authorities about seditious and treasonable intent. Clearly seditious memories did have a provocative, and indeed mobilising, effect. The plots and risings of the 1660s, 1670s, and 1680s are testament to this fact. Nonetheless, this chapter has shown that, by avoiding assumptions about the radical or republican intent of those who expressed seditious memories, additional significance can be adduced about such views from the fact that they were shared. Seditious memories enabled former Parliamentarians and republicans to reproduce identities that Royalist anti-fanatical censure sought to destabilise. By perpetuating the very identities that Royalists had sought to eradicate, those who had opposed, resisted, and overthrown the Stuarts and established church found solidarity in communities of memory. Moreover, sharing alternative future realities in which the 'liberties' of the 1640s and 1650s were restored mediated hope between those who may otherwise have foreseen only a desperate future.

By emphasising the role of seditious remembering as a psychological resource, further conclusions may be drawn about memories that, unlike those to which this and chapter 4 referred, were never externalised in speech and writing.[90] Social psychologists have proposed that, in and of itself, the act of remembering – that is, the *internal* construction of narratives about experiences of reality – can be psychologically significant to those who remember. Of particular significance in this respect is what these scholars have labelled 'nostalgia' or, in the words of social psychologist Clay Routledge, an 'emotional' and 'past-oriented experience focused on fond memories' which emphasises social relationships and in which 'the self is typically the protagonist'.[91] Nostalgia has been described as a cognitive resource, one which connects individuals to 'a past authentic self',[92] and counters isolation by recalling moments of heightened socialness.[93] It has also been branded as 'restorative', possessing what the literary scholar Svetlana Boym has described as 'a utopian dimension'.[94] We will never know what was occurring in the minds of men and women after the Restoration. However, it is surely not far-fetched to suggest that the reflective and restorative uses of the past, which, as we have seen, were a common feature of cases of seditious remembering, offered former Parliamentarians and republicans personal strategies for dealing with the potentially isolating experiences of censorship and censure, and the 'experience of defeat' of which these formed a part. We might speculate, in fact, that the most secure sites in which to secrete away seditious memories after the Restoration were the heads of the people who conjured them.

NOTES

1. Irwin-Zarecka, *Frames of Remembrance*, p. 54.
2. Influential here has been the work of Natalie Zemon Davis, especially *Fiction in the Archives: Pardon Tales and Their Tellers in Sixteenth-Century France* (Cambridge: Polity, 1988).
3. T. Liu, 'Cokayn, George (bap. 1620, d. 1691)', in *ODNB*, xii, p. 443.
4. TNA, SP29/91/22.
5. TNA, SP29/430/38.
6. Marshall, *Intelligence and Espionage*, especially ch. 5.
7. Cited in *ibid.*, p. 154.
8. *Ibid.*, pp. 124–125.
9. TNA, SP29/118/10.
10. TNA, SP29/86/22, I, II.
11. T. Cogswell and A. Bellany, *The Murder of King James I* (New Haven, CT: Yale University Press, 2015), p. 510.
12. T. L. Stoate (ed.), *The Cornwall Protestation Returns, 1641* (Bristol: T. L. Stoate, 1974), p. 163. For the Protestation and proto-Parliamentarianism, see J. Walter, *Covenanting Citizens: The Protestation Oath and Popular Political Culture in the English Revolution* (Oxford: Oxford University Press, 2017), pp. 131–137.
13. Cited in Greaves, *Deliver Us from Evil*, p. 32.
14. TNA, SP89/5/11.
15. 'Sedition Act', *Statutes of the Realm*, v, p. 305.
16. TNA, SP89/5/11.
17. MacRay and Routledge, *Clarendon State Papers*, v, p. 99.
18. I am grateful to Hillary Taylor whose work on subornation and subordination has been formative in the production of this chapter and my general thinking about seditious and treasonable speech. See also H. Taylor, 'Branded on the Tongue: Aspects of Language and Social Relations in Early Modern England' (unpublished PhD dissertation, University of Yale, 2016), ch. 5.
19. Beiner, *Remembering*, p. 23.
20. Hoad and Grime, *Borough Sessions Papers*, p. 17.
21. See, for instance, J. Vansina, 'Memory and Oral Tradition', in J. C. Miller (ed.), *The African Past Speaks: Essays on Oral Tradition and History* (Folkestone: Dawson, 1980), pp. 262–279.
22. Freist, *Governed by Opinion*, p. 242.
23. *MCR*, iii, pp. 315–316.
24. *Ibid.*, p. 316.
25. TNA, PROB11/409/282, Will of William Hammond, mariner of Stepney, Middlesex; and TNA, PROB11/453/292, Will of George Appleby, mariner of St Paul Shadwell, Middlesex.
26. Freist, *Governed by Opinion*, pp. 48–50.
27. See Bardle, *Literary Underground*.
28. For the dating, see W. Johnston, *Revelation Restored: The Apocalypse in Later Seventeenth-Century England* (Woodbridge: Boydell, 2011), p. 77.
29. *A Treatise of the Execution of Justice*, p. 15.

30 M. Jenkinson, *Culture and Politics at the Court of Charles II, 1660–1685* (Woodbridge: Boydell, 2010), p. 39.
31 *SPEECHES AND PRAYERS OF Some of the late King's Judges*, p. 86.
32 Cited in Scott, *Algernon Sidney*, p. 317.
33 Edmund Ludlow, *A Voyce from the Watch Tower, Part Five: 1660–1662*, ed. A. B. Worden (London: Royal Historical Society, 1978), pp. 215–216.
34 Josselin, *Diary*, p. 489.
35 Cited in R. Ollard, *Pepys, A Biography* (London: Hodder and Stoughton, 1974), p. 36.
36 Stocks and Stevenson, *Records of the Borough of Leicester*, p. 488.
37 C. Hill, *Experience of Defeat*, p. 75.
38 See N. H. Keeble and G. F. Nuttall, 'Introduction', in *Calendar*, i, p. xxvii.
39 Keeble and Nuttall, *Calendar*, ii, pp. 70–71.
40 J. Walter, 'Public Transcripts, Popular Agency and the Politics of Subsistence in Early Modern England', in M. J. Braddick and J. Walter (eds), *Negotiating Power in Early Modern Society: Order, Hierarchy and Subordination in Britain and Ireland* (Cambridge: Cambridge University Press, 2001), p. 145.
41 See C. Hill, *Experience of Defeat*, passim; and Woolrych, 'Good Old Cause', 133–161.
42 See Irwin-Zarecka, *Frames of Remembrance*, p. 54.
43 See Matthews, *Calamy Revised*, p. 540.
44 Roger Lowe, *The Diary of Roger Lowe of Ashton-in-Makerfield, Lancashire. 1663–1678*, ed. I. G. Winstanley (Ashton-in-Makerfield: Picks, 1994), p. 32.
45 Hopper, 'Farnley Wood', 285.
46 *History and Proceedings of the House of Commons*, p. 320.
47 E. Legon, 'Bound Up with Meaning: The Politics and Memory of Ribbon Wearing in Restoration England and Scotland', *Journal of British Studies*, 56:1 (Jan., 2017), 27–50.
48 See also Appleby, 'Veteran Politics', 323–342.
49 TNA, SP89/5/11.
50 TNA, SP29/118/10.
51 TNA, SP29/84/70.
52 Samuel Rosewell, *THE ARRAIGNMENT AND TRYAL Of the late REVEREND Mr. Thomas Rosewell, FOR HIGH-TREASON; BEFORE THE Lord Chief Justice Jefferies, at the Court of King's Bench, Westminster, in the Year 1684* (London, 1718), pp. 281–282.
53 TNA, SP29/427/99.
54 TNA, SP29/417/132. See also J. B. Marsh, *The Story of Harecourt: Being the History of an Independent Church* (London: Strahan, 1871), p. 164.
55 Thomas Tillam, *THE TEMPLE Of Lively Stones* (London, 1660), [sig. A3r].
56 [Roger Jones], *Mene Tekel; Or, The Downfal of Tyranny* (n.p. 1663), p. 15.
57 *A Door of Hope: OR, A CALL and DECLARATION for the gathering together of the first ripe Fruits unto the STANDARD of our Lord, KING JESUS* ([London, 1661]), pp. 7–8.
58 Evan Price, *Eye-salve for England: OR, The Grand TRAPPAN Detected, In a plain and faithful NARRATIVE of the horrid and unheard-of Designs of some Justices and Deputy-Lieutenants in Lancashire, treacherously to ensnare the Lives and Estates of*

    many Persons of Quality in that County, as also in the Counties of York and Chester (London, 1667), p. 6.
59 Capp, *Fifth Monarchy Men*, p. 221; and R. L. Greaves, 'The Tangled Careers of Two Stuart Radicals: Henry and Robert Danvers', *Baptist Quarterly*, 29:1 (Jan., 1981), 39.
60 *THE DECLARATION OF JAMES DUKE of MONMOUTH, & The Noblemen, Gentlemen & others, now in Arms, for Defence & vindication of the Protestant Religion, & the Laws, Rights, & Privileges of England, from the Invasion made upon them: & for Delivering the Kingdom from the Usurpation and Tyranny of JAMES DUKE of YORK* (n.p., [1685]), p. 3.
61 See, for instance, *DECLARATION OR REPRESENTATION Of the Actions*, p. 5.
62 TNA, SP29/101/29, I; and TNA/SP29/101/34, I.
63 C. Firth and G. Davies, *The Regimental History of Cromwell's Army* (2 vols, Oxford: University of Oxford Press, 1940), ii, pp. 345–346; and TNA, SP29/233/103.
64 TNA, SP29/21/16.
65 TNA, SP29/21/15.
66 TNA, SP29/113/40.
67 On remembering and 'imagined communities', see Cubitt, *History and Memory*, p. 138.
68 TNA, SP29/431/76.
69 TNA, SP29/420/6.
70 TNA, SP29/69/48. These words were denied by Katharine Gregory: TNA, SP29/69/63.
71 TNA, SP29/65/19.
72 TNA, SP29/42/37, cited in Greaves, *Deliver Us from Evil*, p. 63.
73 N. H. Keeble, *The Restoration: England in the 1660s* (Malden, MA: Blackwell, 2002), ch. 6.
74 Pepys, *Diary*, iv, pp. 52, 374–375; v, pp. 59, 344; vi, pp. 45–46; viii, pp. 250, 332, 377–378, 390–391, 426; and ix, pp. 70–71.
75 Woolf, 'Two Elizabeths?', 184–189.
76 Pepys, *Diary*, vi, pp. 45–46.
77 J. Yonge Akerman (ed.), *Moneys Received and Paid for Secret Services of Charles II. and James II. from 30th March, 1679, to 25th December, 1688* (London: Camden Society, 1851), p. 25.
78 It seems possible that the man behind these words was Thomas Hayter, a 'conventicler' who was dismissed from his role as comptroller of the Navy shortly after these words were spoken; see Pepys, *Diary*, x, p. 171; *CSPD*, 1682, p. 20.
79 TNA, SP29/417/183.
80 TNA, SP29/438/79.
81 *MCR*, iii, p. 304. See also TNA, SP29/419/86.
82 TNA, SP29/46/5, I. For Pestell's role as a government agent, see Capp, *Fifth Monarchy Men*, pp. 205, 207.
83 ERO, Q/SR387/52. See also ERO, Q/SR387/51.
84 TNA, SP29/58/17.
85 TNA, SP29/93/60. See also H. Stewart, *History of the Worshipful Company of Gold and Silver Wyre-Drawers: and of the Origin and Development of the Industry which the Company Represents* (London: Leadenhall, 1891), pp. 49–50.

86 Cressy, *Dangerous Talk*, p. 215.
87 See M. Fisher, *Capitalist Realism: Is There No Alternative?* (Winchester: Zero Books, 2009).
88 See Snyder and Feldman, 'Hope for the Many', p. 409.
89 Bellah *et al.*, *Habits of the Heart*, p. 153.
90 On the difficulty of construing personal memories, see R. E. McGlone, 'Deciphering Memory: John Adams and the Authorship of the Declaration of Independence', *Journal of American History*, 85:2 (Sept., 1998), 411–438.
91 Routledge, *Nostalgia*, p. 14–17. See also M. Vess, J. Arndt, C. Routledge, C. Sedikides, and T. Wildschut, 'Nostalgia as a Resource for the Self', *Self and Identity*, 11:3 (2012), 275.
92 Routledge, *Nostalgia*, p. 80.
93 X. Zhou, C. Sedikides, T. Wildschut, and D. Gao, 'Counteracting Loneliness: On the Restorative Function of Nostalgia', *Psychological Science*, 19:10 (2008), 1023–1029; and T. Wildschut, C. Sedikides, C. Routledge, J. Arndt, and F. Cordaro, 'Nostalgia as a Repository of Social Connectedness: The Role of Attachment-Related Avoidance', *Journal of Personality and Social Psychology*, 98:4 (2010), 575–586.
94 Boym, 'Nostalgia', 9.

Chapter 6

Seditious memories in Scotland and Ireland

The wars and revolutions of the mid seventeenth century were British phenomena.[1] The composite monarchy that Charles I inherited from his father meant that rebellion by Presbyterians in Scotland in 1637 and by Roman Catholics in Ireland four years later sent destructive shockwaves towards England. Ironically, experiences of the ensuing conquest by English 'usurpers' in the late 1640s and 1650s ensured that it was in Irish and Scottish soil that the seeds of Restoration were sown. The mnemonic landscapes that resulted after 1660 appear rather different from those in England and Wales, characterised as they were by the claims of erstwhile 'rebels' to have been the saviours, rather than the scourges, of Crown and established church. Historians of Restoration Scotland and Ireland are beginning to explore the features of these mnemonic landscapes.[2] This is especially the case in Ireland, where examinations of memory and trauma belong to a longer tradition of research into the legacies of conflict.[3] Light is yet to be shone on attempts by governors to exert control over these landscapes after the Restoration, and how and why those attempts were negotiated, resisted, and subverted. Such an inquiry involves revisiting material which, owing to its traditional, and sometimes hagiographical, deployment by historians as evidence of political and religious dissent, has been relatively absent from recent revisionist studies of royalism in Scotland and Ireland following the Restoration.[4]

This chapter explores alternative memories of the wars and revolutions in these kingdoms to the extent that they appear in evidence of efforts to censor those views. In Scotland, seditious or 'unlawful' memories reflect the endurance of sympathies for the National Covenant (1638) and the Solemn League and Covenant (1643), but also the constitutional and ecclesiological revolutions to which these oaths belonged and contributed. Reflecting

Ireland's unique experience of conflict, Irish seditious memories are shown to have been both Protestant and Roman Catholic, ranging from sympathies to the Covenants and Oliver Cromwell to those of the rebellion of 1641 and the subsequent Confederation of Kilkenny.

Having located seditious memories in Scotland and Ireland, their significance to the people who possessed and expressed them is explored. While seditious memories may have lent themselves to radical or republican action, and constituted a direct threat to the Restoration settlements as a result, this was only one way in which they proved significant to Scottish and Irish men and women. The various forms taken by seditious memories, and their inextricability from a broader context of censorship and censure, allows us to identify their role in counteracting the efforts of governments in Scotland and Ireland to secure mnemonic hegemony, efforts that are comparable to those encountered so far in England and Wales. Put differently, the unlawful opinions of the Stuarts' Scottish and Irish subjects can be categorised as counter-memories, the full significance of which is deducible from information about how such views were articulated and how audiences were expected to react to them.

By taking this line, evidence of seditious and treasonable speech and writing in Ireland and Scotland is viewed from a fresh perspective, one that avoids the assumption that such expressions were, as one historian has put it, 'the musings of irate malcontents'.[5] Moreover, by focusing on people from all levels of society, this chapter offers a rare examination of popular participation in politics and religion outside England and Wales after the Restoration.[6] Overall, the chapter seeks to draw together the political and religious cultures of the Stuart realms, but also their cultures of remembering.[7]

LOCATING UNLAWFUL MEMORIES IN SCOTLAND

Raucous scenes accompanied the Restoration in Scotland. The diarist John Nicoll described the 'ringing of bellis, setting out of bailfyres, sounding of trumpetis, roring of cannounes, touking of drums, dancing about the fyres, and using all uther takins of joy for the advancement and preference of thair native King to his croun and native inheritance.'[8] Shortly after these words were written, legislators set about rewinding the threads of episcopacy and monarchy that the Scottish revolution had unravelled. Their progress was swift. It took less than a month for the new parliament to pass legislation that prohibited the king's Scottish subjects from entering into leagues or covenants, and threatened with the 'highest peril' any who should 'presume, upon any pretext of any authority whatsoever, to require the renewing or swearing of the [Solemn] League and Covenant'.[9] This act also countered claims that the Covenants were perpetually binding. Further legislation condemned the deliverance of Charles I into the hands of the English Parliament in 1647 and annulled the 'pretended' committee of estates which sat two years later.[10]

The 'Rescissory Act' of 28 March 1661 proved to be the most retrospective in scope, however, annulling as it did the seven 'pretended parliaments' that sat between 1640 and 1648, and rescinding thereby the statutory authority of the 'reformation' that had been enacted by their members.[11]

The government took further measures to ensure that public discourse was cleansed of any lingering sympathies for the Scottish revolution. On 24 June 1662, an 'Act for preservation of his majesty's person, authority and government' was passed, which, as its name suggests, echoed the English Sedition Act of 1661. This act made 'unlawfull' all 'writing, printing, praying, preacheing, libelling, remonstrating or ... any malicious and advised speiking' which might serve 'to stir up the people to the hatred or dislyk of his majesties' royall prerogative and supremacie in causes ecclesiastick or of the government of the Church by archbishops and bishops, as it is now setled by law'. Outdoing the English equivalent, the Scottish act also made illegal any efforts 'to justifie any of the deeds, actings, practises or things abovementioned and declared against by this present act'. This included 'the miseries, confusions, bondage and oppressions this kingdome hath groaned under since the yeer 1637' and extended to the 'unlawfull meitings and gatherings of the people', 'mutinous and tumultuary' petitioning, 'insolent and sedicious protestations against his majesties' royall and just commands', and, most importantly, 'entering into unlawfull oaths and covenants'.[12] Here, the events of the late 1630s were synonymised with over a decade of Covenanter government, disregarding thereby the assembly of 1640 and its proceedings, including the formal abolition of episcopacy, which had been acknowledged by Charles I.

Through this legislative programme, the Scottish parliament sought to reverse what it described elsewhere as 'all the miseries, confusions and disorders' that the nation had 'groaned under these twenty-three years'. The accompanying glosses were often condescending, dismissing as they did Scotland's 'reformations' as a mere 'pretext'.[13] Rapidly, this censorious version of the Scottish revolution inflected messages from pulpit and print. One individual who took advantage of both media was John Paterson, an Episcopalian whose 1661 parliament sermon – later printed with the telling subtitle *Scotlands Late misery be[w]ailed* – compared the nation's late '*Bondage* and *Captivity* of a Nation' to 'a *Chain*' that had 'depriveth a *Nation* of their Civil and Ecclesiastick *Liberty*.'[14] Another tract from the same year urged Scots to 'look back, and bestow some of your deepest thoughts on so sad a subject' as 'that deplorable condition your poor Countrey have labour'd under for these many years past'.[15]

Historians of Restoration Scotland now acknowledge that the attack on the Scottish revolution after 1660 was as considerable as that in England and Wales.[16] This flew in the face of the nation's Free and General Pardon, Indemnity, and Oblivion, that, when it became law in May 1662, did as little as its English predecessor to prevent 'all seeds of future differences and remembrance of former proceedings'.[17] When, for instance, William Douglas, Earl of Queensberry, the son of Covenanter James Douglas, complained in 1673 that John Paterson, dean of Edinburgh, had used a parliamentary sermon to '[reflect] on some members of Parliament' and their civil war allegiances, the earl's protests received short shrift.[18] Tellingly, in fact, Paterson was able to deny any wrongdoing by highlighting how his sermon had reflected on the *past* rather than the present.[19] By censoring favourable accounts of the Scottish revolution and unfettering those that, like Paterson's, were implicitly hostile, we are witnessing an extension of attempts by the government of Charles II to secure mnemonic hegemony in Scotland, one which was driven by an effort to forestall the reproduction of the 'fanaticism' that wrought rebellion in the late 1630s. Indeed, Alasdair Raffe has suggested that the appellation of the word 'fanatic' to Presbyterians as well as members of the sects after 1660 reflects 'the seizure of political influence at the Restoration by cavaliers and episcopalians'.[20]

Notwithstanding these circumstances, alternative, or what the legislation of the early 1660s referred to as 'unlawful', memories are bequeathed to us in government papers and legal records as a direct consequence of efforts to censor them. The records of the High Court of Justiciary and the Privy Council of Scotland, as well as material pertaining to Scottish affairs from English government papers, overflow with opinions about the wars and revolution which were caught in the net of rescissory legislation. More considerably than in England and Wales, these unlawful memories exist also in surviving print and scribal culture, including pamphlets and the literature that is associated with the rebellions in the middle and at the end of Charles II's reign. Efforts to navigate censorship in the form of personal diaries, journals, and even letters give us further access to these unlawful opinions. Finally, the sympathetic records of like-minded individuals, be they in the form of trial transcripts, the last dying speeches (and writings) of rebels, or the Covenanter martyrologies that were produced in the more favourable climate after 1688–89, further expose unlawful memories of the Scottish revolution.

This evidence is not without its issues. Memories that were mediated by the government or other hostile parties are, like those in England and Wales, vulnerable to the claim that they were confected out of malice or paranoia. Moreover, opinions that were published sympathetically, especially last dying speeches and writings, might be emblematic only of what the editors *wanted* their audiences to read. The same is true for martyrologies which possess the further issue of relying on anecdote. Yet the evidential baby should not be thrown out with its murky bathwater. The sheer extent of sympathies for the revolution in Scotland that are connoted by efforts to contain, if not eradicate, them is evidence enough that such opinion survived the Restoration and continued to preoccupy the authorities. How far the government was willing to go to control what was said on the scaffold, as well as to restrict the capacity of others to record it, implies that the tone, if not the exact substance, of these speeches has been conveyed to us.[21] Even when these speeches were mediated by sympathetic onlookers, and were thus subject to some level of distortion, the very fact that an onlooker was sympathetic is, as we shall discover, revealing of the significance of their content. Elsewhere, martyrologies were written with outspoken, and indeed proto-modern, claims to methodological felicity that ought to be acknowledged by twenty-first-century historians.[22]

With these stipulations in mind, a more complete panorama of the landscape of remembering in Scotland after the Restoration can be depicted. Given the specific targets of the government's assault on the legacy of the revolution in Scotland, it is unsurprising that claims of continued adherence to the Covenants of 1638 and 1643 form the dominant theme of these unlawful memories. The oaths' lingering presence after the Restoration is well known to historians, especially when they accompanied rebellion. When thousands of men and women marched on Edinburgh from the western counties in November 1666, the National Covenant of 1638 was read at the tolbooth at Lanark and renewed by some of those present.[23] When unrest returned in May 1679, the conventiclers who assembled at Rutherglen in Lanarkshire published a paper which 'owned' the Covenants and justified the decision to incinerate, among other acts, the 'Declaration' of 1662, which had been 'imposed upon, and subscribed by all persons in public trust' and in which 'the covenants are renounced and condemned.'[24] Further declarations were published at Glasgow in June 1679, at Queensferry in Fife and Sanquhar in Dumfries in June 1680, and at Lanark in December 1681, all of which took inspiration from, or explicitly stated adherence to, the Covenants of 1638 and 1643.[25]

If these declarations speak of the tenacity of the Covenants in Scotland, then the 'dying testimonies' of the rebels who were executed in 1666 offer more direct accounts of the oaths' enduring significance. John Wilson of Kilmaurs in Ayrshire divulged that his 'ground' for joining the rising had been 'the renewing of the Covenant with my God, and labouring to defend the same, according to my Oath'.[26] When George Crawford, a yeoman, was executed for his involvement in the same rebellion, he spoke of his adherence to 'the way of Church-Government sworn to in the Covenant, which I think and assert to be conform to God's Word.'[27] Speaking at his trial following the Covenanter rebellion at Bothwell Bridge some thirteen years later, James Skene (or Skein) explained similarly that he and his fellow rebels had burned several acts of the Restoration parliaments 'because they were against the Covenant', adding that he 'would not admit the authority of the king or parliament in things that were against the Covenant.'[28] Imprisoned for his own involvement at Bothwell Bridge, John Whitelaw wrote a testimony confessing to his 'owning of the Covenant' and predicting 'the wrath that is coming on th[ese] lands for the qwarrell off [sic] a broken and brwnt [burnt] covinant and all the fals dealings with God'.[29]

The words of Skene and Whitelaw demonstrate the linguistic propinquity of the belief in the Covenants' perpetual obligations and the (often vituperative) accusations that certain individuals had 'abjured', 'broken', and literally 'brwnt' them. James Guthrie, a 'Protestor' who was brought to the scaffold in 1661 for his treasonable authorship of *The Causes of the Lord's Wrath* eight years earlier, reserved some of the most scathing of his dying words for what he termed 'the horrible treachery and perjury that is in the matter of the Covenant and Cause of God, and work of reformation.'[30] Some of those who were condemned to death on 7 December 1666 for their part in the rebellion in the west described with equal force 'the Nationall and Authorized Backsliding of the Land, by Perjury and breach of Covenant'.[31] Reflecting the appearance of this kind of language in print as well as speech, the final four sections of John Brown of Wamphray's famous *An Apologeticall Relation* (1665) were devoted to vindicating the Covenants and decrying those who had abjured them since the Restoration.[32] Replicating the common framing of covenant-breaking in terms of lying under oath,[33] Brown described abjuration of the oaths as 'periury of the deepest dye'.[34]

One individual whose 'perjury' was raised on several occasions in Scotland after 1660 was Charles II. In 1651, Charles had subscribed to the Covenants at his coronation, in exchange for the military backing of Scottish Presbyterians against the English Commonwealth. Charles's sympathies for an episcopal settlement of the church after the Restoration were held by some to have constituted a breach of the Covenants and, indeed, his coronation oath. Shortly after his return, ten ministers and a gentleman were apprehended for subscribing to a supplication that congratulated Charles, but also 'presse[d] [and] exhort[ed] him, in the fear of the Lord, to minde his oaths unto, & covenants with God'.[35] Following the annulment of the Covenants, the attitudes of some ministers had hardened. In April 1663, the Scottish Privy Council recorded that 'severall ministers' had 'in their sermons inveighed highly against his Majesties government, some of them ... daring ... to call him ane apostat or perjured person publictly out of pulpitts or in other places'.[36] Memories of Charles's coronation oath endured. Before his execution in December 1666, Alexander Robertson, a rebel, reminded Charles that he was bound to the 'extirpation of Prelacy' as a result of his taking the Covenant.[37] These views transferred onto Charles's brother and heir, James II, when he ascended to the throne. Together with his part in the rising at Rutherglen, James Boyl was indicted in November 1687 for 'asserting [James II] was not King till he took the Covenant', language that suggests memories of 1638 and 1643 infused contractual theories of monarchy.[38]

The denunciation of Charles as an apostate or perjured person was not a necessary corollary of the belief that the Covenants' obligations endured. Others argued that defences of the Covenants were entirely compatible with loyalty to the Crown. Having been seized six months earlier for a seditious libel, Robert Trail, erstwhile chaplain for the Scottish forces in the First

English civil war, spoke in the newly assembled Scottish parliament in March 1661 of his adherence to 'those blessed *Covenants*, which are now so much spoken against', which he took to be 'a testimony of my loyalty to my king'.[39] Trail's opinions were repeated by those who rose in the west of Scotland in 1666. Ralph Shields, an Englishman who joined the rebellion, used his final testimony to expound on the idea that the rebellion had not been 'against his Majesty, but for the Covenant which is now troden under foot'.[40] John Wilson, a fellow rebel, went further, explaining on the scaffold before his own execution that 'in my judgement, a man's endeavouring to extirpate perjured Prelates and abjured Prelacy, according as he is bound by Oath in a sworn Covenant, may very well stand with a man's Loyalty to King and Countrey'.[41] The issue of whether adherence to the Covenants necessitated resistance came around again in 1679, when some of the signatories to a declaration reciting 'the great injuries done to the church in introducing of prelats' were split over whether to 'declar[e] for the king's interest according to the covenant'.[42]

That adherence to the Covenants was believed by some to be compatible with loyalty to the Crown implies that sympathies for the former extended beyond what one historian has described as a 'narrow and localised, fanatical and extreme' minority.[43] Further evidence suggests, in fact, that commitment to the cause of the 1630s and 1640s penetrated beyond the most outspoken defenders of reformation. Hundreds of Scots disclosed a sense of obligation under the Covenants by refusing to subscribe to the various counter-oaths that were tendered by the government after the Restoration. Holders of public office were required to take several oaths and declarations in which the Covenants were to be renounced, including the Oath of Allegiance and the aforementioned 'Declaration'.[44] In the wake of the crisis of 1679–81, the Test Act called upon all holders of 'public trust' to renounce the Covenants once more.[45] A further act was passed in 1685 which rendered it treason to take or own the Covenants.[46]

References to the failure of magistrates and (more often) ministers throughout Scotland, especially in the west, to take these counter-oaths pepper the records of Scottish government following the Restoration.[47] Occasionally, the opinions of refusers have been recorded. Following his imprisonment in 1660, and having had the Oath of Allegiance tendered to him on his release, John Spreul, the town clerk of Glasgow, protested that he must refuse it on account of 'the tie that lay upon him by the oath of the Covenant'.[48] In addition to these counter-oaths, the Act of Presentation and Collation of June 1662 deposed any minister who had been instituted since 1649 and who could not receive either presentation from former patrons or episcopal collation (appointment).[49] Consequently, many of the 270 ministers who were ejected and did not regain their livings had refused collation from a local bishop on account of the Covenants' obligation to defend Scotland from episcopacy.[50]

Failure to subscribe to the earliest counter-oaths discloses loyalty to the Covenants only insofar as they endured among those who qualified for positions of 'public trust'. Indeed, as Laura Stewart has recently shown, there were thousands of people from below the status of magisterial and ministerial office who, if they chose to, might consider themselves bound by the Covenants after the Restoration.[51] Stewart's work has shown that the National Covenant of 1638 was designed specifically as 'a direct appeal to people ordinarily excluded from governance',[52] adding that the revolution's major consequence was that 'greater numbers of people than ever before, from a wider range of social groupings, were engaged in the controversial – often confrontational – task of directing, explaining, and justifying a more expansive, complex, and coercive state.'[53] It is a cause of no surprise, then, that women were among those who believed themselves to be bound by the Covenants after the Restoration. It was noted in the 1680s that Annabel Gordon, Margaret Lesly, Agnes Steven, Margaret Forrest, Jean Moffat, and Annabel Jackson had left for New Jersey (along with twenty-two men) having signed a 'Testimony against the Evils of the Time' that included a statement of their 'duty' to 'their Covenant Engagements'.[54] That the men and women who continued to adhere to the Covenants were drawn from the lower ranks of society is implied by the words of Ralph Shields, yeoman, who explained in his final written testimony that he was 'a man unlearned and not accustomed to speak in publick'.[55] By referring to the social status of Shields, but also of the other yeomen and merchants whose dying testimonies were documented in his famous *Napthali*, James Stewart of Goodtrees may well have been catering for an audience who were drawn from outside the ranks of Scotland's traditional rulers. Indeed, his 1669 work *Jus Populi Vindicatum* invoked 'The People' 'who have been Spectators of the great and wonderful workings of God in our Land' when it had been bound 'by Solemne Covenants ... and the defence of the Reformed Religion'.[56]

Despite rescissory legislation, the available evidence shows that the Covenants continued to figure prevalently in the Scottish imagination after the Restoration. The peculiar tenacity of the Covenants is worth pursuing further. The gravity of oaths in early modern Britain, and related concerns about apostasy and perjury, are likely to have been sufficient to discourage Scots from turning their backs on the Covenants.[57] And yet it is also plausible that the oaths' endurance owed itself to their sheer ubiquity before the Restoration. Laura Stewart has shown that, besides mass swearing ceremonies, the Covenants were discussed, passed around, learned by rote, and displayed in both public and domestic settings after 1638.[58] The survival of the Covenants in the Scottish imagination was assisted by attempts to republish them, but also the highly provocative acts of burning them publicly.[59] Indeed, Sir John Lauder of Fountainhall was led to question the wisdom of burning the Covenants and thus 'reviving the memory of so old and buried a legend as the Solemne League was ... and set[ting] peeple now a-work to buy it, and read it.'[60]

The ubiquity of the Covenants before the Restoration, together with their physical survival and conspicuous destruction, implies that the oaths were rather more than just their contents to the individuals who took them. They became metonymous with broader sympathies for opposition and resistance in the 1630s and 1640s, something that is borne out by their apparent inextricability from other sources of rival allegiance to the episcopal settlements after the Restoration. The rebels who died together on 7 December 1666 declared their adherence not only to the Covenants, but also to the Propositions concerning Kirk Government and Ordination of Ministers (1645), and the liturgical, confessional, and doctrinal reforms that were associated with the adoption of the Directory of Public Worship, the Confession of Faith, and the Larger and Shorter Catechisms.[61] These texts endured in the collective psyche well into the 1680s. In February 1682, for example, William Harvey, a weaver from Lanark, told the Court of Justiciary, before which he stood indicted for involvement in the rebellion at Bothwell Bridge, that 'he .... adhered to the Confession of Faith, national and *Solemn League* and *Covenant*' as well as 'our Catechisms'.[62] In November 1683, John Whitelaw, then prisoner in the tolbooth, Edinburgh, went further, leaving his 'testimony' to the Covenants, 'the Confeshon of Faith, Larger and Shorter Cathichisems', and what he referred to as the 'Solem Acknowledgment of Sin and Ingadgment to Duty'.[63] Here, Whitelaw cited the *Solemn Acknowledgment* that had been issued by the General Assembly in 1648 for renewing the Covenants in light of the recent 'Engagement' with Charles I, thus emphasising his own identification with 'Remonstrants' and 'Protestors' who refused to commit to the Stuart cause between 1647 and 1660.[64]

The metonymic character of the Covenants is also suggested by the regularity of accompanying references to the Scottish revolution as a 'Golden Age' of Scottish history.[65] Commonly, this took the form of references to the 'Work of Reformation' or, in the formulation of one western rebel, 'our blessed Reformations both from Popery and Prelacy'.[66] More specifically, former proponents of the Work of Reformation highlighted the superiority of the covenanted ministry following the overthrow of episcopacy in Scotland. In December 1666, for instance, Captain Andrew Arnot, another of those who were executed for their part in the western rebellion, described 'that glorious Work of Reformation in *Britain* and *Ireland*, and to Gospel-Ordinances in their Purity, as they have been taught and administrated these 30 Years last by past'.[67] The 1630s and 1640s were also elevated via favourable comparisons with an era of moral decline since the Restoration. The Marquis of Argyll, standing on the scaffold before his own execution in 1661 for complicity in the regicide, explained that though he had 'been a Prisoner' his ears had not been 'shut' and he had 'hear[d] assuredly, that Swearing, Drinking and Whoring were never more common, never more countenanced then now they are'.[68] Whereas critical introspection of this kind was an enduring trope of Scottish Presbyterianism, the revolution appears to have brought events since the Restoration into even starker relief.

Favourable references to the decades before the English invasion of 1650 were also *pro*spective and thus restorative, translating thereby into hopes and expectations about the future. Some erstwhile supporters of the Scottish revolution prayed that God might renew the special favour which he had shown to Scotland and its neighbouring kingdoms. James Guthrie, speaking on the scaffold in 1661, prayed that God might 'direct the Congregations and Presbyteries of *Scotland* once more with faithful Pastors, and grant that the Work of the Lord may be revived through all *Brittain* and over all the World'.[69] Following Guthrie to his fate two years later, and echoing his British focus, Lord Wariston called upon God to 'revive His Name, His Covenant, His Word, His Work, His Sanctuary and His Saints in these Nations, even in the three Covenanted Nations, which were by so Solemn Bonds, Covenants, Subscriptions and Oaths, given away and devoted unto Himself.'[70] The reversion of Scotland to the Covenants was common in such restorative language. Speaking in 1684, the Edinburgh man George Broune, who was described as a 'tailzeor journieman', was accused of having said before the Privy Council that 'he thinks it laufull to take up armes against the King in defence of the Covenant, and that the Covenant will be ouned yet'.[71]

Whether Scots were sympathetic to the Work of Reformation or thought themselves bound by the Covenants, one thing was clear: it was the era *before* the trial and execution of Charles I in 1649, and the subsequent invasion of Scotland by Oliver Cromwell, that provided the foci of such memories.[72] To select one example, James Gray of Chrystoun saw the kingdom's road to regicide as having diverged considerably from that which the Covenants and the Work of Reformation were taking. Having been hauled before the Privy Council in 1682 for a suspected part in the Bothwell Bridge rebellion, Gray (as with other suspects) was asked whether he thought 'King *Charles* I's. Death' was 'Murder or not'. In response, Gray 'signified how much he was surprized at their going so far back,' telling them that 'he was of the same Mind with the then Church and State of *Scotland*, who did highly resent it.' Gray was convinced nonetheless that 'the Matter of the *Covenant* was lawful, and its Obligation binding'.[73] Even the Marquis of Argyll, who used the scaffold in 1661 to promote the cause of the Covenants, distanced himself from the regicide in which he was then implicated.[74]

Not everyone abhorred the radical direction that the revolutions had taken in Britain. Some may even have felt that revolution had not gone far enough. Echoing language that was alleged of radical Whigs in England and Wales, Charles I was likened to the biblical tyrant King Rehoboam in a ballad from early 1688.[75] Elsewhere, Alexander Gordon of Earlston, Kirkcudbright, differed from many of his countrymen and women by lauding the regicide. In the immediate wake of the revelations regarding the Rye House Plot in 1683, Gordon was alleged to have regaled his officers with the elaborate tale of his taking of Threave Castle in Kirkcudbrightshire from Charles I, '"wh[ich] had in it about 200 of the name of Maxwell, of whom the greatest part [were] papists"'. Earlstoun was said to have delighted in the fact that '"*we put them all to the sword*, and demolished the castle ... and now (tho' an old man) I take up arms against the son, whom I hope to see go the same way that his father went: for we can never trust in a covenant breaker: so, gentlemen, your cause is good, ye need not fear to fight against a forsworn king."'[76] Gordon's language melded references to the Covenants with those that are more familiar in the English and Welsh context, a fact which may reflect his connections with a cross-border radical movement.[77] Scots were, in fact, willing to express their favourable interpretations of the Scottish revolution within England itself. In 1664, for instance, one William Rock, a 'petty chapman' from Scotland, was committed to Chester Castle for having said that 'he had been once within this kingdom with a Greate Armye' (i.e. the Covenanter army of 1640) and 'hoped within five yeares at the most, to come againe with a greater Aryme'.[78]

UNDERSTANDING SEDITIOUS MEMORIES IN SCOTLAND

Sympathies for the Scottish revolution existed after the Restoration as expressions of enduring adherence to the Covenants and Work of Reformation. The question which this provokes is how these kinds of memories were meaningful to the men and women who expressed them. Historians of this fractious era in Scottish history have treated evidence of unlawful memories in Scotland as emblematic of political philosophy, Presbyterian theology, and even an 'ideology of protest'.[79] To be sure, the events of 1666 and 1679–81 are evidence enough that unlawful memories inspired actions up to and including rebellion. And yet by synonymising views about the revolution and its oaths with theories whose application concerned the present, we are in danger of overlooking the inherently mnemonic character of such language. Unpicking the multiple ways in which unlawful memories were meaningful to those who expressed them entails an acknowledgment that, as in England and Wales, these opinions belonged to, and are inextricable from, a politics of memory in which they were subjected to censorship while countervailing hostility to the Scottish revolution was given free reign. Put differently, like the seditious memories to which this book has referred so far, unlawful memories in Scotland were counter-memories that resisted attempts by Royalists in Scotland to secure mnemonic hegemony through the public and social delegitimisation of the Scottish revolution. Uncovering how these counter-memories operated requires us to examine closely how audiences were expected to react to their expression.

Unlawful memories were never uttered into the void; they were often intended for audiences of people who were expected to agree with them. The scale of the audiences with which such sentiment could be shared was increased considerably by access to illicit means of print production.[80] We have already encountered John Brown of Wamphray's famous *An Apologeticall*

Relation and the dying testimonies which James Stewart incorporated into his *Napthali*, both of which found considerable audiences, male and female.[81] That these and similar tracts reinforced the unlawful memories contained therein is borne out by the government's concerted efforts at suppression.[82] The same was true of dying testimonies, about which concerns were raised by the government in December 1666 that they 'had to [sic] great Dipping in the hearts of the Commonality'.[83] Thereafter, in fact, officials who presided over public executions in Scotland were more proactive in censoring the transmission of unlawful language from the scaffold. Echoing efforts by the English government to suppress the seditious memories of Sir Henry Vane in 1662, four western rebels had their dying speeches obscured by 'five drummeris going about the scaffold, beatting upone thair drums'.[84] Notwithstanding these measures, the condemned found ways of navigating censorship. When Captain Andrew Arnot was executed in 1666, he was criticised posthumously for having distributed a paper at the scaffold that declared the 'adherence' of him and his fellow sufferers 'to king and covenant and against Bishops'.[85]

Unlawful memories found equally large, if not even greater, audiences at field conventicles, the most familiar symbol of dissent to the ecclesiastical settlements in Restoration Scotland. In November 1670 it was reported that a conventicle at Ayr had culminated in a communal promise 'never [to] hear Curates againe; but [that we] should for ever adhere to and preserve the glorious ends of their League & Covenant.'[86] Later that month, concerns were expressed that 'there were ten thousand' who 'mett armed about glasco [Glasgow] to ... Renew theire Covenant'.[87] The passage of time did not erode the Covenants' bonds. In 1678, Scottish Presbyterians were described as clinging to the notion that the Covenants were 'in force' and 'never need be dissembled'.[88] Later that year, it was reported that 'John Welch with 36 other nonconformist ministers' had 'convocated tenn thousand of the kings ... enemies at Maybol nigh air [Ayr]' and 'there celebrat[ed] the Lords Supper, with great solemnity, preached up the Solemn League and Covenant, and the Lawfulness, conveniency and necessity of defensive arms'.[89]

Imprisonment encouraged others to share their opinions about the Covenants in different ways. In the 1680s, several letters from political prisoners found their way to the Scottish Privy Council, suggesting that these had been intercepted before they were able to reach their intended recipients.[90] One of these was penned by James Mure (or Muir) of Cessford, Roxburghshire, who was imprisoned in the tolbooths at Lanark and Canongate in Edinburgh in the early months of 1684. In March, one of Mure's missives expressed his view that Scotland was God's land, and that 'His rightes is confirmed therto and mead soor by our solem consente quhen we gave away ourselves to Him and band ourselwes in that mariag covinant to be for Him and not for another.' Like others who suffered for their consciences after 1660, Mure saw those 'ingegments' as 'the ground of controvercie this day; for enemies is siking to break that mariag solemnity and twrne us from our first love.'[91] That these letters ended up in the hands of the Scottish Privy Council suggests that his efforts to share his views privately with sympathetic readers failed.

Together, this evidence shows that pamphlets, dying testimonies, conventicle sermons, and letters are not merely representative of the perpetuation of Presbyterian theology or political philosophy. James Mure's contention that the Covenants had 'confirmed' God's 'rightes' by 'solem consente' suggests that, in evidence where unlawful memories were shared with like-minded people, we are witnessing the communal reinforcement of wider-ranging sympathies with the Scottish revolution. Why this occurred can be explained with recourse to the sheer force with which opposition and resistance were targeted by the government's censorship and censure after the Restoration as means of forestalling the reproduction of 'fanatic' identities that, from the point of view of Royalists, endangered the safety and security of the Stuart realms. By legitimising the revolution socially, Scottish men and women were counteracting these attacks, reproducing thereby identities that were anchored in the events of 1637–50 and conjuring communal solidarity in the face of isolating experiences of censorship and censure.

Discussions between ex-Covenanters about the recent past were susceptible to debates that had riven opposition to Scottish episcopacy during the 1640s and 1650s. This is evident from an episode recorded by the Restoration diarist Alexander Brodie, a Presbyterian who had been one of the most fervent supporters of the Covenanting cause from 1638 onwards and had even attempted to dissuade others from engaging with Charles II in the 1650s.[92] Following the Restoration, Brodie's diaries represent conformist anxieties about whether the Covenants were binding.[93] Nonetheless, Brodie was often passionate about defending the 'sense' in which he had subscribed to the oath. This was the case in December 1677 when the diarist recorded his fury at being told by one Thomas Gordon that the Covenants prohibited 'partak[ing] of the Word, or Sacraments, or other Ordinances from officers admitted by Bishops, nor from ani other but Presbyters.' Brodie's response was that 'I [neither] did receav, took, nor understood the Covenant under that sense'.[94] Even if Brodie and Gordon did not agree on the 'sense' of the Covenant, what was left 'unsaid' during their discourse in 1677 was a shared sense that, on some level, subscription to that oath had been legitimate. It is likely that similar opinions were shared by many more Scots after the Restoration.

The audiences of unlawful memories were not always uncritical. When James Guthrie awaited execution in 1661, he broached the fact that most of his audience had come merely 'to gaze rather then to be edified by the carriage and last words of a dying man'.[95] Guthrie's identification of spectators who might not sympathise with his cause has implications for how we understand the unlawful memories that punctuated his dying speech. Rather than preaching to the converted, Guthrie intended to *contest* the notion that instilled the charge of treason against him and that is likely to have prevailed among some of his spectators: namely, the wrongfulness of his actions over the last two and a half decades. Put differently, the cases of Guthrie and some others like him allow us to acknowledge that enduring sympathies for the Covenants and Work of Reformation were not articulated in 'echo chambers', serving 'principally to inspire fellow Covenanters and covenanting enthusiasts'.[96] Instead, they were means of legitimising publicly identities that were inextricable from the Scottish revolution.

Other dying speeches and testimonies lend credence to the role of unlawful memories in contesting the censure to which the events of the 1630s and 1640s were exposed after the Restoration. On 22 December 1666, the minister Hew McKaile explained from the gallows that 'whatever indignity is done unto these Covenants, I do esteem to be no less then doing despite unto the spirit of Grace in his most eminent Exerting of himself'.[97] Particularly ardent in his continued adherence to the Covenants was John Wilson, who held that 'since the day I did first swear and subscribe this Covenant for Reformation, it hath been sweet unto me, for I am persuaded in my Conscience of the warrantableness thereof.'[98] It is possible that John Brown of Wamphray's famous pamphlet *An Apologeticall Relation* had encouraged the western rebels to take part in this public self-vindication. In it, Brown rebuked fiercely those who 'basely ... speak of these holy bonds, & sacred Covenants', demonstrating that '*Scotland* hath no cause to be ashamed of these Covenants.'[99] More seditiously, however, and evoking how the Scottish parliament continued to be elevated by Presbyterians in Scotland as a bulwark against absolutism and popery, Brown contended that 'it was the common practice of the Parliaments of *Scotland* ... to rise in armes against their Kings, when they turned tyrants: And therefore, the Parliament their late taking up of armes in their own sinlesse self defence, can no wayes be condemned'.[100]

Other kinds of evidence are representative of a more conspicuously dialogic contest over the meaning of the Scottish revolution. During Sir James Turner's captivity by the western rebels in November 1666, for instance, he recorded how the minister John Welch had 'enterd in a tedious discourse of the Covenant, which, as he said, had made Scotland glorieous in the eyes of the nations.' Seeing an opportunity to win Turner (who had fought with the Covenanters in the 1640s) around to his way of thinking, but unaware, perhaps, of the futility of attempting to do so, Welch 'confidentlie offerd to allure me [Turner], that the Lord had reveald it unto them, that this was the time appointed by God, for the deliverance of his saints and people, from the persecutions and tirannies of these who had vilipended and contemned the Covenant.' Despite this claim, Turner responded resolutely 'that revelations and miracles were ceasd' and 'that it was not probable that he or his partie could set up their Covenant, with such inconsiderable numbers as either they yet had, or were like to get, against the Kings standing forces'.[101] Turner recorded that a similar attempt was made by Gabriel Semple, minister of Jedburgh, to convince him that 'vice and sinne were ... more punished in the time of Presbiterie, then it was now in the time of Episcopacie.' Unimpressed, Turner contended that 'I never saw either publike or private sinne more abound then in the years 1643 and 1644, when the Solemne League and Covenant was subscrived by many.'[102]

Defences of the Scottish revolution might take other forms – silence, for instance, could be made to speak volumes. In the early 1680s, John Hay, Earl of Tweeddale, was recorded as having sat through a meeting between the Dukes of York and Hamilton and several other high-profile Scots, in which 'the Advocat', presumably Lord Advocate George Mackenzie of Rosehaugh, 'fell to work and for an hour together deduced the case of those late rebellious times ... wherin he omitted nothing materiall, but mentioned no mans name.' Tweeddale, who had changed sides four times during the civil wars, including a period of collaboration with Scotland's English conquerors, was reported to have 'sayd nothing as long as he stayed'. More tellingly, it seems, it was reported that Tweeddale 'had not patience to stay halfe the time, for when the deduction by the Advocat came the lenth of the ... abjuring the King, then our cousin went aside and went off out of the roome.'[103] While Tweeddale was no radical, it is surely significant that his decision to leave the room was viewed by onlookers as a measure of his objection to, and perhaps shame concerning, the censure of the Scottish revolution.

Public statements of adherence to the Covenants also constituted a form of resistance that derived its force from the extent to which the oaths had comprised a target of the authorities in Restoration Scotland. This can be witnessed in a case from 1677, when the Privy Council ordered a Captain Carstares to seize John Balfour at his house in Kinloch in Fife. Not only did Balfour refuse to go quietly, he also mobilised fifteen others who 'discharged a volley of fire-arms from the house, and then pursued the runaways on horseback, calling Carstares to yield, and render himself in the name of the God and of the Covenant.'[104] Defiance against the government of this kind recurred during the interrogation of suspected rebels following the crisis of 1679–81. By responding negatively to questioning regarding the illegality of the Covenants, Scots subverted the expectation that they should admit that the oaths were no longer binding. In March 1681, for instance, Walter Smith contended that 'he is obliged to perform all the Duties of that *Covenant*, conform to the Word of God, and the King is only to be obeyed in the Terms of the *Covenant*.'[105]

Defiance around the issue of the Covenants' illegality was a consistent concern of the state, both in Scotland and England, during the early 1680s, and particularly after the revelation of the Rye House Plot in 1683.[106] This was especially true when it took the form of refusing the 1681 Test, an oath which required its taker to disown both Covenants. Of those who were recorded as having the Test tendered to them in 1684 in the Scottish southwest, several refused to subscribe on principle.[107] Elsewhere, the very fears that drove hostility to the Scottish revolution were exploited by predictions that the kingdom would be restored to the Covenants. In December 1662, for instance, William Dobbie, a Glaswegian weaver, was indicted by the Justiciary Court at Edinburgh for having said to one of the king's commissioners that 'there should be an other Bout of it, and that he should be turned back'.[108]

By examining how people were expected to respond to unlawful memories, we can penetrate deeper into the significance of these opinions to the men and women who expressed them. When these memories were circulated among the like-minded, they served to reproduce identities of which shared experiences of the Scottish revolution were constitutive. And yet unlawful memories were also expressed before less sympathetic Scottish audiences. In these cases, the intentions of the speakers can be interpreted differently. On the one hand, public affirmations of the Covenants and 'Work of Reformation' counteracted attempts by the Scottish government to delegitimise the Scottish revolution. Conversely, public identification with the Scottish revolution constituted forms of resistance that appropriated the 'fanatic' identities which those responsible for the rescissory legislation of the 1660s sought to eradicate. Meanwhile, predictions of the return of the Work of Reformation exploited the very anxieties that undergirded experiences of censorship and censure in Restoration Scotland.

LOCATING SEDITIOUS MEMORIES IN IRELAND

The rebellion, wars, and conquest of Ireland in the 1640s and 1650s left legacies that continue to inform antagonisms to this very day. The first to confront the shadow of the past were those who oversaw the protracted process of 'settling' the kingdom in the 1660s. The thorniest issue with which these men contended was the massive redistribution of land that had taken place over the previous decade from Catholic and Royalist 'rebels' to Protestants who had encouraged, funded, or participated in the nation's conquest by the English Commonwealth between 1649 and 1653. The dilemma of whether these lands should remain in the hands of Protestants or revert to Catholics and Royalists loomed large in the post-conflict settlements, a situation which was complicated further by the competing claims of both Protestants and Roman Catholics to royal favour.[109] The claims of Irish Catholics rested on their efforts to restore Charles II to the Crown in the 1650s and the 'fanatic' political and religious identities of the conquering 'New Protestants', many of whom were Parliamentarian and republican soldiers.[110] Countering these claims were the New Protestants themselves, who martialled emotive memories of the bloodshed of 1641 as a means of prejudicing the notion that 'papists' should be trusted with property or public office.[111] These rival accounts of the wars and revolutions in Britain proved compelling to governors in Dublin and London for different reasons. While anti-popery continued to inform politics and religion in Britain, this was now rivalled by the anti-fanaticism that, as we have seen, drove Royalist resentment in England and Wales.

The synthesis of these competing forces was a settlement that, in theory, prioritised loyalty to the Crown over religious uniformity. In practice, however, a clamorous campaign from press and pulpit about the dangers of a return to 1641 drowned out Catholic efforts to raise the spectre of 'fanaticism'. The consequences were political and religious settlements in Ireland of which New Protestants were beneficiaries, and a mnemonic landscape that looks rather different from those encountered so far across the Irish Sea.[112] Caught in the thicket of competing claims to loyalty, governors proffered no Irish equivalent of the Act of Free and General Pardon, Indemnity, and Oblivion.[113] Meanwhile, the dominance of parliament by Protestants, many of whom remained sympathetic to the Cromwellian land settlements, forestalled anything like the pursuit of mnemonic hegemony by hard-line Royalists which took place in England, Wales, and Scotland.[114]

Corresponding with these different circumstances, the parliament of 1661–66 passed no new legislation prohibiting seditious or treasonable language in Ireland. The bills that did reach the statute book contain nothing like the vituperation of the late 'rebels' and 'usurpers' that characterise those of the English, Welsh, and Scottish settlements. The 1662 Act of Settlement spoke, in fact, of the New Protestants as having 'served or suffered in the suppression of the ... rebellion and war', who then 'as soon as with much difficultie and hazard they had gotten the power of this kingdom into their hands, did according to their bounden dutie, with all humilitie and cheerfulness, invite your Majestie into this [his] kingdom'.[115] The 'rebellion' of 1641 and the 'usurpation' of royal authority thereafter feature much more heavily in legislative memory. Moreover, reflecting the dominance of 1641 in the collective imagination, acts formalised commemoration of the beginning of the Irish rebellion on 23 October and, as in England, Wales, and Scotland, the Restoration on 29 May (see chapter 7).[116]

Memories of 1641 are receiving deserved attention from historians of Ireland.[117] In line with the kingdom's unique mnemonic landscape, memories that were sympathetic to the rebellion of 1641 and the Confederation of Kilkenny had the potential to be treated by Protestant governors as seditious or treasonable, bringing them within the scope of this book. In September 1663, for instance, George Nutt was indicted at the Clonmel assizes for identifying himself with one Garret Wall of Coolnamuck (or Culenemucky), Kilkenny, who, with his father James, had been transplanted following the conquest before being restored to his estate in March 1661.[118] Nutt explained that 'Garrett Wall hath gott his Estate and is King of Culenemucky', adding that 'I will spend my blood before Garrett Wall lose his Enterest at Culenemucky'.[119] The historian Danielle McCormack has identified similar sentiment throughout Ireland after the Restoration, including the words of the Catholic George Codd of Wexford, who said 'that the English in Ireland were more Rebells then the Irish and that they murdered the Irish in the North at the beginning of the Warr', and 'that all the English in Ireland were Rebels and doggs and traytors for sending away the Irish to Spain and Barbados'.[120] What constituted seditious remembering in Ireland might even stretch to criticisms of those who had participated in, or actively supported, the conquest between 1649 and 1653. George Nutt, whose identification with the landowner Garret Wall has been mentioned, was also bound over in September 1663 for describing Roger Boyle, Earl of Orrery – a former supporter of Oliver Cromwell – as 'but a Rebell'.[121] Ten years later, John MacNamara was forced to defend himself from a similar accusation that he had labelled 'those that served Cromwell' as 'rebels'. MacNamara explained that he had only 'reflected' on old Oliverians insofar as he 'believed [them] by their principles to be enemies to the King', for he understood that 'others of them [were] very faithful to his Majesty's service.'[122]

The case of John MacNamara signifies the extent to which the authority to speak for the recent past in Restoration Ireland was held by those who sympathised with the conquest and who, consequently, had a vested interested in defending its legacy from attacks by the indigenous Irish and others. Yet, as we have seen, the mnemonic landscape of Restoration Ireland was considerably more complex than this. New Protestants who benefitted from the conquest were not the only constituency that was represented by the government of Ireland after the Restoration. Equally influential were individuals like James Butler, Duke of Ormond, lord steward and later lord lieutenant of Ireland, who had defended Crown and established church from both Irish and English 'rebels' and 'usurpers' during the 1640s and 1650s. Corresponding with the royalism of figures like Ormond, formal attempts were made to forestall a situation in which sympathies for the rebellion and usurpation of Protestants were given free reign. In 1661, for instance, the Lords ordered the burning of the Solemn League and Covenant and its public renunciation by all ministers who had subscribed to it since 1643.[123] This was followed in 1666 by an Act of Uniformity, which, in addition to enforcing the Book of Common Prayer, enjoined all ministers and teachers to renounce the Covenants and to declare *'that the same was in itself an unlawful oath.'*[124]

In addition to these acts and orders, further evidence suggests that local authorities enforced existing legislation concerning seditious or treasonable language as a means of ridding the public arena of opinions that reflected sympathies with opposition to, resistance against, and the overthrow of the Stuarts between 1637 and 1660. There was also a periodic campaign of government surveillance throughout the Restoration that treated sympathies for Parliamentarianism and republicanism before 1660 as evidence of seditious or treasonable intent. It was through these local and supranational channels that sympathetic parties within Irish government sought to ensure that Charles II's Irish subjects did not frustrate the efforts of hard-line Royalists to eradicate 'fanatic' identities within the Stuart realms.

If, then, we wish to find alternative memories in which people sympathised with the 'rebellion' of the English Parliament, we must turn once more to the records of those who sought to police them. Corresponding with the declaration of 1661 and the act of 1665, seditious references to the Solemn League and Covenant are common in Irish and English government papers after the Restoration. The Covenant was taken by thousands of Protestants in Ireland in 1643, particularly Presbyterians in Ulster.[125] Its enduring significance after the Restoration is represented by how many ministers were unwilling to renounce the oath as instructed in 1661.[126] Others who continued to identify with the Covenants were accused of plotting to continue their work in Ireland. In June 1662, for instance, information was passed to Whitehall that there was soon to be a rising in defence of the Covenant.[127] In 1663, it was reported that the Irishman Fawns Urry had told an Englishman on his arrival at the Isle of Wight that '70000 of ye English Planters [were] listed as armed & in readynesse to rise for ye defence of the English interest & Solemne League & Covinant'.[128]

Reflecting the enduring power of the Covenants in Ireland, the historian Richard L. Greaves has pointed to further declarations for the oaths in Ulster in 1668 and 1669,[129] and, as late as 1677, the Earl of Essex wrote to Secretary of State William Coventry warning him that 'ye old Covenant had bin newly revived and administered in severall of ye Corporations of some parts of ye County of Londonderry'.[130] Writing from Castlemartyr in Cork, the Earl of Orrery aired similar anxieties in June 1679 that 'the Covenant ... is deeply rooted in too many here'.[131] Two years later, it was reported from Raphoe in Donegal that an order had been published regarding a 'general fast and abstinence from labour', which implored 'repentance for forgetting or annihilating that wicked Solemn League and Covenant'.[132] Views such as these were shared across the Irish Sea.[133] Michael Bruce, 'ane Irish minister', was recorded chiding an audience at Cambusnethen in Clydesdale for betraying those 'who travelled many a night and many a day to get the Covenant and work of Reformation'.[134]

This evidence reflects the endurance of a sense of the Covenants' obligations in Ireland after 1660 and their suspected role as a means by which covenanted communities endeavoured to foment sedition and treason. Elsewhere in Ireland, allegations of other forms of identification with the revolutions in Britain came before magistrates. Foremost among these were claims of allegiance to Oliver Cromwell, the leader of the English conquest of Ireland between 1649 and 1653. The historian Sarah Covington has described Cromwell's Irish legacy as 'calamitous', drawing attention to how Cromwell 'was very much remembered, and demonised ... in a variety of forms across oral and popular culture'.[135] Yet the opinions of those who profited from the conquest, particularly through the acquisition of land, could be rather different. In 1683, for instance, Captain Henry Shrimpton, a Commonwealth soldier who had acquired lands in Kerry and Tipperary during the 1650s,[136] was bound over at the Clonmel assizes for having said that 'if Cromwell had lived he was as powerfull and as just a King as ever was'.[137] Daniel O'Quinlyn was indicted, although later cleared, for saying similarly in April 1663 that 'I doe not care for the King Queene or Duke of Yorcke' and 'I gott more by Cromwell then by them.'[138] Others emphasised how particular social classes had benefitted from the conquest. In 1682, information was given on oath that John Hawkins of Rathfriland in Down had lamented tithes, bishops, and the plight of 'poor labourers' in Ireland and had reflected on 'how satisfactorily the poor labourers lived, when the kingdoms were governed by a commonwealth'.[139]

Under similar scrutiny by the authorities in Ireland were sympathies for the trial and execution of Charles I in 1649. In 1662, Thomas Hook was accused of saying 'that the late King was justly put to death and it was a just act of the Parliament.'[140] Richard Tight (or Tighe), who, like Hook, was an alderman of Dublin, was accused of reiterating some of the rumours that had circulated in the late 1640s and were used to justify Charles I's execution, including that 'the late King did poison King James'. Tight also recycled the accusation that 'King James committed an abominable crime ... with the Duke of Buckingham'.[141] Memories of Charles I's demise allowed others to envisage that of his son, Charles II. Henry Feltham stood accused in 1663 of having said that 'I hope his ma[jes]tie ... were served as his father'.[142] Elsewhere, in 1679, James Morley and John Cooper were described as being 'in a very earnest discourse' with John Brogan and Herbert Ferall, saying similarly that 'they did not question to see this King's head off as his father's was and that the King was a rogue ... in endeavouring to dispossess them ... of their estates on the testimony of rogues.'[143] Others imagined a chance to regain their lands through the kinds of violence that had characterised the conquest of Ireland in the first place. One former troop of horse under Oliver Cromwell, Captain Nicolls, was accused in 1681 of having said that 'he will have t'other bout yet'.[144]

Combined, these cases suggest the existence of similar forms of remembering in Ireland to those encountered elsewhere in the Stuart realms. Another point of comparison with England and Wales comes in the form of the disappointment of some that Charles II failed to conserve the ecclesiastical settlement of the 1650s and to confirm New Protestants in their lands. In addition to the restoration of episcopacy, the early years of the 1660s witnessed the incremental restoration of Catholic and Royalist property.[145] Instrumental in this restoration was Ormond, a staunch Royalist who saw Old English Catholics as better guarantors of peace in Ireland than New Protestants.[146] One alleged critic of Ormond was Henry Feltham, who was reported to have spoken to John Fetherston in 1663 'about the Course of the times and newes', advising that the Duke of Ormond 'might be gladd to goe with the Crew that came with him to the place from whence he came 'ere long'.[147]

Anger about the dispossession of Protestants after 1660 contributed to, and thus found its most forceful expression in, the Dublin Plot of 1663.[148] Together with a demand for 'establischeing the Protestant religione in puritie, according to the tenor of the Solemne League and Covenant', the rebels' declaration included the claim that Charles II had been 'seduced by evil counsellors' so that 'justlie forfalted estates' had been returned to Catholics.[149] Not far removed from these scathing attacks on the 'traitors' of the Protestant interest in Ireland were those reflecting continued antagonism against Irish Royalists. John Hawkins of Rathfriland evoked these enduring animosities when he labelled Charles II's supporters in 1682 as 'his confederate rebels'.[150] Catholics might also be regarded as rebels, such as the 'natives, freemen, and inhabitants of Galway' who complained to the Earl of Essex of being described as such in 1672.[151] These cases represent the endurance of identities that were anchored in the events of the 1640s and 1650s in Ireland.

UNDERSTANDING SEDITIOUS MEMORIES IN IRELAND

The evidence above points to a complex mnemonic landscape in Ireland after the Restoration in which the law became a means of censoring and censuring both Protestant and Roman Catholic rebels. Nevertheless, the same evidence suggests that sympathies for the Covenants and the Cromwellian settlements were targeted disproportionately by sedition and treason laws and government surveillance. Given the nature of this evidence, and the detail supplied of the contexts in which seditious memories were expressed, we can draw conclusions about the intentions of those who expressed them. These kinds of opinions, like those that were expressed in England, Wales, and Scotland, tend to be associated either with forms of radicalism and republicanism or with popular complaint.[152] And yet, like those in Scotland, England, and Wales, these opinions cannot be extricated from attempts by governors to censor them, nor from attacks on Parliamentarianism and republicanism which, for instance, took the form of public desecration of the Covenants. Once more, seditious memories can be understood as counter-memories which, as implied by information about how audiences were expected to react, counteracted the public and social delegitimisation of opposition and resistance before the Restoration.

Some evidence of seditious memories in Ireland suggests efforts by individuals to defend political decisions that were made during the 1640s and 1650s. In expressing these thoughts, the censure to which former opponents of the Crown might be subjected was publicly contested. In 1663, for instance, one Sergeant Beverley was referred to as 'one of Cromwell's doggs', to which he responded defiantly that 'Cromwell was the best man that ever reigned in the three nations,' adding that 'if the King intends to take away our lands, gained by our swords, we will have one knock for it first'.[153] In the same year, Abel Warren, one of those who were executed for their part in the Dublin Plot, used the scaffold to contradict what he perceived as attacks on the late 'reformation'. While it was clear to all that godliness lay 'now in the dust', Warren explained that 'not long since it made the Mountaines of the Earth to tremble and terribly shooke the Cedars of Lebanon and will againe revive till all the Enemies of it are dealt withal'.[154] Warren's words suggest that, unlike Sergeant Beverley, he foresaw the 'revival' of Ireland's late revolutions as an inevitable outcome of divine providence. Not all those who sympathised with the conquest of Ireland, in other words, need have pursued what Beverley foresaw as another 'knock'. Indeed, others used similarly restorative language to threaten, such as in June 1665, when one David Davies was accused of having relished telling Mortagh O'Bryen that 'I ... wish [tha]t Oliv[e]r Cromwel ... were alive againe.'[155]

The government was particularly troubled by accusations that seditious memories were the basis of agreement. The cases resulting from these anxieties denote equivalent processes of social legitimisation to those identified in England, Wales, and Scotland. One of the longest-running cases from the English state papers concerns Thomas Walcott, a former Oliverian officer who had acquired lands in Kerry and Limerick for his service under Lieutenant-General Edmund Ludlow during the conquest.[156] Presenting his information to Murrough O'Brien, Earl of Inchinquin, on 3 November 1673, Captain Thomas Cullen, himself an old Oliverian soldier,[157] deposed that Walcott had visited him one afternoon and had 'bewailed the condition of the English in general, and of this kingdom, and said that the Irish were like to have all again, so that he wished himself out of the kingdom'. Of more concern to the government was Cullen's allegation that Walcott had led him from his garden to a 'private chamber' where he produced 'out a paper of at least two sheets, all written' which 'mention[ed] many grievances, occasioned by several Ministers of State ... and demanding first that the perpetual Parliament should be re-established ... and that Popery and Prelacy should be put down and Presbytery established'.[158] Following his arrest, Walcott was examined before Henry O'Brien, Earl of Thormond, on 11 November, where he corroborated some of Cullen's allegations. He confessed at length that 'the cause of his fear and trouble' had been 'remembering how the Irish Papists had in 1641 murdered his father, and turned all his children a-begging, thereof he being one and a spectator, he believed their principles were the same now as then'.[159] Suggesting that Walcott had expressed these kinds of opinions to others, he was also accused of 'tampering with two or three others' who had been officers under the Commonwealth.[160]

Walcott 'utterly denied' Cullen's allegations that he had identified with the Long Parliament and the re-establishment of Presbyterianism, pointing out that 'he being for the Congregational way, none would think he should be for the Presbyterian'.[161] In doing so, of course, Walcott contended that his memories fell within a more acceptable depiction of Irish, and indeed British, history: one that emphasised the horrors of 1641 and cited an Irish

Revolution remembered

Protestant commonplace that Catholics posed a more significant threat to Britain than they did. He knew, in other words, that sympathies for the Long Parliament – especially the view that it ought to be restored – were seditious and were liable to land him rather hotter water. If the allegations against Walcott were more factual than he was willing to admit, then it suggests that he was seeking consensus from Cullen in his favour for the Long Parliament. By leading Cullen into a private room, moreover, Walcott had assumed that their conversation, and indeed consensus, were insulated from those who might contend with such views. In the event, Cullen's provision of information to the government suggests that Walcott misapprehended consensus about the events of the 1640s and 1650s, opinions that he had, perhaps, shared more freely with other old Oliverians.

Another, equally rich example of seditious remembering from Restoration Ireland may represent a similarly mistaken belief that certain views about the 1640s and 1650s were shared. In 1663, Charles Minchin of Knockagh, Tipperary, was indicted at the Clonmel assizes for a series of seditious statements that he was alleged to have spoken between June 1661 and August 1662. Minchin was a former soldier under the Commonwealth who had acquired land in Tipperary following the Oliverian conquest.[162] Steadfast identification with this service is the most striking aspect of the veteran's alleged words. He explained that 'for his owne parte he did never serve the King, nor ever would, and that [ever] since his minoritie he did ever serve against himselfe and his father'.[163] Treading further, Minchin envisioned a time when he might serve Edmund Ludlow once more and 'bring this pretended King to the same end his father came unto'. Indeed, there was also an element of frustrated uchronia in Minchin's words, as he explained that 'he wished rather then 2000ls. that he had 6000 men when Ludloe was at Dunkanane [Duncannon], and if soe, he could have stopped Monkes designe'. He also wished 'that the souldiers that served Cromwell in Ireland, had not sould theire estates unto the Officers, for if they had kept them, it had beene neither the King, nor the Duke of Ormond durst try theire Quallifications'.[164]

Citing the failure of indictments like Minchin's to lead to prosecution, the historian Tim Harris has expressed doubts about the reality of such language.[165] And yet, as we saw in chapter 2, the failure to prosecute is not necessarily a tell-tale sign of malicious information. We must acknowledge that, to a more considerable extent than elsewhere in the Stuart realms, the Irish magistracy represented a constituency that had benefitted considerably from, or who were at least sympathetic to, Parliamentarian opposition to Roman Catholicism and the ensuing conquest of Ireland by the Commonwealth in the early 1650s. Moreover, if we refer back to the case of Charles Minchin, the apparent haste with which the allegations of his seditious memories were recorded by the clerk of the assizes, who later wrote them out in neat, suggests the confidence of the deposing party in recalling them and, perhaps, the authenticity of his or her deposition.[166]

If Minchin's words were real, their significance lies in the identity of his company when he spoke them. In the evidence that was provided against him, Minchin was accused of speaking the words 'in conference and severall communication with one Edmond Morres'.[167] Morres's identity is unknown, but the number of occasions when Minchin 'communicated' his opinions to him would suggest an expectation of agreement about the sentiments that were expressed. Indeed, implying that he thought himself to be on safe ground when exchanging these opinions with Morres, it was recorded that Minchin had speculated that 'if people durst speake the truth he [i.e. Morres] might say soe too, And that he was sorry for the times when he may call them without speakeing treason'.[168] In this striking statement, Minchin appears to have acknowledged that censorship was preventing New Protestants, including, perhaps, Morres, from speaking their minds about the revolution. That Minchin, like many others who expressed seditious memories in Ireland after 1660, evaded conviction for his words may lead us to doubt their validity. It may also suggest, however, that the censorship against which he spoke was not quite as severe as he imagined, and certainly not as severe as it was elsewhere in the Stuart realms.

CONCLUSION

In Ireland and Scotland, as in England and Wales, alternative opinions about the wars and revolution in Britain endured after the Restoration. These can be identified in the records of those who, in attempting to control how the events of 1637–60 were remembered, sought to extirpate 'fanaticism' from the soil of Scotland and Ireland. These memories possess a tone that is distinct from those encountered in England and Wales. In Scotland, the Covenants and so-called 'Work of Reformation' between the outbreak of rebellion in 1637 and the English conquest from 1650 onwards constituted the main objects of unlawful remembering. In Ireland, seditious memories were often expressed regarding the nation's distinct experience of conquest, from which many New Protestants had benefitted. Nevertheless, unlike the situation in any of the other Stuart realms, seditious memories in Ireland extended to the opinions of Catholics who continued to possess sympathies for the rebellion of 1641 and the Confederation, as well as those who attacked 'New Protestant' settlers.

Despite these differences, references to the Covenants and Oliver Cromwell suggest that the mnemonic landscapes of the Stuart realms were not entirely distinct. That this may have enabled Dissenters in the four kingdoms to find common cause after the Restoration is suggested by how infrequently these memories were parochial. In the imaginations of Irish and Scottish men and women, the wars and revolution of 1637–60 had been British phenomena, and, to the extent that the recovery of opposition and resistance was imagined, the implications of the events of the wars and revolution extended far beyond individual kingdoms. This situation may have derived from the fact that seditious and unlawful memories in England, Wales, Scotland, and Ireland responded to similar circumstances. The attempt to eradicate 'fanatic' identities was British in scope, and in both Ireland and Scotland, this mission was undergirded by a programme of censorship and censure comparable to that across the Irish Sea. Seditious and unlawful memories counteracted these efforts, and enabled individuals to reproduce the very identities whose eradication was pursued by hard-line supporters of the Restoration.

One upshot of the interconnectedness of seditious remembering was that the endurance of sympathies for erstwhile opposition and resistance to Crown and established church in Scotland and Ireland buoyed Dissenters in England and Wales. In 1661, for instance, the Essex man John Buck was alleged to have uttered that 'if the Scotts came it was for the renewing of the Covenant, and setleing of the Church government'.[169] His views were shared by 'an eminent person off the presbyterian way' in Hereford, who wrote in December 1666 'that thousands off [sic] the Scots ... are up and declare For K[ing] & Cov[enant]'.[170] On 8 December, it was reported from Chester that Ralph Egg, a man notorious in the north-west for having proclaimed Charles I 'traitor' in 1651, responded to news of rebellion in Scotland with the words that 'the Covinant was now goeing up, & it should goe up.'[171] The aforementioned opinion of Fawns Urry that '70000 of ye English Planters [were] ... to rise for ye defence of the English interest & Solemne League & Covinant' shows that dissent in Ireland might be equally inspirational to Dissenters in England. Together, this evidence suggests that, as it had been in the 1640s, rebellion in Scotland and Ireland remained a considerable source of hope for men and women in England and Wales.

NOTES

1 C. Russell, 'The British Problem and the English Civil War', *History*, 72:236 (Oct., 1987), 397.
2 See R. J. Finlay, 'Keeping the Covenant: Scottish National Identity', in T. M. Devine and J. R. Young (eds), *Eighteenth Century Scotland: New Perspectives* (East Linton: Tuckwell, 1999), pp. 121–133; E. M. Robinson, 'Sacred Memory: The Covenanter Use of History in Scotland and America', *Journal of Transatlantic Studies*, 11:2 (2013), 135–157; and L. Stewart, *Rethinking the Scottish Revolution: Covenanted Scotland, 1637–1651* (Oxford: Oxford University Press, 2016), pp. 314–332.
3 T. C. Barnard, 'Crises of Identity among Irish Protestants 1641–1685', *Past and Present*, 127 (May, 1990), 54–55; S. Covington, '"The Odious Demon from Across the Sea": Oliver Cromwell, Memory and the Dislocations of Ireland', in E. Kuijpers, J. Pollmann, J. Müller, and J. van der Steen (eds), *Memory before Modernity: Practices of Memory in Early Modern Europe* (Leiden: Brill, 2013), pp. 149–164; J. Gibney, *The Shadow of a Year: The 1641 Rebellion in*

Irish History and Memory (Madison, WI: University of Wisconsin Press, 2013); D. McCormack, *The Stuart Restoration and the English in Ireland* (Woodbridge: Boydell, 2016), *passim.*; and N. McAreavey, 'Portadown, 1641: Memory and the 1641 Depositions', *Irish University Review*, 47:1 (Apr., 2017), 15–31.

4   See, for instance, C. Jackson, *Restoration Scotland, 1660–1690: Royalist Politics, Religion and Ideas* (Woodbridge: Boydell, 2003); T. Harris, *Restoration: Charles II*; and T. Harris, 'Restoration Ireland: Themes and Problems', in C. A. Dennehy (ed.), *Restoration Ireland: Always Settling and Never Settled* (Aldershot: Ashgate, 2008), pp. 16–17. For an exception to this trend, see A. Raffe, *The Culture of Controversy: Religious Arguments in Scotland, 1660–1714* (Woodbridge: Boydell, 2012).

5   T. Harris, *Restoration: Charles II*, p. 406.

6   Notable exceptions include R. A. Houston, *Social Change in the Age of Enlightenment: Edinburgh, 1660–1760* (Oxford: Clarendon, 1994), pp. 290–306; T. Harris, *Restoration: Charles II, passim.*; T. Harris, 'Restoration Ireland', pp. 1–19; and Raffe, *Culture of Controversy*, especially ch. 8.

7   T. Harris, 'British Dimension', pp. 131–156.

8   John Nicoll, *A Diary of Public Transactions and Other Occurrences, Chiefly in Scotland, From January 1650 to June 1667*, ed. D. Laing (Edinburgh: Bannatyne Club, 1836), p. 283.

9   National Archives of Scotland (hereafter NAS), PA2/26, fol. 21, 'Act concerning the League and Covenant'.

10 NAS, PA2/26, fols. 46–47, 'Act condemning the delivery of the king'.

11 NAS, PA2/26, fols. 124–126, 'Act rescinding and annulling the pretended parliaments in the years 1640, 1641 etc.' See A. Raffe, 'The Restoration, the Revolution and the Failure of Episcopacy in Scotland', in T. Harris and S. Taylor (eds), *The Final Crisis of the Stuart Monarchy: The Revolutions of 1688–91 in Their British, Atlantic and European Contexts* (Woodbridge: Boydell, 2013), p. 106.

12 NAS, PA2/28, fol. 10–11, 'Act for preservation of his majesty's person, authority and government'.

13 'Act rescinding and annulling the pretended parliaments'.

14 John Paterson, *TANDEM BONA CAUSA TRIUMPHAT. OR SCOTLANDS Late misery bevailed, and the HONOUR AND LOYALTY Of this Ancient KINGDOM, Asserted in a SERMON, Preached before His Majesties High Commissioner, and the Honourable Parliament of the Kingdom of Scotland. At Edinburgh the 17. day of February. 1661* (Edinburgh, 1661), p. 2.

15 *A LETTER CONTAINING An Humble and Serious Advice to some in Scotland, IN Reference to their late Troubles and Calamities* (n.p., 1661), p. [1].

16 L. Stewart, *Rethinking the Scottish Revolution*, pp. 275–276, 318–319.

17 NAS, PA2/28, fols. 47–48, 'The king's majesties' gracious and free pardon, act of indemnity and oblivion'.

18 Robert Law, *Memorialls; Or. The Memorable Things that Fell Out within this Island of Brittain from 1638 to 1684. By the Rev. Mr Robert Law*, ed. C. Kirkpatrick Sharpe (Edinburgh: Constable, 1818), pp. 54–55.

19 See Jackson, *Restoration Scotland*, p. 93.

20 Raffe, *Culture of Controversy*, pp. 122–123. See *ibid.*, ch. 5, for a more general discussion of the appellation after the Restoration.

21 For a positive assessment of scaffold speeches as evidence, see Stewart, *Rethinking the Scottish Revolution*, p. 314.
22 The frontispiece of the first volume of Robert Wodrow's *The History of the Sufferings of the Church of Scotland* (2 vols, Edinburgh, 1721) spoke of its having been 'Collected From the Public Records, Original Papers, and Manuscripts ... and other well attested Narratives.'
23 See James Turner, *Memoirs of His Own Life and Times by Sir James Turner. M.DC.XXXII.–M.DC.LXX* (Edinburgh, 1829), p. 169.
24 Robert Wodrow, *The History of the Sufferings of the Church of Scotland from the Restoration to the Revolution by Rev, Robert Wodrow*, ed. R. Burns (Glasgow: Blackie, Fullarton, 1829), iii, p. 67.
25 For copies of these declarations, see *ibid.*, 94n–95n, 207n–211n, 212n–213n. See also T. Harris, *Restoration: Charles II*, pp. 360–361. The Covenants were conspicuous by their absence in the abortive rebellion of Archibald Campbell, Marquis of Argyll, led in May 1685. John Erskine later offered a reason for this, explaining that 'it was thought best' to leave out specific references to the Covenants, 'the quarrel being now clearly stated – Protestant and Papist'. See John Erskine, *Journal of the Hon. John Erskine of Carnock 1683–1687*, ed. W. MacLeod (Edinburgh: Scottish History Society, 1893), p. 137.
26 [James Stewart], *NAPTHALI, OR The Wrestlings of the Church of SCOTLAND For the KINGDOM of CHRIST; Contained in A true and short Deduction thereof, from the beginning of the Reformation of Religion, until the Year 1667* (n p., 1667), p. 260. See also *ibid.*, p. 261.
27 *Ibid.*, p. 238. See also *ibid.*, pp. 257, 258.
28 T. B. Howell, *State Trials*, viii, pp. 123–124.
29 *RPCS, 1683–84*, p. 634.
30 *The True and Perfect SPEECH of Mr. James Guthrey LATE Minister of Sterling AS It was delivered by himself immediately before his Execution, on June 1. 1661. at Edinbrough* (Edinburgh, 1661), p. 9. See also *ibid.*, p. 11.
31 [James Stewart], *NAPTHALI*, p. 217.
32 [John Brown], *AN Apologeticall Relation, Of the particular sufferings of the faithfull Ministers & professours of the Church of Scotland, since August. 1660* (n.p., 1665), pp. 327–426.
33 For examples of this, see [James Stewart], *NAPTHALI*, p. 232.
34 [Brown], *Apologeticall Relation*, p. 328. See also *ibid.*, p. 276.
35 *Ibid.*, p. 69.
36 *RPCS, 1661–64*, p. 355.
37 [James Stewart], *NAPTHALI*, p. 229.
38 Although Boyl denied this allegation; see, Wodrow, *History of the Sufferings* (1721), ii, p. 612.
39 Wodrow, *History of the Sufferings* (1721), i, p. 75.
40 [James Stewart], *NAPTHALI*, p. 255.
41 *Ibid.*, p. 260.
42 Law, *Memorialls*, p. 150.
43 C. Erskine, 'The Political Thought of the Restoration Covenanters', in S. Adams and J. Goodare (eds), *Scotland in the Age of Two Revolutions* (Woodbridge: Boydell, 2014), p. 157.

44 Jackson, *Restoration Scotland*, p. 148.
45 NAS, PA2/31, fols 9–10v, 'Act anent religion and the test'.
46 NAS, PA2/32, fol. 152. 'Act declaring it treason to take or own the covenants'.
47 See *RPCS, 1661–64*, pp. 302, 311, 601, 617–618; *RPCS, 1665–69*, p. 554; *RPCS, 1673–76*, pp. 17–18, 35, 52, 323; *RPCS, 1676–78*, pp. 545, 564; *RPCS, 1678–80*, pp. 17–18, 404–405; *RPCS, 1681–82*, pp. 110, 113, 214, 238, 242–243, 249–250, 253–256, 262–263, 273, 287–288, 297, 300–301, 304, 327, 351, 418, 471, 547–548, 576, 585, 597, 599, 610, 728–731; *RPCS, 1683–84*, pp. 31, 103, 178, 437–440, 443–444, 446, 508, 519, 642–658; *RPCS, 1684*, pp. 691–700.
48 Jackson, *Restoration Scotland*, p. 48n. See also the cases of George Stirling and James Elphinstone, Lord Balmerino, in *ibid.*, p. 149; and G. MacIntosh, *Scottish Parliament under Charles II, 1660–1685* (Edinburgh: Edinburgh University Press, 2007), p. 22.
49 T. Harris, *Restoration: Charles II*, p. 113.
50 Jackson, *Restoration Scotland*, p. 109.
51 L. Stewart, *Rethinking the Scottish Revolution*, p. 318.
52 *Ibid.*, p. 5.
53 *Ibid.*, p. 26. On the social status of Covenanters, see also I. B. Cowan, *The Scottish Covenanters 1660–1688* (London: V. Gollancz, 1976), p. 157; and V. G. Kiernan, 'A Banner with a Strange Device: The Later Covenanters', in T. Brotherstone (ed.), *Covenant, Charter, and Party: Traditions of Revolt and Protest in Modern Scottish History* (Aberdeen: Aberdeen University Press, 1989), p. 43.
54 Wodrow, *History of the Sufferings* (1721), ii, p. 566.
55 [James Stewart], *NAPTHALI*, p. 226.
56 [James Stewart], *JUS POPULI VINDICATUM OR, The Peoples Right, to defend themselves and their Covenanted Religion Vindicated* (n.p., 1669), sigs *[1]r–*[1]v.
57 On the gravity of oaths in early modern Europe, see J. Spurr, 'A Profane History of Early Modern Oaths', *Transactions of the Royal Historical Society*, 11 (2001), 37–63.
58 L. Stewart, *Rethinking the Scottish Revolution*, pp. 116–117.
59 For an example of the republication of the Covenants, see [James Stewart], *NAPTHALI*, sig. a1r–b2v.
60 John Lauder, *Historical Notices of Scotish Affairs, Selected from the Manuscripts of Sir John Lauder of Fountainhall, Bart., One of the Senators of the College of Justice. Volume First. 1661–1663*, ed. D. Laing (2 vols, Edinburgh: Bannatyne Club, 1848), p. 346.
61 [James Stewart], *NAPTHALI*, pp. 218, 225, 258.
62 Wodrow, *History of the Sufferings* (1721), ii, p. 261. See also *ibid.*, p. 370; and Lauder, *Historical Notices*, p. 453.
63 *RPCS, 1683–84*, pp. 633–634. See also *ibid.*, p. 638.
64 *A Solemn ACKNOWLEDGEMENT OF PUBLICK SINS And breaches of the COVENANT AND A Solemn ENGAGEMENT to all the DUTIES contained therein, namely those, which do in a more speciall way relate unto the Dangers of these Times* (Edinburgh, 1648).
65 Raffe, *Culture of Controversy*, p. 103; Robinson, 'Sacred Memory', pp. 138–144; and C. Erskine, 'Political Thought', p. 161.
66 [James Stewart], *NAPTHALI*, p. 224.

67 Ibid., p. 225. See also ibid., pp. 228–229, 238, 260–261.
68 My Lord Marquis OF ARGYLE HIS SPEECH UPON THE SCAFFOLD, the 27 of May 1661 (n.p., 1661), p. 2.
69 SPEECH of Mr. James Guthrey, p. 13.
70 [James Stewart], NAPTHALI, p. 212. For further discussion of Wariston's behaviour at his death, see C. Hill, Experience of Defeat, pp. 82–83.
71 RPCS, 1684, p. 181.
72 For Covenanter attitudes to the regicide, see Kiernan, 'Banner with a Strange Device', p. 34.
73 Wodrow, History of the Sufferings (1721), ii, p. 248.
74 My Lord Marquis OF ARGYLE, pp. 2, 4.
75 See Goldie et al., Entring Book, iv, p. 206.
76 James Kirkton, The Secret and True History of the Church of Scotland from the Restoration to the Year 1678. By the Rev. Mr James Kirkton, ed. C. Kirkpatrick Sharpe (Edinburgh: James Ballantyne, 1817), p. 472n. See also TNA, SP29/427/43, I.
77 Greaves, Secrets of the Kingdom, p. 84.
78 TNA, SP29/103/147.
79 See Raffe, 'Religious Controversy', pp. 139–144; A. Raffe, 'Presbyterians and Episcopalians: The Formation of Confessional Cultures in Scotland, 1660–1715', English Historical Review, 125:514 (Jun., 2010), 570–598; Raffe, Culture of Controversy, ch. 3; C. Erskine, 'Political Thought', pp. 155–172.
80 For discussions of the political impact of print culture in Restoration Scotland, see Greaves, Enemies under His Feet, pp. 184–190; Finlay, 'Keeping the Covenant, p. 126; and Jackson, Restoration Scotland, p. 146.
81 See Greaves, Enemies under His Feet, p. 186.
82 See, for instance, the suppression of Stewart's Jus Populi Vindicatum: RPCS, 1669–72, p. 265.
83 TNA, SP29/182/98.
84 Nicoll, Diary, p. 452. See also TNA, SP29/406/108.
85 TNA, SP29/180/124. For Arnot, see Robert Blair, The life of Mr Robert Blair, Minister of St Andrews, containing his Autobiography from 1593 to 1636, ed. T. McCrie (Edinburgh: Wodrow Society, 1848), p. 502.
86 TNA, SP29/397/146.
87 TNA, SP29/398/8.
88 TNA, SP29/404/13.
89 TNA, SP29/405/250.
90 RPCS, 1665–69, pp. 671–673; RPCS, 1669–72, pp. 643, 706–707; RPCS, 1673–76, pp. 610–611; RPCS, 1681–82, p. 743; RPCS, 1683–84, pp. 684–685, 701–702, 708; and RPCS, 1684, pp. 213–214.
91 RPCS, 1683–84, p. 685.
92 A. G. Muir, 'Brodie, Alexander, of Brodie, Lord Brodie (1617–1680)', in ODNB, vii, pp. 771–772.
93 Alexander Brodie and James Brodie, The Diary of Alexander Brodie of Brodie, MDCLII.–MDCLXXX. And of his Son, James Brodie of Brodie, M DC LXXX–M DC LXXXV, ed. D. Laing (Aberdeen: Spalding Club, 1863), p. 405. For similar anxieties, see Wodrow, History of the Sufferings (1721), ii, p. 203; and Kirkton, Secret and True History, p. 195.

94 Brodie and Brodie, *Diary*, p. 375.
95 *SPEECH of Mr. James Guthrey*, p. 3.
96 C. Erskine, 'Political Thought', p. 167.
97 [James Stewart], *NAPTHALI*, p. 240.
98 *Ibid.*, p. 261.
99 Brown, *Apologeticall Relation*, p. [xxii].
100 *Ibid.*, p. 143.
101 Turner, *Memoirs of His Own Life*, pp. 155–156.
102 *Ibid.*, p. 159.
103 *RPCS, 1681–82*, p. 743.
104 Kirkton, *Secret and True History*, p. 410n.
105 Wodrow, *History of the Sufferings* (1721), ii, p. 186. See also the case of William Cuthil, *ibid.*
106 Lauder, *Historical Notices*, pp. 332–333; Wodrow, *History of the Sufferings* (1721), ii, p. 312; TNA, SP29/428/196; TNA, SP29/429/60; John Erskine, *Journal*, p. 29; and *RPCS, 1684*, pp. 107–109.
107 *RPCS, 1684*, pp. 691–700.
108 W. G. Scott-Moncrieff (ed.), *The Records of the Proceedings of the Justiciary Court Edinburgh 1661–1678*, vol. I, *1661–1669* (2 vols, Edinburgh: Scottish History Society, 1905), p. 55.
109 McCormack, *Stuart Restoration*, p. 4.
110 *Ibid.*, p. 110.
111 *Ibid.*, p. 112. See also J. Gibney, 'Ireland's Restoration Crisis', in T. Harris and Taylor, *Final Crisis*, p. 139.
112 Gibney, *Shadow of a Year*, pp. 39–42.
113 See C. A. Dennehy, 'The Restoration Irish Parliament, 1661–6', in *Restoration Ireland*, pp. 59–59n.
114 This should be compared with the absence of a comparable penal code to those that were enacted across the Irish Sea; see R. Gillespie, 'Dissenters and Nonconformists, 1661–1700', in K. Herlihy (ed.), *The Irish Dissenting Tradition 1650–1750* (Dublin: Four Courts, 1995), p. 13. For the Protestant dominance of parliament, see McCormack, *Stuart Restoration*, pp. 139–140.
115 'An Act for the better execution of his Majesties gracious declaration for the settlement of his kingdom of Ireland, and satisfaction of the several interests of adventurers, souldiers and other his subjects there', 14 and 15 Car. II, c. 2, *The statutes at large passed in the parliaments held in Ireland: from the third year of Edward the Second, A. D. 1310, to the first year of George the Third, A. D. 1761 inclusive, with marginal notes, and a compleat index to the whole* (20 vols, Dublin: Boulter Grierson, 1765–1801), ii, p. 240.
116 'An act for keeping and celebrating the twenty-third day of October, as an anniversary thanksgiving in this kingdom', 14 and 15 Car. II, c. 23, *ibid.*, pp. 526–528; and 'An Act for a perpetual anniversary thanksgiving on the nine and twentieth day of May in this kingdom', 14 and 15 Car. II, c. 1, *ibid.*, pp. 237–238.
117 See Gibney, *Shadow of a Year*; and McAreavey, 'Portadown, 1641', 15–31.
118 For the transplantation, see R. C. Simington (ed.), *The Civil Survey A.D. 1654–1656 County of Waterford*, vol. VI (Dublin: Stationery Office, 1942), p. 79; and Royal Commission on Historical Manuscripts (ed.), *Second Report of the*

Royal Commission on Historical Manuscripts (London: George Edward Eyre and William Spottiswoode, 1871), p. 212.
119 National Library of Ireland, Dublin (hereafter NLI), MS4908, fol. 16r.
120 See McCormack, *Stuart Restoration*, pp. 102–103.
121 NLI, MS4908, fol. 13v.
122 *CSPD, 1672–73*, pp. 526–527.
123 T. Harris, *Restoration: Charles II*, p. 91.
124 'An act for the uniformity of publique prayers and administration of the sacraments, and other rites and ceremonies; and for establishing the forme of making, ordaining, and consecrating bishops, priests and deacons, in the church of Ireland', 17 and 18 Car. II, c. 6, *Statutes at large*, iii, p. 143. Suggesting a less critical stance to the Covenants than similar legislation across the Irish Sea, the act included a caveat that the declaration would lapse in March 1682. See *ibid.*, p. 144. For the relative tolerance that Covenanters experienced in Ireland, see Gibney, 'Ireland's Restoration Crisis', pp. 143–144.
125 For the impact of Covenanters in Ireland after 1660, see *ibid.*, pp. 143–148.
126 T. Harris, *Restoration: Charles II*, p. 91.
127 TNA, SP29/56/19.
128 TNA, SP29/76/71.
129 Greaves, *Enemies under His Feet*, pp. 113–114.
130 Arthur Capel, Earl of Essex, *Selections from the Correspondence of Arthur Capel Earl of Essex 1675–1677*, ed. C. E. Pike (London: Camden Society, 1913), p. 93.
131 Historical Manuscripts Commission (ed.), *Calendar of the Manuscripts of the Marquess of Ormonde, K.P. preserved at Kilkenny Castle*, New Series (Hereford: HMSO, 1908), v, p. 146.
132 *CSPD, 1680–81*, p. 180.
133 See R. L. Greaves, 'Conformity and Security in Scotland and Ireland, 1660–85', in E. Boran and C. Gribben (eds), *Enforcing Reformation in Ireland and Scotland, 1550–1700* (Aldershot: Ashgate, 2006), pp. 228–250.
134 Kirkton, *Secret and True History*, pp. 272–276. Bruce was cited to appear before the Privy Council in June 1664 for 'seditious preaching'; see *RPCS, 1661–64*, p. 551. He was later banished; see *RPCS, 1665–69*, p. 478.
135 Covington, 'Odious Demon', pp. 150–151.
136 See 'Catalogue of the Reports and Schedules addressed to the Court of Claims', in *The Sixth, Seventh, Eighth, Ninth and Tenth Reports from the Commissioners Appointed by His Majesty to execute the Measures Recommended in an Address of the House of Commons, respecting the Public Records of Ireland; with supplements and appendixes, 1816–1820* (n.p., 1820), p. 291.
137 NLI, MS4909, fol. 30r.
138 NLI, MS4908, fol. 3v.
139 *CSPD, 1682*, p. 202.
140 *Calendar of the State Papers relating to Ireland preserved in the Public Record Office. 1663–1665* (London: HMSO, 1907), p. 499.
141 *Ibid.*
142 NLI, MS4908, fol. 14r.
143 *CSPD, 1680–81*, p. 581.

144 Historical Manuscripts Commission, *Manuscripts of the Marquess of Ormonde*, iii, p. 576.
145 McCormack, *Stuart Restoration*, p. 166.
146 *Ibid.*, p. 134.
147 NLI, MS4908, fol. 14v. See also the information against one P. Duckinfield in 1662, TNA, SP Ireland 333/202, II.
148 See Greaves, *Deliver Us from Evil*, pp. 140–150; and McCormack, *Stuart Restoration*, p. 153.
149 See 'Declaration of Colonel Blood and his Accomplices in Ireland', in William Veitch and George Brysson, *Memoirs of Mr. William Veitch, and George Brysson, Written by themselves: With Other Narratives Illustrative of the History of Scotland, from the Restoration to the Revolution*, ed. T. McCrie (Edinburgh: William Blackwood, 1825), pp. 508–509.
150 *CSPD, 1682*, p. 201.
151 *CSPD, May–Sept. 1672*, pp. 503–504.
152 Greaves, *Deliver Us from Evil*, pp. 135–157; and Greaves, *Enemies under His Feet*, pp. 103–120.
153 J. P. Prendergast, *The Cromwellian Settlement of Ireland* (New York: P. M. Haverty, 1868), p. 271.
154 Cited in Greaves, *Deliver Us from Evil*, pp. 148–149.
155 NLI, MS 4908, fol. 31v.
156 See 'Catalogue of the Reports and Schedules', p. 295; and TNA, SP Ireland 332/52. For further testimonies of Walcott's character, positive and negative, see TNA, SP29/330/49; TNA, Ireland 332/70; and TNA, Ireland 332/74.
157 TNA, SP29/335/7.
158 *CSPD, 1672–73*, pp. 120–121.
159 *Ibid.*, pp. 152–153.
160 *Ibid.*, pp. 281–282.
161 *Ibid.*, p. 153.
162 'Catalogue of the Reports and Schedules', p. 281.
163 NLI, MS 4908, fol. 7v.
164 NLI, MS 4908, fol. 7v.
165 T. Harris, *Restoration: Charles II*, p. 98.
166 See NLI, MS 4908, fols 7v, 8r.
167 NLI, MS 4908, fol. 4r.
168 NLI, MS 4908, fols 7r–7v.
169 ERO, Q/SR 389/54.
170 TNA, SP29/180/41. See also TNA, SP29/180/85.
171 TNA, SP29/181/14. See also TNA, SP29 404/13.

Chapter 7

Mis-commemoration after the Restoration

Speech and writing were not the only means by which British people articulated memories after the Restoration. Historians have shown that the mnemonic landscapes of the four kingdoms during the reigns of the later Stuarts were also characterised by a culture of annual commemoration. Together with the anniversaries of the Gunpowder Plot and the coronation of Elizabeth I on 5 and 17 November, people were called to remember the execution of Charles I on 30 January and the Restoration of his son on 29 May.[1] These anniversaries are usually portrayed as presenting Crown and established church with opportunities to encourage obedience via the remembrance of Charles I's 'martyrdom' and memories of the joyous scenes that accompanied the return of Charles II.[2] To the extent that disobedience has been touched upon at all by historians of the anniversaries, it has been ascribed to a minority of recalcitrant troublemakers or identified with the era after the Glorious Revolution of 1688–89.[3] Even work that has highlighted the controversial nature of commemorative culture after 1660 tends to contrast these anniversaries, which are labelled 'royal and dynastic occasions that were especially satisfying to the Tories', with those of the Gunpowder Plot and coronation of Elizabeth I in 'the later autumn season for the Whigs.'[4]

The assumption that the dominant form that commemoration took after the Restoration corresponded with a 'loyal' and thus 'Royalist' interpretation of British history ignores the extent to which it served the government to propagate an image of obedience on the anniversaries. This chapter highlights instances of what I term 'mis-commemoration' by attending to evidence of the failure of subjects to live up to expectations of behaviour that were codified in acts and proclamations concerning 30 January and 29 May between 1660 and 1662. This analysis is supplemented by further consideration of seditious or treasonable speech and writing to which the anniversaries offered a backdrop, as well as efforts to elude government censorship via personal writings such as diaries. Through an exploration of this material, the chapter develops a typology of mis-commemoration that illustrates how men and women throughout Britain failed to attend church, down tools, and take part in other activities that were expected of them by the government and supporters of narrow political and religious settlements. In doing so, this chapter draws inspiration from accounts of government-sponsored rituals that have accounted for mishap and subversion.[5]

Once more, this chapter is interested in both locating and explaining behaviour that was, or had the potential to be, labelled as seditious or treasonable. Rather than synonymising mis-commemoration with what previous chapters have described as seditious and unlawful memories, these actions are identified with a range of objections to the anniversaries that derived from the experiential and theological worlds of political and religious dissent. This includes dissenting scruples at the liturgy of the Church of England as well as doubts about the legitimacy of days of humiliation and thanksgiving that were appointed by the magistrate. Thereafter, mis-commemoration is associated with opposition to the messages that, increasingly, were disseminated from press and pulpit on the anniversaries. These included discourses of loyalty to the political and religious settlements, but also the censure of Dissenters throughout Britain who were, as we have seen, associated with the 'rebellion' and 'usurpation' of the 1640s and 1650s. The chapter finishes with examples of mis-commemoration that are emblematic of opposition to these hostile interpretations of the civil wars and revolution. Put differently, in the final analysis, some instances of mis-commemoration are associated with the kinds of seditious remembering to which this book has referred.

In these ways, the chapter shows that the commemorative culture of Restoration Britain was one that offered numerous opportunities to express political and religious opinions not only about the Restoration settlements, but also about the events that had preceded them. In doing so, it challenges the notion that commemoration was an aspect of early modern popular culture that filtered from the centre outwards and that men and women were largely unable to contest the messages that were conveyed by sermons, bells, and bonfires.[6] This involves drawing on studies that have shown that, as a 'performance' of social memory,[7] commemoration is likewise open to negotiation, contestation, and subversion.[8]

COMMEMORATING OBLIVION

The short-lived era of oblivion that followed the Restoration was not one of total amnesia. The Convention Parliament that welcomed Charles II prioritised the enforcement of annual national commemorations of his return on 29 May 1660, a date that coincided with his thirtieth birthday, and the execution of his father on 30 January 1649. 'An Act for a Perpetuall Anniversary

Thanksgiving on the nine and twentyeth day of May' was passed into law on 29 August 1660 following an initial thanksgiving for the Restoration on 28 June.[9] Then, just before the dissolution of the Convention Parliament, the 'Act for the Attainder of severall persons guilty of the horrid Murther of his late Sacred Majestie King Charles the first' was added to the statute book, incorporating provision for a 'Yearly Anniversary of Humiliation on 30th Jan. for ever',[10] and officialising thereby an event that had been observed illicitly by Royalists ever since 1649.[11] Royal proclamations were then issued on 25 January and 20 May 1661 that, as a means of reinforcing expectations of behaviour, were to be read in church during services prior to the anniversaries of the regicide and Restoration, respectively.[12] Separate acts were passed in 1661 and 1662 for thanksgiving on 29 May by the parliaments of Scotland and Ireland,[13] although no additional legislation materialised in those kingdoms pertaining to 30 January.

By stirring memories of the recent past, these acts and proclamations were dangerously close to undermining a programme of reconciliation in which the differences of the civil wars were to be buried in oblivion. English legislators were thus careful to delineate exactly how Charles's subjects were to conduct themselves on the anniversaries and what was to be remembered. 30 January was to be observed by people 'of what degree, quality or condition soever ... as a day of Fasting and Humiliation'. This required 'all persons whatsoever ... to abstain from all servile Works and Business on that day, and meekly and orderly to repair to the Publick place for Divine Worship'.[14] The proclamation explained that the purpose of the fast was to implore God that 'the guilt of that Sacred and Innocent Blood [i.e. that of Charles I]' might not 'at any time after be visited upon [the Three Kingdoms]'.[15] The proclamation ended with the coercive message that 'such persons as shall be faulty herein, shall be esteemed by [U]s, Contemners and Infringers of Our Laws and Commands, and Prophane persons, who wilfully shut their eyes, both against the [J]udgements and Mercie of Almighty God.'[16]

The royal proclamation concerning 29 May was much the same, but with the obvious difference that the anniversary was to be observed as one of 'publick Praises and Thanksgivings unto Almighty God, for all the [recent] extraordinary Mercies, Blessings and Deliverances received'. The proclamation also sponsored a celebratory atmosphere, instructing subjects to relive the 'dutifull and joyful demonstrations of ... Allegiance' that had attended Charles II on his entry to London in May 1660.[17] This included the usual ceremonies and rituals of civic and popular culture, including processions, feasts, drinking (sometimes from conduits that ran with wine instead of water), the decoration of buildings and streets, bell-ringing, and the lighting of bonfires in public places. The proclamation for observing 29 May, like that for 30 January, also made it clear that subjects were 'to abstain from all servile works and business ... and chearfully and orderly to repair to the publick place of Gods Divine Worship, for the due performance of the Duties of that day' and ended with a similar warning to 'such persons as shall be faulty herein'.[18]

The official messages of the anniversarial acts and proclamations of 1660–61 were thus clear: 30 January and 29 May were occasions for imploring God's mercy for the murder of Charles I and giving thanks for the Restoration of his son. Recrimination against Parliamentarians and republicans, such as imbued later acts of parliament, was exchanged for a tale of seduction in which 'a Party of wretched men, desperately wicked and hardened in their Impiety' beguiled the four kingdoms first into dissolving 'this Excellent Monarchy, and with it the true Reformed Protestant Religion' and then 'the very being and constitution of Parliament' itself.[19] In this account of the recent past, most of the MPs of the Long Parliament were given special dispensation, since 'not a tenth part of the whole' had brought Charles I to the block. Even the soldiers of the New Model Army, who had played a rather more conspicuous part in the events that led to the regicide, were exonerated as the victims of a republican 'seduction', 'chiefly for fear of losing their Imployments and Arrears'. The cataclysmic events of the 1640s and 1650s were thus reduced to what the proclamation labelled as 'the Fanatick rage of a few miscreants'.[20]

Although the royal proclamation for the observance of 29 May was produced in the much less conciliatory atmosphere of the recently assembled Cavalier Parliament, it contained much of the spirit of oblivion in which the act concerning 30 January had been produced. The wars and revolution figured even less in the proclamation, consigned as they were to a bracketed, and self-consciously vague, passage about those who had undergone 'sundry years forced Extermination into Foreign parts, by the most Trayterous Conspiracies and armed Power of Usurping Tyrants, and execrable and perfideous Traytors'. In the spirit of 'thanksgiving', much more of the proclamation was devoted to 'that most joyful day' in 1660 when, 'without the least opposition or effusion of blood', Charles II returned to his cities of London and Westminster 'with all possible expressions of their publick joy, and Loyal affections'.[21] Both proclamations made it clear that commemoration was to be inclusive as long as services took place within 'every Church, Chappel, and other usual place of Divine Service and publick Prayer'.[22]

By reiterating the official account of war and revolution, the anniversarial acts and proclamations reinforce the idea that the authority to remember those events was vested in Charles II in the immediate aftermath of his restoration. Some of Charles's subjects conformed to this spirit of oblivion by showing an unwillingness to rake over the still-warm coals of the recent past. On 30 January 1661, for instance, Samuel Pepys recorded that he had attended the sermon of one Daniel Milles, the minister of St Olave's, Hart Street, who spoke on Psalm 79:8: 'Remember not against us the iniquities of our forefathers'. Pepys was pleased with the sermon, writing that Milles had '[spoken] excellently of the justice of God in punishing men for the sins of their ancestors'.[23] Milles's efforts to dissociate himself from the 'iniquitous' judges of Charles I were echoed in the prayers of the Presbyterian Philip Henry on 30 January 1665 that God might 'forgive ye sin wch is cald to remembr. this day' and, perhaps more significantly, that he might 'let ye innocency of ye Innocent bee cleared up'. This theme recurred in Henry's anniversarial writings. On 30 January 1671, he prayed again that God might 'deliver ye nation from bloud-guiltines'.[24]

The writings of Mary Rich, Countess of Warwick, speak of her comparable efforts to highlight the 'innocency' of the 'innocent' after the Restoration. In 1670, she wrote of how she had 'beg[ged] of God to give repentance to those that had been so wicked as to have a hand in the death of our late sovereign,' praying that he 'would take away the guilt of his innocent blood from this kingdom.' For Rich, the annual commemoration of the regicide was a time of heightened, almost uncontrollable, emotion; so much so, in fact, that her prayers had been accompanied in 1670 'with some self-abhorrence, and with some tears'.[25] Together with an emphasis on innocence, others glossed the wars that had preceded the regicide in ways that conspicuously avoided the 'names and termes of distinction' of the 1640s. It was for this reason that the ex-Covenanter Alexander, Lord Brodie, eschewed a partisan explanation of what he called 'the long bloodi war in thes lands' on 30 January 1662. He did so by evoking the uncontrollable force of the sea, describing how, since the beginning of the Scottish revolution, 'one has bein dashd against the other'.[26]

By emphasising innocence and avoiding recrimination, the prayers of these individuals can be read as efforts to abdicate responsibility. This is likely to derive from the fact that they had all been involved, or otherwise complicit in, the 'rebellions' and 'usurpations' of 1637–60 in some form or other. Although the son of a Royalist, Philip Henry was a Presbyterian minister during the 1650s.[27] While supportive of the return of Charles II, Alexander Brodie was, as we saw in chapter 6, a staunch Presbyterian and a leader of the Scottish Covenanter movement in the 1630s and 1640s.[28] Likewise, we have seen that Samuel Pepys was a servant of the Commonwealth, and Daniel Milles, his minister, was appointed in 1657 under the Protectorate.[29] Despite retaining a distance from the events of the revolution, Mary Rich had married into the staunchly Parliamentarian family of the same name on the eve of the civil wars. In each of these cases, prayers that implored God to clear the 'innocent' disclose anxieties that, however conciliatory the acts and proclamations of 1660–61, recriminations were still a disturbing possibility.

MIS-COMMEMORATION

Not everyone conformed as enthusiastically to the officialised commemoration of 30 January and 29 May. If we look to other evidence from after 1660, we find several examples of mis-commemoration; that is, the failure of other people to observe the anniversaries in the ways that were prescribed by the acts and proclamations of 1661–62. Commonly, this involved deviating from the order to 'abstain from all servile Works and Business' and to attend church on the anniversaries. It was reported with unease that not 'John Nichollson, nor any of his family, nor Ralph Barber, nor his wife nor Robert Wood, nor his wife, nor John Wetwan, nor Francis Wettwan, nor Peter Johnson, nor Thomas Eshbon, nor Richard Hardy' attended the parish church at Hollym in East Yorkshire on 30 January 1665.[30] Elsewhere, the Puritan diarist and minister Ralph Josselin highlighted the extent of absenteeism in his parish of Earls Colne, Essex. His 1661 thanksgiving sermon for the Restoration had 'very few hearers', while 'not above 70 persons' heard him preach on 30 January 1662.[31] Things had not improved by 30 January 1663, when Josselin recorded a similar number of hearers at his fast sermon on Romans 6:23.[32] Seventeen years later, attendance reached a nadir when 'not 30' turned up to his thanksgiving sermon on 29 May.[33] Josselin was not alone in observing a decline in commemorative activity. The diarist John Evelyn, who, unlike Josselin, had been a firm Royalist during the 1640s and 1650s, recorded that 'there was so thin a Congregation' at his parish church on 29 May 1680 'that our Viccar who came prepar'd to Preach, omitted [the sermon]', adding his concern that his fellow countrymen and women had 'slight[ed] & forgot[ten] Gods benefits.'[34]

Not all evidence of absenteeism on the anniversaries comes to us secondhand. The diarist Bulstrode Whitelocke, who served as lord keeper of the great seal under the Commonwealth, recorded his own failure to attend church on anniversaries throughout the period between the Restoration and his death in 1675. On one of these occasions – 30 January 1661 – Whitelocke recorded that he stayed at home, or, in his words, 'went not abroad'.[35] On the same day in 1662, he also 'did not goe abroade', while he 'had sadness enough to keep home' four months later on 29 May 1662.[36] Remarkably, Whitelocke's attendance at church was recorded on only two of the anniversaries through which he lived, and only on the latter occasion (29 May 1673) because he had attended the funeral of Henry Hungerford, a Presbyterian MP in the Long Parliament.[37] Other diaries suggest that Whitelocke was not alone in his absenteeism. Despite his opinion that 30 January 1662 was 'a day of darkness in regard of the wrath of God on thes lands', eighteen years passed before Alexander Brodie referred to observing the fast.[38] Between these occurrences, his diary entries on 30 January are characterised by references to visits abroad.[39] The Presbyterian Oliver Heywood wrote similarly on 30 January 1680 that he 'stayd at home [and] studyed' rather than attending church, 'except that I visited John Learoyd, [and] went to Alice Holts at Cockil.' Heywood was thus able to conclude that 'god made me of use.'[40]

Lapses in church attendance on the anniversaries of the regicide in the 1660s are a feature of the most famous diary of the Restoration: that of Samuel Pepys. On 30 January 1665, Pepys recorded that 'I kept my house, putting my closett to rights again, having lately put it out of order in removing my books and things in order to being made clean.'[41] Indeed, while Pepys observed the 1660 proclamation by attending his parish church, he did not do so when it came to 'abstain[ing] from all servile Works and Business'. Pepys recorded that, like Oliver Heywood, he had worked from home on the anniversaries of the regicide in 1663, 1664, 1665, 1667, and 1668, as well as that of the Restoration in 1668.[42] On one of these occasions, 30 January 1667, his wife Elizabeth had to stop him from singing in his back garden, reminding her diarist husband that it was a day set aside for fasting and prayer.[43] Fellow diarist Bulstrode Whitelocke also carried on with business on the anniversaries throughout the 1660s. As they came at the end of the month, Whitelocke often devoted these days to settling accounts.[44]

While Pepys and Whitelocke conducted business in private on the anniversaries, the lapses of others in this regard were rather more conspicuous, attracting allegations of seditious intent as a result. The Dorset Quaker John Askew was accused of continuing his work in 1661 despite it being a 'day of Thanksgiveing for the Kings birthday & Restoration'.[45] Elsewhere, entire communities might refuse to down tools on 30 January, suggesting, perhaps, that if one person continued to work then others followed. In 1663, the Dissenter Philip Henry recorded that the local market had been kept in Whitchurch, Shropshire, on 29 May, which, he wrote, 'should not bee.'[46] The refusal to close places of business was a cause of especial anxiety for governors when it occurred on the anniversary of the regicide. On 30 January 1664, it was reported with alarm in a government newspaper that York's Dissenters had '[kept] open their Shops, and make it a day of Common Business'.[47] This kind of behaviour continued into the 1670s, including on 30 January 1676, when Samuel Fox, a Quaker living in Rochester in Kent, refused to shut his shop windows, despite being told to do so repeatedly by the town's aldermen, common councillors, and a constable.[48] That observance of the anniversary was a more widespread issue in Kent is hinted at by the palpable relief with which solemnities were reported by a government correspondent at Deal in the same year.[49]

Obedience to the commands regarding commemoration was not an expectation merely of parishioners, but also of their ministers, whose task it was to read the proclamation on the Sunday preceding the anniversaries, and then on the days themselves to lead prayers of humiliation or thanksgiving. In both respects, there is evidence to suggest that ministers failed to live up to what was expected of them. The government was informed on 29 May 1662 that James Bradshaw, the Presbyterian minister at Macclesfield in Cheshire, had refused to 'celebrate [the] day of thanksgiving for his sacred ma[jes]tie's Restauration'.[50] Elsewhere, Nathaniel Wilmott of Faversham, Kent, a Congregationalist, was accused of denying 'a p[er]formance of his duty' to preach a sermon on 30 January.[51] Other ministers overlooked their responsibility to give warning to their parishioners one week in advance of the anniversaries. *Kingdomes Intelligencer*, a government newspaper, reported on 31 January 1661 that the parishioners of Dorchester were 'somewhat troubled for that we had no Proclamation for observing yesterday ... as a solemn Humiliation.' The reporter offered his assurances that '[we] are only sorry we were deprived of the opportunity of expressing [our loyalty] yesterday.'[52] So widespread did these kinds of lapses become, in fact, that in 1676 the Privy Council ordered all bishops 'to take Care that ye day annually Observd uppon ye Martyrdom of ye late King may be kept wth all sollemnity'.[53]

Ministerial observance of 29 May was a more significant issue in Scotland. Suggesting that the initial act of 1661 concerning the anniversary failed to take root north of the border, a special proclamation was issued in June 1662 that made failure to observe the anniversary punishable by removal from ecclesiastical benefice.[54] This did not prevent Presbyterians from absenting themselves from the pulpit on 29 May, and John Brown of Wamphray was provoked to write in 1665 that many had 'suffer[ed]' owing to their refusal 'to observe the Anniversary Day.'[55] One of these was Donald Cargill, then minister of Barron church in Glasgow, who was reported in October 1662 to have 'disobeyed the acts of Parliament for keeping ane anniversary thanksgiving for his Majestys happy restauration'.[56] Suggesting that the disobedience continued, the Privy Council was forced to issue an order in July 1671 that any 'ministers as shall not give due obedience' to the act 'shall be removed from the churches at which they presently serve, and discharged to preach at any tyme thereafter'.[57] Subsequent references to mis-commemoration of 29 May in Scotland suggest that this proclamation was as ineffective as others in preventing such behaviour.[58] References to commemoration of 30 January are even rarer in Scotland. So unusual was it for Scottish Presbyterians to commemorate the anniversary that a riot broke out when Glaswegian Episcopalians observed the day in 1704.[59]

Together with the expectation to attend church, the injunction to *fast* was one of the most crucial aspects of appropriate behaviour on 30 January. It is surprising, then, that there are conspicuously few references in the archive to men and women who upheld this expectation. So far from fasting was Samuel Pepys on 30 January 1663 that he was provoked to write that 'we were forced to keep [the fast] *more than we would have done*, having forgot to take any victuals into the house' (my italics).[60] Whereas Oliver Heywood provides one of the few examples of someone who did follow the direction to fast, his efforts to do so seem decidedly lacklustre. On 30 January 1679, Heywood reported that his 'solemne fasting and prayer' lasted 'from 11 to 3', a somewhat unimpressive duration of four hours.[61] Rather more conspicuous than the actions of these two diarists were those of the Worshipful Company of Salters in January 1682. Sir Leoline Jenkins recorded that the company's members refused to move their annual feast, which fell on 30 January, and concluded that the Company 'had not respect enough for ye Royall Martyr nor obedience to ye kings law sufficient to adjourne their mirth but held a solemne feast on [tha]t day'.[62] That at least one London company produced printed *pro forma* 'reminders' of forthcoming anniversaries of the regicide suggests that a more general failure to attend special livery events on 30 January remained a significant issue into the last decades of the century.[63] This hypothesis is borne out by the evidence of one Joseph Browne, the clerk of the Worshipful Company of Coopers, who was accused in 1683 of being not 'with the m[aste]r & wardens of his company at St Mary Bow at the Late Comemoracon of that Abhorred 30th of January.'[64]

Attending church, refraining from servile works and business, and fasting and praying were not the only commemorative activities that were disobeyed after the Restoration. More abstractly, others failed to get into the spirit of events that replicated the celebratory atmosphere of 29 May 1660. This was the case in 1683 when the notoriously 'factious' inhabitants of Taunton in Somerset were reproached for refusing to contribute to the construction of a bonfire in the town on the anniversary.[65] Others appear to have gone to considerable lengths to undermine celebrations on 29 May. On that date in 1664, eleven of the inhabitants of Towcester in Northamptonshire complained that Thomas Jones, the town's constable, 'together with his Tapster & ye rest of his family violently together with his watch' went about 'Squenching' a bonfire that had been erected in the centre of town, 'beateing abuseing and haleing towards the Stockes' the 'Loyall Subiects' who had constructed it.[66]

Obstructive behaviour on the anniversary of the Restoration continued into the 1680s. When the sessions of oyer and terminer met at London's Old Bailey in September 1682, one Benton, an ensign in the Trained Bands, was accused of attacking Andrew Williams, who had 'attempt[ed] to destroy the Bone-fire made before his door' on the 29 May beforehand.[67] That, as this case suggests, the anniversary of the Restoration, but also the regicide, might boil over into violence is hinted at by the government's efforts to pre-empt disorder on those days. It was for this reason that Peter Mews, the vice-chancellor of the University of Oxford, had a proclamation 'stuck up on all comon places in ye university' and 'all comon places of [tha]t city' on 30 January 1672, enjoining the city's constables 'diligently to look after all Disorders on the said Day, and to give an account of all such Persons, as shall be found offending therein, to some of his Majesties Justices of the Peace, to the end they may be proceeded against with all severity.'[68]

For some of those who experienced multiple anniversaries throughout Charles II's reign, there was a sense that participation in the construction of public bonfires was not only sporadic, as these cases suggest, but also in decline. On 29 May 1666, Samuel Pepys was provoked to comment on the lack of bonfires on the 'City side of the Temple' as compared with the Westminster side, which 'would make one wonder the difference between the temper of one sort of people and the other: and the difference among all between what they do now, and what it was the night when [General] Monk come into the City' (i.e. on 3 February 1660).[69] In 1682, the Oxford diarist

Anthony Wood spoke of his own surprise that 29 May had been ushered in with 'but one bonfier ... in the four great streets, made by any townsman, wheras there hath been seen twenty.'[70] These perceptions of a decline in bonfire construction since the Restoration should be viewed together with Ralph Josselin's observations that his anniversarial sermons were attracting fewer and fewer hearers. These shifts are mirrored in what the historian Ronald Hutton has described as the waning contribution of parishes to commemorative bell-ringing during the reign of Charles II.[71]

Despite dwindling church attendance, Ralph Josselin was at least conscientious in his annual commemoration of the regicide and Restoration. Even Dissenters showed diligence in preaching on the anniversaries. The Congregationalist minister Thomas Jolly wrote on 29 May 1673 that while he and his flock at Slade in Lancashire 'could not keep the 29th [May] ... as enjoyned by autority and therfore judged it not convenient to meet publiquly', he nonetheless 'kept that day in way of thanksgiving at my hous privately what the lord had done by the king and that wee might come as nigh to obedience unto autority as wee could', adding that 'it was a good day.'[72] Likewise, in 1680, but this time on 30 January, Jolly wrote how 'though wee could not spend [it] in the way and manner others did, yet could wee not follow our calling to the offence of others, but wee spent it together in prayer and fasting.'[73] These diligent efforts to observe the anniversaries outside official places of worship appear to have left Dissenters vulnerable to arrest, such as when the Baptist congregation at Broadmead near Bristol 'resolved to keep a day at Mr. Jackson's, over the down' on 29 May 1682 only for 'the bailiff of the hundred and half a dozen more' arriving 'to disturb' them.[74]

The diligence of these Dissenters to commemorate the anniversaries should not lead us to assume enthusiasm. That, on the contrary, some of them clearly felt compelled to observe the anniversary of the Restoration is evident in a diary entry by Thomas Jolly from 29 May 1672, shortly after the Declaration of Indulgence and his own success in securing a license to preach at Slade in Lancashire. Although Jolly spoke of the fact that he had taken 'occasion to begin a new service at Slade (one of our Licensed places) upon ... the (day of his majesty's return)', he recorded having done so only 'to avoid offence' such as might have resulted 'if wee had taken noe notice of [the day of thanksgiving]'.[75] The diary of Alexander Brodie is even more explicit in illustrating compulsion to commemorate the anniversaries. On 30 January 1680, he wrote that Thomas Hogg, a Presbyterian, 'cam heir from Ed[inbu]r[gh], to sie me' and that he 'scrupld to preach', it being the anniversary of the regicide, 'to them that heard the conform ministers.' Looking to divine inspiration, Brodie prayed that, 'as to Mr Th. Hog's cariag and exercis, Lord! direct him and us anent it in a way that He approvs off.'[76] That fear of conspicuous non-compliance drove anniversarial observance is implied also by the palpable distress of Ralph Josselin when he forgot to preach on 29 May 1664, an oversight that the minister described as 'a great error'.[77] By enforcing commemoration, the acts and proclamations of 1660–61 encouraged displays of loyalty that speak of compulsion as much as willing compliance.

UNDERSTANDING MIS-COMMEMORATION

Rather than one of all-round enthusiasm, we are left with the impression that adherence to the acts and proclamations of 1660–61 was sporadic, in decline, and, in some communities, verging on non-existent. On occasions when commemoration did occur, diligence in preaching or attending sermons should be understood within the context of the compulsion to exhibit such diligence. If this evidence speaks of a more widespread phenomenon of mis-commemoration after the Restoration, how can it be explained? Clearly, any answer to this question must acknowledge that, as we have seen, the actions that constituted mis-commemoration ranged considerably from resistance to varieties of absenteeism. Equally important to bear in mind is that the men and women who were guilty of mis-commemoration differed to a considerable degree in terms of politics and religion. Evidently, then, no single motivation for mis-commemoration can be identified. Fortunately, additional evidence allows us to explore the range of objections that may have fomented mis-commemoration.

For Dissenters, the command to attend a 'Church, Chappel, and other usual place of Divine Service and publick Prayer' on the anniversaries could prove to be a stumbling block to commemoration. Quakers were particularly prone to avoiding church and remaining at work on the anniversaries, something that derived, at least in part, from their objections to worshipping in what they labelled 'steeple houses'. The inclusion of orders of service for 30 January and 29 May in the new Book of Common Prayer (1662) meant that a broader constituency, including, for instance, Thomas Jolly, felt unable to attend church on the anniversaries 'as enjoyned by autority'.[78] Meanwhile, the dilemma that some Scottish Presbyterians faced about whether to hear 'curates' who had conformed to the episcopal church accounts for similar varieties of mis-commemoration in Scotland.[79] One absentee from the designated place of worship was Alexander, Lord Brodie, who, despite having written on 29 May of his intention to attend the parish church, would do so 'not out of any superstition or esteem of the day: but not thinking it sinful, ... to remov som preiudice of myself, as if I wer wholli against hearing of thes who conform'. In the event, Brodie was stopped in his tracks when he heard 'the bell-ringing'. 'Turn[ing] asid,' Brodie 'lookd up to God for direction', where, 'after som struggling', he 'did wholli forbear, lest I should stumbl and offend honest men, in hearing, and countenancing ther holi days, both at once.'[80]

Brodie's sense that 29 May was 'superstitious' represented his belief, expressed elsewhere in his diaries, that while the anniversary was 'lawful' as 'a civil remembranc', it was in 'noe way differing from other days.'[81] Others were less sure than Brodie about the 'lawfulness' of the anniversary of 29 May, scrupling that there was no scriptural mandate for what were described as *pro re nata* days of thanksgiving (i.e. those that arose as necessity dictated). Gilbert Burnet, then a minister in the episcopal Church of Scotland, was thus convinced that much of the absenteeism on 29 May was a consequence of the conviction that days of thanksgiving 'should not be enjoyned by the Magistrate, but by the Church, who ought only to order the worship of God.'[82] One proponent of this view was William Weir, the minister of West Calder, Linlithgow, who not only failed to observe 29 May 1674, but was also accused of preaching on another occasion 'that the civill magistrat had no power to appoint a day to be keeped holy and to be observed in publick worship'.[83] Similar objections were raised by Presbyterians in England and Wales, such as those of the minister Philip Henry, who cavilled at 'Humiliation dayes for sin committed' such as the anniversary of the regicide, 'esp. ... after ye Judgmt caus'd by that sin is at an end'.[84] For Henry, bloodguilt belonged only to a limited period.

Dissenting objections to 29 May extended beyond their lawfulness to the ways in which they were observed. This was especially true of the lighting of bonfires and drinking in the streets, activities that, by the estimations of some, preceded debauchery, drunkenness, and even disorder. Alexander Brodie prayed on 29 May 1663 that his fellow Scots might not 'mock God, and think that ther carnal, profan mirth, loosnes, drunkennes, and inordinatnes, is an acceptabl way of thankfulnes to God for ani merci or deliuer-anc'.[85] Seventeen years later, Ralph Thoresby spoke similarly of his 'great dissatisfaction' when he returned home on 29 May to find 'some company ... too merry for our circumstances, too many profane words, and much precious time spent idly if not sinfully'.[86] So considerable were the objections of some dissenting ministers that they utilised 29 May sermons as a way of dissuading their hearers from such behaviour. Henry Newcome, recorded that his sermon on 29 May 1662, on Psalm 102:18 ('This shall be written for the generation to come: and the people that shall be created shall praise the Lord'), had 'prevayled so far [tha]t all were afraid of being overseene in drinke, and it was not observed [tha]t any were overcharged.'[87] Even if this evidence does not suggest opposition to the anniversaries of the Restoration themselves, it suggests the strength of Puritan resentment at one of the forms that commemoration was expected to take.

The framing of mis-commemoration as a matter of conscience was given short shrift by hostile witnesses like the indomitable Sir Roger L'Estrange. Reporting on the failure of York's Dissenters to close their shops on 30 January 1664, the licenser of the press drew attention to the numerous 'dayes of Humiliation, or Thanksgiving' that had been so 'superstitiously observe[d]' during the 1640s and 1650s by the self-same '*Phanatiques*'. For L'Estrange, mis-commemoration epitomised nothing more than the 'fanatic' refusal to abide by 'any thing, which Authority Commands'.[88] Evidence exists to support this interpretation of mis-commemoration, if only in a handful of cases. Here, anniversarial sermons became opportunities for the Puritanically minded to broadcast grievances with the Restoration settlements. On 29 May 1661, for instance, John Sacheverell, the Presbyterian minister at Wincanton in Somerset, used his sermon to preach on 1 Samuel 12:25 ('But if ye shall still do wickedly, ye shall be consumed, both ye and your king'), a text that had appeared on the frontispiece of the 1644 Covenanter pamphlet *Lex, Rex*.[89] Sacheverell's unconcealed attack on Charles II found an echo on 30 January 1662 when Henry Newcome attended the sermon of a Mr Richardson, who preached on 2 Samuel 21:1, a verse in which God explained to David that the cause of a recent famine was Saul (a biblical monarch with whom Charles II was often compared by Dissenters), as well as 'his bloody house' and 'because he slew the Gibeonites.'[90]

Unsurprisingly, these kinds of sermons could lead to accusations of sedition against preachers. One of these was Henry Godman, who 'preached to a numerous auditory' in Sussex on 29 May 1670, only for audience members to inform the authorities about his choice of text: 'Redeeming the time, because the days are evil' (Ephesians 5:16).[91] Whatever the concerns of some of Godman's audience, further evidence suggests that people from outside the established church expected topical sermons on the anniversaries and were disappointed if the minister did not deliver. Alexander Brodie was apparently underwhelmed when his minister, one Mr Douglas, 'preach'd sound and smooth things' on 29 May 1662, failing thereby to admonish 'the present estat of the [Scottish] church.'[92] Matters of state continued to instil sermons on the anniversaries during the 1680s, although the subject matter had, by then, transformed into the likelihood of a Roman Catholic successor in the form of James, Duke of York. The future archbishop of Canterbury, John Tillotson, was heard to have 'declare[d]' on 30 January 1682 'his abhorrence of [the regicide]' and had given 'His Late Maj[es]tie ye character of ye best Prince [tha]t ever lived', sentiments that did not stop him from warning that 'Our Relligion and Liberty in all humane probability woud expire wth [Charles II].'[93]

Other media could be used to subvert what was expected of subjects on the anniversaries. One of these was the drinking of 'loyal healths',[94] as became evident on 29 May 1683 when a man was accused of refusing a health to James, Duke of York, only to drink to his rival for the Crown, James, Duke of Monmouth, instead.[95] Pamphleteering provided a rather more conspicuous means by which individuals could air grievances on the anniversaries. In one intriguing case from 30 January 1664, the *Kingdomes Intelligencer* reported that, far from being universally observed, 'this day was both Usher'd in and Enterteyn'd with seditious Practices against his most Sacred and Merciful Majesty'.[96] Helping to fill in the gaps of this commentary, the Venetian ambassador recorded how 'libels [had been] scattered abroad in divers places against the royal honour, the quiet of the kingdom and the safety of the first ministers of the state.'⁹⁷ While the content of these libels is unknown, we do know that libellous material had been published over recent months in which the perceived immorality and insobriety of Charles II and his court were indicted.⁹⁸

This behaviour stood in stark contrast to the message of loyalty that imbued the anniversaries of the regicide and Restoration, one that was characterised increasingly by a narrow vision of church and state.⁹⁹ By the late 1660s, the tone of anniversarial sermons had changed markedly from those that, as we have seen, emphasised the 'innocency' of the 'innocent'. When Thomas Stanhope preached before a congregation at St Margaret's, Leicester, on 29 May 1669, he was drawn to a denunciation of 'Rebellion' as 'a *most grievous sin*', asserting that 'it is *impossible* a *Rebel* should ever be *reconciled to God* without *a very great measure* of *repentance*.'¹⁰⁰ Here, the implication was clear: by continuing to dissent from the church, 'fanatics', including, no doubt, some of his parishioners, had yet to repent for the events of the 1640s and 1650s. As well as providing men like Stanhope with an opportunity to beat the drum for a narrow vision of conformity to church and state, the anniversaries amplified contrasting opinions. That absence from church and other forms of mis-commemoration were so conspicuous to the authorities may suggest that these actions constituted silent, but no less powerful, statements of political, as well as religious, dissent after the Restoration.

DISSENTERS HATTERED

Loyalty was not the only message that prevailed on the anniversaries of the regicide and Restoration. Notwithstanding the spirit of oblivion that was espoused by the English acts and proclamations of 1660–61, the normal experiences of Dissenters on 30 January and 29 May were of censure for their 'rebellion' and 'usurpation' before the Restoration. The diaries of Dissenters after the Restoration offer a window on to these experiences. Oliver Heywood recorded on 30 January 1679 that he had attended the funeral of one Thomas Lister of Halifax in West Yorkshire, during which he and his fellow Dissenters had endured the 'censures' of the Church of England minister Dr Richard Hooks,¹⁰¹ an experience that may explain his heart having 'drawn out' a year later on the biblical commandment 'shalt thou serve thine enemies which the Lord shall send against thee, in hunger, and in thirst.'¹⁰² Other Dissenters referred to how extensive such abuse could be. On 29 May 1681, Philip Henry wrote of having heard of 'a general rayling ... in all the churches & chapels round about, which I am wel assured the lord hims[el]f wil in due time reckon for'.¹⁰³ Ralph Josselin spoke likewise of 'poor dissenters' being 'hatterd' (harassed, or badly treated) in London on 30 January 1683.¹⁰⁴

Quite how intense this 'hattering' of Dissenters could be is evident in the diaries of John Evelyn and Anthony Wood, two Royalists who were regular attendees at anniversary sermons throughout the reign of Charles II. On 30 January 1666, the former reported attending a sermon in which 'the vile treatchery of his late Majesties Enemies' was expounded, with reference to 'the simple meaning of some, & [the] abominable treason & malice of others'. Forestalling any interpretation of these words as an appeal to oblivion, Evelyn related that the minister had also 'proved exceedingly well' that 'no pretence of doing good, by evil meanes was justifiable'.[105] Much more vitriolic than this was the sermon that Evelyn heard on 30 January 1677, in which the defence of taking up arms against Charles I was heavily criticised, or, two years later, when Ralph Cudworth related how the *'Treasons'* of the 1640s and 1650s had been committed 'under a forme [i.e. pretence] of Reformation & Godlinesse'.[106] In 1684, this time on 29 May, Evelyn noted simply that a preacher at Temple church had 'perstring[ed] our present dissenters'.[107] Anthony Wood reported hearing similar attacks on Dissenters, including on 30 January 1683, when Francis White of Balliol College had preached a sermon at St Mary's, Oxford, that was 'very satyricall and bitter against the phanaticks.'[108]

The tradition of bonfire building on 29 May comprised yet another opportunity to carry out deeply symbolic attacks on those who were associated with the revolution of the 1640s and 1650s. This was especially the case on 29 May 1661, only a week after the House of Lords ordered that all extant copies of the Solemn League and Covenant in England and Wales should be burned by the common hangman.[109] One of the most elaborate of these ritual destructions occurred in the Suffolk town of Bury St Edmunds on 29 May 1661, when the parishioners of St James, one of the town's principal parishes, built an effigy of the regicide Hugh Peter, 'that grand Impostor', who was made to hold the Solemn League and Covenant and the Presbyterian Directory for Public Worship. It was reported that Peter's effigy was then carried to a gibbet in the centre of the town where it was burned along with '[a] Picture of *Oliver* [Cromwell], and a List of the bloody Regicides'. Just in case the symbolism was lost on the audience, it was also recorded that 'on the top of all was painted in Capital letters THE COVENANT EXALTED.'[110] Similar events were reported in Halesworth, on the other side of Suffolk, where the Solemn League and Covenant was burned with an effigy of Cromwell and a copy of the Engagement to the Commonwealth 'in a Bonfire of above Five hundred Faggots.'[111]

These elaborate rituals reappeared in the 1680s amid attempts to enjoin Charles II's subjects to reject the 'fanatic' efforts of the Whigs to exclude James, Duke of York. On 29 May 1682, 'the Loyal Inhabitants' of Norwich built 'a very great Bonfire ... in the very same place it was on Coronation day'. In the centre of the bonfire was a 'mawkin' (an East Anglian word for a scarecrow) that had been dressed up as *'Baal's Presbyterian Priest ...* with the Commonwealth Arms standing over his head, having a long Cloak on, and on his breast these expressions written (*viz*) *The Petitioners for the*

Murder of King Charles I'. The scarecrow was destroyed in the flames with an impressive catalogue of 'Seditious and Rebellious Papers', including 'The *Solemn League and Covenant, the Engagement. The Directory; The Long Members Speech in the Long Parliament to king* Charles I. *The Bill of Comprehension. The Exclusion Bill*; [and] *The Association*.' With these documents were also burnt effigies of an impressive catalogue of Whig booksellers, printers, publishers, and writers, including Richard Baldwin, Henry Care, Langley Curtis, Richard Janeway, Francis 'Elephant' Smith, and Thomas Vile.[112] Only a little less elaborate than Norwich's commemoration of the Restoration in 1683 was that in the former Parliamentarian stronghold of Coventry a year later, where likenesses of the Earl of Shaftesbury and Robert Ferguson were burned, along with 'a [live] *Cat* in my Lord [Shaftesbury]'s *breeches*'.[113]

In these examples, the Tories' claims about the continuities between the fanaticism of the 1640s and that of the 1680s were at their most explicit and creative. Yet they were also methods by which former Royalists, and later Tories, sought to target specific individuals whose allegiances during the civil wars and revolution were, at least on a local level, well known. When, for instance, the residents of York celebrated the first anniversary of the Restoration on 29 May 1661 by burning the Solemn League and Covenant and effigies of Oliver Cromwell and his fellow regicide John Bradshaw, the bonfire was lit on Coney Street, outside the door of the lord mayor, James Brooke. That the location of the bonfire was intentional is implied by a reference in a government newspaper to the fact that, during his previous spell as mayor in 1651, Brooke had 'feasted *Oliver* [Cromwell]'.[114] Here, bonfires were not serving as means of symbolically eradicating the past; rather, they drew attention to those who were held to have been culpable for, or heavily implicated in, the events of the 1640s and 1650s.

Considering the extent of efforts to target Dissenters, it should be no source of surprise that, like those who absented themselves from sermons on 29 May and 30 January, others refused to get into the spirit of public celebrations. The report of the bonfire in Bury St Edmunds on 29 May 1661 included a reference to the fact that the parishioners of St Mary's parish – who, it was implied, were either former Parliamentarians or Dissenters – had skulked off between the end of their anniversary sermon and the town's bonfire in order to 'mourn in private for their sins'.[115] It may be that recriminatory attacks on Dissenters led to instances of violence on the anniversaries. On 29 May 1682, the *Observator in Dialogue* reported that one reveller in Durham 'broke' the head of a man who, having taken offence at his consumption of 'a whole *Hatfull*' of wine, had 'bad[e] him be *Civil*'.[116] Given the extent of recrimination on 29 May, it is possible that the civility that had been requested by the deceased corresponded with an experience of censure.

In Scotland, experiences of censure on 29 May were especially acute. This was a symptom of the recriminatory language in which the act enforcing commemoration of the anniversary in the kingdom was couched. Mirroring the language of the rescissory legislation of the 1660s (see chapter 6), the act included references to 'the sad condition, slavery and bondage this ancient kingdom has groaned under during these twenty years' troubles in which, under the specious pretences of reformation, a public rebellion has been, by the treachery of some and mis-persuasion of others, violently carried on against sacred authority'. This statement was followed by several rhetorical questions that belied any nuanced distinction between traitors and the 'mis-persuaded', including the query as to '[whether it had] been pretended to for the warrant of all those vile and bloody murders, which in high contempt of Almighty God and of his majesty's authority and laws, were under colour of justice committed upon his majesty's good subjects, merely for the discharge of their duty to God and loyalty to the king?'[117] In contrast to England and Wales, the official language in which commemoration of 29 May in Scotland was couched reflected a broad-brushed attack on the Covenanters' revolution.

The ferocity of the act concerning 29 May did not pass without comment in Scotland. The exiled Presbyterian Robert McWard used his 1671 work *The True Nonconformist* to indict the Scottish government for encouraging attacks on his co-religionists, citing 'the disservice done to the King, in rendering the celebration of that day (which in its righteous and proper use might have been an acceptable & kindly warming of his Subjects affection) a very odious provocation to aversion and alienation'. Significantly, McWard also countered the claim that mis-commemoration was a result of objections to 'the Magistrates power in appointing *pro re nata* dayes of solemne thanks-giving'.[118] McWard's writings found an echo in the *Mirabilis Annus* tracts of 1660–62, which abounded with tales of God's disfavour for those who attacked Dissenters on 29 May. One such tale related how efforts to light an effigy of John Sacheverell, minister at Wincanton on 29 May 1661, had ended in failure.[119] The tracts also referred to a rather more graphic case, in which a resident of Grantham in Lincolnshire reputedly 'wor[e] away to nothing but skin and bone' because he had been one of those who were 'very forward in abusing the *Solemn League and Covenant*' on 29 May 1661.[120] Intriguingly, this account made its way to the Presbyterian Philip Henry, who, implying that he was reassured by the tale, described how Sacheverell had 'offended the prophane of ye Town' with his sermon.[121] Print was also deployed as a way of ridiculing ministers who 'hattered' Dissenters from the pulpit. In February 1681, the Whig activist Stephen Colledge challenged ministers who, on 30 January beforehand, could be heard '*Pelt-ing* pay them off, with [16]40 and [16]48 ... t[elling] the Hereticks plainly ... [that] the Martyrs Blood out did the *Blood of Jesus*'.[122] Even sermons might be used as a source of comfort for Dissenters on the anniversaries. It was for this reason, no doubt, that the Presbyterian Richard Heyrick used his 'thanksgiving' on 29 May 1663 to reassure his congregation that 'no weapon forged against you will prevail'.[123]

One fleeting moment during the Exclusion Crisis appears to have provided Dissenters with a rather more effective means of defending themselves on the anniversary of the Restoration. In the build-up to 29 May 1680, rumours spread that London's apprentices were planning on burning effigies of Oliver Cromwell and 'the rump' (i.e. a rump steak representing the 'Rump Parliament' that had condemned Charles I to death),[124] and were 'afterwards to have pull'd down both the Meeting-houses & Bawdy-howses in *London*'.[125] Having heard of the plans, London's Common Council, which was then dominated by Whigs who were sympathetic to dissent, rounded up the ringleaders and, in April, published an order for 'preventing Tumultuous disorders which happen hereafter on pretence of Assembling to make Bonefires and Publick Fireworks, and for Disappointing the Evil Designs of Persons Disaffected to the Government, who commonly make use of such Occasions to turn those Meetings into Riots and Tumults.'[126] That this was a remarkably successful exercise is reflected in the fact that Anthony Wood, a staunch Royalist, noted mournfully, and perhaps even resentfully, in his diary that 29 May 1680 had been 'forbidden at London'.[127] The conclusion to which we are drawn by the actions of the Common Council is that, far from being willing to acquiesce in the verbal and symbolic attacks upon them, Dissenters found ways of defending themselves from, or, at the very least, steeling themselves against, Royalist censure on the anniversaries. To be sure, it is likely that at least a handful of examples of absenteeism from church and other commemorative events on the anniversaries is representative of the avoidance of censorious sermons and other forms of public shaming.

MIS-COMMEMORATION AND SEDITIOUS MEMORIES

If Dissenters objected to the use of the anniversaries to censure them, then some of their number were almost certainly opposed to the interpretations of the civil wars and revolution in which that censure was couched. To be sure, Royalist onlookers had few doubts that lingering Parliamentarianism and republicanism were a, if not the, major cause of mis-commemoration. We have already met with Sir Roger L'Estrange's suspicions that the failure to attend church on the anniversaries belied the enthusiasm for fast days and days of thanksgiving in the 1640s and 1650s, many of which were appointed to commemorate Parliament's victories in the civil wars. Elsewhere, informants of mis-commemorative activity took the opportunity to cite the former Parliamentarian or republican allegiances of those who failed to attend anniversarial services or other events. When Edward Tucker, a woollen draper from Weymouth in Dorset, refused to shut his shop (with several others) on 30 January 1665, the agent who reported the indiscretion to Whitehall felt it necessary to point out that Tucker was 'formerly a Rump officer.'[128] Likewise, Thomas Jones, whose efforts to obstruct Towcester's annual commemorations of the Restoration were mentioned earlier, was labelled as 'formerly in actuall Armes against this prsent Government'.[129] So close was this association of mis-commemoration with erstwhile Parliamentarianism and republicanism that the failure of Dissenters to attend church on 30 January and 29 May was listed by one author as among the *'several things, which [they] do for the propagation of the good Old Cause'*.[130]

Given that the anniversaries became opportunities to conjure memories of the era 1637–60, it is hardly surprising that Royalists synonymised deviancy with the endurance of 'fanaticism'. And yet there is evidence to suggest that mis-commemoration did indeed embody seditious memories. It was reported on 30 January 1682, for instance, that Thomas Birch, the minister of Preston in Lancashire who 'doth not Christen Children According to ye forme and Custome of the Church', had been provoked into telling his curate that 'noe preaching should be on ye Kings martyrdome' as 'hee was not Convinced nor Satisfyed [tha]t ye late King was murdered but died by providence.'[131] Similar views were aired on the same day when a government informant visited the school of William Roberts at Southwark, Surrey. When Roberts was asked 'w[ha]t. made him keep schoole that day', being the anniversary of the regicide, he responded that 'he would work [tha]t. day rather than any other, and that [he] was a knave for saying King Charles was murthered being he had his tryall by due course of law And that the beheading of his late ma[jes]tie was the best deed that ever the Parliament did.'[132] Not all reflections on the justice of the regicide were expressed in public. Suggesting enduring identification with his own high-profile part in the regicide, Colonel John Hutchinson was provoked at some point in 1662 or 1663 to scrawl the words 'for the 30th of January' in his personal bible next to Hosea 4:11 ('whoredom and wine and new wine take away the heart').[133]

Objections to the central message of 30 January – that the regicide was a national sin – are unlikely to have been held beyond a coterie of the most radical former Parliamentarians and republicans. And yet further evidence implies that the broader attacks on the civil wars and revolution to which the anniversaries of 30 January and 29 May gave rise provoked seditious memories that looked beyond the events of 1648–49. On 30 January 1680, for instance, John Sherstone, a member of the corporation in Bath, Somerset, made his opinions about an earlier element of the wars in England abundantly clear during the anniversary sermon at the city's abbey. According to evidence that was provided against him, Sherstone took issue with commendatory references to Thomas Wentworth, Earl of Strafford, who was executed by Parliament in 1641, and Archbishop William Laud, who faced a similar fate in 1645, holding forth that 'I wonder Mr. Williams ... should speak in their commendation, when they were two of the greatest rogues in the kingdom.'[134] Here, the anniversary of the regicide led to contestation of an account of the early 1640s that, in the context of the Exclusion Crisis, was considerably more threatening to the authorities than may have been the case at other times of relative domestic peace.

Sympathies for Parliament and the Republic are rather more likely to have provoked mis-commemoration on 29 May, a day on which the regicide featured relatively less prominently than on 30 January. This is borne out by evidence of Dissenters who actively subverted the order to celebrate the anniversary by upholding an atmosphere of solemnity instead. This inversion is evident on two notable occasions during the reign of Charles II: on 29 May 1664, when it was recorded that Dissenters in London had 'generally lamented' the Restoration, and then fourteen years later, when Dissenters kept the day of thanksgiving as one of 'humiliation' in London.[135] Intriguing evidence from the diary of the Presbyterian Oliver Heywood suggests that the inversion of the celebratory mood of 29 May was not the recourse of those willing to resist the government. Writing on 29 May 1672, Heywood described how, having secured a license to preach as a result of the Declaration of Indulgence, 'we had a private fast in my meeting-house, the first week-day fast we had there'.[136]

In Scotland, opposition to commemoration of 29 May was explicitly associated with the way in which the so-called Work of Reformation had been censured by the government since the Restoration. Referring to the censorious language of the 1661 act concerning 29 May, the Presbyterian John Brown of Wamphray argued in 1665 'That none could so much as preach on that day or give any countenance to [the act], unlesse they would condemn all which had been done for twenty three yeers space, in carrying on of the work of Reformation, as being the height of treachery & rebellion, designedly & purposely carryed on, under the specious pretexts of Reformation'.[137] Echoing Brown's criticisms, the rebels of 1679 included a reference in their declaration to the anniversary as having 'given Glory to the Creature that is due to our Lord Redeemer, and rejoiced over the setting up an usurping Power to the destroying the Interest of Christ in the Land.'[138] Others objected to the burning of the Covenants, an activity that was as common on the anniversary of the Restoration in Scotland as it was in England and Wales. In 1662, for instance, one pamphlet responded in verse to the notorious destruction of the Solemn League and Covenant on the first anniversary of the Restoration, entreating the reader to remember that 'Poor *Scotland* thy great Glory was, / Thy Covenanting times / Tho afterwerd by Backslidings; / They were accounted Crimes.'[139]

As this case suggests, the inversions of 29 May as a day of mourning or humiliation are comparable to a form of seditious remembering that has been encountered throughout this book: namely, the idea that, since the Restoration, the Stuart realms had experienced military, economic, and (especially) spiritual decline, and indeed 'Backslidings' from the courageous, prosperous, and godly era of the 1640s and 1650s. That the anniversary of the Restoration was liable to provoke this sentiment is evident in efforts by ministers from within the Church of England and beyond to dissuade their flocks from nostalgia. Preaching on the anniversary in 1673, for instance, one unnamed Devonian minister went to considerable lengths to remind his congregation of 'what our condition was' in the 1650s and how, while 'some things did please *a part* of these Nations, yet the *whole body* reeled to and fro as having no firm ground to stand upon.' The minister concluded that the Restoration was evidence that 'it pleased God himself to interpose, and *to prepare a way in the Desart*, a way where none was.'[140] Elsewhere in Devon, the former Royalist Thomas Long injected a dose of realism into his sermon at Exeter on 29 May 1681, enjoining his audience to 'Say not thou, What is the cause that the former days were better than these? for thou dost not enquire wisely concerning this.'[141]

Not all ministers were as diligent as Long in dissuading nostalgia. Others appear to have gone to some lengths to accentuate how far the four kingdoms had descended since the Restoration. Ralph Josselin, the Essex minister who retained his living after the ejection of Nonconformist ministers in 1662, was nonetheless moved to use his sermon on 30 January 1662 to speak on Jeremiah 3:22, beseeching his congregation to 'Return, ye backsliding children, and I will heal your backslidings'.[142] Josselin's implied nostalgia for the revolution took a rather more explicit form exactly two years later when Francis Griffin, an inhabitant of Taunton, spent the fast not in church or at home, but propping up the bar in a local alehouse. It was alleged, in fact, that Griffin sang the Parliamentarian song *Essex's March*, an act that elicited complaints from at least one of those present. Defiantly, Griffin 'fell on vindicating Oliver Cromewell', to which the informant of his words 'bid him forebeare speaking any more of a fellow that was buried under the Gallowes'. Griffin responded to this effort to censor him with the words 'Cromwell was as Good a man as the King'.[143] It is possible that the nostalgia for the revolution that is evident in these cases influenced the decisions of others to stray from the spirits of 'humiliation' and 'thanksgiving' in which 30 January and 29 May were supposed to have been conducted, leading them to avoid anniversarial services and other forms of public commemoration.

By highlighting the discrepancy between past and present, nostalgia was particularly concerning to the Restoration government, who saw these memories as having the potential to inspire rebellion. Other evidence suggests that these concerns were merited. The famous Covenanter rebellion of 1679 not only began on the anniversary of the Restoration, it was also ushered in by the burning of both 'the Act appointing an anniversary of 29 May' and that for burning the Solemn League and Covenant.[144] A fascinating incident from Bristol suggests that the anniversary of the regicide may have inspired the disorder that broke out there on 30 January 1680. It was reported by the *London Gazette* that fifty or sixty 'young Fellows (most of them Carpenters) ... marched together in a tumultuous manner through some of our principle Streets' on the anniversary, 'one of them bearing on his shoulder a great wooden Ax, painted red, with a Lyon carved thereon ... and drawing a multitude after them, to the great Terror of all His Majesties Loyal Subjects here'.[145] Although the local militia intervened, and some of the participants were arrested, the events provoked a brief period of moral panic.[146]

Interpretations of the riot have tended to overlook the significance of the date, choosing instead to focus on how it 'ar[ose] from an old disorderly Custome' on Shrove Tuesday in which 'the Free Carpinders of the Citty ... goe through the Towne to search out all ... who use that trade & are not Freemen'.[147] That the riot occurred just over three weeks before Shrove Tuesday in 1680, and that the rioters chose to carry a red axe, suggests that there was more to the symbolism of the riots than these accounts suggest.

The case of the Bristol apprentices on 30 January 1680 reinforces the idea that alternative opinions about the execution of Charles I were not the preserve of those who wished to see his son befall the same fate. On the contrary, this extraordinary case suggests that the inextricability of memory and authority imbued counter-memories with efficacy as forms of cultural resistance (see chapter 4). Speculatively, this interpretation of seditious memories may help to explain one of the most famous, but least credited, episodes of remembering from the late seventeenth century: the Calves Head Club. Rumours of the existence of the club emerged in the 1690s when it was reported by pamphlets such as the *Secret History of the Calves-Head Club* that its membership engaged in bizarre acts on 30 January as a means of expressing their support for the verdict of the High Court of Justice in 1649. Most memorably, it was claimed that members of the club dined on a selection of offal, including a calf's head, which represented that of Charles I. Historians have given little credence to the notion that the club existed, and Richard L. Greaves, one of the most prominent historians of Restoration radicalism, concluded that such rumours were 'preposterous'.[148] Elsewhere, Michelle Orihel has depicted the club as a literary fiction that was used by the Tories to 'discredit [their] enemies by connecting them to the regicide.'[149]

It could be argued that to locate any truth in the activities of the Calves Head Club is to stretch credulity about seditious memories to breaking point. What is striking, however, is that accounts of the club in the 1690s were not the first, and, in terms of detail, closely followed those provided in 1685 by Colonel John Rumsey, a former New Model Army officer who had been imprisoned for participation in the Monmouth Rebellion of that summer and the Rye House Plot two years earlier. From prison, Rumsey provided some two thousand words of information concerning 'every discourse that ever I had with my Lord Stamford', another of the Monmouth rebels, which included an account of an annual gathering on the 30 January to which Rumsey had been invited, at a 'blind taverne' in London's Watling Street, by fellow plotter Robert West. Rumsey explained that 'when I came into the chamber the table was covered and noething but heads'. Among Rumsey's list of attendees (which, together with some who were unknown to Rumsey, numbered as many as twenty) were a range of men with connections to the radical Whig cause, including West (the chairman), Sir Walter Yonge, Richard Duke, John Trenchard, John Freke, Richard Goodenough, Nathaniel Wade, John Row, and Robert Blaney. Rumsey explained that his fellow diners 'told me the meaning and magnified the deed [i.e. the regicide] and the Glorious Men that did it and Dranke health to theyr memory', before drinking another health to those who should assassinate 'the two sparks his sons [i.e. Charles II and James, Duke of York]'. Rumsey concluded that 'there was severall such meeting[s] in London and they had bene keepe ever since the Restauration of the Royall Family'.[150]

Rumsey's inclusion of this information as an addendum to earlier statements – because, as he put it, it had been 'drove out' of his thoughts – might lead us to question its authenticity.[151] Nonetheless, it is perhaps significant that most of those to whom Rumsey referred had more or less conspicuous links with the Parliamentarian and republican causes. Yonge, Duke, Trenchard, and Wade all had Parliamentarian fathers, while Robert Blaney was the son-in-law of Parliamentarian antiquarian John Rushworth. Richard Goodenough, meanwhile, was hauled before the Privy Council in 1683 for expressing his own sympathies with those who had overthrown the Stuarts in the 1640s.[152] The bizarreness of the Calves Head Club ritual makes it an improbable feature of the late seventeenth century. Yet, given the extent of mis-commemorative activity on the anniversary of the regicide, and the degree to which the events of 1649 continued to be contested, it is possible that the spirit, if not the letter, of Rumsey's evidence against the Calves Head Club was truthful. If nothing else, Colonel Rumsey's mythical club may have been confected from examples of genuine, and much less bizarre, forms of mis-commemoration of 30 January 'ever since the Restauration of the Royall Family.'

CONCLUSION

This chapter has demonstrated the extent to which the anniversaries of the regicide and Restoration were mis-commemorated during the reign of Charles II. In contrast to the image that historians have painted of the obedience of subjects on 30 January and 29 May, there are numerous cases of men and women who did not live up to the expectations of behaviour as set out by the acts and proclamations of 1660–62. Instead, these individuals refused to close their places of business, abstained from attending church, and failed to participate in other public rituals, such as processions and bonfires. Since those who mis-commemorated came from diverse political and religious backgrounds, the reasons for this behaviour are numerous and cannot be explained with recourse to a single motivation. Nevertheless, objections that derived from Puritan scruples and experiences of Royalist recrimination were evidently at the forefront. Moreover, that both dates gave rise to a narrow conception of conformity to church and state meant that sermons and other displays of loyalty were appropriated as fora for the articulation of political and religious grievances that, in turn, may account for other forms of mis-commemoration. On some occasions, and reflecting the wellspring of seditious memories to which previous chapters have referred, mis-commemoration resulted from differences of opinion about the events that were being remembered. Indeed, the tendency for the pulpit, press, and pavement to act as fora for lambasting Dissenters for their role (perceived or otherwise) in the revolution of the 1630s, 1640s, and 1650s resulted in countervailing justification of, nostalgia for, and identification with the Covenants, Parliamentarianism, and republicanism.

That, in some instances, mis-commemoration embodied seditious memories suggests that we can look beyond speech and writing for the articulation of political and religious opinion in early modern Britain.[153] In a society where sedition and treason were to an unprecedented extent defined by what one said and wrote, what people did or, perhaps, *what they did not do* can tell us a great deal about what they thought. Distinguishing too starkly between action and inaction is clearly not always helpful, though. As we have seen in this chapter, there was a considerable 'grey area' between commemoration and mis-commemoration that was defined by extremes of unenthusiastic obedience (such as of Thomas Jolly and others who were 'enjoyned' by authority to commemorate) and unintentional disobedience (as characterised by the forgetfulness of Ralph Josselin and Samuel Pepys). And yet it is from within this ambiguous space that some of the most intriguing possibilities about Restoration Britain emerge. The pains of hard-line Royalists to recall the 'rebellion' and 'usurpation' of 'fanatics' are less suggestive of how 'popular' their memories were than they are of their terror at the consequences of forgetting. After all, it was this anxiety that drove their opposition to oblivion in 1660 and their seizure of the authority to speak for the past thereafter. That, as we have seen, there were numerous objections to their appropriation of commemoration after the Restoration suggests that the pursuit of mnemonic hegemony by Royalists was necessarily doomed to failure. By raking over the coals of war and revolution, the anniversaries of the regicide and Restoration, like the Royalist interpretation of recent history itself, encouraged the perpetuation of the very identities that Royalists sought to forestall. Most troublingly of all for Royalists was that 'fanaticism' was perpetuated among a generation of people who, like some of those who Colonel Rumsey implicated as members of the Calves Head Club, were too young to have served Parliament or the Republic. It is to these men and women that the final chapter of this book attends.

NOTES

1 See, for instance, Stoyle, 'Remembering the English Civil Wars', pp. 19–30.
2 B. S. Stewart, 'The Cult of the Royal Martyr', *Church History*, 38:2 (Jun., 1969), 175–187; K. Sharpe, '"So Hard a Text"? Images of Charles I, 1612–1700', *Historical Journal*, 43:2 (Jun., 2000), 394–397; A. Lacey, *The Cult of King Charles the Martyr* (Woodbridge: Boydell, 2003), pp. 129–171; and Neufeld, *Civil Wars after 1660*, p. 241.

3 L. Potter, 'The Royal Martyr in the Restoration: National Grief and National Sin', in T. N. Corns (ed.), *The Royal Image: Representations of Charles I* (Cambridge: Cambridge University Press, 1999), p. 247; and Lacey, *Cult of King Charles*, pp. 148–149, 164–165, 248.
4 D. Cressy, *Bonfires and Bells: National Memory and the Protestant Calendar in Elizabethan and Stuart England* (London: Weidenfeld and Nicolson, 1989), p. 187.
5 B. Klein, '"Between the Bums and the Bellies of the Multitude": Civic Pageantry and the Problem of the Audience in Late Stuart London', *London Journal: A Review of Metropolitan Society Past and Present*, 17 (1992), 18–26; and E. Tierney, 'Strategies for Celebration: Realising the Ideal Celebratory City in London and Paris, 1660–1715' (unpublished PhD dissertation, University of Sussex, 2012).
6 D. Cressy, *Society and Culture in Early Modern England* (Aldershot: Ashgate, 2003), pp. 38–39.
7 Connerton, *How Societies Remember*, ch. 2.
8 R. Higgins, *Transforming 1916: Meaning, Memory and the Fiftieth Anniversary of the Easter Rising* (Cork: Cork University Press, 2012), pp. 4, 22.
9 'An Act for a Perpetuall Anniversary Thanksgiving on the nine and twentyeth day of May', 12 Car. II, c. 14 (1660), *Statutes of the Realm*, v, p. 237.
10 'An Act for the Attainder of severall persons guilty of the horrid Murther of his late Sacred Majestie King Charles the first', 12 Car. II, c. 30, *Statutes of the Realm*, v, pp. 288–290.
11 Lacey, *Cult of King Charles*, p. 130.
12 [Charles II], *By the King. A PROCLAMATION, For Observation of the Thirtieth day of January as a day of Fast and Humiliation according to the late Act of Parliament for that purpose* (London, 166[1]); and [Charles II], *By the King. A PROCLAMATION, For the observation of the Nine and twentieth day of May instant, as a day of Publick Thanksgiving, according to the late Act of Parliament for that purpose* (London, 1661).
13 NAS, PA2/26, fols 297–298, 'Act for a solemn anniversary thanksgiving for his majesty's restitution to his royal government etc.'; and 'Act for a perpetual anniversary thanksgiving on the nine and twentieth day of May in this kingdom'.
14 [Charles II], *PROCLAMATION, For Observation of the Thirtieth day of January*, p. 3.
15 *Ibid.*, p. 2.
16 *Ibid.*, p. 3.
17 [Charles II], *PROCLAMATION, For the observation of the Nine and twentieth day of May*, p. 2.
18 *Ibid.*, p. 3.
19 [Charles II], *PROCLAMATION, For Observation of the Thirtieth day of January*, p. 1.
20 *Ibid.*, pp. 1–2.
21 [Charles II], *PROCLAMATION, For the observation of the Nine and twentieth day of May*, p. 1.
22 *Ibid.*, pp. 1–2.
23 Pepys, *Diary*, ii, p. 26.
24 Henry, *Diaries*, pp. 166, 236.

25 Mary Rich, Countess of Warwick, *Memoir of Lady Warwick: Also Her Diary from A.D. 1666 to 1672, Now First Published*, ed. A. Walker (London: Religious Tract Society, 1847), p. 197.
26 Brodie and Brodie, *Diary*, p. 239.
27 R. L. Greaves, 'Henry, Philip (1631–1696)', in *ODNB*, xxvi, pp. 587–588. See also Achinstein, *Literature and Dissent*, p. 86.
28 Muir, 'Brodie, Alexander, of Brodie'.
29 Pepys, *Diary*, i, p. 225n.
30 TNA, SP29/113/63, I.
31 Josselin, *Diary*, pp. 480, 486.
32 *Ibid.*, p. 495.
33 *Ibid.*, p. 628.
34 John Evelyn, *The Diary of John Evelyn*, ed. E. S. De Beer (6 vols, Oxford: Clarendon, 1955), iv, p. 204.
35 Whitelocke, *Diary*, p. 625.
36 *Ibid.*, pp. 642, 649.
37 *Ibid.*, pp. 683, 810.
38 Brodie and Brodie, *Diary*, pp. 239, 420.
39 See, for instance, *ibid.*, pp. 287, 325.
40 Heywood, *Diaries*, ii, p. 115.
41 Pepys, *Diary*, vi, p. 25.
42 *Ibid.*, iv, p. 29; v, pp. 30–31; vi, p. 25; viii, p. 37; ix, pp. 42–43, 216–217.
43 *Ibid.*, viii, p. 37.
44 See, for instance, Whitelocke, *Diary*, pp. 705, 789, 795, 806.
45 TNA, SP29/56/134.
46 Henry, *Diaries*, p. 138.
47 *Newes* (4 February 1664).
48 *CSPD, 1675–76*, p. 536.
49 *Ibid.*, p. 536.
50 TNA, SP29/55/16.
51 TNA, SP29/50/22.
52 *Kingdomes Intelligencer* (4–11 February 1661).
53 Hines, *Newdigate*, 278 (20 January 1675).
54 NAS, PA2/28, fols 8v–9, 'Proclamation for the anniversary thanksgiving'.
55 Brown, *Apologeticall Relation*, p. 88.
56 *RPCS, 1661–64*, p. 270.
57 *RPCS, 1669–72*, p. 347.
58 *RPCS, 1672–73*, pp. 71–73, 83, 101–102.
59 Raffe, *Culture of Controversy*, p. 225.
60 Pepys, *Diary*, iv, p. 29.
61 Heywood, *Diaries*, ii, p. 84.
62 TNA, SP29/422/68.
63 With thanks to Tim Somers for this information. For a discussion of the use of *pro formas* and tickets as a tool of mass organisation during the English Revolution, see J. Peacey, *Print and Public Politics in the English Revolution* (Cambridge: Cambridge University Press, 2013), pp. 334–338.
64 TNA, SP29/422/56.

65 TNA, SP20/424/133.
66 TNA, SP29/145/32, I.
67 *A Full and True ACCOUNT of the PROCEEDINGS AT THE Sessions of Oyer and Terminer, Holdern for the City of London, County of Middlesex, and Goal-Delivery of Newgate; WHICH BEGAN AT THE SESSIONS-House in the Old-Baily, On Wednesday, Septemb. 6th. and Ended on Thursday, Septemb. 7th.* 1682 (London, 1682), p. 4. For a similar case, see *THE TRYALS OF THE PRISONERS AT THE SESSIONS Holdern in the Sessions-House in the Old-Baily. Which began on the Twelfth of July, 1682 and ended the Thirteenth of the same Month* (London, 1682), p. 2.
68 P[eter] Mews, *VVHEREAS Tuesday next, being the Thirtieth day of this instant January* (Oxford, 167[2]).
69 Pepys, *Diary*, vii, p. 136.
70 Anthony Wood, *The Life and Times of Anthony Wood, Antiquary of Oxford, 1632–1695*, ed. A. Clark (5 vols, Oxford: Clarendon, 1891–1900), iii, p. 16.
71 R. Hutton, *Stations of the Sun: A History of the Ritual Year in Britain* (Oxford: Oxford University Press, 1996), p. 289.
72 Thomas Jolly, *The Note Book of the Rev. Thomas Jolly, A.D. 1671–1693*, ed. H. Fishwick (Manchester: Chetham Society, 1894), p. 11.
73 *Ibid.*, p. 39.
74 E. B. Underhill (ed.), *The Records of a Church of Christ, Meeting in Broadmead, Bristol. 1640–1687* (London: J. Haddon, 1847), p. 456.
75 Jolly, *Note Book*, p. 7.
76 Brodie and Brodie, *Diary*, p. 420.
77 Josselin, *Diary*, p. 508.
78 [Henry Hammond,] *Private Forms of Prayer, Fitted for the late Sad-Times. Particularly, A Form of Prayer for THE Thirtieth of January, Morning and Evening* (London, 166[1]); *A FORM OF PRAYER, WITH THANKSGIVING To be used Of all the Kings MAJESTIE'S Loving Subjects The 29th May Yearly, For His MAJESTIE'S Happy Return to His KINGDOMS, It being also the Day of His Birth* (London, 1661); *THE BOOK OF COMMON-PRAYER, AND Administration of the Sacraments, and other Rites and Ceremonies of the CHURCH, According to the Use OF THE CHURCH OF ENGLAND, Together with the Psalter or Psalms OF DAVID, Pointed as they are to be Sung or Said in CHURCHES* (London, 1662).
79 Raffe, *Culture of Controversy*, ch. 7.
80 Brodie and Brodie, *Diary*, p. 356.
81 *Ibid.*, p. 299.
82 [Gilbert Burnet], *A MODEST AND FREE CONFERENCE BETWIXT a Conformist and Non-conformist, about the Present Distempers of Scotland* (n.p., 1669), pp. 9–10.
83 *RPCS, 1673–76*, pp. 101–102.
84 Henry, *Diaries*, pp. 283–284.
85 Brodie and Brodie, *Diary*, p. 299.
86 Ralph Thoresby, *The Diary of Ralph Thoresby, F.R.S.: Author of the Topography of Leeds (1677–1724.)*, ed. J. Hunter (2 vols, London: Henry Colburn and Richard Bentley, 1830), i, pp. 45–46.
87 Henry Newcome, *The Diary of the Rev. Henry Newcome, from September 30, 1661,*

to September 29, 1663, ed. T. Heywood (Manchester: Chetham Society, 1849), p. 91.
88 *Newes* (4 February 1664).
89 [Cockayne, et al.], *MIRABILIS ANNUS, OR, The year of Prodigies and Wonders*, p. 56.
90 Newcome, *Diary*, p. 51.
91 M. A. Lower, *The Worthies of Sussex: Biographical Sketches of the Most Eminent Natives or Inhabitants of the County, from the Earliest Period to the Present Time* (Lewes: G. P. Bacon, 1865), p. 328.
92 Brodie and Brodie, *Diary*, p. 255.
93 TNA, SP29/422/67.
94 Keblusek, 'Wine for Comfort', p. 63; and A. J. McShane, 'Roaring Royalists and Ranting Brewers: The Politicisation of Drink and Drunkenness in Political Broadside Ballads from 1640 to 1689', in Smyth, *Pleasing Sinne*, pp. 69–87.
95 TNA, SP29/432/38.
96 *Kingdomes Intelligencer* (1 February 1664).
97 A. B. Hinds (ed.), *Calendar of State Papers and Manuscripts relating to English Affairs, existing in the Archives of Venice, and in other libraries of Northern Italy*, vol. xxxii, 1661–1664 (London: HMSO, 1932), p. 286, cited in Lacey, *Cult of King Charles*, p. 164.
98 See Josselin, *Diary*, p. 501.
99 Lacey, *Cult of King Charles*, p. 137.
100 Thomas Stanhope, *FOUR SERMONS Preached upon Solemne Occasions* (London, 1670), p. 62.
101 Heywood, *Diaries*, ii, p. 54.
102 *Ibid.*, ii, p. 84.
103 Henry, *Diaries*, p. 299.
104 Josselin, *Diary*, p. 641.
105 Evelyn, *Diary*, iii, p. 429.
106 *Ibid.*, pp. 105, 163.
107 *Ibid.*, p. 381.
108 Anthony Wood, *Life and Times*, iii, p. 35.
109 *Journals of the House of Commons. From April the 25th 1660, to July the 29th 1667, In the Nineteenth Year of the Reign of King Charles the Second* (n.p., 1803), p. 256.
110 *Kingdomes Intelligencer* (3–10 June 1661).
111 *Ibid.*
112 *Loyal Protestant and True Domestick Intelligence* (8 June 1682).
113 *Observator in Dialogue* (19 September 1683).
114 *Kingdomes Intelligencer* (3–10 June 1661).
115 *Ibid.*
116 *Observator in Dialogue* (8 June 1682).
117 'Act for a solemn anniversary thanksgiving'.
118 [Robert McWard], *The True NON-CONFORMIST in Answere to the Modest and Free Conference Betwixt a CONFORMIST and a NON-CONFORMIST, About the present Distempers of SCOTLAND* (n.p., 1671), pp. 32–34.
119 [Cockayne, et al.], *MIRABILIS ANNUS, OR The year of Prodigies and Wonders*, p. 56.

120 [Cockayne, et al.], SECOND PART OF THE SECOND YEARS PRODIGIES, p. 47.
121 Henry, *Diaries*, p. 104.
122 [Stephen Colledge], *A True Copy OF A LETTER (intercepted) going for Holland, Directed Thus For his (and his Wives) never Failing Friend Roger Le Strange At the Oranges Court with Care and Speed, hast, hast, post hast* (London, 168[1]), p. 2.
123 Newcome, *Diary*, p. 188.
124 A. J. McShane, 'The Roasting of the Rump: Scatology and the Body Politic in Restoration England', *Past & Present*, 196:1 (2007), 253–272.
125 *Mercurius Civicus or A True Account of Affairs Both Foreign and Domestick* (24 March 1680).
126 *Protestant (Domestick) Intelligence or News Both from City and Country* (13 April 1680).
127 Anthony Wood, *Life and Times*, ii, p. 487.
128 TNA, SP29/111/103.
129 TNA, SP29/145/32, I.
130 [John Birkenhead], *CABALA, OR AN Impartial Account OF THE NON-CONFORMISTS Private Designs, Actings and Wayes from August 24. 1662 to December 25. in the Same Year* (London, 1663), pp. 36–37; see also *The Occasional Doctor HIS EXAMINATION BEFORE A Committee of Whigg-Priests* (n.p., [1682?]), p. [1].
131 TNA, SP29/429/233.
132 TNA, SP29/421/162.
133 Norbrook, 'Memoirs and Oblivion', 275.
134 *CSPD, Jan.–June 1683*, pp. 60–61.
135 TNA, SP29/99/7; and TNA, SP29/404/90.
136 Heywood, *Diaries*, i, p. 290.
137 Brown, *Apologeticall Relation*, p. 89.
138 Wodrow, *History of the Sufferings* (1721), ii, p. 45.
139 *A Dismal Account of the Burning of our Solemn LEAGUE and National COVENANT* (n.p., 1662), p. [2].
140 *A SERMON Preach'd on May the 29th. 1673. IN ONE OF His Majesties LICENS'D MEETINGS in DEVON* (London, 1673), p. 19.
141 Neufeld, *Civil Wars after 1660*, p. 220.
142 Josselin, *Diary*, p. 486.
143 SHC, Q/SR105, fol. 35r.
144 *CSPD, 1679–80*, p. 169.
145 *London Gazette* (29 January–2 February [1680]), p. 2.
146 See, for instance, Narcissus Luttrell, *A Brief Historical Relation of State Affairs from September 1678 to April 1714. By Narcissus Luttrell* (6 vols, Oxford: Oxford University Press, 1857), i, p. 33.
147 Hines, *Newdigate*, 896 (5 February 1679). See also J. Barry, 'Popular Culture in Seventeenth-Century Bristol', in B. Reay (ed.), *Popular Culture in Seventeenth-Century England* (London: Croom Helm, 1985), p. 74.
148 Greaves, *Secrets of the Kingdom*, p. 135.
149 M. Orihel, '"Treacherous Memories" of Regicide: The Calves-Head Club in the Age of Anne', *Historian*, 73:3 (2011), 438.

150 British Library, London (hereafter BL), Lansdowne MS 1152, fols 249v–250v.
151 *Ibid.*, 249v.
152 *CSPD, 1683*, pp. 381–384.
153 M. J. Braddick (ed.), *The Politics of Gesture: Historical Perspectives* (Oxford: Oxford University Press, 2009); and E. Vallance, 'The Captivity of James II: Gestures of Loyalty and Disloyalty in Seventeenth-Century England', *Journal of British Studies*, 48:4 (Oct., 2009), 848–858.

Chapter 8

Seditious memories across generations

Through speech, writing, and mis-commemoration, people from across the Stuart realms articulated opinions about the civil wars and revolutions that were deemed by the authorities to be seditious and unlawful. The risks taken to articulate these views connote the degree to which certain political and religious identities were bound up with a sense that various aspects of opposition to, and resistance against, the Crown and established church had been legitimate. And yet some of the Parliamentarian and republican sympathies that exist in the archive, including some of those encountered so far in this book, were expressed by people whose experiences of 1637–60, if they existed at all, were those of children or teenagers. This chapter begins by illustrating that individuals who are unlikely to have been politically active during the civil wars and revolution – a group that I describe as the 'Restoration generation' – were enamoured nonetheless by the opposition and resistance that occurred during that era. This identification with Parliament and the Commonwealth is viewed as having derived from the experiences that proved formative to this generation: namely, anxieties about the threat to parliament and Protestants that took the form of an absolutist monarch (Charles II), his Roman Catholic heir (James, Duke of York), and what were, by the estimation of many of their subjects, persistent attempts by so-called 'papists' to commit bloodshed on British soil.[1] Building on the work of Gary De Krey, the defence of these institutions from 'popery' and 'arbitrary government' before 1660 is taken to have been inspirational among a new generation of men and women thereafter.[2]

The remainder of the chapter is devoted to interrogating the issue that arises from this analysis: how was it that the Restoration generation came to sympathise with Covenants, Parliament, and the Republic when, as we have seen, these symbols were subjected to public and social delegitimisation after 1660? In order to answer this question, inspiration is taken from recent studies of 'cultural' memory, or what Jan Assmann terms 'the store of knowledge from which a group derives an awareness of its unity and peculiarity.'[3] Correspondingly, social milieux, including familial and political networks, and the preponderance of former Parliamentarians and republicans within them, are identified as having offered touchpoints between the Restoration generation and seditious or unlawful memories. This entails research into the social networks of notable individuals, such as the Whig activist Stephen Colledge, but also the interrogation of evidence that exposes the very moments at which alternative opinions about the civil wars and revolution were transmitted between the older and younger generations. Finally, the chapter moves on to consider how, in addition to orality, scribal and print culture were also responsible for the passage of Parliamentarian and republican sympathies from one generation to the next.

SEDITIOUS MEMORIES AND GENERATION

Seditious memories were sometimes expressed by people who were born after the events to which those memories referred. One of these was Strange Southby, a scholar who was denied his degree from the University of Oxford in June 1682 for contending a year beforehand that the regicide 'was a glorious action, and done in the face of the nation' since 'the common fame was that the old king was a man of ill principles'. Contradicting those who laid blame for the civil wars at the door of the Long Parliament, Southby added that 'he would not excuse' either Charles I or Charles II from the 'guilt' of that conflict.[4] Southby, who was described as 'a green ribband man' – that is, a member of the radical Green Ribbon Club – had matriculated at Magdalen Hall, Oxford, in April 1674 aged seventeen, and was thus only a toddler when Charles II returned to his kingdoms in 1660.[5] Given low life expectancy, the likelihood is that others who were guilty of sharing these kinds of opinions, including some of those mentioned earlier in this book, were born after the events to which they referred. The demographic data that the haberdasher John Graunt compiled in 1662 suggests that only forty per cent of Londoners who were born sixteen years beforehand (in 1646) were still alive. The cohort that had been born in 1636, meanwhile, had, by 1662, reduced to almost one quarter.[6] If this rate of depletion is transposed to 1681, the year in which Strange Southby uttered his views about the regicide, we can speculate that about three quarters of London's population would have been his age or younger. This proportion is likely to be significantly higher given the demographic shock of the plague in 1665.[7]

In the case of Strange Southby and any others of his age group who sympathised with Parliament or the Republic, the events to which their seditious memories referred fell beyond the horizon of lived experience. Rather than civil war and revolution in the 1640s and 1650s, fears for parliaments and Protestants during the decades that followed proved formative to these men and women. Of particular importance to them were the alleged 'firing' of London in 1666, the pursuit of a Francophile foreign policy by Charles II, the revelation that his brother, James, Duke of York, was a Roman Catholic, the 'arbitrary' proceedings of his chief minister, Thomas Osborne, Earl of Danby, and the Popish Plot revelations of 1678.[8] Using the sociologist Karl Mannheim's definition of generations, these events constituted the 'specific range of potential experience' that 'predispos[ed] them for a certain characteristic mode of thought and experience, and a characteristic type of historically relevant action.'[9] In this instance, the 'historically relevant action' was the defence of parliaments and Protestantism from the twin threats of 'popery' and 'arbitrary government' that culminated in the deposal of the Duke of York, then James II, from the throne in 1688–89.

To what we might refer as the 'Restoration generation', then, seditious memories, like those of Strange Southby, became meaningful amid the crises of Charles II's reign.[10] Defined as such, the generation can be extended to encompass people who were born earlier than the 1650s. One of these is the satirist John Ayloffe (or Ayliffe), who was born in 1645 and matriculated at Oxford two years after the Restoration.[11] Despite his youth, Ayloffe is held to have authored *A Dialogue between Two Horses* in late 1675, a poem that is replete with explicitly favourable references to Parliament and the Commonwealth.[12] Ayloffe contrived the poem's dialogue as taking place between the horses of Charles I and Charles II as they were depicted in equestrian statues at Charing Cross in Westminster and St Mary Woolnoth in the City of London, respectively. In an attention-grabbing act of street theatre, copies of the poem were attached to the statues in early December 1675, making public thereby their seditious content. The statue of Charles II's horse – notable for trampling a likeness of Oliver Cromwell[13] – began by asking mockingly, 'where is thy King gone?' to which his counterpart in the City answered, 'to see Bishop Laud'. The Charing Cross horse probed further: 'What has thou to say against my royal rider [i.e. Charles I]?', to which Woolnoth replied that 'Thy priest-ridden King turn'd desperate fighter / For the surplice, lawn sleeves, the cross, and the mitre, / Till at last on the scaffold he was left in the lurch / By knaves that cri'd up themselves for the Church.'[14] This strikingly candid account of Charles I and the Arminian Revolution of the 1630s was followed by a comparison between father and son: 'Though father and son be different rods, / Between the two scourges we find little odds. / Both infamous stand in three kingdoms' votes: / This for picking our pockets, that for cutting our throats.' The Charing Cross horse went further, comparing his royal rider unfavourably with Oliver Cromwell, who 'had ... a brave soul'. To this Woolnoth agreed, arguing, 'I freely declare, I am for old Noll. / Though his government did a tyrant's resemble, / He made England great and its enemies tremble.'[15] The poem closed with a declaration for 'A commonwealth! a commonwealth!' since 'gods have repented the King's

Restoration',[16] and a warning that 'they that conquer'd the father won't be slaves to the son.'[17]

A Dialogue between Two Horses incorporated the main forms of seditious remembering to which this book has referred: justification of, and identification with, Parliament's opposition and resistance in the 1640s and the establishment of a Commonwealth thereafter; unfavourable, and possibly nostalgic, comparisons between Oliver Cromwell and his royal successor; and the (implied) prospection of the restoration of the Commonwealth. As a young teenager, it is likely that Ayloffe was able to remember the final years of the revolution, but it is improbable that the political and religious significance of those events became evident to him until after the Restoration. This is probably also true of three individuals whose references to Ayloffe's pamphlet suggest their sympathies for its content. One of these was Edward Stysted (or Stisted), who was accused in December 1675 of crediting Ayloffe's account, which he had seen at the statue of Charles II near St Mary Woolnoth.[18] Stysted had only been admitted to the Middle Temple two years beforehand, suggesting that he was probably younger even than Ayloffe.[19] Further up the social scale, Theophilus Hastings, Earl of Huntingdon, who was born in 1650, was sent a transcript of the poem by his younger sister, Mary. Huntingdon was a supporter of the exclusion of the Duke of York, and his brother-in-law, Mary's husband Sir William Joliffe (born 1622), was the son of a man who had served the Commonwealth, implying that the siblings identified with the content of Ayloffe's pamphlet.[20] This is borne out by Mary's apparent caginess in sending a short passage of the satire to her brother, telling him of her concerns that 'the letters are sometimes opened'.[21]

The case of another notable publicist of seditious memories, the Whig activist Stephen Colledge, invites us to extend the breadth of the Restoration generation to include individuals who were born even earlier than Ayloffe. Colledge was a joiner by trade who, from at least the late 1670s, moonlighted as the author of numerous critical satires of the established church, court, and royal family.[22] Eventually, Colledge's scurrilous output brought him to the attention of a government that, by 1681, was prepared to exert the full force of the law against those who were identified as exhibiting 'fanatic' principles. Having audaciously attended the Oxford Parliament of March 1681 armed and wearing a full suit of armour, and disseminated seditious material on his arrival, Colledge was hauled before the Middlesex grand jury in July 1681 on a sedition charge. Packed with sympathetic tradesmen, the jury acquitted the joiner, although he was tried for a second time, convicted, and then executed at Oxford in late August.

The government's case against Colledge was entirely in keeping with the anti-fanatical claims of hard-line Royalists and Tories that sympathies for Parliamentarianism – including those that explicitly condemned the regicide – were *ipso facto* representative of treasonable intent (see chapter 2). The prosecution called Mr Masters, a neighbour of Colledge, who testified that he had heard the joiner justifying the actions of the Long Parliament in levying war against Charles I. Masters recalled that, around Christmas 1680, Colledge had vindicated 'the late long Parliament['s] Actions in 1640' and had said that 'That Parliament was as good a Parliament as ever was chosen in the Nation'. Damningly, when Masters had reproved Colledge for these words, and what he felt was an implicit justification of the regicide, the joiner responded that 'They did nothing but what they had just Cause for, and the Parliament that sate last at *Westminster* was of their Opinion'.[23]

Colledge's failure to acknowledge that a defence of the Long Parliament was necessarily a defence of the regicide was referred to on several occasions at his trial, not merely as a means of imputing treasonable intent to him, but also of casting doubt on his understanding of the civil wars. One of his judges, Sir Thomas Jones, who was a Royalist in the first civil war, accused Colledge of 'mak[ing] mirth of the blackest Tragedy that ever was'; that is, 'That horrid Rebellion, and the Murther of the late King.'[24] Rather than backtracking, Colledge defended his seditious memories, attesting later at his trial that he understood the Long Parliament 'to be an honest Parliament, that minded the true Interest of the Nation, and much of the same opinion with the Parliament that sate last at *Westminster*', and clarifying that 'I said they were persons altogether innocent of the Kings murder, and raising the War against the King.'[25] Colledge also contended that 'the Papists began the War' and 'did all the mischief in the late times'.[26] The joiner was upbraided for these sentiments by Lord Chief Justice Francis North, who declared that a vindication of Parliamentarianism exposed Colledge's 'temper', and, capturing the mood of Royalist and Tory anti-fanaticism, that 'they that justifie such things as to the time passed, would lead us to the same things again if they could.' 'The War was a Rebellion on the Parliaments part,' explained North, 'let us not mince the matter'.[27]

North's rebuttal forced from Colledge a curious confession: 'I was then a child,' he contended, 'and do not know all the passages, but I speak my sence.'[28] Colledge was born in the mid-1630s, so he was already in his early teens when Charles I was executed.[29] This raises interesting questions about age and the development of 'political consciousness' in early modern Britain.[30] The early confrontations between Crown and Parliament are likely to have had an impact on young Colledge. His native Watford was known for the Puritanism of its minister, Cornelius Burges, a man who was one of the most vehement supporters of the Protestation in 1641–42.[31] Moreover, in 1645, at around the time of Colledge's tenth birthday, hundreds of troops assembled at Watford before the Battle of Naseby.[32] And yet despite these events, Colledge's evocation of his being 'a child' during this time implies that, like John Ayloffe and Strange Southby, his 'sence' of, and thus identification with, the Long Parliament as a bulwark of parliaments and Protestants belonged to a later era. To be sure, Colledge's final words on the executioner's cart within the grounds of Oxford Castle in August 1681 included prayers that 'mine may be the last protestant blood, that murdering church of Rome may shed in Christendome: and that my death may be a far greater blow to theire bloody cause, that I either have or could have by my life'.[33] Having contributed to the reconstruction of London as a joiner during the 1670s, it was anxiety about the slaughter of Protestants that had driven Colledge to identify so strongly with the opposition and resistance of the Long Parliament thirty years earlier.

SEDITIOUS MEMORIES AND WHIG IDENTITY

The strength of Colledge's identification with Parliamentarianism is represented by the volume of evidence of seditious and treasonable sentiment that the government compiled against him, both before and after his death. It was alleged at his trial, for instance, that he had authored a tract entitled *Queries*, including 'a Vindication ... of the proceedings of that Parliament of 41'.[34] Other evidence suggests that Colledge had expressed his proclivities for the Long Parliament in speech as well as writing. Sir Roger L'Estrange, with whom Colledge famously locked satirical horns in 1680–81, wrote a year before the joiner's trial that Colledge had been heard to '[whip] up two or three Blades t'other day ... upon the War of *Forty One*', telling his audience 'to their very Noses, that the Parliament men of those days were the bravest *Patriots* that ever *England* bred; that they fought for the *Liberty* of the *Subject*; and in one word exalted them to the skyes.'[35] This nostalgic sentiment matches that of a ballad by Colledge in which England and Wales before 1660 were similarly 'exalted' as a nation of 'men' that had since become 'slaves again'.[36]

The most useful evidence to the government was that in which Colledge imagined the restoration of rebellion. In January 1681, Colledge had been heard to say that 'We must e'en draw our swords and fight it over againe.'[37] Two years later, Don Lewis deposed that he had heard Colledge say that 'there were men ready to justify the Remnant of ye Long Parliamt.'[38] That, in the final moments before his execution, Colledge identified with what he called 'the Church of England according to the best and last Reformation, as it was purged from idolatry and superstition', suggests that his sympathies lay not only with Parliament's defences of English law, but also with its promotion of 'further reformation'.[39] That Colledge had gone further, and justified the regicide itself, or at least failed to condemn it, is not inconceivable. The joiner was much less respectful of Charles I than the martyrisation of the late king dictated. In a 1678 version of *A Ra-ree Show*, the ballad that was used at his trial as evidence of treasonable intent, Colledge described Charles I as 'like a Fool' who had 'Lost his life, to save his Soul'.[40] Provocatively, Colledge even used the language that the New Model Army had coined to describe Charles I, by labelling the father of Lord Chief Justice William Scroggs, a butcher, as 'a man of Blood'.[41]

By far the most common theme of Colledge's work, however, were comparisons between Charles II and his father, Charles I. The aforementioned ballad *A Ra-ree Show* asks the reader or listener to 'Remember old *Dry Bobbs* [i.e. Charles I] ... For Fleecing *Englands* Flocks'.[42] More seditiously, and suggesting that the ballad was intended to incite rebellion, the piece also contains lines that declare, 'Ha-loo the *Hunts* begun ... Like Father, Like Son.'[43] Meanwhile, Colledge's *Truth Brought to Light Or Murder Will Out* laments England as a 'poor nation' that had been 'undone' both 'By a bad father, and now a worse, his son!'[44] Earlier in 1681, Colledge had been tried in London for, among other speeches, a more explicit desire 'to serve [the King] as [the logger-head his] father was served.'[45] Colledge's work also identified those who had fought for Charles I with the followers of his son. His *The Catholick Gamesters* thus describes how there were 'some among us for this fifty Years / Have Traitors been; engaged by the Ears'.[46]

Like his fellow Whigs John Ayloffe and Strange Southby, Stephen Colledge justified, identified with, and imagined the restoration of elements of the civil wars and revolution. The question arising at this juncture is whether this common esteem for Parliament and the Republic among these younger activists characterises the Whig movement. Tellingly, perhaps, Colledge was not alone among the Whigs in identifying strongly with the Long Parliament. The solicitor Edward Whitaker (or Whitacre), who was nicknamed the 'Protestant Attorney' for his advocacy of several notable Whig defendants, including Stephen Colledge himself,[47] was also accused of vindicating the Parliament in a case of seditious speech that bound Whitaker up in legal proceedings over the next decade.[48] It was alleged by three witnesses that, amid a heated debate in a Bath coffee house with the Royalist veteran Sir James Long, Whitaker had said 'hee knew of noe Rebellion [parliament] made for twas in Justification of their rights & that the King was not Murdered but taken of by a Legall Tryall.' Rather than being a spontaneous outburst, Whitaker's words had been spoken to contest Long's claim that annual parliaments had 'caused rebellion and murdered the late King.'[49] Whitaker had children in the London parish of St Thomas the Apostle in the 1670s,[50] and given that he was still alive, and indeed active, in 1709, and did not die for another ten years, it is improbable that he was born before the 1630s.[51] Indeed, he may be the Putney gentleman of the same name whose marriage at the age of 23 was recorded in 1661.[52] For Whitaker, then, as for Colledge, the Long Parliament's defence of its rights against an absolutist monarch is likely to have become meaningful to him only in the context of the 1670s and 1680s.

Whigs among the Restoration generation are characterised not only by their Parliamentarian and republican sympathies, but also, as the cases of Stephen Colledge and John Ayloffe imply, their apparent willingness to publicise these views. In Stephen Colledge's case, this willingness can be accounted for by the relative freedom to publish that had resulted from the lapse of the Licensing Act in 1679. However, it is also conceivable that there was something peculiar to this generation – what Mannheim referred to as 'a certain characteristic mode of thought and experience' – that also encouraged such unabashed identification with Parliamentarianism and even republicanism during the 1640s and 1650s. The relative indifference with which resistance was invoked as a response to the threats of 'popery' and 'arbitrary' government reflects the lack of experience of civil conflict that tied the Restoration generation together. This nonchalance is displayed most clearly in the House of Commons speech by Sir Thomas Player during a debate about the exclusion of James, Duke of York, in 1680. Player told his fellow MPs that 'As for that one argument, of a Civil War that may come upon this Exclusion, I would let the World know, that we are not afraid of War upon that occasion.'[53] Given that his parents married in 1641, it is unlikely that Player was born before the outbreak of civil war.[54] That he, and others of his age group, were willing to draw swords in the name of Protestantism probably derived from not having witnessed the human cost of those actions.

That individuals like Player had a different attitude when it came to the taking up of arms in defence of parliaments and Protestantism sheds light on an aspect of memory after the Restoration that has received considerable attention from historians: the concerted effort by hard-line Royalists and Tories between 1680 and 1685 to rearticulate their warnings about a return to 'rebellion' and 'usurpation'. Historians have usually seen this scaremongering campaign as a means by which the Whigs were discredited, the assumption being that the 'centre ground' of political and religious opinion in the final years of Charles II's reign was conquerable by tarring those who opposed the succession of the Duke of York, and supported the toleration of Dissenters, as the inheritors of civil war 'fanaticism'.[55] The extent to which Whigs like Sir Thomas Player, for whom we have little evidence of radical or republican intent, were willing to discount what he termed 'that one argument, of a Civil War that may come upon this Exclusion', belies this interpretation. So too does the evident panic with which popular sympathies for civil war Parliamentarianism, such as those of Stephen Colledge, were met by the authorities. Rather than a means of discrediting the Whig movement, what have been described as 'Tory caterwauling', the references to '[16]41 come again' that typified the 'Tory Reaction' of the 1680s, might be viewed as a concerted effort by Tories to win over a new generation from the kinds of favourable interpretations of the civil wars and revolution to which people were increasingly exposed.[56]

MODES OF TRANSMISSION: FAMILIES

The question that arises from this analysis is how the Restoration generation was exposed to seditious memories when, as we have seen, such sentiment was censored and its referents censured. We may answer this question by turning once more to recent studies of remembering, especially those in which memory is understood to be intrinsically social in origin. In the words of Elizabeth Tonkin, 'the contents or evoked messages of memory are ... ineluctably social insofar as they are acquired in the social world'.[57] The implication of studies of 'social memory' is that there also exists something called 'cultural memory', which, in the words of Jan Assmann, 'preserves the store of knowledge from which a group derives an awareness of its unity and peculiarity.'[58] This association of cultural memory with the process of socialisation has led the Holocaust scholar Marianne Hirsch to refer to 'post-memories' or, in her words, the product of '[growing] up with overwhelming inherited memories' and being 'dominated by narratives that preceded one's birth or one's consciousness'.[59] These explorations into memory, society, and generation invite us to examine the affinities of the Restoration generation for opposition and resistance during the 1640s and 1650s not as some spontaneous condition of their distance from those events, but as a set of opinions that were inherited from individuals who had been active participants. Put differently, the likelihood that individuals espoused seditious memories was increased significantly by the Parliamentarianism or republicanism of their social milieux.

For those, like Stephen Colledge, who were in their twenties when Charles II returned in 1660, it is likely that exposure to the kinds of opinions that became potentially seditious or treasonable after the Restoration occurred during the decades of civil war and revolution themselves. In Marianne Hirsch's conception, the 'narratives' that dominated the first two decades of the lives of these elder members of the Restoration generation were, owing to the political and religious climate of the era, those that continued to justify Parliament's taking up arms against Charles I. Most famously, the crisis at the end of the 1650s witnessed an outpouring of reappraisals of the so-called 'good old cause' in an effort to justify post-Oliverian settlements that were variously monarchical, republican, Presbyterian, and sectarian.[60] It may be that Colledge's exposure to William Prynne's claims that civil war and regicide had been fomented by Jesuit conspirators (see chapter 2) had encouraged his opinion, which he appears to have accepted as common sense, that 'the Papists began the War'. Colledge's apparently Presbyterian upbringing no doubt increased his exposure to these kinds of opinions.[61]

Colledge's upbringing in Puritan Watford may also have informed his sympathies for the Long Parliament. At his trial, Colledge called several witnesses to attest to his having attended Anglican communion, one of whom was Thomas Deacon, presumably the same of Wiggen Hall in the parish of Watford, who had served Parliament as lieutenant-colonel.[62] New evidence also suggests that Colledge's family were actively supportive of Parliament. It was recorded by the diarist Anthony Wood that Colledge was a nephew of the Oxford musician and Puritan Edward Golledge, who became a notable target of Royalist ire during the early 1640s.[63] It was reported widely in 1641 that a maypole was set up in the Oxford parish of Holywell, to the top of which was affixed an effigy of Edward Golledge ('or College') preaching from a tub.[64] If this man was the son of another musician, Thomas Golledge of Ware in Hertfordshire, then his will (dated 1613) provides us with the names of the joiner's uncles and, of course, his father.[65] One of his uncles was Thomas Golledge (or Gollidge), who shares his name with another Oxford man who was wrongfully imprisoned by Archbishop William Laud following the murder of his brother, Richard (also named in the aforementioned will) in 1632.[66] These events may have driven Colledge's uncle Thomas into the arms of Parliament in 1642, as there is a man of that name listed in the Oxfordshire regiment of Lord Saye and Sele.[67] Stephen Colledge's father, Stephen, also shares his name with one of those mentioned in the 1613 will.[68] Colledge's father was also active for Parliament as marshal to the Hertfordshire county committee in 1644.[69]

Parliamentarian families would have remained important media for the transmission of what became seditious memories of the 1640s and 1650s to those who were born just before or after the Restoration. It is surely significant that Strange Southby, whose justification of the regicide was considered at the beginning of this chapter, was the grandson of John Southby, who served Parliament between 1647 and 1660, and the son of Richard Southby, who was MP for Cirencester in 1659.[70] The significance of Parliamentarian or republican heritage was self-evident to the authorities, who, as we saw in chapter 3, were prone to extrapolating people's 'fanatic' principles from the disloyalty of their parents or grandparents. This stereotyping continued long into the 1680s. In July 1686, the mayor of Liverpool saw fit to describe a local bailiff as 'the sonne of an old Oliverian sequestrator ... and the same Principles for sometime imbibed by this his sonne'.[71]

Tellingly, accusations of seditious remembering were themselves often informed by the heritage of the accused. In April 1681, a little over two weeks after Charles II dissolved the final parliament of his reign at Oxford, an allegation of seditious words was made against one Edmund Gibons (or Gibbon), who was believed by his accuser, former Royalist Captain Gregory Alford, to be the son of a 'Cromwellite', perhaps the Parliamentarian officer Major Robert Gibbon.[72] Gibons was alleged by Alford to have launched into a tirade against the king, including an allegation that he had dissolved parliament in exchange for a pension from Louis XIV. Echoing the views that were alleged of Stephen Colledge, Gibons added that 'now thare was a nessesyty that Thare must and would be a warr wth the King as thare was wth and a gaynst the Late King To desyd the matter'.[73] While we have no biographical information about Edmund Gibons, the fact that Alford referred to his father's participation in the civil wars may suggest that his son was not old enough to have acted 'a gaynst the Late King' himself. It may be significant, in fact, that Gibons's travelling companion, the Earl of Stamford, was himself the son of a Parliamentarian, and indeed regicide (Thomas Grey, Lord Grey of Groby), and was not born until 1654.

The association of seditious memories with Parliamentarian and republican heritage extended to what I referred to in chapter 7 as mis-commemoration. One detailed case of this behaviour from the Exclusion Crisis reflects how closely it was associated with the actions of an individual's parents during the civil wars and revolution. It was reported on the anniversary of the regicide in January 1681 that, as the congregation of St Stephen's church in Sparsholt, Hampshire, spilled out into the cold winter air after a sermon by their minister Edward Lane, several men '[rode] into ye ... Parish' and 'did Then and There together Follow their Game of Hunting, When they were in Duty Bound, As all other People likewise in the Nation were, To Humble themselves before God in Fasting and Prayer.' Appended to the witness statements of several villagers was a note from the minister Edward Lane himself, explaining that it was 'the Common Voice of the Parish' that two of the huntsmen were 'Mr Oliver St John Esq' (born *circa* 1642), a Whig MP, and 'Mr Oliver Cromwell' (born in 1656), who, it was explained, was the 'Eldest sonne of Richard, [himself the] eldest sonne of Oliver Cromwell ye usurper, & murder [*sic*] of his Master; o[u]r late king of Ever blessed Memory'.[74] The men who failed to commemorate the regicide were, in other words, a nephew of former Parliamentarian Oliver St John and, far worse, the grandson of the most famous regicide of all, Oliver Cromwell. It is possible that the failure of both men to observe the regicide in the expected manner derived from a culture of mis-commemoration that had been passed down through the Cromwell and St John families.

Other cases of seditious remembering that entailed identification with Parliamentarian or republican parents and grandparents are also suggestive of the transmission of these sympathies through families. This is illustrated in a case of seditious speech from September 1683 when a mariner living in Shadwell, Middlesex, named John Robinson declared that 'I care not a fart for the King of England himselfe' since 'my father was a soldier to Oliver and fought against the King, and I would do the like if there were occasion.' Robinson had been responding to a claim that he had been 'rash' to call James, Duke of York, 'a Papist' and to say that the Rye House Plot was 'his Plott', reflecting thereby how seditious remembering informed cultural resistance (see chapter 4).[75] In a similar case from two years earlier, it was a grandfather, rather than a father, with whom an individual identified. The individual in question was Colonel Edward Dering, who 'dranke confusion to Lawne sleeves' and said that 'he was of his Gran: fathers opinion, neither for Lord Bishops nor Duke Bishops.'[76] Here, Dering was probably referring to Sir Edward Dering, an MP in the Long Parliament who, while later an active Royalist, was notable for having spoken out against Archbishop Laud.[77] That Stephen Colledge's speeches and writings regularly disclose an obsession with paternity – he often referred to the Royalist parentage of those who he attacked, including William Scroggs, up to and including Charles II himself – suggests that his own seditious memories originated in a specific identification with his father.[78]

We may speculate that similar kinds of identification with Parliamentarian and republican ancestors took place during what some historians have described as the swansong of the good old cause. Studies of the Monmouth Rebellion of 1685 have often evoked the idea that the rising was informed, in part, by nostalgia for the 1640s and 1650s that had been passed down through successive generations of West Country men and women. Peter Earle has lent credence to the image that the Victorian novel *Micah Clarke* painted of the Monmouth Rebellion, in which '[Oliverian] fathers fitt[ed] out their sons, and indeed their servants, for the rebellion.'[79] Here, Parliamentarian identities were passed from father to son in an evocatively literal way. That the rebels' declaration alluded to the civil wars suggests that this image was not merely a figment of Victorian romanticism. In a thinly veiled allusion to Parliamentarianism, the declaration identified explicitly with 'our noble & generous *Ancestours,* who conveyed our *Priviledges* to us at the expence of their blood & treasure'.[80] That the rebels' ancestors were invoked suggests that opposition and resistance during the 1640s, and the victories of Parliament in the civil wars, proved inspirational not only to those who, as we saw in chapter 5, had witnessed them, but also to their children.

The actions of the Covenanters in the late 1630s, and the 'Work of Reformation' that followed, were formative for the generation of Scottish men and women whose experiences were defined by government persecution. Commonly, this is illustrated by claims that the Covenants were binding on the descendants of those who had subscribed to them in 1638 and afterwards. In July 1683, for instance, a thirty-three-year-old Scotsman named John Heborn was hauled before the English Privy Council for interrogation regarding the recent foiled Rye House Plot. Perhaps in response to a query about his father's involvement in the Scottish revolution, he responded that 'he hope[d] none taught him his principles but The Lord', but conceded that 'His fathers taking the Covenant obliges him [to it]'. When he was asked if he had taken 'the Test' – an oath of commitment to the royal supremacy[81] – Heborn responded that he had never taken it, since 'he cannot maintain ye Covenant and take the Test.'[82] Pressed about his adherence to the Covenants, Heborn cited the notion of 'descending obligation'– the idea that the Covenants were obliging not only upon those who subscribed to them, but also upon all subsequent generations – as a justification for his identification with it.[83] Evidence of this belief can be located elsewhere during the 1680s. In July 1683, for instance, one James Frazer responded to his own interrogation by the government with his belief that 'He judged himself by the Word of God, Laws of the Land, yea, and the Covenant itself, tho' never personally taken by him, bound thereunto.'[84] If the Parliamentarianism and republicanism of the civil war generation inspired opposition and even resistance in England and Wales after the Restoration, then the bond of the Covenants guaranteed that influence on some Presbyterians in Scotland.

MODES OF TRANSMISSION: POLITICAL COMMUNITIES

Family was not the only touchpoint between the Restoration generation and sympathies for Parliament and the Republic. Younger activists such as Stephen Colledge and Edward Whitaker were, as we have seen, also embedded within political and religious networks after the Restoration whose links to those who had been involved in opposition and resistance during the 1640s and 1650s are well known to historians.[85] Gary De Krey has gone as far as to describe London's Whigs as 'a cross-generational alliance of older and younger advocates of reformation in church and state', adding that 'Friendships and cooperation among the older and younger Whig leaders connected some who could remember the personal rule of Charles I to some who would guide the city through the turmoil of 1688–89.'[86] Indeed, if the Whigs were, or included, a community of memory in which Parliamentarian and republican sympathies were exchanged, this must have been inspirational to people for whom the threats of 'popery' and 'arbitrary government' in the 1660s, 1670s, and 1680s were formative.

One individual whose embeddedness within the Whig movement is well documented is Stephen Colledge. Despite his 'humble' origins, Colledge was connected to Whig leaders like Anthony Ashley Cooper, Earl of Shaftesbury.[87] Indeed, suggesting that Shaftesbury was himself influential in transmitting seditious opinions about the 1640s and 1650s to individuals like Stephen Colledge, it was claimed at the earl's trial in 1681 that he had made similar comparisons between Charles II and his father.[88] Colledge is also likely to have known Shaftesbury's servant Samuel Wilson,[89] who was accused in the same year of condemning those who sentenced the joiner to death, alleging that Charles II had perjured himself by breaking the Solemn League and Covenant, and for quoting Oliver Cromwell's 'witty' view that 'a shoulder of mutton and a whore' were 'all [the king] Cares for'.[90] Colledge was likewise associated with other Whig-sympathising former Parliamentarians like Captain Brown[91] and Captain Clinton,[92] and he travelled to Oxford in March 1681 with Lord Howard of Escrick, who was dismissed from Cromwell's lifeguards in the mid-1650s for his Leveller views.[93] Colledge was also visited in prison in August 1681 by John Martin, Oxford's Parliamentarian town clerk during the revolution, who had notably changed his last name from Bishop, 'being a hater of Bishops'.[94] It is conceivable, of course, that Martin, as an Oxford resident, had been associated with Colledge's uncles during the early 1640s.

The embeddedness of Whigs within networks of former Parliamentarians appears to have served them in digging up dirt against former Royalists. In 1682, Colledge's friend and fellow Whig Edward Whitaker, whose opinions about the Long Parliament were encountered earlier, wrote a tract that sought to discredit Sir William Smyth, the author of a vehemently anti-fanatical speech before the Middlesex Grand Jury in April 1682, which was later printed.⁹⁵ Responding to a conspicuous reference in the speech to Smyth's civil war royalism, Whitaker took the opportunity to dig further into his war service, explaining that, in his native Buckinghamshire, he had 'g[iven] Councel to kill and destroy all the Gentlemen, Yeomen, Farmers, their wives and Children, with out regard either to Sex, Age, or condition'.⁹⁶ Whitaker also mocked Smyth for the questionable loyalty of his having been 'the chief promoter in the County of *Bucks*, and other places, to procure Addresses to *Richard Cromwel*, and was then the most zealous and forwardest man in that Service.'⁹⁷ That Whitaker wrote of having been 'informed' of Smyth's service in the wars and that he been forced to 'rake in Dunghills ... after so long an intervale' denotes that he had researched Smyth's actions during the civil wars.⁹⁸ That he was able to may reflect his connection to Whigs in Buckinghamshire, the county seat of his notable former client, the Duke of Buckingham.⁹⁹

In Scotland, covenanted communities continued to act as media for the transmission of seditious memories. This was noted gravely by the government agent Matthew Mackaile in October 1678, who disclosed his fears that adherence to Presbyterianism was evident 'not only' among 'old folks and these that have seen former tymes', but also 'many of the young' who were 'as willing to suffer ... as any are'.¹⁰⁰ The risings in Scotland at the beginning and end of Charles II's reign, in which, as we saw in chapter 6, the Covenants played a crucial symbolic role, constituted moments when their significance was transmitted to a new generation. The memoir of the Presbyterian minister William Veitch, who fled Scotland following his participation in the Pentland Rising of 1666, conveys the enduring appeal of the Covenants among those who were willing to defend Presbyterianism by taking up arms after the Restoration.¹⁰¹ Veitch related having been brought before the Committee of Public Affairs in February 1679, which was then presided over by James Sharp, the archbishop of St Andrews who was assassinated later that year. Sharp sought to 'ensnare' Veitch by questioning whether he had ever taken the Covenant. Like Stephen Colledge at his trial in 1681, Veitch, who was born two years after the signing of the National Covenant in 1638, answered that 'all that see me at this honourable board may easily perceive that I was not capable to take the Covenant, when you and the other ministers of Scotland tendered it'. Riled by this reference to his own Covenanting past, Sharp pressed Veitch to answer whether he had taken the Covenant since the Restoration. Veitch answered only evasively that 'I judge myself obliged to covenant myself away to God, and frequently to renew it.'¹⁰²

The Covenants had an impact on individuals who are not usually associated with the radical intentions of Veitch and others who rose against the authorities during the reigns of Charles II and James II. Gilbert Burnet, an Episcopalian and later bishop of Salisbury, was described by fellow historian Robert Wodrow as having aired views that, given their immediate context, had the potential to be treated as sedition or treason. Writing in his *History of the Sufferings of the Church of Scotland*, Wodrow described how the Presbyterian Anne, Duchess of Hamilton, had heard Burnet 'sp[eak] of the national Covenant, with a great deal of Respect,' saying 'He believed it would never be well with Scotland, until we returned to that Covenant, and renewed it.'[103] Whether Burnet had identified this explicitly with the Covenant is unclear. If he did, then he broke ranks with his father, Robert Burnet, who had refused to subscribe to the Solemn League and Covenant in 1643.[104] Nonetheless, the younger Burnet's association with the Whig leadership in London during the 1680s, including those who were tried and executed for involvement in the Rye House Plot in 1683, suggests that he had been won round to the resurgent respect for the Covenants that, as the historian Edward Vallance has shown, inspired the Protestant 'associations' of the Exclusion Crisis.[105]

GLIMPSES OF TRANSMISSION

The inherent socialness of memory encourages us to think about seditious memories that were articulated by members of the Restoration generation as having been informed by social milieux. We are fortunate enough that some evidence affords us with fleeting glimpses of the very moments at which these memories were transmitted from one generation to the next. Remaining in Scotland, we find that last dying speeches and testimonies offered those who were indicted for rebellion with an opportunity to encourage a new generation of Scots to act in the name of the Covenants. Shortly before the Covenanter John Nilson was executed in 1666, he laid 'an express charge' upon his wife that she might 'shew all my Children, that I have bound them all to the Covenant, for which now I lay down my life, and ... that they adhere to every Article thereof.'[106] Following the Pentland Rising in 1666, the Glasgow merchant John Wodrow recommended that the readers of his final testimony, including their 'young-ones', 'keep [to God's] Covenant.'[107] That Wodrow's testimony was included with others in James Stewart's *Napthali, Or the Wrestlings of the Church of Scotland For the Kingdom of Christ*, in 1667 ensured that his message reached a large audience.

Evidence of seditious remembering in England and Wales offers us comparable glimpses of the transmission of Parliamentarian and republican sympathies. The informant Edward Massey spoke in September 1683 of having encountered conspirators in Essex, London, and the West Country who, despite being drawn from different generations, referred regularly to the civil wars and revolution. One of these was Samuel Hensman, a Baptist preacher from Braintree, Essex, who Massey recalled having bumped into while on business in London in September 1680. Massey was told by Hensman that 'he would bring [him] to a brave ould bead', who turned out to be none other than Major John Gladman, sometime New Model Army agitator who was later implicated in the Rye House Plot.[108] Having been taken to Gladman's lodgings in Bishopsgate,[109] Massey heard the veteran speak of his pride that Hensman 'did so much imitate his father as hee doth to tread in his steps as i heard he doth.'[110] Massey did not elaborate upon these words in his evidence, but it seems likely that Gladman was referring here to Hensman's Parliamentarian heritage. Hensman was a member of John Bunyan's Bedford congregation in the 1670s before he was transferred to Braintree,[111] and it is possible that his father was the Robert Hensman who, like Bunyan, had been garrisoned in the Bedfordshire town of Newport Pagnell during the first civil war.[112] That Gladman appears to have been from Bedfordshire himself may explain the connection between the pair.[113]

Hensman's description of Gladman as a 'brave ould bead' implies that he was in awe of his father's generation. Indeed, that those of Hensman's age group saw opposition to and resistance against the Stuarts as inherently venerable is a major theme of Edward Massey's evidence. Samuel Hensman was himself accused by Massey of lamenting the pusillanimity of his younger comrades, suggesting that they might search instead for 'too [sic] or three thousand of such ould boyes as [J]oseph Smitheman'.[114] 'Ould boyes' was, as we have seen, a signifier of active service for Parliament in the 1640s, and it is likely that Hensman was referring here to the Essex man Joseph Smitheman (or Smytheman) who had been accused of plotting against the government in 1661.[115] Smitheman was himself accused by Massey of sedition for having stated that 'we will have our land governed by [j]udges as it was in the days of ould', a reference, we might speculate, to the English Commonwealth.[116] Massey accused another conspirator, the brazier Joseph Clarke, of echoing Smitheman's nostalgia when he remarked that 'Olivers days' had been 'brave Tymes'.[117]

Since Joseph Clarke's age is unknown, his reference to Oliver Cromwell may be read either as a declaration of the courage of his own generation in fighting the Stuarts or as a wide-eyed identification with the generation before him. Further evidence shows that the latter offered younger activists a means of currying favour with those who had fought for Parliament and the Commonwealth. At the height of the Rye House Plot revelations in July 1683, the clerk Samuel Starkey made a series of allegations against four men who had met four years earlier at the house of his employer Aaron Smith, a friend of Stephen Colledge who acted as the joiner's solicitor at his Oxford trial in 1681.[118] Starkey recalled that the company 'fell into discourse concerning their then affaires in agitation', leading Smith to aver that 'he that destroyed them & their whole family root & branch did God good service,' words that his audience 'by their constant discourse seem'd well pleased at'. Indeed, one of those present, Thomas Haselrig, added his view 'that ye Old King deserv'd his death for entertaining private conferences wth. Priests & Jesuits, & that this King exactly follow'd his Fathers Steps & would assuredly receive his Fate', sentiment which, according to Starkey, the speaker of these words had 'often suggested'.[119]

Starkey was at pains to identify who had been his master's company when these words were spoken. Haselrig was referred to as 'a kinsman' of the notorious Parliamentarian and republican Sir Arthur Haselrig. He is thus likely to have been the Thomas Haselrig who lived at St Andrew, Holborn, and whose guardian had once been another Sir Thomas Hesilrig (or Haselrig), son of Sir Arthur.[120] Given that his guardian had only married in the mid-1660s, this Thomas Haselrig was probably still a young man at the time of the Restoration. Aaron Smith's age is unknown, although it has been recorded by his biographer that he tended to associate with 'roundheads' sons', including, judging by the evidence examined above, his client Stephen Colledge.[121] Indeed, another man who was present when these seditious words were spoken was 'Simon Maine Esq.', who Starkey described as being 'son to Maine that was one of his late Ma[jes]ties Judges'. This is a reference to Simon Maine (or Mayne), born in 1644 to the regicide of the same name.[122]

Not all Smith's guests belonged to the Restoration generation. It was also mentioned that 'one Dr. Harrington (brother to ye. late Sr. James Harrington)' was in their company when the words were spoken.[123] Sir James Harrington, a former Parliamentarian, had no brothers who survived into adulthood, so this is likely to have been a mistaken reference to the republican theorist James Harrington, cousin to the Earl of Shaftesbury, who did have a brother, William Harrington.[124] That this was indeed the man to whom Starkey was referring is corroborated by the fact that the same William Harrington had written in September 1679 of the death of one 'Honest Tom Haselrige', a reference to the man who had spoken the seditious words at the house of Aaron Smith.[125] Indeed, suggesting a close connection between the pair, the will of this Thomas Haselrig (spelled Hesilrige) was signed by a 'Wm Harington' in August 1679.[126] If this was, as suspected, *the* William Harrington, then he had been on parliamentary committees in the 1640s and was, for a time, brother-in-law to the Parliamentarian Ralph Assheton (or Asheton).[127] This suggests, then, that the seditious memories of Smith and Haselrig had been aimed specifically at securing Harrington's approval.[128]

Efforts to curry favour with the civil war generation by expressing seditious memories could backfire. This appears to have been what happened in July 1682 when 'a Babtist [Baptist] widow-woman' from Stepney in Middlesex informed the authorities of having been approached by two youngsters who had told her that 'they must shortly pull downe Babylon and all the greate ones ... And that they must fight as Resolute as her husband or any other in the Late Warrs'.[129] It was noted that the individuals in question belonged to the congregation of Matthew Meade, who, following ejection from his lectureship at St Sepulchre in London in 1662, had continued preaching in the parish of Stepney, a dissenting hotspot. He was, like many other dissenting preachers, a vocal opponent of 'popery' and 'arbitrary government' in the 1680s, and yet he distanced himself from involvement in the Rye House Plot in 1683.[130] Nevertheless, Meade's writings from the Restoration suggest a more or less implicit nostalgia for the era before the Restoration, something that, as we saw in chapter 2, is a common feature of dissenting writing. For Meade, the catastrophic plague of 1665 was a divine judgement for the kingdom's sins and would be remedied only when 'the guiltie [are] humbled, wickedness rooted out, God appeased, and all our mercies, both spiritual and temporal, restored and continued'.[131] Indeed, he called on the godly to 'think of that matchless Love, that continued Patience, that clear Light, those great Engagements, Purposes, and frequent Promises, that thou hast sinned against', language that is evocative of the Solemn League and Covenant.[132]

Gary De Krey has interpreted the words reported by the 'Babtist widow-woman' as implying that 'the use of language resonant with hidden suggestions was, perhaps, [safe] for the clergy, but it was dangerous for their auditory, who could easily ... apply them in unforeseen manners.'[133] In this specific example, the mistaken expectation of the accused was that, since her husband had fought 'in the Late wars', the widow would concur with their belief that renewed conflict was on the horizon. A similar case of misconstrual led to one of the most lucid examples of an attempt to transmit seditious memories between generations. In November 1680, William Serocold informed the authorities that he had heard Stephen Standen espouse seditious sentiment while the former was recuperating at Standen's home at Whitefriars in London. This included Standen's belief that the Bill of Exclusion 'was out of kindnesse to his R[oyal] H[ighness]', and that he believed that 'now they would proceed in a severer way ag[ains]t Him.' Intriguingly, having inspected his ailing guest, Standen told Serocold that he 'was not old enough to remember what sorte of men they were; as for Example in ye late Civil Warrs of England'. Standen went on to explain that 'whatever they did sett upon, they never left off till they had performed it; and that they were ye same men still; and that they would never leave off till they had Turnd ye Duke of Yorke out of ye Succession.'[134]

The case of Stephen Standen is not the only evidence of an explicit attempt to inform a member of the Restoration generation of 'what sorte of men' had opposed the Crown in the 1640s. One surprising source of similar sentiment is the diary of the Presbyterian minister Philip Henry, who lived at Worthenbury in Flintshire. In December 1661, Henry wrote of having 'inform'd T. Pr. of ye state of publique affaires, as to the late war & Covenant, concerning which hee knew little, the result whereof was, that though partic. Instrumts might miscarry, yet twas in general the Cause of God & Religion, and will in due time bee made so to appear.'[135] While the identity of the person to whom Henry spoke these words is unknown, the implication was that it was someone who was too young to have lived through the 1640s. Here, Henry invoked the idea that, at some point in the future, and perhaps through divine revelation, the legitimacy of the godly cause would be made manifest.

Standen and Henry provide some of the most explicit evidence of the transmission of seditious memories from the civil war generation to its Restoration successor. Their cases also imply that one of the chief reasons for expressing seditious memories was to reproduce identities not only among those who had experienced the civil wars and revolution, and thus synchronically, but also among those who had not experienced those events, and thus diachronically. Put differently, the motivation for sharing Parliamentarian and republican sympathies was to ensure the perpetuation of political and religious identities of which those sympathies were constitutive. This was true for individuals like Standen, who expected, and perhaps desired, that a 'severer way' would be taken against Charles II, but also Philip Henry, who was a notable supporter of the Restoration.[136]

OTHER MEDIA OF TRANSMISSION

The exposure of the Restoration generation to seditious memories was not confined to oral culture. The government was conscious that other means by which Parliamentarian and republican sympathies were articulated had the potential to spread 'fanaticism' to a new generation. One official observed in 1683 that the annual commemoration of the Parliamentarian relief of the siege of Taunton was a means by which rebellion was being 'transmit[ted] ... as a thing of imitation to posterity.'[137] Similar concerns were shared in Scotland. In 1680, the Edinburgh students who rioted against James, Duke of York, were accused of deliberately adopting the behaviour of those who rose against the Crown over forty years earlier by 'enter[ing] into Bonds and Combinations' (that is, Covenants) and 'putting up blew Ribbans, as Signs and Cognisances, not only to difference them from others, but likewise for Convocating themselves, in pursuance of those Seditious and Tumultuous Designs'. The proclamation that was produced in the immediate aftermath of the riot described the students as 'studiously imitat[ing]' the 'disloyal and mutinous persons' who 'did, in the last age, bring on all their dreadful Rebellion'.[138] Recognising the hazards of being associated with the Covenanters of the 1630s and 1640s, a defence of the rioters entitled *A Modest Apology for the Students of Edenburgh* was published in 1681 in order to insist (tenuously) that, rather than a covenant, with which 'that Kingdom has been so burnt in the hand', the 'bond' had been 'no more than a mutual promise to meet on such a day, at such a place, to play a *Game at Foot-ball*.'[139]

In terms of its staying power, or 'fixity', the residue of civil war print culture was of considerably greater concern to the government as a means by which 'fanatic' principles were transmitted between the civil war and Restoration generations.[140] In 1663, Sir Roger L'Estrange wrote that print had the potential for 'discouraging Loyalty *to Future Generations, by transmitting the whole Party of the Royalists ... to Posterity, for a prostitute Rabble of* Villeins, *and* Traytors.'[141] It was concerns like these that motivated the opposition of former Royalists to the policy of oblivion in the early 1660s. As we saw in chapter 3, the Church of England minister Thomas Tomkins hoped for 'an act of Oblivion, that all that is past may be not only pardoned but forgot.' The specific context for these words was the written works of Richard Baxter during the 1640s and 1650s, and particularly his *Holy Commonwealth* of 1659, the persistence of which after the Restoration was described by Tomkins as perpetuating the 'folly' and 'impiety ... in our late Proceedings'.[142]

It was a cause of consternation to Tomkins and L'Estrange, then, that during the Exclusion Crisis at the end of Charles II's reign, material that had been produced before the Restoration was still being reprinted.[143] Elsewhere, tracts produced and consumed during the 1640s and 1650s are likely to have been accessible to the Restoration generation within the private collections of their elders. Arthur Annesley, Earl of Anglesey, had numerous 'treasonable, seditious and scandalous Books' in his library when he died, including texts from the civil war era.[144] Publications from the civil war were also to be found in the library of 'puritan Whig' Roger Morrice.[145] In Scotland, we know that a conscious effort was made to disseminate seditious works in which the Covenanters of the 1630s and 1640s were held in high esteem (see chapter 6). Elsewhere, during his imprisonment in 1683, James Mure detailed the bequest of several books to friends and family, including the 1635 work *A Short Explanation of the Epistle of Pavl to the Hebrewes* by David Dickson, a Presbyterian opponent of Arminianism.[146] He also bequeathed James Stewart's *Jus Populi Vindicatum*, a 1669 tract notable for having reminded readers of 'indissoluble' engagements to 'Solemne Covenants ... and the defence of the Reformed Religion'.[147]

The abundance of scribal material that was produced after the Restoration, especially in the form of diaries, journals, and memoirs, was also intended as a means of conveying an alternative narrative about the civil wars and revolution to future generations who, if censorship was to continue, would never know the 'truth' of what happened during the 1640s and 1650s. We know, for instance, that the Dissenter John Shawe produced a private account of his life after the Restoration, in which he included a series of references to Parliamentarian sympathies, so that it could be read by his young child (see chapter 2).[148] Meanwhile, Andrew Hopper has identified Sir Thomas Fairfax's decision to justify his own Parliamentarianism in a Restoration journal as a means of protecting his reputation among future generations.[149] For former Parliamentarians and republicans who were concerned about being ensnared by sedition and treason laws, posterity was a safer target audience.

CONCLUSION

Seditious memories of the civil wars and revolution in Britain did not end with the generation that had fought for Parliament and Republic. Cases of seditious remembering from the reigns of Charles II and James II suggest instead that counter-memories were taken on by men and women whose formative experiences were the creeping threats of 'popery' and 'arbitrary government' that typified the Restoration era. It is probable that the social milieux of the Restoration generation were such that these people inherited exactly the kinds of seditious memories to which this book has referred. Given their relative distance from the brutal conflict of the 1640s and 1650s, these opinions were influential in the opposition and resistance that were pursued in the 1680s and that culminated in the deposal of James II from the throne in 1688–89.

That, in part, Parliamentarian (and even republican) sympathies informed Whig identity and fuelled later opposition and resistance is surely one of the ways in which the continued espousal of seditious memories by the civil war generation can be regarded as a success. So far in this book, the very nature of the evidence of these alternative opinions has led us to think of them as illustrating efforts to eradicate 'fanaticism' from the Stuart realms. And yet the fact that hard-line Royalists and, later, Tories were unable to dispel sympathies for Parliament and the Republic is represented by the extent to which those who were born immediately before or after the civil wars and revolution continued to espouse these views. What the seditious memories of the Restoration generation represent above all is the failure of the Stuarts' most strident backers to achieve the mnemonic hegemony that had been pursued ever since Charles II's return in 1660.

NOTES

1. P. Hinds, *"The Horrid Popish Plot:" Roger L'Estrange and the Circulation of Political Discourse in Late Seventeenth-Century London* (Oxford: Oxford University Press, 2009); and C. Walker, 'Remember Justice Godfrey', 117–38.
2. G. S. De Krey, 'London Radicals and Revolutionary Politics, 1675–1683', in T. Harris, P. Seaward, and M. Goldie (eds), *The Politics of Religion in Restoration England* (Oxford: Basil Blackwell, 1990), pp. 133–162. See also G. S. De Krey, *London and the Restoration 1659–1683* (Cambridge: Cambridge University Press, 2005), *passim*.
3. J. Assmann, 'Collective Memory', 130.
4. Anthony Wood, *Life and Times*, iii, pp. 19–20.
5. Anthony Wood, *Athenae Oxonienses: An Exact History of all the Writers and Bishops who have had their Education in the University of Oxford* (4 vols, London, 1813–20), i, pp. lxxxviii, 1392.
6. John Graunt, *Natural and Political OBSERVATIONS, Mentioned in a following INDEX, and made upon the Bills of Mortality* (London, 1662), p. 62.
7. For the demographic impact of the 1665 plague on London, see E. A. Wrigley and R. Schofield, *The Population History of England 1541–1871: A Reconstruction* (London: Edward Arnold, 1981), pp. 79–80.
8. For the particular significance of the Great Fire of London for radical Whig political identities, see Zook, *Radical Whigs*, pp. 99–100.

9 K. Mannheim, 'The Sociological Problem of Generations', in *Essays on the Sociology of Knowledge by Karl Mannheim*, ed. P. Kecskemeti ([1928]; London: Routledge and Kegan Paul, 1952), p. 291. See also A. Assmann, 'Four Formats of Memory', p. 23.
10 The authors William Strauss and Neil Howe differentiated between 'Cavalier' and 'Glorious' generations in addition to their more famous label, 'Millennials'. See W. Strauss and N. Howe, *Generations: The History of America's Future, 1584 to 2069* (New York: Morrow, 1991).
11 Warren Chernaik, 'Ayloffe, John (c.1645–1685)', in *ODNB*, iii, p. 31.
12 For the attribution to Ayloffe, see T. Harris, *London Crowds*, p. 92. For a discussion of the pamphlet, see Montaño, *Courting the Moderates*, pp. 194–196.
13 John Stow, *A SURVEY OF THE CITIES OF London and Westminster, Borough of SOUTHWARK, And PARTS Adjacent* (2 vols, London, 1734–35), i, p. 490.
14 [John Ayloffe], 'A Dialogue between Two Horses' (1676), in G. Lord (ed.), *Poems on Affairs of State: Augustan Satirical Verse, 1660–1714* (7 vols, New Haven, CT: Yale University Press, 1963–75), i, p. 280.
15 *Ibid.*, p. 281.
16 *Ibid.*, p. 282.
17 *Ibid.*, p. 283.
18 TNA, SP29/375/170.
19 *Register of Admissions to the Honourable Society of the Middle Temple* (5 vols, London: Honourable Society of the Middle Temple, [1949]), i, p. 187.
20 P. Walker, 'The Political Career of Theophilus Hastings (1650–1701), 7th Earl of Huntingdon', *Transactions of the Leicestershire Archaeological and Historical Society*, 71 (1997), 60–71; and P. Watson, 'Joliffe, William (c. 1622–1712), of London and Caverswall Castle, Staffs.', in D. Hayton, E. Cruickshanks, and S. Handley (eds), *The History of Parliament: The House of Commons 1690–1715* (Cambridge: Cambridge University Press, 2002), iv, p. 519.
21 Royal Commission on Historical Manuscripts (ed.), *Report on the Manuscripts of the Late Reginald Rawdon Hastings, Esq., of the Manor house, Ashby de la Zouche* (4 vols, London: HMSO, 1928–47), ii, p. 169.
22 For Colledge's life, see H. Weber, *Paper Bullets: Print and Kingship under Charles II* (Lexington, KY: University of Kentucky Press, 1996), ch. 5; and G. S. De Krey, 'College, Stephen (c.1635–1681)', in *ODNB*, xii, pp. 616–618.
23 *ARRAIGNMENT, TRYAL AND CONDEMNATION*, p. 31.
24 *Ibid.*, p. 39.
25 *Ibid.*, p. 81.
26 *Ibid.*, p. 82.
27 *Ibid.*
28 *Ibid.*
29 De Krey, 'College, Stephen', p. 616.
30 I am grateful to Jonah Miller for his thoughts on this issue.
31 Walter, *Covenanting Citizens*, p. 56.
32 A. Thomson, 'Troop Movements during the Civil Wars, 1642–8', in D. Short (ed.), *An Historical Atlas of Hertfordshire* (Hatfield: University of Hertfordshire Press, 2011), p. 172.
33 TNA, SP 29/416/112, 113.

34 *ARRAIGMENT, TRYAL AND CONDEMNATION*, p. 93.
35 [Roger L'Estrange], *L'Estrange's CASE In a CIVIL DIALOGUE Betwixt ZEKIEL AND EPHRAIM* (London, 1680), p. 4.
36 [Stephen Colledge], 'A New Ballad' (1679), in Lord, *Poems on Affairs of State*, ii, p. 176.
37 TNA, SP29/416/172.
38 TNA, SP29/427/81.
39 TNA, SP29/416/133.
40 BL, Harley MS 7319, fols 35v–37r. For the mutations of *A Ra-ree Show*, see C. M. Simpson, *The British Broadside Ballad and its Music* (New Brunswick, NJ: Rutgers University Press, c. 1966), p. 333.
41 [Stephen Colledge], *A SATYR AGAINST IN-JUSTICE; OR, Sc[rog]gs upon Sc[rog]gs* (n.p., [1681]), p. 2.
42 [Stephen Colledge], *A RA-REE SHOW. To the Tune of I am a Senceless Thing* (London, 1681).
43 Ibid.
44 [Stephen Colledge], 'Truth Brought to Light Or Murder Will Out' (1679), in Lord, *Poems on Affairs of State*, ii, p. 16.
45 T. B. Howell, *State Trials*, viii, p. 717.
46 [Stephen Colledge], *THE CATHOLICK GAMESTERS or A DUBBLE MATCH OF BOWLEING With an Account of a Sharp Conference held on the Eve of St. Jago, between his HOLINESS and the Mahometan DONS in St. Katherines Bastile: wherein their Nine-pins are wholly condemned, and their Worships severely checkt, for pleying at that small Game now in the heat of his Harvest* (London, 1680). For a discussion of this pamphlet, see A. Morton, 'Intensive Ephemera: The Catholick Gamesters and the Visual Culture of News in Restoration London', in S. F. Davies and P. Fletcher (eds), *News in Early Modern Europe: Currents and Connections* (Leiden: Brill, 2014), pp. 115–140.
47 Knights, *Politics and Opinion*, p. 290n; and *A LETTER FROM Mr. Edward Whitaker TO THE Protestant Joyner Upon his Bill being sent to OXFORD* (London, 1681).
48 *CSPD, Jan. 1686–May 1687*, p. 1107.
49 Hines, *Newdigate*, 1294 (31 October 1682).
50 J. L. Chester (ed.), *The Parish Registers of St. Thomas the Apostle, London, containing the marriages, baptisms, and burials from 1558 to 1754* (London, 1881), pp. 141–142.
51 Goldie et al., *Entring Book*, vi, p. 221; and Shaw, *Calendar of Treasury Books*, xxiii, 1709, pt 2, *Treasury Minutes, Warrants, etc., with Index*, p. 55. See also TNA, PROB 11/571/110, Will of Edward Whitaker, Gentleman of London, that lists one of his sons as 'Edward Whitaker Serjeant at Law', thus confirming that he is the same Whig solicitor who was listed as living at St Thomas the Apostle in London in 1681; see *CSPD, 1680–81*, p. 348; and W. R. Williams, *The History of the Great Sessions in Wales 1542–1830* (Brecknock: E. Davies, 1899), p. 145.
52 J. Foster (ed.), *London Marriage Licenses, 1521–1869* (London: Benard Quaritch, 1887), p. 1447. Edward Whitaker had lands in Surrey on his death and was married to a woman named Elizabeth, see *CSPD, Jan.–Jun. 1683*, p. 229.

53 A. Grey (ed.), *Debates of the House of Commons, From the Year 1667 to the Year 1694* (10 vols, London, 1769), vii, p. 406, cited in Zook, *Radical Whigs*, pp. 85–86.
54 E. Cruickshanks, 'Player, Sir Thomas (d. 1686), of Hackney, Mdx. and Basinghall Street, London.', in B. D. Henning (ed.), *The History of Parliament: The House of Commons, 1660–1690* (3 vols, London, 1983), iii, p. 250.
55 T. Harris, *Restoration: Charles II*, especially ch 4.
56 Zook, *Radical Whigs*, p. xix.
57 Tonkin, *Narrating Our Pasts*, p. 112.
58 J. Assmann, 'Collective Memory', p. 130.
59 Hirsch, *Generation of Postmemory*, p. 107.
60 Woolrych, 'Good Old Cause', 133–161.
61 De Krey, 'College, Stephen', p. 616.
62 E. Deacon, *The Descent of the Family of Deacon of Elstowe and London, with some Geological, Biographical and Topographical Notes, and Sketches of Allied Families including Reynes of Clifton, and Meres of Kirton* (Bridgeport, CT, 1898), p. 27. This may be the same Thomas Deakan who volunteered for the parliamentary army at Watford in 1642; see TNA, SP28/17, fol. 1r.
63 Anthony Wood, *Life and Times*, ii, p. 552. See also M. Fleming, 'Phillippe Golledge: Another Oxford Musical Instrument Dealer?', *Galpin Society Journal*, 61 (Apr., 2008), 333. I am grateful to Dr Fleming for information regarding the Golledges of Oxford.
64 Cited in Anthony Wood, *Life and Times* ii, p. 552. See also M. G. Hobson and H. E. Salter (eds), *Oxford Council Acts, 1626–1665* (5 vols, Oxford: Oxford University Press, 1928–62), ii, p. 366.
65 ERO, D/ABW 17/150, 'Will of Thomas Gollidge of Ware, Hertfordshire, musician'.
66 HL/PO/JO/10/1/46. A 'Thomas Gollege' was teaching viol lessons in Oxford in 1620–21, suggesting that he may also have been a musician. See P. M. Gouk, 'Music', in N. Tyacke, *The History of the University of Oxford, vol. iv, Seventeenth-Century Oxford* (Oxford: Clarendon, 1997), p. 632.
67 Firth and Davies, *Regimental History*, i, p. 337.
68 TNA, SP44/54, fol. 81.
69 TNA, SP28/231, *passim*.
70 See L. Naylor and G. Jaggar, 'Southby, Richard (c.1624–1704), of Somerford Keynes, Wilts. and Carswell, Buckland, Berks.', in Henning, *History of Parliament*, iii, p. 458.
71 TNA, SP31/3, fol. 61.
72 See Firth and Davies, *Regimental History*, i, pp. 116, 119–120, 123, 325, 381; *ibid.*, ii, pp. 507, 519–521, 532, 556.
73 TNA, SP29/415/120.
74 TNA, SP29/415/96, 96 I. For the birth dates, see P. Watson, 'St. John, Oliver (c.1642–89), of Farley Chamberlayne, Hants.', in Henning, *History of Parliament*, iii, 382; and [R. Gough], *A SHORT GENEALOGICAL VIEW OF THE FAMILY OF OLIVER CROMWELL TO WHICH IS PREFIXED A COPIOUS PEDIGREE* (London: J. Nichols, 1785), p. 27.
75 MCR, iv, p. 224.
76 TNA, SP29/416/92.

77 S. P. Salt, 'Dering, Sir Edward, first baronet (1598–1644)', in *ODNB*, xv, pp. 875–880. For Dering's allegiances during the early 1640s, see also J. Peacey, 'Sir Edward Dering, Popularity, and the Public, 1640–1644', *Historical Journal*, 54:4 (Dec., 2011), 955–983.

78 Brian Haynes testified at Colledge's trial that he had said, 'we cannot endure [the Duke of Monmouth], because he is against his own Father.' *ARRAIGNMENT, TRYAL AND CONDEMNATION*, p. 29. In 1682, Simpson Tonge, son of Israel, spoke of having been approached by Colledge while he was in prison, where he was told that '*I should be damn'd, if I offer'd to accuse my own father.*' *Observator in Dialogue* (23 January 1682).

79 P. Earle, *Monmouth's Rebels: The Road to Sedgemoor 1685* (London: Weidenfeld and Nicolson, 1977), pp. 18–19. See also *ibid.*, pp. 22–23, 30. For the importance of family connections to radical Whig politics, see also Zook, *Radical Whigs*, pp. 30–36.

80 *DECLARATION OF JAMES DUKE of MONMOUTH*, p. 3.

81 Greaves, *Secrets of the Kingdom*, p. 80.

82 TNA, SP29/428/60, pp. 24–25.

83 Robinson, 'Sacred Memory', 138.

84 Wodrow, *History of the Sufferings* (1721), ii, p. 289.

85 R. Ashcraft, *Revolutionary Politics and Locke's Two Treatises of Government* (Princeton, NJ: Princeton University Press, 1986), pp. 247–248.

86 De Krey, *London and the Restoration*, p. 316.

87 De Krey, 'College, Stephen', p. 617.

88 T. B. Howell, *State Trials*, viii, pp. 759–843.

89 TNA, SP29/416/125.

90 TNA, SP29/417/29. This allegation has been described as an 'entrapment' by one sympathetic nineteenth-century historian; see Marsh, *Story of Harecourt*, p. 172.

91 *ARRAIGNMENT,TRYAL AND CONDEMNATION*, pp. 21, 24.

92 TNA, SP16/506/66. A newsletter dated 28 July 1681 described Clinton as 'next heir to the Earldom of Lincoln'; see *CSPD, 1681*, p. 378.

93 *ARRAIGNMENT,TRYAL AND CONDEMNATION*, pp. 37–28.

94 TNA, SP29/416/120.

95 See *THE CHARGE GIVEN BY Sr William Smith, Brt. At the Quarter-Sessions of the Peace held for the County of Middlesex, at Westminster, on Monday the 24th of April, 1682* (London, 1682).

96 *Ibid.*, p. 2.

97 *Ibid.*, p. 3.

98 *Ibid.*, p. 1.

99 Marshall, *Intelligence and Espionage*, p. 221.

100 TNA, SP29/407/105.

101 G. Gardner, 'Veitch, William [alias William Johnston, George Johnston] (1640–1722)', in *ODNB*, lvi, p. 238.

102 Veitch and Brysson, *Memoirs*, pp. 94–95.

103 Wodrow, *History of the Sufferings* (1721), ii, p. 521.

104 M. Greig, 'Burnet, Gilbert (1643–1715)', in *ODNB*, viii, p. 908.

105 E. Vallance, 'Loyal or Rebellious?: Protestant Associations in England 1584–1696', *Seventeenth Century*, 17:1 (2002), 10.

106 [James Stewart], *NAPTHALI*, p. 236.
107 *Ibid.*, p. 253.
108 R. Zaller, 'Gladman, John (*fl.* 1644–1685)', in *ODNB*, xxii, pp. 370–371.
109 TNA, SP29/431/76; and Greaves, *Secrets of the Kingdom*, p. 99.
110 TNA, SP29/431/76.
111 R. L. Greaves, *John Bunyan and English Nonconformity* (London: Hambledon, 1992), p. 98; and *The Church Book of Bunyan Meeting, 1650–1821* (London: J. M. Dent and Sons, 1928), p. 30.
112 C. Hill, *Turbulent, Seditious and Factious*, p. 8; and Samuel Luke, *The Letter Books of Sir Samuel Luke, 1644–45, Parliamentary Governor of Newport Pagnell*, ed. H. G. Tibbutt (London: HMSO, 1963), p. 200.
113 I am grateful to Professor Jason Peacey for this information.
114 TNA, SP29/431/76.
115 ERO, D/DEb95/118.
116 TNA, SP29/431/76.
117 TNA, SP29/431/108.
118 *ARRAIGNMENT, TRYAL AND CONDEMNATION, passim*.
119 TNA, SP29/427/99.
120 See TNA, DG21/89.
121 P. Hopkins, 'Smith, Aaron (*d.* 1701)', in *ODNB*, li, p. 11.
122 E. Cruickshanks and S. Handley, 'Mayne, Simon (c.1644–1725), of Dinton, nr. Aylesbury, Bucks.', in Hayton, *et al.*, *History of Parliament*, pp. 780–781.
123 TNA, SP29/427/99.
124 See Scott, *Algernon Sidney*, p. 160.
125 See Historical Manuscripts Commission (ed.), *The Manuscripts of Sir William Fitzherbert, Bart., and Others* (London: Eyre and Spottiswoode, 1893), p. 21.
126 TNA, PROB11/360/660, Will of Thomas Hesilrige of London.
127 See J. Peacey, 'Politics, Accounts and Propaganda in the Long Parliament', in J. Peacey and C. Kyle (eds), *Parliament at Work: Parliamentary Committees, Political Power and Public Access in Early Modern England* (Woodbridge: Boydell and Brewer, 2002), p. 68.
128 William Harrington and Aaron Smith were also members of the Green Ribbon Club; see Knights, *Politics and Opinion*, p. 164; and Hopkins, 'Smith, Aaron', p. 11.
129 TNA, SP29/421/30.
130 R. L. Greaves, 'Meade [Mead], Matthew (1628/9–1699)', in *ODNB*, xxxvii, p. 649.
131 M[atthew] M[eade], *SOLOMON'S PRESCRIPTION For the Removal of PESTILENCE: OR, The Discovery of the PLAGUE of our Hearts, in order to the Healing of that in our Flesh* (London, 1665), sig. A4v.
132 *Ibid.*, p. 14.
133 De Krey, 'London Radicals', p. 153.
134 TNA, SP29/414/159.
135 Henry, *Diaries*, p. 102.
136 Greaves, 'Henry, Philip', p. 588.
137 *CSPD, Jan.–Jun. 1683*, p. 266.

138 *A PROCLAMATION Concerning the Students in the Colledge of Edinburgh* (Edinburgh, 1681), p. 1.
139 N. M., *A MODEST APOLOGY FOR THE Students of Edenburgh BURNING A POPE December 25, 1680* (London, 1681), p. 9.
140 E. L. Eisenstein, *The Printing Revolution in Early Modern Europe* (Cambridge: Cambridge University Press, 1983).
141 Roger L'Estrange, *Considerations and Proposals In Order to the Regulation OF THE PRESS: TOGETHER WITH Diverse Instances of Treasonous, and Seditious Pamphlets, Proving the Necessity thereof* (London, 1663), p. 9.
142 [Tomkins], *Rebels Plea*, p. 45.
143 See, for instance, Achinstein, *Literature and Dissent*, p. 19.
144 TNA, SP44/337, fol. 123. See also A. Patterson and M. Dzelzainis, 'Marvell and the Earl of Anglesey: A Chapter in the History of Reading', *Historical Journal*, 44:3 (2001), 712, 712n.
145 See Goldie, *Roger Morrice*, pp. 167–168.
146 *RPCS, 1683–84*, p. 702.
147 [James Stewart], *JUS POPULI VINDICATUM*, sig. A1.
148 Jackson, *Yorkshire Diaries*, i, pp. 121–122.
149 Hopper, *'Black Tom'*, p. 225.

Conclusion

Burying the good old cause

The experiences of Edward Bowles were typical of godly clergy who lived through the mid seventeenth century. A supporter of Parliament's cause, he was appointed chaplain to a regiment of foot in the early months of the civil war. In the next decade, Bowles ministered at York, where he corresponded with Oliver Cromwell's spymaster John Thurloe. Despite his support for the Protectorate, Bowles saw the restoration of Charles II as the surest method of reaching a political and religious compromise, and, with it, peace and stability. In the final year of the Commonwealth, he actively mediated discussions between General George Monck and Thomas, Lord Fairfax, who were then preparing to declare for a free parliament at Westminster. Despite his active support for the Restoration, Bowles, with other Presbyterians, suffered exclusion in its immediate aftermath. And yet, dying on the eve of the infamous 'Black Bartholomew's Day' in August 1662, he did not quite live long enough to see the ejection of hundreds of his fellow Nonconformist ministers from their livings.

Shortly before his death, Bowles paid one last visit to none other than George Monck, by then ennobled as Duke of Albemarle. On encountering the duke, Bowles is said to have explained that 'I have buried the good old cause, and am now going to bury myself.'[1] The word 'burial' was on the lips of many of Charles II's subjects in the first months of his reign. The king himself spoke of his 'wish[es] that the memory of what is past, may be buried to the world'.[2] It was his earnestness in this regard that stirred the anxieties of his most ardent supporters that, along with the 'names and terms of distinction' of the civil war, their 'dear-bought experience', as Sir Roger L'Estrange put it, would be buried in oblivion. Some Royalists saw exhumation and posthumous justice as the wisest methods of forestalling renewed war, 'rebellion', and 'usurpation'. Writing from Constantinople in January

1662, Benjamin Denham, chaplain to the Royalist Heneage Finch, Earl of Winchelsea, explained his desire to reveal some information concerning the Marquess of Dorchester's behaviour in the 1640s, 'wch otherwise had beene buryed in the grave of oblivion, and dyed wth my owne person'.[3]

The metaphor of exhumation became a lucid and disturbing reality in the first winter of Charles II's reign. In January 1661, Oliver Cromwell's body and those of his son-in-law Colonel Henry Ireton and the regicide John Bradshaw were exhumed from their tombs at Westminster Abbey and mutilated at Tyburn. Their decollated heads were then displayed on the roof of Westminster Hall, the building in which Charles I had been condemned. Lauded by Royalists like Secretary of State Sir Edward Nicholas as 'a wonderful example of justice',[4] these highly symbolic acts were imitated eight months later when the bodies of a further twenty-one men and women were disinterred from Westminster Abbey, in which they had been given honourable burial during the 1640s and 1650s. Unlike the trio that had been exhumed in January, these individuals were to be buried, albeit unceremoniously in a nearby pit.[5]

What these vindictive actions imply is that, if Royalists were to support the burial of the late troubles after the Restoration, it was to be on their terms. In doing so, they were counteracting the cover-up of which individuals like Edward Bowles were suspected when they spoke of 'burying' their former actions. Those, like Bowles, who had opposed Crown and established church were not to be let off the hook so easily. Bowles's fellow Presbyterian William Bates was one who was acutely conscious of this hostility to the spirit of oblivion and the ends to which it was leading. Speaking from the pulpit on the day of his ejection from his living at Tottenham in Middlesex, Bates explained that, notwithstanding recent 'promises' which had been 'made to bury all differences as rubbish under the foundation ... nevertheless the great work of many persons [had been] only to revive those former animosities ... to promote divisions and disturbances amongst us, clothe their enemies with the livery of shame and reproach, that so they may be baited by their fury'.[6]

The Restoration's politics of memory was one in which attempts were made to take control of how, if at all, the events of the civil wars were to be buried. The acquisition of positions of central and local office by Royalists in the first year of Charles II's reign ensured that this authority to speak for the recent past was theirs. The result was, as we have seen in this book, not far from what Bates predicted: the clothing of former opponents of Crown and established church in what he described as 'the livery of shame and reproach'. This was accompanied by the censorship of opinions that differed from the Royalists' censorious account of the civil war and revolution as a 'rebellion' and 'usurpation' driven by the cancerous ideology of 'fanaticism'. By delegitimising Parliamentarianism and republicanism publicly and by preventing their social circulation, Royalists sought to forestall the reproduction of an ideology that was, by their estimation, inextricable from rebellion and regicide.

And yet the major contention of this book has been that experiences of censorship and censure were not unchallenged by those who were on the receiving end. Former opponents of Crown and established church discovered ways of moulding the mnemonic landscapes of the Stuart realms. Often, this involved counteracting the Royalists' delegitimisation of the old cause and expounding instead the ideas that taking up arms had been for the 'true Protestant religion', that Oliver Cromwell and 'Lord' Lambert had been 'honest' men, and even, on occasion, that the regicide had been 'just', 'legal', and 'right'. Others corrected what they felt was the obsequious praise that had been heaped on those who had brought about the Restoration, especially General Monck. It is also clear that these kinds of statements infused the conversations of like-minded men and women. In spaces that were (often wrongly) held to be conducive to private conversations, the old cause was justified and nostalgised. In these ways, erstwhile opponents of Crown and established church found ways of publicly and socially legitimising their actions and the decisions upon which they were based, perpetuating thereby identities that were, as Royalists had feared, entangled with the weighty decisions to resist and oppose Crown and established church before the Restoration.

But sympathies for Parliament and the Republic served other purposes within the politics of memory in the reigns of Charles II and James II. In the context of Royalist uses of the 'rebellion' and 'usurpation' to undermine 'fanatics', enduring allegiances provided people with methods of framing opposition and resistance not only to old Cavaliers, but also to those whose positions of authority derived from Restoration settlements. Moreover, the articulation of opinions about the recurrence of war and revolution in the future exploited the very anxieties that had driven the Royalists' pursuit of mnemonic hegemony. When these kinds of opinions were shared between men and women who were like-minded, they had the potential to inspire rebellion, but also hope. In each of these forms, sympathies for Parliament and the Republic continued to serve the people who had opposed Crown and established church in ways that did not entail conspiracy or political and religious violence.

The story does not end with England and Wales. The claims of former rebels in Scotland and Ireland that they were instrumental in the return of Charles II to his 'rightful' throne did nothing to preclude similar experiences of Royalist censure and censorship in those kingdoms. In Scotland, rescissory legislation sought to sever people from the 'pretended Work of Reformation' between 1637 and 1650. The same was true in Ireland, where, notwithstanding the retention of land and authority by New Protestants, the symbols of Parliament's rebellion, such as the Covenants, were publicly desecrated. In these contexts, we can consider comparable sympathies for opposition to, and resistance against, the Stuarts and established church after the Restoration as evidence of the contestation and subversion of Royalist attempts to reconfigure public and social representations of the recent past. Together, we can speak of mnemonic landscapes that, rather than being distinct, were intersected by inspiring reflections on how far rebellion in each of the four kingdoms had resulted in the transformation of the political, religious, and socio-economic status quo throughout Britain.

Seditious memories took forms other than speech and writing. Most intriguingly, this involved what has been described in this book as 'mis-commemoration'. In the failure to comply with the acts and proclamations concerning commemoration of the anniversaries of the regicide on 30 January and the Restoration on 29 May, men and women may have been displaying opinions about the Royalists' interpretations of these events or, at the very least, challenging the use of these occasions as means of disseminating an anti-fanatical interpretation of the recent past. Mis-commemoration discloses other beliefs, including dissenting opinions regarding government-sponsored fasting and thanksgiving, and especially the excesses to which the latter might lead. The anniversaries were also given over to statements about the political and religious settlements of Britain which, owing to the messages of loyalty that were broadcast from the pulpit and in other places on these occasions, were imbued with peculiar potency.

A source of considerable discomfort to the government was the fact that many of those who articulated seditious memories had not experienced the events in question, or had done so only as children or teenagers. This speaks of how far those who had supported Parliament and the Republic sought to transmit their sympathies to those who were born immediately before, during, or even after the era of wars and revolution. That they did so is a measure of the failure of Royalists to forestall the reproduction of 'fanatic' ideologies through censorship and censure. What it suggests, in fact, is that the desperate efforts of Royalists to expound their 'dear-bought experience' had the effect of perpetuating the kinds of opinions that we have referred to here as seditious memories. To continue the metaphor, the exhumation of the civil wars and revolution, as well as their very public desecration, only served to prolong their presence in the British imagination. The result was that, when 'popery' and 'arbitrary' government reared their heads once more in the 1670s, a new generation of Protestants looked back to the actions of their elders for inspiration. It may be that this provided at least some of the motivation behind the deposal of James II from the throne in 1688–89.

To be sure, the Glorious Revolution witnessed the freeing up of discourse around the events of the wars and revolution. Speaking in the House of Commons in 1689, the long-standing MP and former Parliamentarian officer John Birch spoke boldly that for 'these 40 years' he and his fellow Protestants had 'been scrambling for [their] Religion' and that, having fought for Parliament in the 1640s, he had been 'on the right side'.[7] That, shortly after the Restoration, Birch had attracted the attention of the government for referring to his disbanded New Model Army regiment as 'his Lyons', and adding that 'hee hoped they wold serve him againe if hee had occasion', shows how far the mnemonic landscape had shifted over the previous three decades.[8] Indeed, Birch was even in a position to leave a monumental inscription at Weobley Church in Herefordshire containing his belief that, in supporting Parliament during the civil wars, he had been 'vindicating ye Laws and Liberties of his Country in War, and of promoting its Welfare and Prosperity in Peace'.[9] In the shadow of 1688, even those who had been brought up in Royalist households during the 1640s, such as sometime Speaker of the House of Commons Sir Edward Seymour, were moved to speak with equanimity of 'what a miserable case the Subject was brought [to]' by the reign of Charles I.[10]

The transition that took place in the mnemonic landscape after the Glorious Revolution deserves closer scrutiny. The commemoration of 30 January and 29 May continued into the next century and beyond, and, as historians have pointed out, it took a long time for the events of 1648–49 to be extricated from the martyr cult of Charles I.[11] Whether there is scope for a study of 'alternative' memories of the civil wars and revolution insofar as they penetrated society after 1688–89 is difficult to ascertain. The kinds of opinions about the past that became seditious or treasonable after the Glorious Revolution shifted to sympathies for the exiled James II and his descendants. This, together with the fact that James, Duke of Monmouth, became the major reference point for alternative memories after his rebellion in 1685, bears out the idea that seditious memories were always those which the government feared most. This does not mean, of course, that the events of the 1640s and 1650s became any less incendiary. We look forward to the publication of Edward Vallance's research into the issue of how sensitivities regarding involvement in the regicide endured into the eighteenth century.[12]

There are other areas that have been touched upon in this study, but that are worthy of more concerted attention elsewhere. Methodologically, this book has taken seriously the kinds of sentiment that were recorded in cases of sedition and treason, and it has involved construing the intentions of these words from the contexts in which they were spoken, especially how audiences were expected to react to controversial views. It may be that this methodology can be applied not only to the articulation of interpretations of the past in other historical contexts for which we have evidence of seditious and treasonable language, but also more general political and religious opinions. One such area could be the expressions of alternative opinions about events of enduring social significance by women. Whereas women have figured in this study, I am conscious that, owing to the nature of the evidence, references to them have been sparse. Yet if we look to dangerous opinions after the Restoration that extend beyond memories, including, for instance, those that attacked Charles II and James II directly, we encounter the voices of many more women. The ways in which these memories were expressed, and expectations of how their authors' audiences were to react, are likely to provide us with a greater sense of the role of women in strategies of cultural resistance and the formation of political and religious solidarities such as those to which this book has referred.

For these and other reasons, this study does not pretend to be the final word on the landscapes of remembering across the Stuart realms. The mnemonic landscapes of Scotland and Ireland – kingdoms in which, as we have seen, memories wove in and out of the complex, and enduring, legacies of civil conflict and rebellion – deserve closer scrutiny. The study of Scotland in this book penetrates only shallowly into the wealth of material that reflects enduring sympathies for the Covenants and 'Work of Reformation'. Other archives of central and local government, such as burgh records, may offer a window on to how men and women at the lower rungs of society remembered the Scottish revolution and, more importantly, how such views were circulated publicly and socially. The geographical reach of studies of remembering might also extend beyond the 'Atlantic Archipelago', taking thereby a less Brittano-centric approach than I have offered here.[13]

Whereas elements of this book, and another article that derived from it, have considered the forms which remembering took outside speech and writing, there is much more to say on this matter.[14] Further research into the relationship between memory and objects, such as might draw inspiration from recent studies of Jacobitism and material culture, would enrich our understanding of the mnemonic landscape of Restoration Britain.[15] These might cast light on the shadowy area that lies beyond Royalist souvenirs of the 1640s and 1650s. Indeed, this book has focused on only three of the five media that the cultural historian Peter Burke has identified as the transmitters of memory: orality, writing, and actions (such as rituals). Together with further studies of these media, future work on how the civil wars and revolution were remembered might also consider how images and spaces served the transmission of interpretations of those events.[16] In terms of the latter, we look forward to the work of Ian Atherton on the commemoration of battles and sieges.[17] Others might pick up where I left off in chapter 5 by thinking further about sequestered sites in urban and rural landscapes and how these perpetuated identities born of conflict. This all suggests that the myriad approaches labelled 'memory studies' still have a great deal to tell us about the legacies of the civil wars and revolution in Britain.

I have only been able to survey a limited period of British history from the Restoration to the Glorious Revolution. Pleasingly, further chronologies of memory are being explored by others. Of particular interest will be the research of Imogen Peck into memory and the numerous forms that it took in the immediate aftermath of the civil wars until the Restoration.[18] So too will be the PhD research of Michael Sewell, who is exploring how the civil wars and revolution have been remembered over a much longer period.[19]

Speaking in a Commons debate about the tercentenary of the Glorious Revolution in 1988, the future leader of the Labour Party, Jeremy Corbyn, declared his misgivings that 'We have chosen to celebrate the tercentenary of the so-called glorious revolution of 1688 rather than the triumph of the armies of Parliament over the armies of the King during the civil war'.[20] To be sure, even if we do not agree with Corbyn's depiction of Parliament's 'triumph', we may ask why it is that the revolutions of 1637–1660 fail to stir the British imagination in the same way of those in other countries throughout the world. It is surely significant that, at the time of writing, the desecration of those who were exhumed from Westminster Abbey and deposited in an unmarked pit nearby has attracted only a commemorative plaque. The Royalists' burial of the old cause continues to effect how we understand it today.

NOTES

1 S. Wright, 'Bowles, Edward (*bap.* 1613, *d.* 1662)', in *ODNB*, vi, pp. 959–960.
2 Cited in H. Nenner, 'The Trial of the Regicides: Retribution and Treason in 1660', in *Politics and the Political Imagination*, p. 22.
3 TNA, SP29/49/97.
4 *CSPD, 1660–61*, p. 500.
5 J. G. Nichols, *Collectanea Topographica et Genealogica* (8 vols, London: John Bowyer Nichols and Son, 1843), viii, pp. 153–154.
6 *Farewell Sermons*, p. 164.
7 *Cobbett's Parliamentary History of England. From the Norman Conquest, in 1066 to the Year 1803* (36 vols, London, 1809), v, p. 51.
8 TNA, SP29/23/71, I.
9 This inscription still survives and can be seen in Weobley Church (Herefordshire).
10 Goldie et al., *Entring Book*, iv, p. 505.
11 Lacey, *Cult of King Charles*.
12 E. Vallance, 'Writing the Regicide in an Age of Revolution: The Case of Mark Noble', in Vallance, *Remembering Early Modern Revolutions*.
13 For studies which have investigated memories of the British civil wars outside Britain, see G. Cubitt, 'Revolution, Reaction and Restoration: The Meanings and Uses of Seventeenth-Century English History in the Political Thinking of Benjamin Constant, c. 1797–1830', *European Review of History* 14:1 (2007), 21–47; and P. Walker, 'The Church Militant: The American Émigré Clergy and the Making of the British Counterrevolution, 1763–92' (unpublished PhD dissertation, University of Columbia, 2016).
14 Legon, 'Bound Up with Meaning'.
15 M. Pittock, *Material Culture and Sedition, 1688–1760: Treasured Objects, Secret Places* (Basingstoke: Palgrave Macmillan, 2013).
16 P. Burke, 'History as Social Memory', in T. Butler (ed.), *Memory: History, Culture and the Mind* (Oxford: Blackwell, 1989), pp. 100–102.
17 For an introduction to that research, see Atherton, 'Remembering (and Forgetting)', pp. 95–119.

18 For an introduction to that research, see I. Peck, 'The Great Unknown: The Negotiation and Narration of Death by English Civil War Widows, 1647–1660', *Northern History* (2016), 220–235.
19 The title of his PhD, which is currently under way at the University of Essex, is 'The Meanings of Modern Commemoration of the British Civil Wars in the 1640s.'
20 House of Commons Debate, 7 July 1988, 'Revolutions of 1688–89 (Tercentenary)', *Hansard*, vol. 136, col. 1253, https://api.parliament.uk/historic-hansard/commons/1988/jul/07/revolutions-of-1688-89-tercentenary#column_1253 (accessed 7 May 2018).

Select bibliography

MANUSCRIPTS

British Library, London

Harley MS 7319   'A Collection of Choice Poems'
Lansdowne MS 1152   A Collection of the Papers of William Bridgeman, Esq.

Essex Record Office, Chelmsford

D/ABW17   Commissary of Bishop of London: Wills
Q/SR387–389   Quarter Sessions Rolls, 1660–1685

House of Lords Record Office, London

PO/JO/10/1   Main Papers, 1–12 January 1641

National Archives of Scotland, Edinburgh

PA2   Acts of the Parliaments of Scotland

National Library of Ireland, Dublin

MS4908, 4909   Assize Books Clonmel, 1663–69, 1674–75, 1683

Somerset Heritage Centre, Taunton

Q/SR99, 100–103, 105, 155   Quarter Sessions Rolls, 1660–64, 1683

Select bibliography

Surrey History Centre, Woking

LM1058   Papers relating to *The King v. Thomas Hall of Godalming*

The National Archives, London

ASSI5/5   Assizes: Oxford Circuit: Indictment Files, 1681–83
PROB11   Prerogative Court of Canterbury: Wills
SP16   State Papers Domestic: Charles I
SP28   State Papers Domestic: Interregnum
SP29   State Papers Domestic: Charles II
SP31   State Papers Domestic: James II
SP44   State Papers Domestic: Entry Books
SP89   State Papers Foreign: Portugal

The Victoria & Albert Museum, London

F   Forster MS

EARLY PRINTED SOURCES

Amy, S[amuel], *A Præfatory DISCOURSE TO A Late PAMPHLET Entituled, A MEMENTO FOR English PROTESTANTS, &c* (London, 1682).
AN ANSWER TO THE GENEVA BALLAD ([London], 1674).
THE ARRAIGNMENT, TRYAL AND CONDEMNATION OF Stephen Colledge FOR HIGH-TREASON, IN Conspiring the Death of the KING, the Levying of WAR, and the Subversion of the GOVERNMENT (London, 1681).
[Ashley Cooper, Anthony], *TWO SEAONSABLE DISCOURSES Concerning this present Parliament* (Oxford, 1675).
[Ashley Cooper, Anthony], *A LETTER From a Person of QUALITY, To His FRIEND In the COUNTRY.* (n.p., 1675).
[Bagshaw, Edward], *A LETTER unto a PERSON of Honour & Quality, Containing some ANIMADVERSIONS upon the Bishop of Worcester's LETTER* (London, [1662]).
Baxter, Richard, *THE TRUE HISTORY OF COUNCILS Enlarged and Defended* (London, 1682).
Baxter, Richard, *Reliquiae Baxterianae: OR, Mr. Richard Baxters NARRATIVE OF The most Memorable Passages OF HIS LIFE AND TIMES.*, ed. Matthew Sylvester (London, 1696).
Beaton, Nehemiah, *NO TREASON TO SAY, Kings are Gods Subjects: OR THE SUPREMACY OF God, opened, asserted, applied, In some Sermons preached at Lurgarshal in Sussex by N.B. then Record there* (London, 1661).
Behn, Aphra, *Sir Patient Fancy: A COMEDY* (London, 1678).
[Brown, John], *AN Apologeticall Relation, Of the particular sufferings of the faithfull Ministers & professours of the Church of Scotland, since August. 1660* (n.p., 1665).
[Burnet, Gilbert], *A MODEST AND FREE CONFERENCE BETWIXT a Conformist and Non-conformist, about the Present Distempers of Scotland* (n.p., 1669).
[Butler, Samuel], *THE GENEVA BALLAD. To the Tune of 48* (London, 1674).

The Cavaleers Letany (London, 1661).
THE CHARGE GIVEN BY Sr William Smith, Brt. At the Quarter-Sessions of the Peace held for the County of Middlesex, at Westminster, on Monday the 24th of April, 1682 (London, 1682).
[Charles II], *By the King. A PROCLAMATION, For Observation of the Thirtieth day of January as a day of Fast and Humiliation according to the late Act of Parliament for that purpose* (London, 166[1]).
[Charles II], *By the King. A PROCLAMATION, For the observation of the Nine and twentieth day of May instant, as a day of Publick Thanksgiving, according to the late Act of Parliament for that purpose* (London, 1661).
[Cockayne, George, Henry Danvers, and Henry Jessey], ENIAUTOS TERASTIOS MIRABILIS ANNUS, OR *The year of Prodigies and Wonders, being a faithful and impartial Collection of several Signs that have been seen in the Heavens, in the Earth, and in the Waters; together with many remarkable Accidents and Judgments befalling divers Persons, according as they have been testified by very credible hands; all which have happened within the space of one year last past, and are now made publick for a seasonable Warning to the People of these three Kingdoms speedily to repent and turn to the Lord, whose hand is lifted up amongst us* ([London], 1661).
[Cockayne, George, Henry Danvers, and Henry Jessey], MIRABILIS ANNUS SECUNDUS: Or, The SECOND YEAR OF PRODIGIES ([London], 1661).
[Cockayne, George, Henry Danvers, and Henry Jessey], MIRABILIS ANNUS SECUNDUS: OR, THE SECOND PART Of the SECOND YEARS PRODIGIES ([London], 1662).
[Colledge, Stephen], THE CATHOLICK GAMESTERS or A DUBBLE MATCH OF BOWLEING *With an Account of a Sharp Conference held on the Eve of St. Jago, between his HOLINESS and the Mahometan DONS in St. Katherines Bastile: wherein their Nine-pins are wholly condemned, and their Worships severely checkt, for pleying at that small Game now in the heat of his Harvest* (London, 1680).
[Colledge, Stephen], A RA-REE SHOW. *To the Tune of I am a Senceless Thing* (London, 1681).
[Colledge, Stephen], A SATYR AGAINST IN-JUSTICE; OR, Sc[rog]gs upon Sc[rog]gs (n.p., [1681]).
[Colledge, Stephen], *A True Copy OF A LETTER (intercepted) going for Holland, Directed Thus For his (and his Wives) never Failing Friend Roger Le Strange At the Oranges Court with Care and Speed, hast, hast, post hast* (London, 168[1]).
C[ooper], A[ndrew], STATOLOGIA OR THE HISTORY OF THE ENGLISH CIVIL VVARS, *In English Verse* (London, 166[0]).
A COUNTREY SONG, INTITULED THE RESTORATION ([London], 1661).
[Crofton, Zachary], *Berith Anti-Baal, OR Zach. Croftons Appearance Before the Prelate-Justice of Peace, Vainly pretending to binde the Covenant and Convenanters to their good Behaviour* (London, 1661).
THE DECLARATION OF JAMES DUKE of MONMOUTH, & *The Noblemen, Gentlemen & others, now in Arms, for Defence & vindication of the Protestant Religion, & the Laws, Rights, & Privileges of England, from the Invasion made upon them: & for Delivering the Kingdom from the Usurpation and Tyranny of* JAMES DUKE of YORK (n.p., [1685]).
A Dismal Account of the Burning of our Solemn LEAGUE and National COVENANT (n.p., 1662).

Select bibliography

A Door of Hope: OR, A CALL and DECLARATION for the gathering together of the first ripe Fruits unto the STANDARD of our Lord, KING JESUS ([London, 1661]).
D'Urfey, Thomas, *The Whig Rampant: OR, EXALTATION. Being a Pleasant New Song of 82* (London, 1682).
Eaton, Nathaniel, *De Fastis Anglicis, SIVE CALENDARIVM SACRUM* (London, 1661).
A FORM OF PRAYER, WITH THANKSGIVING To be used Of all the Kings MAJESTIE'S Loving Subjects The 29th May Yearly, For His MAJESTIE'S Happy Return to His KINGDOMS, It being also the Day of His Birth (London, 1661).
A Full and True ACCOUNT of the PROCEEDINGS AT THE Sessions of Oyer and Terminer, Holdern for the City of London, County of Middlesex, and Goal-Delivery of Newgate; WHICH BEGAN AT THE SESSIONS-House in the Old-Baily, On Wednesday, Septemb. 6th. and Ended on Thursday, Septemb. 7th. 1682 (London, 1682).
Graunt, John, *Natural and Political OBSERVATIONS, Mentioned in a following INDEX, and made upon the Bills of Mortality* (London, 1662).
[Hammond, Henry], *Private Forms of Prayer, Fitted for the late Sad-Times. Particularly, A Form of Prayer for THE Thirtieth of January, Morning and Evening* (London, 166[1]).
Hill, William, *A BRIEF NARRATIVE Of that Stupendious Tragedie Late intended to be Acted by the Satanical SAINTS of these Reforming Times* (London, 1663).
Howell, James, *A CORDIAL FOR THE CAVALIERS* (n.p., [1661]).
AN Impartial Account OF THE NATURE and TENDENCY Of the Late ADDRESSES, IN A LETTER TO A Gentleman in the COUNTRY (London, 1681).
Intelligencer.
[Jones, Roger], *Mene Tekel; Or, The Downfal of Tyranny* (n.p., 1663).
[Jordan, Thomas], *Here is some comfort for Poor Cavaleeres* (London, [1661]).
Kennet, White, *A REGISTER AND CHRONICLE Ecclesiastical and Civil: CONTAINING MATTERS of FACT, Delivered in the WORDS of the most Authentick BOOKS, PAPERS, and RECORDS; Digested in Exact Order of TIME* (London, 1728).
Kingdomes Intelligencer.
[Leigh, Richard], *THE TRANSPROSER REHEARS'D: OR THE Fifth ACT OF Mr. BAYES's PLAY* (Oxford, 1673).
[L'Estrange, Roger], *A CAVEAT TO THE Cavaliers* (London, 1661).
L'Estrange, Roger, *A Modest Plea Both for the CAVEAT, AND The AUTHOR of It* (London, 1661).
L'Estrange, Roger, *Considerations and Proposals In Order to the Regulation OF THE PRESS: TOGETHER WITH Diverse Instances of Treasonous, and Seditious Pamphlets, Proving the Necessity thereof* (London, 1663).
[L'Estrange, Roger], *L'Estrange's CASE In a CIVIL DIALOGUE Betwixt ZEKIEL AND EPHRAIM* (London, 1680).
A LETTER CONTAINING An Humble and Serious Advice to some in Scotland, IN Reference to their late Troubles and Calamities (n.p., 1661).
A LETTER FROM Mr. Edward Whitaker TO THE Protestant Joyner Upon his Bill being sent to OXFORD (London, 1681).
London Gazette.
Loyal Protestant and True Domestick Intelligence.

Select bibliography

M., N., *A MODEST APOLOGY FOR THE Students of Edenburgh BURNING A POPE December 25, 1680* (London, 1681).

[Marvell, Andrew], *THE REHEARSAL TRANSPROS'D; Or, Animadversions Upon a late Book, Intituled, A PREFACE SHEWING What Grounds there are of Fears and Jealousies of Popery* (London, 1672).

[McWard, Robert], *The True NON-CONFORMIST in Answere to the Modest and Free Conference Betwixt a CONFORMIST and a NON-CONFORMIST, About the present Distempers of SCOTLAND* (n.p., 1671).

M[eade], M[atthew], *SOLOMON'S PRESCRIPTION For the Removal of PESTILENCE: OR, The Discovery of the PLAGUE of our Hearts, in order to the Healing of that in our Flesh* (London, 1665).

Mercurius Civicus or A True Account of Affairs Both Foreign and Domestick.

Mews, P[eter], *VVHEREAS Tuesday next, being the Thirtieth day of this instant January* (Oxford, 167[2]).

My Lord Marquis OF ARGYLE HIS SPEECH UPON THE SCAFFOLD, the 27 of May 1661 (n.p., 1661).

A NARRATIVE OF THE APPREHENDING, COMMITMENT, ARRAIGNMENT, CONDEMNATION, And EXECUTION of JOHN JAMES Who Suffered at TIBURNE, Novemb. the 26th 1661 (London, 1662).

Newes.

Observator in Dialogue.

The Occasional Doctor HIS EXAMINATION BEFORE A Committee of Whigg-Priests (n.p., [1682?]).

Ogilby, John, *THE ENTERTAINMENT OF His Most Excellent MAJESTIE CHARLES II, IN His PASSAGE through the CITY of LONDON TO HIS CORONATION* (London, 1662).

Paterson, John, *TANDEM BONA CAUSA TRIUMPHAT. OR SCOTLANDS Late misery bevailed, and the HONOUR AND LOYALTY Of this Ancient KINGDOM, Asserted in a SERMON, Preached before His Majesties High Commissioner, and the Honourable Parliament of the Kingdom of Scotland. At Edinburgh the 17. day of February. 1661* (Edinburgh, 1661).

[Phillips, John], *New News from TORY-LAND AND Tantivy-Shire* (London, 1682).

[Phillips, John], *Speculum Crape-Gownorum, THE SECOND PART* (London, 1682).

Phillips Thomas, *The Long Parliament REVIVED: OR, An Act for Continuation, and the Not Dissolving the Long Parliament (call'd by King CHARLES the First, in the Year 1640.) but by an Act of Parliament* (London, 1660).

Price, Evan, *Eye-salve for England: OR, The Grand TRAPPAN Detected, In a plain and faithful NARRATIVE of the horrid and unheard-of Designs of some Justices and Deputy-Lieutenants in Lancashire, treacherously to ensnare the Lives and Estates of many Persons of Quality in that County, as also in the Counties of York and Chester* (London, 1667).

A PROCLAMATION Concerning the Students in the Colledge of Edinburgh (Edinburgh, 1681).

Protestant (Domestick) Intelligence or News Both from City and Country.

Prynne, William, *THE RE-PUBLICANS AND OTHERS SPURIOUS Good Old Cause, briefly and truly Anatomized* (n.p., 1659).

Select bibliography

Rosewell, Samuel, THE ARRAIGNMENT AND TRYAL Of the late REVEREND Mr. Thomas Rosewell, FOR HIGH-TREASON; BEFORE THE Lord Chief Justice Jefferies, at the Court of King's Bench, Westminster, in the Year 1684 (London, 1718).

Rushworth, John, *Historical Collections* (8 vols., London, 1721), iv.

A SERMON Preach'd on May the 29th. 1673. IN ONE OF His Majesties LICENS'D MEETINGS in DEVON (London, 1673).

[Simon, Patrick], A Further CONTINUATION AND DEFENCE, OR, A Third Part OF THE Friendly Debate (London, 1670).

A Solemn ACKNOWLEDGEMENT OF PUBLICK SINS And breaches of the COVENANT AND A Solemn ENGAGEMENT to all the DUTIES contained therein, namely those, which do in a more speciall way relate unto the Dangers of these Times (Edinburgh, 1648).

THE SPEECHES AND PRAYERS Of JOHN BARKSTEAD, JOHN OKEY, and MILES CORBET (London, 1662).

The SPEECHES AND PRAYERS OF Some of the late King's Judges, viz. Major Gen. Harrison, Octob. 13. Mr. John Carew, Octob. 15. Mr. Justice Cooke, Mr. Hugh Peters Octob. 16. Mr. Tho. Scot, Mr. Gregory Clement, Col. Adrian Scroop, Col. John Jones, Oct. 17. Col. Dan. Axtell, Col. Fran. Hacker, Octob. 19. 1660 ([London], 1660).

Stanhope, Thomas, FOUR SERMONS Preached upon Solemne Occasions (London, 1670).

[Stewart, James], NAPTHALI, OR The Wrestlings of the Church of SCOTLAND For the KINGDOM of CHRIST; Contained in A true and short Deduction thereof, from the beginning of the Reformation of Religion, until the Year 1667 (n.p., 1667).

[Stewart, James], JUS POPULI VINDICATUM OR, The Peoples Right, to defend themselves and their Covenanted Religion Vindicated (n.p., 1669).

Tillam, Thomas, THE TEMPLE Of Lively Stones (London, 1660).

[Tomkins, Thomas], The Rebels Plea, OR. Mr. Baxters judgement, Concerning the late Wars (London, 1660).

A Treatise of the Execution of Justice, wherein is clearly proved, that the Execution of Judgment and Justice, is as well the Peoples as the Magistrates Duty; And that if Magistrates pervert Judgement, the People are bound by the Law of God to execute Judgement without them, and upon them (n.p., [1663]).

The True and Perfect SPEECH of Mr. James Guthrey LATE Minister of Sterling AS It was delivered by himself immediately before his Execution, on June 1. 1661. at Edinbrough (Edinburgh, 1661).

A TRUE NARRATIVE OF THE Horrid PLOT AND CONSPIRACY OF THE POPISH PARTY Against the LIFE of His Sacred Majesty, THE GOVERNMENT, AND THE Protestant Religion (London, 1679).

THE TRYAL OF Sir Henry Vane, Kt. AT the KINGS BENCH, Westminster, June the 2d. and 6th. 1662 (n.p., 1662).

THE TRYALS OF THE PRISONERS AT THE SESSIONS Holdern in the Sessions-House in the Old-Baily. Which began on the Twelfth of July, 1682 and ended the Thirteenth of the same Month (London, 1682).

W., J., Some REMARKS UPON A SPEECH MADE TO THE GRAND JURY For the County of MIDDLESEX CONCERNING THE Execution of PENALTIES UPON THE Churches of Christ, Which worship God in MEETING-HOUSES, For their so doing (London, 1682).

[Wharton, George], *Select and Choice POEMS Collected out of the LABOURS OF CAPTAIN George Wharton* (London, 1661).

THE Wheel of Time turning Round TO THE GOOD OLD VVAY; OR, The Good Old Cause Vindicated (n.p., [1661]).

Williams, Griffith, *SEVEN TREATISES, Very necessary to be observed in these very bad Days To prevent the Seven last Vials of God's wrath, that the Seven Angels are to pour down upon the Earth* (London, 1661).

Wodrow, Robert, *The History of the Sufferings of the Church of Scotland* (2 vols, Edinburgh, 1721–22).

LATER PRINTED SOURCES

Atkinson, J. C. (ed.), *Quarter Sessions Records [North Riding of Yorkshire]* (9 vols, London: North Riding Record Society, 1888), vi.

Blair, Robert, *The life of Mr Robert Blair, Minister of St Andrews, containing his Autobiography from 1593 to 1636*, ed. T. McCrie (Edinburgh: Wodrow Society, 1848).

Brodie, Alexander, and James Brodie, *The Diary of Alexander Brodie of Brodie, MDCLII.–MDCLXXX. And of his Son, James Brodie of Brodie, M DC LXXX–M DC LXXXV*, ed. D. Laing (Aberdeen: Spalding Club, 1863).

Brown, P. H. (ed.), *The Register of the Privy Council of Scotland*, third series (Edinburgh: HM General Register House, 1908–24), i–ix.

Calendar of State Papers Preserved in the Public Record Office, Domestic Series, James II, vol. i, *February–December, 1685* (3 vols, London: HM Stationery Office (HMSO), 1960).

Calendar of the State Papers relating to Ireland preserved in the Public Record Office. 1663–1665 (London: HMSO, 1907).

Capel, Arthur, Earl of Essex, *Selections from the Correspondence of Arthur Capel Earl of Essex 1675–1677*, ed. C. E. Pike (London: Camden Society, 1913).

Cockburn, J. S. (ed.), *Calendar of Assize Records: Kent Indictments, Charles II, 1660–1675* (London: HMSO, 1995).

Cockburn, J. S. (ed.), *Calendar of Assize Records: Kent Indictments, Charles II, 1676–1688* (London: HMSO, 1997).

Collections of the Massachusetts Historical Society, vol. VIII, fourth series (Boston, MA: Wiggin and Lunt, 1868).

Cox, J. C. (ed.), *Three Centuries of Derbyshire Annals. As Illustrated by the Records of the Quarter Sessions of the County of Derby, From Queen Elizabeth to Queen Victoria* (2 vols, London: Bemrose and Sons, 1890), ii.

Erskine, John, *Journal of the Hon. John Erskine of Carnock 1683–1687*, ed. W. MacLeod (Edinburgh: Scottish History Society, 1893).

Farewell Sermons of Some of the Most Eminent of the Nonconformist Ministers Delivered at the Period of their Ejectment by the Act of Uniformity in the Year 1662 (London: Gale and Fenner, 1816).

Goldie, M., J. Spurr, T. Harris, S. Taylor, M. Knights, and J. McElligott (eds), *The Entring Book of Roger Morrice 1677–1691* (7 vols, Woodbridge: Boydell, 2007).

Green, M. A. E., F. H. B. Daniell, and F. Bickley (eds), *Calendar of State Papers,*

Select bibliography

    Domestic Series, of the Reign of Charles II (28 vols, London: Longman, Green, Longman, and Roberts, 1869–1936).
Hardy, W. J. (ed.), *Hertford County Records, Notes and Extracts from the Sessions Rolls, 1581–1698* (4 vols, Hertford: Simon, 1905), i.
Henry, Philip, *Diaries and Letters of Philip Henry of Broad Oak, Flintshire, 1631–1696*, ed. M. H. Lee (London: Kegan Paul, Trench, 1882).
Heywood, Oliver, *The Rev. Oliver Heywood, B.A., 1630–1702; His Autobiography, Diaries, Anecdote and Event Books*, ed. J. Horsfall Turner (4 vols, Bingley: T. Harrison, 1882–85).
Hinds, A. B. (ed.), *Calendar of State Papers and Manuscripts relating to English Affairs, existing in the Archives of Venice, and in other libraries of Northern Italy*, vol. xxxii, *1661–1664* (London: HMSO, 1932).
Hines, P. Jr. (ed.), *Newdigate Newsletters: Numbers 1 through 2100 (3 January 1673/4 through June 1692)* (n.p., 1994).
Historical Manuscripts Commission (ed.), *Calendar of the Manuscripts of the Marquess of Ormonde, K.P. preserved at Kilkenny Castle*, New Series, vol. v (Hereford: HMSO, 1908).
The History and Proceedings of the House of Commons from the Restoration to the Present Time (London, 1742), i.
Hoad, M. J., and R. P. Grime (eds), *Portsmouth Record Series: Borough Sessions Papers, 1653–1688: A Calendar* (Chichester: Phillimore, 1971).
Hobson, M. G., and H. E. Salter (eds), *Oxford Council Acts, 1626–1665* (5 vols, Oxford: Oxford University Press, 1928–62), ii.
Howell, T. B. (ed.), *A Complete Collection of State Trials and Proceedings for High Treason and Other Crimes and Misdemeanours from the earliest period to the year 1783, with notes and other illustrations* (34 vols, London: T. C. Hansard: 1816–28).
Jackson, C. (ed.), *Yorkshire Diaries and Autobiographies in the Seventeenth and Eighteenth Centuries* (2 vols, Durham: Andrews, 1877), i.
Jeaffreson, J. C. (ed.), *Middlesex County Records* (4 vols, London: Middlesex County Records Society, 1886–92).
Jolly, Thomas, *The Note Book of the Rev. Thomas Jolly, A.D. 1671–1693*, ed. H. Fishwick (Manchester: Chetham Society, 1894).
Josselin, Ralph, *The Diary of Ralph Josselin, 1616–1683*, ed. A. Macfarlane (Oxford: Oxford University Press, 1991).
Keeble, N. H., and G. F. Nuttall (eds), *Calendar of the Correspondence of Richard Baxter*, (2 vols, Oxford: Clarendon, 1991).
Kirkton, James, *The Secret and True History of the Church of Scotland from the Restoration to the Year 1678. By the Rev. Mr James Kirkton*, ed. C. Kirkpatrick Sharpe (Edinburgh: James Bannatyne, 1817).
Larkham, Thomas, *The Diary of Thomas Larkham, 1647–1669*, ed. S. H. Moore (Woodbridge: Boydell, 2011).
Lauder, John, *Historical Notices of Scotish Affairs, Selected from the Manuscripts of Sir John Lauder of Fountainhall, Bart., One of the Senators of the College of Justice. Volume First. 1661–1663*, ed. D. Laing (2 vols, Edinburgh: Bannatyne Club, 1848).
Law, Robert, *Memorialls; Or. The Memorable Things that Fell Out within this Island of Brittain from 1638 to 1684. By the Rev. Mr Robert Law*, ed. C. Kirkpatrick Sharpe (Edinburgh: Constable, 1818).

Select bibliography

Lord, G. (ed.), *Poems on Affairs of State: Augustan Satirical Verse, 1660–1714* (7 vols, New Haven, CT: Yale University Press, 1963–75).
Lowe, Roger, *The Diary of Roger Lowe of Ashton-in-Makerfield, Lancashire. 1663–1678*, ed. I. G. Winstanley (Ashton-in-Makerfield: Picks, 1994).
Ludlow, Edmund, *A Voyce from the Watch Tower, Part Five: 1660–1662*, ed. A. B. Worden (London: Royal Historical Society, 1978).
Luttrell, Narcissus, *A Brief Historical Relation of State Affairs from September 1678 to April 1714. By Narcissus Luttrell* (6 vols, Oxford: Oxford University Press, 1857), i.
Newcome, Henry, *The Diary of the Rev. Henry Newcome, from September 30, 1661, to September 29, 1663*, ed. T. Heywood (Manchester: Chetham Society, 1849).
Nicoll, John, *A Diary of Public Transactions and Other Occurrences, Chiefly in Scotland, From January 1650 to June 1667*, ed. D. Laing (Edinburgh: Bannatyne Club, 1836).
Pepys, Samuel, *The Diary of Samuel Pepys: A New and Complete Transcription*, ed. R. Latham and W. Matthews (11 vols, London: G. Bell and Sons, 1983).
Raine, J. (ed.), *Depositions from the Castle of York, relating to offences committed in the Northern Counties in the seventeenth century* (Durham: Francis Andrews, 1861).
Rich, Mary, Countess of Warwick, *Memoir of Lady Warwick: Also Her Diary from A.D. 1666 to 1672, Now First Published*, ed. A. Walker (London: Religious Tract Society 1847).
Royal Commission on Historical Manuscripts (ed.), *Report on Manuscripts in Various Collections* (8 vols, London: [HMSO], 1901–13), i.
Royal Commission on Historical Manuscripts (ed.), *Report on the Manuscripts of the Late Reginald Rawdon Hastings, Esq., of the Manor house, Ashby de la Zouche* (4 vols, London: HMSO, 1928–47), ii.
Scott-Moncrieff, W. G. (ed.), *The Records of the Proceedings of the Justiciary Court Edinburgh 1661–1678*, vol. I, *1661–1669* (2 vols, Edinburgh: Scottish History Society, 1905).
Shaw, W. A. (ed.), *Calendar of Treasury Books: Preserved in the Public Record Office*, vol. iii, pt 1, *1669–1672* (London: HMSO, 1908).
The statutes at large passed in the parliaments held in Ireland: from the third year of Edward the Second, A. D. 1310, to the first year of George the Third, A. D. 1761 inclusive, with marginal notes, and a compleat index to the whole (20 vols, Dublin: Boulter Grierson, 1765–1801).
The Statutes of the Realm (10 vols, n.p.: Great Britain Record Commission, 1810–28), v.
Stocks, H., and W. H. Stevenson (eds), *Records of the Borough of Leicester: Being a Series of Extracts from the Archives of the Corporation of Leicester, 1603–1688* (Cambridge: Cambridge University Press, 1923).
Thoresby, Ralph, *The Diary of Ralph Thoresby, F.R.S.: Author of the Topography of Leeds (1677–1724.)*, ed. J. Hunter (2 vols, London: Henry Colburn and Richard Bentley, 1830), i.
Townsend, Henry, *Diary of Henry Townsend of Elmley Lovett, 1640–1663*, ed. J. W. Willis Bund (2 vols, London: Mitchell Hughes and Clarke, 1930), ii.
Turner, James, *Memoirs of His Own Life and Times by Sir James Turner. M.DC. XXXII.–M.DC.LXX* (Edinburgh, 1829).
Underhill, E. B. (ed.), *The Records of a Church of Christ, Meeting in Broadmead, Bristol. 1640–1687* (London: J. Haddon, 1847).

Select bibliography

Veitch, William, and George Brysson, *Memoirs of Mr. William Veitch, and George Brysson, Written by themselves: With Other Narratives Illustrative of the History of Scotland, from the Restoration to the Revolution*, ed. T. McCrie (Edinburgh: William Blackwood, 1825).

Whitelocke, Bulstrode, *The Diary of Bulstrode Whitelocke, 1605–1675*, ed. R. Spalding (Oxford: Oxford University Press, 1990).

Wodrow, Robert, *The History of the Sufferings of the Church of Scotland from the Restoration to the Revolution by Rev, Robert Wodrow*, ed. R. Burns (Glasgow: Blackie, Fullarton, 1829), iii.

Wood, Anthony, *Athenae Oxonienses: An Exact History of all the Writers and Bishops who have had their Education in the University of Oxford*, ed. P. Bliss (4 vols, London, 1813–20).

Wood, Anthony, *The Life and Times of Anthony Wood, Antiquary, of Oxford, 1632–1695*, ed. A. Clark (5 vols, Oxford: Clarendon, 1891–1900).

ARTICLES AND BOOKS

Achinstein, S., *Literature and Dissent in Milton's England* (Cambridge: Cambridge University Press, 2003).

Adams, B., 'The Experience of Defeat Revisited: Suffering, Identity and the Politics of Obedience among Hertford Quakers, 1655–65', in C. Durston and J. Maltby (eds), *Religion in Revolutionary England* (Manchester: Manchester University Press, 2006), pp. 249–268.

Appleby, D. J., *Black Bartholomew's Day: Preaching, Polemic and Restoration Nonconformity* (Manchester: Manchester University Press, 2007).

Appleby, D. J., 'The Restoration County Community: A Post-conflict Culture', in J. Eales and A. Hopper (eds), *The County Community in Seventeenth-Century England and Wales* (Hatfield: University of Hertfordshire Press, 2012), pp. 100–124.

Appleby, D. J., 'Veteran Politics in Restoration England, 1660–1670', *Seventeenth Century*, 28:3 (2013), 323–342.

Ashcraft, R., *Revolutionary Politics and Locke's Two Treatises of Government* (Princeton, NJ: Princeton University Press, 1986).

Assmann, A., 'Four Formats of Memory: From Individual to Collective Constructions of the Past', in C. Emden and D. Midgley (eds), *Cultural Memory and Historical Consciousness in the German-Speaking World Since 1500: Papers from the Conference "The Fragile Tradition", Cambridge 2002*, vol. 1 (Oxford: Peter Lang, 2004), pp. 19–38.

Assmann, J., 'Collective Memory and Cultural Identity', trans. J. Czaplika, *New German Critique*, 65 (Spring–Summer, 1995), 125–133.

Atherton, I.. 'The Press and Popular Political Opinion', in B. Coward (ed.), *Companion to Stuart Britain* (Malden, MA: Blackwell, 2003), pp. 88–110.

Atherton, I., 'Remembering (and Forgetting) Fairfax's Battlefields', in A. Hopper and P. Major (eds), *England's Fortress: New Perspectives on Thomas, 3rd Lord Fairfax* (Farnham: Ashgate, 2014), pp. 95–119.

Bardle, S., *The Literary Underground in the 1660s: Andrew Marvell, George Wither, Ralph Wallis, and the World of Restoration Satire and Pamphleteering* (Oxford: Oxford University Press, 2012).

Barnard, T. C., 'Crises of Identity among Irish Protestants 1641–1685', *Past and Present*, 127 (May, 1990), 39–83.

Barry, J., 'Popular Culture in Seventeenth-Century Bristol', in B. Reay (ed.), *Popular Culture in Seventeenth-Century England* (London: Croom Helm, 1985), pp. 59–90.

Beiner, G., *Remembering the Year of the French: Irish Folk History and Social Memory* (Madison, WI: University of Wisconsin Press, 2007).

Bellah, R. N., R. Madsen, W. M. Sullivan, A. Swidler, and S. M. Tipton, *Habits of the Heart: Individualism and Commitment in American Life* (Berkeley, CA: University of California Press, 1985).

Bodnar, J., *Remaking America: Public Memory, Commemoration, and Patriotism in the Twentieth Century* (Princeton, NJ: Princeton University Press, 1992).

Booth, W. J., *Communities of Memory: On Witness, Identity, and Justice* (Ithaca, NY: Cornell University Press, 2006).

Bowen, L., 'Seditious Speech and Popular Royalism, 1649–60', in J. McElligott and D. L. Smith (eds), *Royalists and Royalism during Interregnum* (Manchester: Manchester University Press, 2010), pp. 44–66.

Boym, S., 'Nostalgia and Its Discontents', *Hedgehog Review*, 9:2 (2007), 7–18.

Braddick, M. J. (ed.), *The Politics of Gesture. Historical Perspectives* (Oxford: Oxford University Press, 2009).

Braddick, M. J., and J. Walter (eds), *Negotiating Power in Early Modern Society: Order, Hierarchy and Subordination in Britain and Ireland* (Cambridge: Cambridge University Press, 2001).

Burke, P., 'History as Social Memory', in T. Butler (ed.), *Memory: History, Culture and the Mind* (Oxford: Blackwell, 1989), pp. 97–113.

Bywaters, D., 'Representations of the Interregnum and Restoration in English Drama of the Early 1660s', *Review of English Studies*, 60:244 (2009), 255–270.

Capp, B., *The Fifth Monarchy Men: A Study in Seventeenth-Century Millenarianism* (London: Faber, 1972).

Clark, J. C. D, *Revolution and Rebellion: State and Society in England in the Seventeenth and Eighteenth Centuries* (Cambridge: Cambridge University Press, 1986).

Clifton, R., *The Last Popular Rebellion: The Western Rising of 1685* (Harlow: Maurice Temple Smith, 1984).

Cogswell, T., and A. Bellany, *The Murder of King James I* (New Haven, CT: Yale University Press, 2015).

Collins, J., 'Restoration Anti-Catholicism: A Prejudice in Motion', in C. W. A. Prior and G. Burgess (eds), *England's Wars of Religion Revisited* (Farnham: Ashgate, 2011), pp. 281–306.

Connerton, P., *How Societies Remember* (Cambridge: Cambridge University Press, 1989).

Cooper, T., *John Owen, Richard Baxter and the Formation of Nonconformity* (Farnham: Ashgate, 2011).

Corns, T. N. (ed.), *The Royal Image: Representations of Charles I* (Cambridge: Cambridge University Press, 1999).

Covington, S., '"The Odious Demon from Across the Sea": Oliver Cromwell, Memory and the Dislocations of Ireland', in E. Kuijpers, J. Pollmann, J. Müller, and J. van der Steen (eds), *Memory before Modernity: Practices of Memory in Early Modern Europe* (Leiden: Brill, 2013), pp. 149–164.

Select bibliography

Cowan, I. B., *The Scottish Covenanters 1660–1688* (London: V. Gollancz, 1976).
Coward, B. (ed.), *Companion to Stuart Britain* (Malden, MA: Blackwell, 2003).
Cressy, D., *Bonfires and Bells: National Memory and the Protestant Calendar in Elizabethan and Stuart England* (London: Weidenfeld and Nicolson, 1989).
Cressy, D., *Society and Culture in Early Modern England* (Aldershot: Ashgate, 2003).
Cressy, D., *England on Edge: Crisis and Revolution, 1640–1642* (Oxford: Oxford University Press, 2006).
Cressy, D., *Dangerous Talk: Scandalous, Seditious, and Treasonable Speech in Pre-modern England* (Oxford: Oxford University Press, 2010).
Cubitt, G., *History and Memory* (Manchester: Manchester University Press, 2007).
Cubitt, G., 'Revolution, Reaction and Restoration: The Meanings and Uses of Seventeenth-Century English History in the Political Thinking of Benjamin Constant, c. 1797–1830', *European Review of History*, 14:1 (2007), 21–47.
Davis, M., 'Is Spain Recovering Its Memory? Breaking the "Pacto del Olvido"', *Human Rights Quarterly*, 27:3 (Aug., 2005), 858–880.
De Krey, G. S., 'London Radicals and Revolutionary Politics, 1675–1683', in T. Harris, P. Seaward, and M. Goldie (eds), *The Politics of Religion in Restoration England* (Oxford: Basil Blackwell, 1990), pp. 133–162.
De Krey, G. S., 'Reformation in the Restoration Crisis, 1679–1682', in D. Hamilton and R. Strier (eds), *Religion, Literature, and Politics in Post-Reformation England, 1540–1688* (Cambridge: Cambridge University Press, 1996), pp. 231–252
De Krey, G. S., 'Radicals, Reformers, and Republicans: Academic Language and Political Discourse in Restoration London,' in A. Houston and S. Pincus (eds), *A Nation Transformed: England after the Restoration* (Cambridge: Cambridge University Press, 2001), pp. 71–99.
De Krey, G. S., *London and the Restoration 1659–1683* (Cambridge: Cambridge University Press, 2005).
Dennehy, C. A. (ed.), *Restoration Ireland: Always Settling and Never Settled* (Aldershot: Ashgate, 2008).
Dennehy, C. A., 'The Restoration Irish Parliament, 1661–6', in *Restoration Ireland*, pp. 53–68.
Devine, T. M., and J. R. Young (eds), *Eighteenth Century Scotland: New Perspectives* (East Linton: Tuckwell, 1999).
Earle, P., *Monmouth's Rebels: The Road to Sedgemoor 1685* (London: Weidenfeld and Nicolson, 1977).
Eisenstein, E. L., *The Printing Revolution in Early Modern Europe* (Cambridge: Cambridge University Press, 1983).
Erskine, C., 'The Political Thought of the Restoration Covenanters', in S. Adams and J. Goodare (eds), *Scotland in the Age of Two Revolutions* (Woodbridge: Boydell, 2014), pp. 155–172.
Esser, R., *The Politics of Memory: The Writing of Partition in the Seventeenth-Century Low Countries* (Leiden: Brill, 2012).
Fentress, J., and C. Wickham, *Social Memory* (Oxford: Blackwell, 1988).
Finlay, R. J., 'Keeping the Covenant: Scottish National Identity', in T. M. Devine and J. R. Young (eds), *Eighteenth Century Scotland: New Perspectives* (East Linton: Tuckwell, 1999), pp. 121–133.

Firth, C., and G. Davies, *The Regimental History of Cromwell's Army* (2 vols, Oxford: University of Oxford Press, 1940).
Fisher, M., *Capitalist Realism: Is There No Alternative?* (Winchester: Zero Books, 2009).
Fleming, M., 'Phillippe Golledge: Another Oxford Musical Instrument Dealer?', *Galpin Society Journal*, 61 (Apr., 2008), 332–335.
Foucault, M., 'An Interview with Michel Foucault', trans. M. Jordin, *Radical Philosophy*, 11 (Summer, 1975), 24–29.
Freist, D., *Governed by Opinion: Politics, Religion and the Dynamics of Communication in Stuart London, 1637–1645* (London: I.B. Tauris, 1997).
Gibney, J., 'Ireland's Restoration Crisis', in T. Harris and S. Taylor (eds), *The Final Crisis of the Stuart Monarchy: The Revolutions of 1688–91 in Their British, Atlantic and European Contexts* (Woodbridge: Boydell, 2013), pp. 133–156.
Gibney, J., *The Shadow of a Year: The 1641 Rebellion in Irish History and Memory* (Madison, WI: University of Wisconsin Press, 2013).
Gille., Z., 'Postscript', in M. Todorova and Z. Gille (eds), *Post-Communist Nostalgia* (New York: Basic Books, 2010), pp. 279–289.
Gillespie, R., 'Dissenters and Nonconformists, 1661–1700', in K. Herlihy (ed.), *The Irish Dissenting Tradition 1650–1750* (Dublin: Four Courts, 1995), pp. 11–28.
Glăveanu, V., and K. Yamamoto, 'Bridging History and Social Psychology: What, How and Why', *Integrative Psychological and Behavioral Science*, 46:4 (2012), 431–439.
Goldie, M., *Roger Morrice and the Puritan Whigs* (Woodbridge: Boydell, 2016).
Greaves, R. L., 'The Tangled Careers of Two Stuart Radicals: Henry and Robert Danvers', *Baptist Quarterly*, 29:1 (Jan., 1981), 32–43.
Greaves, R. L., *Deliver Us from Evil: The Radical Underground in Britain, 1660–1663* (Oxford: Oxford University Press, 1986).
Greaves, R. L., *Enemies under His Feet: Radicals and Nonconformists in Britain, 1664–1677* (Stanford, CA: Stanford University Press, 1990).
Greaves, R. L., *John Bunyan and English Nonconformity* (London: Hambledon, 1992).
Greaves, R. L., *Secrets of the Kingdom: British Radicals from the Popish Plot to the Revolution of 1688–1689* (Stanford, CA: Stanford University Press, 1992).
Greaves, R. L., 'Conformity and Security in Scotland and Ireland, 1660–85', in E. Boran and C. Gribben (eds), *Enforcing Reformation in Ireland and Scotland, 1550–1700* (Aldershot: Ashgate, 2006), pp. 228–250.
Greaves, R. L., and R. Zaller (eds), *Biographical Dictionary of British Radicals in the Seventeenth Century* (3 vols, Brighton: Harvester, 1984).
Greenberg, J., and L. Martin, 'Politics and Memory: Sharnborn's Case and the Role of the Norman Conquest in Stuart Political Thought', in Nenner, *Politics and the Political Imagination*, pp. 121–142.
Griffiths, P., A. Fox, and S. Hindle (eds), *The Experience of Authority in Early Modern England* (Basingstoke: Macmillan, 1996).
Hall, S., *Cultural Studies 1983: A Theoretical Study* (Durham, NC: Duke University Press, 2016).
Halliday, P. D., *Dismembering the Body Politic: Partisan Politics in England's Towns, 1650–1730* (Cambridge: Cambridge University Press, 1998).
Harris, M., 'The "Captain in Oliver's Army" and the Wixford Catholics: Clerical/Lay

Select bibliography

Conflict in South Warwickshire, 1640–1674', *Warwickshire History*, 16:4 (Winter, 2015/16), 170–186.

Harris, T., *London Crowds in the Reign of Charles II: Propaganda and Politics from the Restoration until the Exclusion Crisis* (Cambridge: Cambridge University Press, 1987).

Harris, T., *Politics under the Later Stuarts: Party Conflict in a Divided Society, 1660–1715* (London: Longman, 1993).

Harris, T., 'The British Dimension, Religion, and the Shaping of Political Identities during the Reign of Charles II', in T. Claydon and I. McBride (eds), *Protestantism and National Identity: Britain and Ireland, c. 1650–c.1850* (Cambridge: Cambridge University Press, 1998), pp. 131–156.

Harris, T., 'The Legacy of the English Civil War: Rethinking the Revolution', *European Legacy*, 5:4 (2000), 501–514.

Harris, T., 'The Leveller legacy: From the Restoration to the Exclusion Crisis', in M. Mendle (ed.), *The Putney Debates of 1647: The Army, the Levellers and the English State* (Cambridge: Cambridge University Press, 2001), pp. 219–240.

Harris, T. (ed.), *The Politics of the Excluded, c.1500–1850* (Basingstoke: Palgrave, 2001).

Harris, T., 'Understanding Popular Politics in Restoration Britain', in A. Houston and S. Pincus (eds), *A Nation Transformed: England after the Restoration* (Cambridge: Cambridge University Press, 2001), pp. 125–153.

Harris, T., *Restoration: Charles II and his Kingdoms* (London, Allen Lane: 2005).

Harris, T., 'Restoration Ireland: Themes and Problems', in Dennehy, *Restoration Ireland*, pp. 1–19.

Harris, T., P. Seaward, and M. Goldie (eds), *The Politics of Religion in Restoration England* (Oxford: Basil Blackwell, 1990).

Harris, T., and S. Taylor (eds), *The Final Crisis of the Stuart Monarchy: The Revolutions of 1688–91 in Their British, Atlantic and European Contexts* (Woodbridge: Boydell, 2013).

Hayton, D., E. Cruickshanks, and S. Handley (eds), *The History of Parliament: The House of Commons 1690–1715* (Cambridge: Cambridge University Press, 2002), iv.

Henning, B. D. (ed.), *The History of Parliament: The House of Commons, 1660–1690* (3 vols, London, 1983).

Higgins, R., *Transforming 1916: Meaning, Memory and the Fiftieth Anniversary of the Easter Rising* (Cork: Cork University Press, 2012).

Hill, C., *Some Intellectual Consequences of the English Revolution* (London: Weidenfeld and Nicolson, 1980).

Hill, C., *The Experience of Defeat: Milton and Some Contemporaries* (London: Penguin, 1985).

Hill, C., *A Turbulent, Seditious and Factious People: John Bunyan and his Church, 1628–1688* (Oxford: Clarendon, 1988).

Hill, C., *England's Turning Point: Essays on 17th Century English History* (London: Bookmarks, 1998).

Hill, C., 'Republicanism after the Restoration', in *England's Turning Point*, pp. 61–73.

Hinds, P., *"The Horrid Popish Plot:" Roger L'Estrange and the Circulation of Political Discourse in Late Seventeenth-Century London* (Oxford: Oxford University Press, 2009).

Select bibliography

Hirsch, M., *The Generation of Postmemory: Writing and Visual Culture after the Holocaust* (New York: Columbia University Press, 2012).
Hobsbawm, E., 'Introduction: Inventing Traditions', in E. Hobsbawm and T. Ranger (eds), *The Invention of Tradition* (Cambridge: Cambridge University Press, 1983), pp. 1–14.
Hodgkin, K., and S. Radstone (eds), *Memory, History, Nation: Contested Pasts* (New Brunswick, NJ: Transaction, 2003).
Hopper, A., 'The Farnley Wood Plot and the Memory of the Civil Wars in Yorkshire', *Historical Journal*, 45:2 (2002), 281–303.
Hopper, A., *'Black Tom': Sir Thomas Fairfax and the English Revolution* (Manchester: Manchester University Press, 2007).
Hopper, A., *Turncoats and Renegadoes: Changing Sides during the English Civil Wars* (Oxford: Oxford University Press, 2012).
Hopper, A., and P. Major (eds), *England's Fortress: New Perspectives on Thomas, 3rd Lord Fairfax* (Farnham: Ashgate, 2014).
Houston, A., and S. Pincus (eds), *A Nation Transformed: England after the Restoration* (Cambridge: Cambridge University Press, 2001).
Houston, R. A., *Social Change in the Age of Enlightenment: Edinburgh, 1660–1760* (Oxford: Clarendon, 1994).
Howell, R., *Newcastle upon Tyne and the Puritan Revolution: A Study of the Civil War in North England* (Oxford: Clarendon, 1967).
Hughes, A., 'A "Lunatick Revolter from Loyalty": The Death of Rowland Wilson and the English Revolution', *History Workshop Journal*, 61 (Spring, 2006), 192–204.
Hughes, A., *Gender and the English Revolution* (Abingdon: Routledge, 2012).
Hutton, R., *The Restoration: A Political and Religious History of England and Wales, 1658–1667* (Oxford: Clarendon, 1985).
Hutton, R., *Stations of the Sun: A History of the Ritual Year in Britain* (Oxford: Oxford University Press, 1996).
Irwin-Zarecka, I., *Frames of Remembrance: The Dynamics of Collective Memory* (New Brunswick, NJ: Transaction, 1994).
Jackson, C., *Restoration Scotland, 1660–1690: Royalist Politics, Religion and Ideas* (Woodbridge: Boydell, 2003).
Jenkins, P., '"The Old Leaven": The Welsh Roundheads after 1660', *Historical Journal*, 24:4 (1981), 807–823.
Jenkinson, M., *Culture and Politics at the Court of Charles II, 1660–1685* (Woodbridge: Boydell, 2010).
Johnson, N. C., 'The Contours of Memory in Post-conflict Societies: Enacting Public Remembrance of the Bomb in Omagh, Northern Ireland', *Cultural Geographies*, 19:2 (Nov., 2011), 237–258.
Johnston, W., *Revelation Restored: The Apocalypse in Later Seventeenth-Century England* (Woodbridge: Boydell, 2011).
Jones, J. R. (ed.), *Liberty Secured? Britain before and after 1688* (Stanford, CA: Stanford University Press, 1992).
Kansteiner, W., 'Finding Meaning in Memory: A Methodological Critique of Collective Memory Studies', *History and Theory*, 41:2 (May, 2002), 179–197.
Keblusek, M., 'Wine for Comfort: Drinking and the Royalist Experience, 1642–1660',

in A. Smyth (ed.), *A Pleasing Sinne: Drink and Conviviality in Seventeenth-Century England* (Cambridge: Boydell and Brewer, 2004), pp. 55–68.

Keeble, N. H., *The Literary Culture of Nonconformity in Later Seventeenth-Century England* (Leicester: Leicester University Press, 1987).

Keeble, N. H., *The Restoration: England in the 1660s* (Malden, MA: Blackwell, 2002).

Kemp, G., 'L'Estrange and the Publishing Sphere', in J. McElligott (ed.), *Fear, Exclusion and Revolution: Roger Morrice and Britain in the 1680s* (Aldershot: Ashgate, 2006), pp. 47–90.

Kidson, R. M. (ed.), 'Active Parliamentarians during the Civil Wars', in Staffordshire Record Society (ed.), *Collections for a History of Staffordshire*, fourth series, vol. II (Shrewsbury: Wilding and Son, 1958), pp. 43–70.

Kiernan, V. G., 'A Banner with a Strange Device: The Later Covenanters', in T. Brotherstone (ed.), *Covenant, Charter, and Party: Traditions of Revolt and Protest in Modern Scottish History* (Aberdeen: Aberdeen University Press, 1989), pp. 25–49.

Kishlansky, M., *A Monarchy Transformed: Britain 1603–1714* (London: Allen Lane, 1996).

Klein, B., '"Between the Bums and the Bellies of the Multitude": Civic Pageantry and the Problem of the Audience in Late Stuart London', *London Journal: A Review of Metropolitan Society Past and Present*, 17 (1992), 18–26.

Knights, M., *Politics and Opinion in Crisis, 1678–81* (Cambridge: Cambridge University Press, 1994).

Knights, M., *Representation and Misrepresentation in Later Stuart Britain: Partisanship and Political Culture* (Oxford: Oxford University Press, 2005).

Knights, M., 'The Tory Interpretation of History in the Rage of the Parties', *Huntington Library Quarterly*, 58:1–2 (Mar., 2005), 353–373.

Lacey, A., *The Cult of King Charles the Martyr* (Woodbridge: Boydell, 2003).

Lake, P., 'Calvinism and the English Church, 1570–1635', *Past and Present*, 114 (Feb., 1987), 32–76.

Lake, P., 'Anti-popery: The Structure of a Prejudice', in R. Cust and A. Hughes (eds), *Conflict in Early Stuart England: Studies in Religion and Politics, 1603–1642* (Harlow, 1989), pp. 72–106.

Le Goff, J., *History and Memory*, trans. S. Rendall and E. Claman (New York: Columbia University Press, 1977).

Legon, E., 'Bound Up with Meaning: The Politics and Memory of Ribbon Wearing in Restoration England and Scotland', *Journal of British Studies*, 56:1 (Jan., 2017), 27–50.

Lindley, K., *Fenland Riots and the English Revolution* (London: Heinemann, 1982).

Lindley, K., 'London and Popular Freedom in the 1640s', in R. C. Richardson and G. M. Ridden (eds), *Freedom and the English Revolution: Essays in History and Literature* (Manchester: Manchester University Press, 1986), pp. 111–150.

Lowenthal, D., *The Past Is a Foreign Country* (Cambridge: Cambridge University Press, 1985).

Macgillivray, R., *Restoration Historians and the English Civil War* (The Hague: Martinus Nijhoff, 1974).

MacIntosh, G., *Scottish Parliament under Charles II, 1660–1685* (Edinburgh: Edinburgh University Press, 2007).

Mannheim, K., 'The Sociological Problem of Generations', in K. Mannheim, *Essays on*

the Sociology of Knowledge by Karl Mannheim, ed. P. Kecskemeti ([1928]; London: Routledge and Kegan Paul, 1952), pp. 286–320.
Marshall, A., *Intelligence and Espionage in the Reign of Charles II, 1660–1685* (Cambridge: Cambridge University Press, 1994).
Matthew, H. C. G., and B. Harrison (eds), *Oxford Dictionary of National Biography* (61 vols, Oxford: Oxford University Press, 2004).
Matthews, A. G., *Calamy Revised: Being a Revision of Edmund Calamy's Account of the Ministers and Others Ejected and Silenced, 1660–2* (Oxford: Clarendon, 1934).
McAreavey, N., 'Portadown, 1641: Memory and the 1641 Depositions', *Irish University Review*, 47:1 (Apr., 2017), 15–31.
McCall, F., *Baal's Priests: The Loyalist Clergy and the English Revolution* (Farnham: Ashgate, 2013).
McCall, F., 'Children of Baal: Clergy Families and Their Memories of Sequestration during the English Civil War', *Huntington Library Quarterly*, 76:4 (Winter, 2013), 617–638.
McCormack, D., *The Stuart Restoration and the English in Ireland* (Woodbridge: Boydell, 2016).
McCullough, P., H. Adlington, and E. Rhatigan (eds), *The Oxford Handbook of the Early Modern Sermon* (Oxford: Oxford University Press, 2011).
McElligott, J. (ed.), *Fear, Exclusion and Revolution: Roger Morrice and Britain in the 1680s* (Aldershot: Ashgate, 2006).
McElligott, J., *Royalism, Print and Censorship in Revolutionary England* (Woodbridge: Boydell, 2007).
McGlone, R. E., 'Deciphering Memory: John Adams and the Authorship of the Declaration of Independence', *Journal of American History*, 85:2 (Sept., 1998), 411–438.
McShane, A. J., 'Roaring Royalists and Ranting Brewers: The Politicisation of Drink and Drunkenness in Political Broadside Ballads from 1640 to 1689', in A. Smyth (ed.), *A Pleasing Sinne: Drink and Conviviality in Seventeenth-Century England* (Cambridge: Boydell and Brewer, 2004), pp. 69–87.
McShane, A. J., 'The Roasting of the Rump: Scatology and the Body Politic in Restoration England', *Past and Present*, 196:1 (2007), 253–272.
McShane, A. J., '"Ne Sutor Ultra Crepidam": Political Cobblers and Broadside Ballads in Late Seventeenth Century England', in P. Fumerton, A. Guerrini, and K. McAbee (eds), *Ballads and Broadsides in Britain, 1500–1800* (Farnham: Ashgate, 2010), pp. 207–228.
McShane, A. J., 'Broadsides and Ballads from the Beginnings of Print to 1660', in J. Raymond (ed.), *The Oxford History of Popular Print Culture*, vol. 1, *Britain and Ireland to 1660* (Oxford: Oxford University Press, 2011), pp. 342–396.
McShane, A. J., *Political Broadside Ballads of Seventeenth-Century England: A Critical Bibliography* (London: Pickering and Chatto, 2011).
Miller, J., *Popery and Politics in England: 1660–1688* (Cambridge: Cambridge University Press, 1973).
Miller, J. C. (ed.), *The African Past Speaks: Essays on Oral Tradition and History* (Folkestone: Dawson, 1980).
Milton, A., 'Licensing, Censorship, and Religious Orthodoxy in Early Stuart England', *Historical Journal*, 41:3 (Sept., 1998), 625–651.

Milton, R., 'The Unscholastic Statesman: Locke and the Earl of Shaftesbury', in J. Spurr (ed.), *Anthony Ashley Cooper, First Earl of Shaftesbury, 1621–1683* (Farnham: Ashgate, 2011), pp. 153–181.

Misztal, B. A., *Theories of Social Remembering* (Maidenhead: Open University Press, 2003).

Molden, B., 'Resistant Pasts versus Mnemonic Hegemony: On the Power Relations of Collective Memory', *Memory Studies*, 9:2 (2016), 125–142.

Monod, P. K., *Jacobitism and the English People, 1688–1788* (Cambridge: Cambridge University Press, 1993).

Montaño, J. P., *Courting the Moderates: Ideology, Propaganda, and the Emergence of the Party, 1660–1678* (Newark, DE: University of Delaware Press, 2002).

Morton, A., 'Intensive Ephemera: *The Catholick Gamesters* and the Visual Culture of News in Restoration London', in S. F. Davies and P. Fletcher (eds), *News in Early Modern Europe: Currents and Connections* (Leiden: Brill, 2014), pp. 115–140.

Mosse, G. L., *Fallen Soldiers: Reshaping the Memory of the World Wars* (New York: Oxford University Press, 1990).

Nenner, H. (ed.), *Politics and the Political Imagination in Later Stuart Britain: Essays Presented to Lois Green Schwoerer* (Rochester, NY: University of Rochester Press, 1997).

Nenner, H., 'The Trial of the Regicides: Retribution and Treason in 1660', in *Politics and the Political Imagination*, pp. 21–42.

Neufeld, M., *The Civil Wars after 1660: Public Remembering in Late Stuart England* (Woodbridge: Boydell, 2013).

Neufeld, M., 'Introduction: Putting the Past to Work, Working through the Past', *Huntington Library Quarterly*, 76:4 (Winter, 2013), 483–497.

Norbrook, D., 'Memoirs and Oblivion: Lucy Hutchinson and the Restoration', *Huntington Library Quarterly*, 75:2 (Summer, 2012), 233–282.

Olick, J. K., and J. Robbins, 'Social Memory Studies: From "Collective Memory" to the Historical Sociology of Mnemonic Practices', *Annual Review of Sociology*, 24 (1998), 105–140.

Ollard, R., *Pepys, A Biography* (London: Hodder and Stoughton, 1974).

Orihel, M., '"Treacherous Memories" of Regicide: The Calves-Head Club in the Age of Anne', *Historian*, 73:3 (2011), 435–462.

Patterson, A., *Reading between the Lines* (London: Routledge, 1993).

Patterson, A., and M. Dzelzainis, 'Marvell and the Earl of Anglesey: A Chapter in the History of Reading', *Historical Journal*, 44:3 (2001), 703–726.

Peacey, J., 'Politics, Accounts and Propaganda in the Long Parliament', in J. Peacey and C. Kyle (eds), *Parliament at Work: Parliamentary Committees, Political Power and Public Access in Early Modern England* (Woodbridge: Boydell and Brewer, 2002), pp. 59–78.

Peacey, J., 'Sir Edward Dering, Popularity, and the Public, 1640–1644', *Historical Journal*, 54:4 (Dec., 2011), 955–983.

Peacey, J., *Print and Public Politics in the English Revolution* (Cambridge: Cambridge University Press, 2013).

Peck, I., 'The Great Unknown: The Negotiation and Narration of Death by English Civil War Widows, 1647–1660', *Northern History* (2016), 220–235.

Peters, E., *Commemoration and Oblivion in Royalist Print Culture, 1658–1667* (Cham, Switzerland: Palgrave Studies in the History of Media, 2017).

Pittock, M., *Material Culture and Sedition, 1688–1760: Treasured Objects, Secret Places* (Basingstoke: Palgrave Macmillan: 2013).

Pollman, J., *Memory in Early Modern Europe: 1500–1800* (Oxford: Oxford University Press, 2017).

Popular Memory Group, 'Popular Memory: Theory, Politics, Method', in R. Johnson, G. McLennan, B. Schwarz, and D. Sutton (eds), *Making Histories: Studies in History-Writing and Politics* (London: Hutchinson in association with the Centre for Contemporary Cultural Studies, University of Birmingham, 1982), pp. 205–252.

Portelli, A., 'Uchronic Dreams: Working-Class Memory and Possible Worlds', in R. Samuel and P. Thompson (eds), *The Myths We Live By* (London: Routledge, 1990), pp. 143–160.

Potter, L., 'The Royal Martyr in the Restoration: National Grief and National Sin', in T. N. Corns (ed.), *The Royal Image: Representations of Charles I* (Cambridge: Cambridge University Press, 1999), pp. 240–248.

Poynting, S., 'Deciphering the King: Charles I's Letters to Jane Whorwood', *Seventeenth Century*, 21:1 (2006), 128–140.

Prager, J., *Presenting the Past: Psychoanalysis and the Sociology of Misremembering* (Cambridge, MA: Harvard University Press, 1998).

Raffe, A., 'Presbyterians and Episcopalians: The Formation of Confessional Cultures in Scotland, 1660–1715', *English Historical Review*, 125:514 (Jun., 2010), 570–598.

Raffe, A., *The Culture of Controversy: Religious Arguments in Scotland, 1660–1714* (Woodbridge: Boydell Press, 2012).

Raffe, A., 'The Restoration, the Revolution and the Failure of Episcopacy in Scotland', in T. Harris and S. Taylor (eds), *The Final Crisis of the Stuart Monarchy: The Revolutions of 1688–91 in Their British, Atlantic and European Contexts* (Woodbridge: Boydell, 2013), pp. 87–108.

Reece, H., *The Army in Cromwellian England, 1649–1660* (Oxford: Oxford University Press, 2013).

Richardson, R. C., *The Debate on the English Revolution* (London: Methuen, 1977).

Rigney, A., 'Reconciliation and Remembering: (How) Does It Work?', *Memory Studies*, 5:3 (Jul., 2012), 251–258.

Robinson, E. M., 'Sacred Memory: The Covenanter Use of History in Scotland and America', *Journal of Transatlantic Studies*, 11:2 (2013), 135–157.

Routledge, C., *Nostalgia: A Psychological Resource* (New York: Routledge, 2016).

Roy, I., 'Royalist Reputations: The Cavalier Ideal and the Reality', in J. McElligott and D. L. Smith (eds), *Royalists and Royalism during Interregnum* (Manchester: Manchester University Press, 2010), pp. 89–111.

Russell, C., 'The British Problem and the English Civil War', *History*, 72:236 (Oct., 1987), 395–415.

Rydgren, J., 'Shared Beliefs about the Past: A Cognitive Sociology of Intersubjective Memory', *Frontiers of Sociology*, 11 (2009), 307–330.

Sangha, L., 'Personal Documents', in L. Sangha and J. Willis (eds), *Understanding Early Modern Primary Sources* (London: Routledge, 2016), pp. 107–128.

Schivelbusch, W., *The Culture of Defeat: On National Trauma, Mourning, and Recovery*, trans. J. Chase (London: Granta, 2003).

Select bibliography

Schwoerer, L., 'Liberty of the Press and Public Opinion: 1660–1695', in Jones, *Liberty Secured?*, pp. 199–230.
Scott, J., 'Radicalism and Restoration: The Shape of the Stuart Experience', *Historical Journal*, 31:2 (1988), 453–467.
Scott, J., 'England's Troubles: Exhuming the Popish Plot', in T. Harris *et al*., *Politics of Religion*, pp. 107–131.
Scott, J., *Algernon Sidney and the Restoration Crisis, 1677–1683* (Cambridge: Cambridge University Press, 1991).
Scott., J., *England's Troubles: Seventeenth-Century English Political Instability in European Context* (Cambridge: Cambridge University Press, 2000).
Scott, J. C., *Domination and the Arts of Resistance: Hidden Transcripts* (New Haven, CT: Yale University Press, 1990).
Seaward, P., *The Cavalier Parliament and the Reconstruction of the Old Regime, 1661–1667* (Cambridge: Cambridge University Press, 1988).
Sharp, B., 'Popular Political Opinion in England, 1660–1865', *History of European Ideas*, 10:1 (1989), 13–29.
Sharpe, K., '"So Hard a Text"? Images of Charles I, 1612–1700', *Historical Journal*, 43:2 (Jun., 2000), 383–404.
Snyder, C. R. (ed.), *Handbook of Hope: Theory, Measures, and Applications* (San Diego: Academic Press, 2000).
Spurr, J., *The Restoration of the Church of England, 1646–1689* (New Haven, CT: Yale University Press, 1991).
Spurr, J., 'A Profane History of Early Modern Oaths', *Transactions of the Royal Historical Society*, 11 (2001), 37–63.
Starn, R., 'Meaning-Levels in the Theme of Historical Decline', *History and Theory*, 14:1 (Feb., 1975), 1–31.
Stewart, B. S., 'The Cult of the Royal Martyr', *Church History*, 38:2 (Jun., 1969), 175–187.
Stewart, H., *History of the Worshipful Company of Gold and Silver Wyre-Drawers: and of the Origin and Development of the Industry which the Company Represents* (London: Leadenhall, 1891).
Stewart, L., *Rethinking the Scottish Revolution: Covenanted Scotland, 1637–1651* (Oxford: Oxford University Press, 2016).
Stoyle, M., *Loyalty and Locality: Popular Allegiance in Devon during the English Civil War* (Exeter: Exeter University Press, 1994).
Stoyle, M., 'Memories of the Maimed: The Testimony of Charles I's Former Soldiers, 1660–1730', *History*, 88:290 (2003), 204–226.
Stoyle, M., 'Remembering the English Civil Wars', in P. Gray and K. Oliver (eds), *The Memory of Catastrophe* (Manchester: Manchester University Press, 2004), pp. 19–30.
Stryker, S., and P. J. Burke, 'The Past, Present, and Future of an Identity Theory', *Social Psychology Quarterly*, 63:4 (Dec., 2000), 284–297.
Tajfel, H., *Differentiation between Social Groups: Studies in the Social Psychology of Intergroup Relations* (London: Academic Press, 1978).
Tapsell, G., *The Personal Rule of Charles II, 1681–85* (Woodbridge: Boydell, 2007).
Terdiman, R., *Present Past: Modernity and the Memory Crisis* (Ithaca, NY: Cornell University Press, 1993).

Select bibliography

Tonkin, E., *Narrating Our Pasts: The Social Construction of Oral History* (Cambridge: Cambridge University Press, 1992).
Toscano, A., *Fanaticism: The Uses of an Idea* (London: Verso, 2010).
Vallance, E., 'Loyal or Rebellious?: Protestant Associations in England 1584–1696', *Seventeenth Century*, 17:1 (2002), 1–24.
Vallance, E., *Revolutionary England and the National Covenant: State Oaths, Protestantism and the Political Nation, 1553–1682* (Woodbridge: Boydell, 2005).
Vallance, E., *The Glorious Revolution: 1688 – Britain's Fight for Liberty* (London: Abacus, 2006).
Vallance, E. (ed.), *Remembering Early Modern Revolutions* (London: Routledge, forthcoming).
Vansina, J., 'Memory and Oral Tradition', in J. C. Miller (ed.), *The African Past Speaks: Essays on Oral Tradition and History* (Folkestone: Dawson, 1980), pp. 262–279.
Vess, M., J. Arndt, C. Routledge, C. Sedikides, and T. Wildschut, 'Nostalgia as a Resource for the Self', *Self and Identity*, 11:3 (2012), 273–284.
Walker, C., '"Remember Justice Godfrey": The Popish Plot and the Construction of Panic in Seventeenth-Century Media', in D. Lemmings and C. Walker (eds), *Moral Panics, the Media and the Law in Early Modern England* (Basingstoke: Palgrave Macmillan, 2009), pp. 117–138.
Walter, J., 'Grain Riots and Popular Attitudes to the Law: Maldon and the Crisis of 1629', in J. Brewer and J. Styles (eds), *An Ungovernable People: The English and Their Law in the Seventeenth and Eighteenth Centuries* (London: Hutchinson, 1980), pp. 47–84.
Walter, J., 'Public Transcripts, Popular Agency and the Politics of Subsistence in Early Modern England', in Braddick and Walter, *Negotiating Power*, pp. 123–148.
Walter, J., *Covenanting Citizens: The Protestation Oath and Popular Political Culture in the English Revolution* (Oxford: Oxford University Press, 2017).
Weber, H., *Paper Bullets: Print and Kingship under Charles II* (Lexington, KY: University of Kentucky Press, 1996).
Weber, H., *Memory, Print, and Gender in England, 1653–1759* (New York: Palgrave, 2008).
Wertsch, J., *Voices of Collective Remembering* (Cambridge, Cambridge University Press, 2002).
Wildschut, T., C. Sedikides, C. Routledge, J. Arndt, and F. Cordaro, 'Nostalgia as a Repository of Social Connectedness: The Role of Attachment-Related Avoidance', *Journal of Personality and Social Psychology*, 98:4 (2010), 575–586.
Withington, P., 'Company and Sociability in Early Modern England', *Social History*, 32:3 (Aug., 2007), 291–307.
Wood, Andy, 'Custom, Identity and Resistance: English Free Miners and their Law, c.1550–1800', in P. Griffiths, A. Fox, and S. Hindle (eds), *The Experience of Authority in Early Modern England* (Basingstoke: Macmillan, 1996), pp. 249–285.
Wood, Andy, '"Poore Men Woll Speke One Day": Plebeian Languages of Deference and Defiance in England, c.1520–1640', in T. Harris, *Politics of the Excluded*, pp. 67–98.
Wood, Andy, *Riot, Rebellion and Popular Politics in Early Modern England* (Basingstoke: Palgrave: 2002).

Select bibliography

Wood, Andy, *The 1549 Rebellions and the Making of Early Modern England* (Cambridge: Cambridge University Press, 2007).
Wood, Andy, '"The Queen Is a Goggyll Eyed Hoore": Gender and Seditious Speech in Early Modern England', in N. Tyacke (ed.), *The English Revolution c. 1590–1720: Politics, Religion and Communities* (Manchester: Manchester University Press, 2007), pp. 81–94.
Wood, Andy, *The Memory of the People: Custom and Popular Senses of the Past in Early Modern England* (Cambridge: Cambridge University Press, 2013).
Wood, Andy, 'Coda: History, Time and Social Memory', in K. Wrightson (ed.), *A Social History of England 1500–1750* (Cambridge: Cambridge University Press, 2017), pp. 373–391.
Woolf, D., 'Two Elizabeths? James I and the Late Queen's Famous Memory', *Canadian Journal of History*, 20:2 (Summer, 1985), 167–191.
Woolf, D., 'Memory and Historical Culture in Early Modern England', *Journal of the Canadian Historical Association*, 2:1 (1991), 283–308
Woolf, D., *The Social Circulation of the Past: English Historical Culture: 1500–1730* (Oxford: Oxford University Press, 2003).
Woolf, D., 'Afterword: Shadows of the Past in Early Modern England', *Huntington Library Quarterly*, 76:4 (Winter, 2013), 639–650.
Woolrych, A. H., 'The Good Old Cause and the Fall of the Protectorate', *Cambridge Historical Journal 2*, 13 (1957), 133–161.
Worden, B., *Roundhead Reputations: The English Civil Wars and the Passions of Posterity* (London: Allen Lane, Penguin, 2001).
Wrightson, K. (ed.), *A Social History of England 1500–1750* (Cambridge: Cambridge University Press, 2017).
Zemon Davis, N., *Fiction in the Archives: Pardon Tales and Their Tellers in Sixteenth-Century France* (Cambridge: Polity, 1988).
Zhou, X., C. Sedikides, T. Wildschut, and D. Gao, 'Counteracting Loneliness: On the Restorative Function of Nostalgia', *Psychological Science*, 19:10 (2008), 1023–1029.
Zook, M., *Radical Whigs and Conspiratorial Politics in Late Stuart England* (University Park, PA: Pennsylvania State University Press, 1999).

UNPUBLISHED THESES

Bell, R., 'The Politics of Imprisonment in Early Modern England' (unpublished PhD dissertation, University of Stanford, 2017).
Legon, E., 'Remembering Revolution: Seditious Memories in England and Wales, 1660–1685' (unpublished PhD dissertation, University College London, 2015).
Raffe, A., 'Religious Controversy and Scottish Society, c. 1679–1714' (unpublished PhD dissertation, University of Edinburgh, 2007).
Taylor, H., 'Branded on the Tongue: Aspects of Language and Social Relations in Early Modern England' (unpublished PhD dissertation, University of Yale, 2016)
Tierney, E., 'Strategies for Celebration: Realising the Ideal Celebratory City in London and Paris, 1660–1715' (unpublished PhD dissertation, University of Sussex, 2012).
Walker, P., 'The Church Militant: The American Émigré Clergy and the Making of the British Counterrevolution, 1763–92' (unpublished PhD dissertation, University of Columbia, 2016).

Index

Note: literary works can be found under the names of authors. Footnote numbers are included in references to footnotes. Towns and cities are included as (or beneath) the counties in which they lie.

agents provocateurs 91–92
alehouses *see* drinking
Anglicanism *see* Church of England
Anglo-Dutch Wars (1652–54; 1665–67; 1672–74) 23–24, 71, 78, 81
Annesley, Arthur (Earl of Anglesey) 58, 191
Arminianism 174 ,191
Axtell, Daniel 95
Ayloffe, John 174–178 *passim*
Ayrshire 114, 121

Bagshaw, Edward 19, 57–58
Baptists 76, 83, 100, 151, 186, 188–189
Barkstead, John 96
Bates, William 59–60, 200
Battle of Bothwell Bridge (1679) 114, 118–120, 161, 162, 185
Baxter, Richard 2, 35, 36–38, 56–60 *passim*, 96, 191
    Reliquiae Baxterianae (1696) 36–37
Bedfordshire 90, 187
Behn, Aphra 1–2
bell-ringing 144, 151, 152

Bennet, Henry (Earl of Arlington) 35, 54, 74
Berkshire 38, 54, 56, 83
Birch, John 83, 98, 202–203
Birkenhead, (Sir) John 52
Book of Common Prayer (1662) 27, 95, 127, 152
bonfires 143, 144, 150–153 *passim*, 156–159, 164
Bowles, Edward 199–200
Boyle, Roger (Earl of Orrery) 127, 128
Bradshaw, John 157, 200
Bristol 151, 162–163
broadside ballads 51, 54, 58, 77, 119, 177–178
Brodie, Alexander (Lord Brodie) 122, 146, 147, 151–154 *passim*
Brown, John (of Wamphray) 115, 120–123 *passim*, 149, 161
Buckinghamshire 56, 185
Bunyan, John 2, 187
Burges, Cornelius 176
Burnet, Gilbert (Bishop of Salisbury) 153, 185–186

Index

Butler, James (Duke of Ormond) 127, 129, 132

Caethnes, John 60, 72, 82
Calves-Head Club 163–165
Cambridgeshire 101
Campbell, Archibald (Marquis of Argyll) 118, 119, 136n.25
Capell, Arthur (Earl of Essex) 128, 130
Carew, John 31
censorship 6, 7, 30–31, 48, 50–59, 72, 74, 82, 83, 89, 95, 97, 110–114 *passim*, 120–122, 125, 128, 130, 133, 134, 142–143, 162, 179, 191, 200–202
Charles I 28, 29, 56, 72, 79, 80, 110–112, 118, 134, 144, 154, 156, 180, 182, 203, 205
    cases of seditious words involving 28–32 *passim*, 36, 70–78 *passim*, 81–85 *passim*, 91–96 *passim*, 99, 103, 119, 120, 129, 132, 160, 173–178 *passim*, 181, 184, 187, 201
    Personal Rule 58, 69, 184
    trial and execution (1649) 28, 30–32, 36, 37, 51, 59, 67, 69–75 *passim*, 78, 81–85 *passim*, 90–96 *passim*, 103, 119, 129, 132, 142–146 *passim*, 149, 156–160 *passim*, 163–164, 173–178 *passim*, 180, 187, 188, 200–203
    anniversary of execution 9, 49, 75, 143–165, 182, 202, 203
Charles II 1, 24, 34, 54, 56, 58, 78, 115, 116, 121, 122, 127, 151, 154, 158, 172, 181
    cases of seditious words involving 20–29 *passim*, 32, 33, 36, 70, 73–74, 78–84 *passim*, 94, 99, 101, 103, 115–116, 119, 120, 124, 129–132 *passim*, 154–155, 162, 164, 173–175, 178, 181–184 *passim*, 187, 189, 190
Declaration of Breda (1660) 22, 36
Declaration of Indulgence (1672) 151, 161

and his Free and General Pardon, Indemnity and Oblivion (1660) 7, 48–51 *passim*, 57–61 *passim*, 67, 94, 103, 199
restoration of *see* Restoration (1660)
Cheshire 148
Chester 26, 38, 120, 134
Church of England 1, 3, 20, 21, 31, 47–48, 50, 52, 56, 60, 77–78, 95, 103, 134, 143, 149, 152, 155, 160–164 *passim*, 174, 177, 180–184 *passim*, 191
Church of Ireland 126–129
Church of Scotland 112, 115–124 *passim*, 152–154, 186
Clydesdale 128
Cockayne, George 90–91
Colledge, Stephen 35, 158, 173–185 *passim*, 187, 188, 196n.78
Commonwealth (1649–60) 1, 19, 20–24 *passim*, 32, 34, 37, 50, 51, 54, 56, 71, 72, 77–80 *passim*, 82–84, 91, 97, 99, 115, 119, 125–132 *passim*, 146, 147, 156, 157, 161–162, 174–175, 180, 185, 187, 199
Confederation of Kilkenny (1642–49) 111, 126, 130, 133
Congregationalism 19, 32, 50, 119, 131, 148, 151
Constantinople 199
conventicles 97, 99, 114, 121
Cooper, Anthony Ashley (Earl of Shaftesbury) 55, 60, 103, 157, 184, 188
Corbet, Miles 96
Cork (County) 128
Cornwall 60, 80–81, 92
Covenants
    counter-oaths to 114, 116–117, 124, 127, 183
    Covenanters 110, 113, 114, 120, 123, 146, 154, 158, 162, 183, 185–186, 190, 191
    National Covenant (1638) 110–125 *passim*, 133, 136n.25, 183–186 *passim*, 190, 191, 201, 204

230

Solemn League and Covenant (1643) 18, 19, 22, 23, 32, 38, 73, 85, 110–130 *passim*, 133, 134, 136n.25, 156–158 *passim*, 161, 162, 183–186 *passim*, 189–191, 201, 204
Coventry, (Sir) William 128
Crofton, Zachary 19
Cromwell, Henry 20
Cromwell, Oliver 1, 2, 21, 54, 60, 72, 73, 83, 101, 119, 127, 131, 132, 156, 157, 159, 174, 181–184, 199, 200
  cases of seditious words involving 19–26 *passim*, 32–36 *passim*, 71, 74, 77–79, 83, 85, 91–95 *passim*, 101, 111, 128–133 *passim*, 162, 174–175, 184, 187, 201
  government of *see* Commonwealth (1649–60)
Cromwell, Richard 54, 77, 185
Cumbria 24

De Krey, Gary 172, 184, 189
Denbighshire 54
Derbyshire 27–28, 58, 59
Devon 32, 37, 78, 161–162
diaries *see* life writings
Directory of Public Worship 118, 156, 157
Dissenters 1, 2, 7, 17, 21, 22, 36–39 *passim*, 51–59 *passim*, 71, 84, 98, 101–103, 110, 121, 133–134, 143, 148, 151–162, 165, 179, 188–191 *passim*, 199, 202
Donegal (County) 128
Dorset 20, 34, 35, 38, 52, 74, 83, 148, 149, 159
Douglas, William (Earl of Queensberry) 113
Down (County) 129, 130
drinking 58, 70, 77, 84, 97, 98, 144, 153, 162
  health-drinking 77, 154, 164
Dublin (County) 125, 129–131
Dublin Plot (1663) 130–131
Dumfriesshire 114
Durham (County) 78, 157

Edinburgh 113, 114, 118–121 *passim*, 125, 151, 190
Engagement (1650) 19, 22, 71, 72, 156, 157
Engagers (Scotland) 118
English Parliament 27, 32, 51, 58, 75, 79, 80–81, 88n.66, 90, 98, 103, 111, 156, 179, 202–205 *passim*
Legislation
  Act of Free and General Pardon, Indemnity, and Oblivion (1660) 3, 7, 47–53 *passim*, 56–62 *passim*, 62n.9, 67, 76, 94, 103, 126, 143–146, 155–156, 165, 190–191, 199–200
  Act of Uniformity (1662) 38, 48, 52, 53, 59, 96, 162, 188, 199, 200
  Corporation Act (1661) 38, 52
  Licensing Act (1662) 30–31, 52–53, 178
  Sedition Act (1661) 4, 17, 18–20, 26, 34, 35, 38, 45n.121, 48, 52–53, 88n.74, 93, 112
  Triennial Act (1664) 54
Parliaments
  Cavalier Parliament (1661–79) 17, 18, 48, 51–54, 67, 145
  Convention Parliament (1660) 49, 51, 61, 143–144
  Long Parliament (1640–48; 1660) 19, 27, 28, 32, 35–38 *passim*, 78, 131–132, 145, 147, 157, 173, 176–178, 180, 182, 184
  Oxford Parliament (1681) 80, 175, 181, 184
  Rump Parliament (1648–53; 1659–60) 21, 22, 59, 81–82, 129, 159, 160
Episcopalianism (Scotland) 112–118 *passim*, 122, 124, 149, 152, 153, 185
Essex 27, 54, 56, 77–78, 134, 147, 162, 186–187
Evelyn, (Sir) John 147, 155–156
Exclusion Crisis (1678–81) 1–2, 31–32, 58, 60, 69, 98, 103, 154, 156–160 *passim*, 175, 179–182 *passim*, 186, 189, 191

231

Index

Fairfax, Thomas (Lord Fairfax) 37, 191, 199
Farnley Wood Plot (1663) 5, 57, 69, 81, 100
Fife 114, 124
Fifth Monarchism 99, 101
   Fifth Monarchists' rebellion (1661) 5, 18, 51, 57, 100
Flintshire 189

Galway (County) 130
Gladman, John 186–187
Glorious Revolution (1688–89) 2, 4, 25, 37, 53, 113, 142, 174, 184, 192, 202–205 *passim*
Gloucestershire 27, 181
   Bristol 151, 162–163
good old cause 1, 21, 31, 32, 60–61, 72, 73, 95–96, 99, 100, 160, 180, 199
Gordon, Alexander (of Earlston) 119–120
Goring, George (Lord Goring) 78
Greaves, Richard L. 5, 128, 163
Green Ribbon Club 173
Greville, Robert (Baron Brooke) 98
Grey, Thomas (Earl of Stamford) 163, 181
Guthrie, James 115, 119, 122–123

Hampshire 29, 30, 73, 182
Harrison, Thomas 95–96
Harris, Tim 5, 11n.6, 132
Hearth Tax 28–29, 82
Henry, Philip 38, 146, 148, 153, 155, 158, 189–190
Herefordshire 134, 203, 205n.9
Hertfordshire 54, 76, 176, 180–181
Heywood, Oliver 21, 147–149, 155, 161
Hill, Christopher 7, 48, 55, 97
hope 9, 26, 28, 89–90, 104, 201
Hopper, Andrew 21, 54, 98, 191
House of Commons *see* English Parliament
House of Lords *see* English Parliament
Hutchinson, John 160
Hyde, Edward (Earl of Clarendon) 51–52, 57

Ireton, Henry 20, 200
Irish Confederate Wars (1641–52) 125, 126
Irish Parliament 126–130 *passim*
Irish Rebellion (1641) 9, 30, 111, 125–127, 131–133
Isle of Wight 128

James I 56, 92, 110, 129
James II 1, 2, 5, 31, 32, 124, 156, 172–175 *passim*, 179, 190, 192, 202, 203
   cases of seditious words involving 20, 34, 103, 115, 129, 154, 164, 182, 189, 203–204
Jeffreys, George (Baron Jeffreys) 35
Jenkins, (Sir) Leoline 149
Johnston, Archibald (Lord Wariston) 119
Jolly, Thomas 151, 152, 165
Josselin, Ralph 56, 96, 147, 151–152, 155, 162, 165

Kent 20, 25, 29, 30, 81, 102, 148
   Canterbury 20, 34, 70, 86n.10
Kerry (County) 128, 131
Kilkenny (County) 126
Kirk *see* Church of Scotland
Kirkcudbrightshire 119–120

Lambert, John (Lord Lambert) 20, 26, 77, 98, 201
Lanarkshire 114, 115, 186
   Glasgow 114, 116, 121, 125, 149, 186
   Lanark 114, 118, 121
Lancashire 98, 151, 160, 181
Larkham, Thomas 37
Lauder, John (of Fountainhall) 117
Laud, William (Archbishop of Canterbury) 104, 160, 174, 181, 182
Leicestershire 38, 155
L'Estrange, (Sir) Roger 3, 50–53 *passim*, 60, 64n.55, 153–154, 159, 177, 190–191, 199
Levellers 28, 55, 184
life writings 6, 18, 36–38, 113, 143, 155, 191

Lilburne, John 20–21, 55
Limerick (County) 131
Lincolnshire 26, 82, 91, 158
Linlithgow 153
London 18–24 *passim*, 28, 31–32, 54–57 *passim*, 51, 59, 72, 76, 79, 81, 91–92, 96, 100–103 *passim*, 125, 128, 144, 145, 149–150, 155, 156, 159–164 *passim*, 173–178 *passim*, 184–189 *passim*, 199, 200
   Great Fire of (1666) 174, 177
Londonderry (County) 128
Lowe, Roger 98
Ludlow, Edmund 96, 131, 132

Mannheim, Karl 174, 179
Marvell, Andrew 2, 57
Massey, Edward (informant) 101, 186–187
Mayne, Simon 188
McWard, Robert 158
Meade, Matthew 188–189
Members of Parliament (MPs) *see* English Parliament
memory
  communities of memory 8, 97
  counter-memories 7, 68
  cultural memory 173, 180
  and historians 1–3, 10, 25, 42n.60, 47–48, 69, 77, 110, 120, 126, 142–143, 179, 184, 204–205
  intergenerational memories 10, 172–174, 180, 193n.10
  mnemonic hegemony 7–8, 51
  myths of betrayal 21–22
  nostalgia 25, 105
  prospective memories 8, 26
  public memory 62n.1, 69
  social memory 6, 90, 179–180
  uchronia 27, 132
Middlesex 20, 27, 29, 30, 94, 175, 182, 184, 188
  Tottenham 23, 59, 200
Milles, Daniel 145–146
Milton, John 2, 58
Molden, Berthold 7, 51–54 *passim*

Monck, George (Duke of Albemarle) 22, 37–38, 41n.33 71–72, 74, 81–82, 85, 99, 101–102, 132, 150, 199, 201
Monmouth Rebellion (1685) *see* Scott, James (Duke of Monmouth)
Morrice, Roger 191
Mure, James 121–122, 191

Neufeld, Matthew 2–3, 53
Newcastle-upon-Tyne 70–74 *passim*, 86n.17
Newcome, Henry 153, 154
Newcomen, Matthew 55–56
New Model Army 20, 22, 60, 73, 83, 92, 98, 101, 145, 163, 177, 184, 186, 203
  Army Remonstrance (1648) 28
New Protestants (Ireland) 125–133 *passim*, 201
Nicholas, (Sir) Edward 200
Nicoll, John 111
Nonconformists *see* Dissenters
Norfolk 79
  Great Yarmouth 38, 54, 78
  Norwich 156–157
Northamptonshire 26, 28, 150, 159, 176
North, (Sir) Francis (Baron Guildford) 35, 176
Northumberland 71
Nottinghamshire 36

Oates, Titus 31
Okey, John 27, 31, 96
Osborne, Thomas (Earl of Danby) 174
Oxfordshire 75
  Oxford 30, 80, 150–151, 156, 175–177, 180–181, 184, 187
  University of 150, 156, 173, 174

Paterson, John 112
Paterson, John (Dean of Edinburgh) 113
Penruddock's Rising (1655) 21
Pentland Rising (1666) 114–116, 118, 120, 123, 134, 185, 186

Index

Pepys, Samuel 24, 96, 102, 145–150 *passim*, 165
Perthshire 36, 115
Peter, Hugh 156
Phillips, John 58
Plague (1665–66) 173, 189
Popish Plot (1678) 31, 174
Portugal 93
Presbyterianism 25, 31, 36, 38, 50, 54, 56, 91, 96, 98, 110, 113, 115, 118–124 *passim*, 128, 131, 134, 146–158 *passim*, 161, 180, 183–186 *passim*, 189, 191, 199, 200
prisoners 22, 24, 76, 91–92, 93, 97, 102, 103, 114, 116, 118, 121, 163, 181, 184, 191
Protectorate (1653–59) *see* Commonwealth (1649–60)
Protestation oath (1641) 18, 19, 72–73, 92, 176
Protestors (Scotland) 115, 118
Prynne, William 31, 180
Puritanism 1, 3, 21, 47–48, 55–56, 58–61 *passim*, 147, 153, 154, 164, 176, 180, 191

Quakerism 24, 29, 78, 148, 152

Reformation (English) 21, 25
regicide *see* Charles I
Remonstrants (Scotland) 118
Restoration (1660) 2, 5, 9, 18, 19, 22, 28, 34, 38, 47–49, 55, 58, 60, 67, 70–72, 91–94 *passim*, 99, 110–113 *passim*, 125, 126, 129, 134, 142–148 *passim*, 151, 161, 162, 173–175, 180, 192, 199, 201
    anniversary of 9, 126, 142–165, 202
Rich, Mary (Countess of Warwick) 146
Roman Catholicism 1, 2, 9, 25, 27, 30–32, 51, 69, 78, 83, 84, 99, 110, 111, 118–120, 123–133 *passim*, 154, 172–174, 177, 179, 180, 184, 188, 192, 202
Roxburghshire 121, 124
Rumsey, John 163–165

Rye House Plot (1683) 5, 21, 32, 119, 124, 163, 182, 183, 186–188

Sacheverell, John 154, 158
scaffold speeches 9, 31, 73, 95–96, 113–123 *passim*, 130–131
Scot, Thomas 54
Scottish Parliament 111–116 *passim*, 123
Scott, James (Duke of Monmouth) 33, 154, 203
    rebellion (1685) 5, 9, 32–33, 100, 163, 183, 203
Scroggs, (Sir) William 177, 182
sermons 1, 19, 21, 24, 30, 37, 48, 53, 59, 67, 89–92 *passim*, 96, 99–102 *passim*, 112–115 *passim*, 121, 126, 143–165 *passim*, 180–182, 200, 202
Sharp, James (Archbishop of St Andrews) 185
Shawe, John 36, 191
Shropshire 24, 148
Sidney, Algernon 95–96
Smith, Aaron 99, 187–188
Smyth, (Sir) William 184–185
social psychology 4, 10, 23, 25, 90, 104, 105
solidarity 8, 82, 90, 97–98, 122
Somerset 20, 22, 59, 76, 82, 102, 103
    Bath 160, 178
    Taunton 77, 101, 150, 162, 190
    Wincanton 21, 154, 158
Southby, Strange 173–176 *passim*, 178, 181
Staffordshire 35, 54, 71, 72, 76
Stewart, James 117, 121, 186, 191
St John, Oliver 182
Succession Crisis (1678–81) *see* Exclusion Crisis (1678–81)
Suffolk 23, 34, 156, 157
    Bury St Edmunds 156, 157

Surrey 30, 32, 60, 72, 99, 101, 160, 178
Sussex 22, 30, 32, 154
Sympson, John 92, 96

Tangiers 78
Thoresby, Ralph 153

234

Index

Tillotson, John (Archbishop of Canterbury) 154
Tipperary (County) 128, 132
  Clonmel 126, 132
toasts *see* drinking
Tonge Plot (1662) 73, 95
Tories 1–2, 58, 60, 142, 157, 163, 175, 179, 192
Trail, Robert 115–116
Trelawney, (Sir) Jonathan 78
Trenchard, John 163–164
turn coats 21–23, 77, 80–83 *passim*
Turner, James 123–124
Twyn, John 24–25, 73

Vane, (Sir) Henry 96, 121
Villiers, George (second Duke of Buckingham) 55, 185

Walwyn, William 55
Ward, (Sir) Patience 1
Warwickshire 157
Welch, John 121, 123
Wentworth, Thomas (Earl of Strafford) 70, 160

Westminster *see* London
Westmorland 54
Wexford (County) 126, 132
Whigs 1–2, 5, 58, 69, 75, 85n.6, 119, 142, 156–159 *passim*, 163–164, 173–179, 182, 184–186, 191, 192
Whitaker, Edward 178, 184–185, 194n.51–52
Whitelocke, (Sir) Bulstrode 38, 56–58, 147, 148
Whorwood, Brome 75
Whorwood, Jane (*née* Ryder) 75
Wildman, John 55
Williamson, (Sir) Joseph 78
Wiltshire 21, 35, 73–74
Wood, Anthony 150–151, 155–156, 159, 180
Worcestershire 22
  Kidderminster 37, 38, 96

Yorkshire 19, 20, 24, 26, 28, 29, 32, 36, 54, 69–70, 72, 76–77, 80–84 *passim*, 99, 100, 147
  Halifax 26, 84, 155
  York 19, 32, 78, 148, 153, 157, 199

235

EU authorised representative for GPSR:
Easy Access System Europe, Mustamäe tee 50,
10621 Tallinn, Estonia
gpsr.requests@easproject.com